THE HIDDEN SUN

WITHDRAWN

Also of Interest

† *Japan: Profile of a Postindustrial Power*, Ardath W. Burks

† *Japan's Economy: Coping with Change in the International Environment*, edited by Daniel P. Okimoto

† *Women of Rural Asia*, Robert Orr Whyte and Pauline Whyte

† *A Theory of Japanese Democracy*, Nobutaka Ike

Women and Revolution in Iran, Guity Nashat

Women and Work in Africa, edited by Edna Bay

International Law and the Status of Women, Natalie Kaufman Hevener

Women in Rural Development, Donald R. Mickelwait, Mary Ann Riegelman, and Charles F. Sweet

Introduction to Library Research for Women's Studies, Susan F. Searing

† *Women and Technological Change in Developing Countries*, edited by Roslyn Dauber and Melinda L. Cain

Scientific-Technological Change and the Role of Women in Development, edited by Pamela M. D'Onofrio-Flores and Sheila M. Pfafflin

† *The Underside of History: A View of Women Through Time*, Elise Boulding

Women and Minorities in Science: Strategies for Increasing Participation, edited by Sheila M. Humphreys

Working Women: A Study of Women in Paid Jobs, Ann Seidman

† *New Space for Women*, edited by Gerda R. Wekerle, Rebecca Peterson, and David Morley

† Available in hardcover and paperback.

About the Book and Author

The Hidden Sun: Women of Modern Japan
Dorothy Robins-Mowry

Ever since Japan and the West discovered one another, Western observers have extolled the surface virtues of Japanese women but attended very little to what they are really like. In this new, balanced view of the role of Japanese women in their country's swiftly changing society, Dr. Robins-Mowry destroys the Western stereotype of the shy, perhaps slightly coquettish, doll-like figure and replaces it with a sober, realistic portrait of a woman whose attitudes and activities influence the policies and trends of modern Japan, both domestically and internationally. She analyzes as well the extensive and often unrecognized constraints tradition places on women's performance in Japan's highly industrialized democracy, revealing uniquely Japanese customs and interrelationships in all facets of the nation's culture and society. The result is a penetrating overview of the changes in the whole of Japanese society since World War II—changes in which women have been catalysts, not bystanders.

The central part of the book examines the emergence of the postwar Japanese woman and her impact on her country's affairs, set against the background of critical historical and traditional factors. It is an intimate portrayal of the way the Japanese woman lives, the way she relates to her family and her work, how she sees herself within Japan's social and political contexts, and how she views the contribution she makes or can make to Japan's prosperity in general. Dr. Robins-Mowry writes with insight, sympathy, and understanding derived from years of immersion in the complex social, economic, and political life of Japan and its women. She illustrates her narrative with the comments of scores of Japanese women from all walks of life, culled from hundreds of interviews. A broad spectrum is represented—from well-known figures like Ichikawa Fusae and Ogata Sadako to leaders of rural cooperatives and environmental groups to women concentrating on raising their families.

A foreign service officer in the U.S. Information Agency (USIA) since 1963, Dr. Robins-Mowry has served overseas in Japan and Iran. From 1963 to 1971 she was chief of educational exchanges, cultural programs officer, and women's activities officer in the U.S. Information Service in Tokyo. She currently holds the position of policy officer in USIA for the Office of North Africa, the Middle East, and South Asia. In 1980 and 1981 Dr. Robins-Mowry was visiting professor of political science at the University of Maryland, teaching courses on women and politics.

In the beginning, woman was really the sun.
She was a true person.
Now woman is the moon.
She depends on others for her life
And reflects the light of others.
She is sickly as a wan, blue-white moon.

We, the completely hidden sun, must now restore ourselves.
"We must reveal the hidden sun—our concealed genius."
This is our constant cry and the inspiration of our
  unified purpose.
The climax of this cry, this thirst, this desire will
  impel the genius in ourselves to shine forth.

—Proclamation of Emancipation, *Bluestocking Journal (Seitō)*, 1911

THE HIDDEN SUN: WOMEN OF MODERN JAPAN

Dorothy Robins-Mowry

with a Foreword by
Edwin O. Reischauer

Westview Press / Boulder, Colorado

Copyright © 1983 by Westview Press, Inc.

Published in 1983 in the United States of America by
  Westview Press, Inc.
  5500 Central Avenue
  Boulder, Colorado 80301
  Frederick A. Praeger, President and Publisher

Library of Congress Cataloging in Publication Data
Robins-Mowry, Dorothy, 1921-
The hidden sun.
Bibliography: p.
Includes index.
1. Women—Japan—Social conditions. I. Title.
HQ1762.R6 1982   305.4'0952   82-20230
ISBN 0-86531-421-7
ISBN 0-86531-437-3 (pbk.)

Printed and bound in the United States of America

10   9   8   7   6   5   4   3   2

To the Many Japanese Women
Whose Friendship Inspired This Book
and Made It Possible

Contents

Tables and Illustrations

Foreword

Very shortly after I went to Japan as the U.S. Ambassador in April 1961, my wife, Haru, and I discovered that there was a great demand on the part of Japanese women for meetings with her to discuss Japanese-American relations and, still more, the roles and life of women in the United States and Japan. Soon she found herself with a crushing load of work of this sort to add to her already heavy burdens as an ambassador's wife. It became clear that there was a very real need for a women's activities officer in the United States Information Service branch of the embassy, and we started a search for the right person. The wheels of government, however, move slowly, and it was not until October 1963 that Dr. Dorothy Robins-Mowry, who was simply Dr. Dorothy Robins at the time, arrived in Japan.

A more happy choice could not have been found. Dr. Robins-Mowry had already established herself in the fields of women's work and international relations, and during her eight years in Japan she became a thorough expert on women's affairs there. Through her enthusiastic enterprise, unflagging energy, and warm personality, she established deep and lasting contacts with the women leaders of Japan. She came to know their work and the problems of Japanese women as well as any foreigner ever has. She has continued her interest in Japan and her contacts with the women since her departure, devoting two further years to research on this book. The result is an extraordinarily thorough account, told largely through the activities and words of the Japanese women leaders themselves.

The subject of women in Japan has always been one of the most baffling to foreign observers. The surface evidence seems to point in very contradictory directions. The flirtatious, beautiful *geisha* has been one cliché for Japanese women, the browbeaten *hausfrau* drudge another. The neat, cute office girl has contrasted with the dreary, exploited female factory worker. The exacting mother—the famous *kyōiku mama*, or "education mama"—and the tight-fisted mistress of the family finances form still another picture. Recently we have seen the rise of rebellious women authors and spectacular feminine figures in the world of the arts. Japanese women seem to combine meekness and ironlike strength, docility and domestic dominance, gentle beauty and daring action. It is not a picture that easily blends into a comprehensible whole.

Variations are naturally to be found in all large groupings of people, but Japanese women seem to show greater contrasts than most. Perhaps it is the result of the mixing of clashing heritages. There is reason to believe that Japan has an ancient underlying matriarchal background, which has survived in aspects of its culture all the way through history. At the same time, the main cultural heritage of Japan became more than a thousand years ago the strongly patriarchal tradition of Confucian China, and this was reinforced by the male dominance of a feudal age in which military prowess was all-important. Together these forces produced the extreme male chauvinism that at least superficially characterized the Japan of the nineteenth century. But then came the more liberalizing concepts of the nineteenth-century West, which called for a more equal role for women. These were followed by the still more liberating views of the twentieth-century West. The resulting conflict of cultural influences could well account for the confusing mixture of impressions that the outside world has of Japanese women.

Dr. Robins-Mowry has not tried to analyze all these tangled threads of the lives of women in Japan or explore in depth the attitudes and emotions of the various categories of Japanese women over time or even in the present age. She focuses on the central story of the conscious effort of women leaders in the development of a more coherent and self-respecting role for women in modern Japan from the 1870s until the 1980s. She has given us our most complete account of the activities of a remarkable group of women who became aware of the possible roles of women in society and started movements that have grown to large proportions, deeply affecting the society, economy, and also the politics of contemporary Japan. It is a story of great significance, not only for Japan but for other countries going through some of the same changes. It is also a fascinating account, for many of the women leaders have been truly extraordinary persons, and the spread of their movement from a few individuals to mass organizations that helped shape society and politics is a crucial aspect of the story of our times. Much more will be written about the perplexing place of women in Japanese society, but Dr. Robins-Mowry's book will always serve as a basic introduction to the story of a conscious women's movement in Japan.

Edwin O. Reischauer
University Professor, *Emeritus*
Harvard University

Preface

> . . . *the most wonderful aesthetic products of Japan*
> *are not its ivories, nor its bronzes, nor its porcelains,*
> *nor its swords, nor any of its marvels in metal or*
> *lacquer—but its women.*
> —Lafcadio Hearn, *Japan: An Attempt*
> *at Interpretation,* 1904[1]

Ever since Japan and the West discovered each other, Western observers have extolled the graces of Japanese women. This fundamental fact I knew when I walked down the gangplank of the *President Cleveland* in the rain and fog in October 1963 to start an assignment as women's activities officer at the U.S. Embassy in Tōkyō. Other qualities of Japanese women were not so apparent. The mist enveloping Yokohama port that morning seemed appropriately symbolic.

Ambassador and Mrs. Edwin O. Reischauer, who had urged that a new program to increase contact and understanding between the women of our two countries be initiated at the embassy, encouraged me in my assignment. My first task was to assume nothing and strive to discover what the Japanese woman was really like and what she wanted of her life and for her family and her society.

For the first year I traveled the reaches of Japan, from Kyūshū to Hokkaidō, asking questions, listening to ideas, and meeting a cross-section of girls in schools and textile mills and women in local, provincial, and national leadership positions in organizations, the professions, the media, and politics. I talked about women with men in decision-making positions. I asked about women's interests and problems to discover areas of mutuality between U.S. and Japanese societies and women's role in them. On the basis of this intercommunication, I started building opportunities of exchange and programs that actively grew for nine years, linking Japanese women not only with U.S. women, but also with those of other countries, particularly their neighbors in North and Southeast Asia.

In that time and the years since, I welcomed and cherished the Japanese friends I made and delighted in visits with them and their families in their homes and in taking part in their festivities. I also gained perceptions about how Americans and other Westerners tend to view the Japanese, particularly the women. The longer I lived in Japan, the more I became aware that outsiders were prone to regard women's roles primarily in simplistic terms. How often when explaining to a visitor what my job was at the embassy came the response, "You are working with the Japanese women? Whatever you do don't change them." What the person really meant was, "Do not shatter illusions"— the "remote aesthetic viewpoint," as one Japanese described it.[2]

Japanese men are equally guilty of limited visions about the distaff members of their society. Their inadequate knowledge points up a serious problem within the society, namely poor communication. Unhappily, such deficiencies compound the problem, for it is the men of Japan who normally have most of the encounters with Westerners.

The stock image of Japanese women was not created overnight. From early Dutch and Portuguese traders to the men of Commodore Perry's Black Ships, from the missionaries and diary-keeping tourists of the Meiji and Taishō eras down to their modern counterparts, from the Occupation-era GI to his contemporary military colleague, Western visitors have admired the modesty and delicacy of Japanese women. Lafcadio Hearn, writing the tribute that opens these pages, reflected more eloquently but no less truthfully the reactions of others.

Only a few have penetrated the surface to become aware of the individual woman's aspirations and personality. There is the inevitable language barrier. More pertinently, Japanese society, traditionally keeping the woman secluded in the inner house, figuratively spun for her a protective cocoon that enhanced her mysterious and romantic aura in the foreigner's imagination. Thus, this wonderment molded the Japanese woman into a doll-like figure—lovely but not quite real. The image of the doll, dressed either as an entertaining courtesan, coquettishly mincing with short steps beneath her colorful parasol, or as a docile wife and mother kneeling on the *tatami* mat floor and serving her family with decorously bowed head, in time hardened into stereotype. The world gently placed this living, breathing woman into the glass box used throughout Japan to encase all treasured kimono-clad and artistically hand-wrought dolls. She was entrapped in the legends of her own perfections—a likeness that harmonized with those other perpetuated symbols of Japan: cherry blossoms and Mount Fuji.

Contemporary mass media present an equally superficial point of view, featuring updated variations on the same themes: the modern bar girl; sex life and the office girl, Japanese style; the feminist movement; and the housewife. International diplomatic dignitaries, businessmen, and tourists, stepping off the plane, are eager to see and meet examples for themselves. Japanese government and business hosts order elaborate, expense-account geisha parties in luxurious settings for their guests. Only rarely is a visitor taken to a Japanese home, where the wife and mother will most likely slip in and out of the room, busy with her obligations of serving the honored guest. As far as most of the world can discern, the Japanese doll is still encased in her glass box.

Japanese women with first-hand experience of the outside world have long recognized their predicament. Some contemporaries of Lafcadio Hearn wrote a pamphlet about themselves for distribution at the Chicago World's Columbian Exposition in 1893, advising that they "are misunderstood to a great extent."[3] In the mid-1930s, an organizational leader, after visiting in North and South America, started an English-language newsletter to correct false impressions and give voice to the Japanese woman because "Japanese women to most of the people abroad are *Geisha* Girls or hostesses in bamboo houses with paper lantern. They must be heard, they must be known that they are real women with flesh and blood who experience joy, sorrow, aspirations and struggles."[4] A few Japanese women, such as Sugimoto Inagaki Etsu, Katō (Ishimoto) Shidzue, Kawai Michi, Mishima Sumie, and Matsuoka Yoko, opened a curtain to the West by writing autobiographies in English.

From time to time Western women who lived and worked with Japanese women have reported on the women's way of life. Alice Mabel Bacon, friend of Tsuda Umeko, was perhaps the first. The rationale for her book in 1891 was her belief that the whole fabric of Japanese social life would be better comprehended when the women and the homes that they made were better known.[5] In 1953, Mary R. Beard, pioneer specialist in the history of women, who helped Japanese women organize after the 1923 earthquake, took Japanese-compiled biographies of Japanese women since Amaterasu Ōmikami and "put them in their times and places where their meanings have their significance as a traditional force of women in history."[6] Others, more recently, have portrayed the historical atmosphere through personality sketches or have taken a functional or single-track view.

Emboldened by the enthusiastic support of my Japanese colleagues, here I attempt to look at Japanese women truly as half of their society. I want others to see them as I came to know them, actively influencing all aspects of Japanese affairs. The historical base is included to show the continuum of its influence. Without recognition of historical traditional forces, understanding of modern development is at best qualified—only a seeking of a mirror image of Western society rather than an assessment of a traditional society in the process of change.

The section on the contemporary period emphasizes fundamental themes of development: social, economic, political, and—the aspect that has been the most neglected—international. In each, I have tried to illustrate development through the activities and comments of outstanding women, such as Ichikawa Fusae in the feminist and political fields, Oku Mumeo in the economic, and Katō (Ishimoto) Shidzue in the social and international. These women, recognized by Japanese women themselves as leaders and symbols of progress, can serve similarly to foreigners who would look more deeply into the hearts and minds of Japanese women.

Throughout I have tried to let the women speak for themselves—in the early historical periods through their poetry, memoirs, autobiographies, and novels, adding for this century personal remembrances and direct interviews. In my ten years in Japan from 1963 to 1973, working full-time with Japanese women and their organizations, I kept copious notes of the many discussions and conferences in which I took part. I made notations about my interpretation of the whys of Japanese reactions—very important to a larger understanding.

My purpose is to open the glass case guarding the stereotype and lend a hand to help the active, modern woman step forth. As my friend and mentor Ichikawa Fusae enjoined while urging me to undertake this book, "Tell about the Japanese women as you see them, both favorable and unfavorable, but tell their story."

What follows, therefore, is neither a feminist argument nor a plea for the Japanese woman. Japanese women need no such help from outsiders. It is, rather, a broad-brush study of the Japanese woman's attitudes and activities and their effect on herself, her society, and her country's policies. It describes her influence and how she exerts it. It shows her remarkable capacity to pinpoint domestic problems well in advance of national recognition, making her a forecaster of social and economic need and change.

Given a research assignment in the fall of 1971 by the United States Information Agency (USIA), I was able for the next two years to undertake more formal research in the United States and Japan, and carry out systematic, in-depth interviewing with more than one hundred women and men. The interviews, which were conducted in Japanese and/or English and taped, cut across age groups, life-styles, professions, political viewpoints, and geography. To all the interviewees my deep appreciation. They revealed much more of interest than could possibly be encompassed by just one book. Incidentally, except where used with a Western honorific title, all Japanese names are written with surname first and given name last.

Grants from the National Endowment for the Humanities and the American Association of University Women Educational Foundation helped support my research. To them, as to USIA, I am most grateful. The Radcliffe Institute for Women made me a research fellow, 1971–1972, providing valuable research resources. Working with me through the research and early writing periods were many Japanese companions, who readily assisted whenever I asked. Especially I would mention Ichikawa Fusae, Sakanishi Shio, and Shiraishi Tsugi, all recently deceased, and also Oshima Kiyoko and Sōma Yukika. Yamamoto Kazuko and Ishii Reiko, daily research and translating-interpreting aides who came to me through these friends, in turn became my friends, and the book, a project of joint interest. Together with fifteen to twenty Japanese colleagues working for the U.S. Embassy and Cultural Centers, they did all the translating and interpreting not otherwise credited. Several people reviewed the manuscript; the comments of Ardath W. Burks were particularly detailed, incisive, and encouraging. Philip M. Nagao of the Japanese Division of the Library of Congress kindly spent many hours helping to find illustrations for the historical portion of the text.

Typists in three countries labored diligently. Especially I thank Murate Hiroko in Japan, Bernice Richards in Iran, and Helen Nakki, Frances Kaspar, and Catherine Mike in the United States. Special thanks go to Carolyn Spatta Karlow for editing and putting the final version into shape.

The manuscript in process is well traveled, having crossed from Japan to the United States for my reassignment there in 1973 and then on to Tehran in 1978 for my reassignment there as cultural attaché. I carried the manuscript with me as one of my most valued belongings as I flew out of Iran in December 1978 when revolutionary turmoil possessed the country.

To Mildred Marcy, my colleague at USIA, who sometimes despaired but never lost faith in the long years of this book, and to my husband, David T. Mowry, who also lived with its making, advising, reading manuscript, and editing, "thank you" is hardly sufficient, but most truly it is the finest phrase there is.

Dorothy Robins-Mowry

PART 1
BACKGROUND:
THE LOOM OF HISTORY

*I would like the rest of the world to study Japanese
history so that they will understand the background
of today's Japanese women. Unlike America, where
men and women joined together in founding the
country, Japan has been a country of men. The
quickest way to discover this is to read Japanese
history.*
—Community Leader, Fukuoka, Spring 1972

Past and present mingle freely in Japanese daily life.

At no time is this more apparent than during the observances for
New Year, the most important holiday of the year. Tolling temple bells
ring out at midnight to exorcise the one hundred and eight Buddhist
evils. Family members stop routine daily chores to travel the length
and breadth of Japan for traditional reunions. In the spirit of the event,
modern young women shed their short skirts and workaday uniforms.
They revert to the time-honored, gaily flowered kimono, enveloping
shrugs, and tinsel hair decorations worn proudly as they promenade
the shrine walkways or gather with companions in coffee shops and
restaurants. Their change of dress to honor the season symbolizes the
ease with which the habits of the past intertwine with the customs of
the present. The ongoing traditions weave as naturally into modern
living as the colorful skeins of silk interlace to form patterns in the
brocaded *obi* sashes that tie the kimonos of the celebrating Japanese
women.

At other times of the year, in day-to-day encounters, a graceful
kimono is less likely to be on view to signal to the foreign observer
the juxtaposition of old and new. Nonetheless, the lingering forces of
history and culture are subtly present to guide thinking and action.
Often, the individual woman may not fully realize the basis of her own
actions. She knows only that this is the Japanese way.

The traditional Japanese way embraces the heritage of centuries. The
modern Japanese way evolved during the last one hundred years under
the impact of a series of revolutionary changes. First, Emperor Meiji
and his kindred modernizers superimposed new ideas and revamped

---

Illustration opposite: Lady Murasaki, author of the *The Tale of Genji*, the world's
first novel, sits at her writing table facing out onto her garden. Illustration
courtesy Ise Grand Shrine.

3

methods. Then came General Douglas MacArthur and the Occupation policies and programs. In the last few decades, the miracle of economic growth has added further ferment to the modernization process. The interplay of these various dimensions creates the drama of the present time.

To understand the nature and extent of these adjustments of old and new, we must turn to history. In particular, let us peer at those special threads used on the loom of history to fashion the life design of the Japanese woman: family relationships, social status, education, political prerogatives, and economic well-being.

CHAPTER 1
THE WAY OF TRADITION

EARLY JAPAN—
GODDESSES AND EMPRESSES

> *Our great Sovereign who rules in peace,*
> *Offspring of the Bright One on high,*
> *Wills, as a goddess, to rule her dominion*
> *And to decree her towering Palace*
> *On the plain of Fujiwara.*
> —*Manyōshū*, seventh century[1]

In the dawn of Japanese history women held positions of prestige and authority.

As mothers, women represented fertility and life for the primitive and superstitious familial bands. As queens of Yamatai in western Japan, they brought order to the land and engaged in international diplomacy with the rulers to the west on the mainland of Asia.

Legend made the female deity, the Sun Goddess Amaterasu Ōmikami, the founder of the Japanese imperial family. This "Heaven-Shining-Great Deity" commissioned her grandson Ninigi-no-Mikoto to descend from Heaven upon the Japanese Isles, carrying the three sacred insignia of the mirror, sword, and jewel, to govern and bring prosperity as enduring as that of Heaven and Earth. Thus was established the divine ancestry of the imperial line, which has reigned for more than a thousand years, combining within itself religious and dynastic supremacy. Imperial princesses became the high priestesses to care for the most holy of the Shintō religious shrines at Ise, dedicated to the worship of the Sun Goddess.

Popular lore and early chronicles set forth the position and power held by women in family, religion, and government in the Japanese

Isles in the period through the seventh century. One recent writer has called these early years the golden age of women in Japan. Modern women, from time to time, are strengthened by this heritage in their feminist endeavors.[2]

Queen Himiko

Chinese chroniclers, who gave the first sophisticated records of Japan, pointed to female dominance among the "people of Wa," as they called the Japanese in their third-century *History of the Kingdom of Wei* (*Wei chih*). They told of a Queen Himiko, a mature, unmarried ruler in western Japan whose name probably means sun daughter or princess. She is said to have practiced magic, revealing messages of the gods. Rarely seen, and living in a well-guarded palace with 1,000 women attendants, she maintained strict laws, ruling through her brother. In A.D. 238 she dispatched envoys to pay homage to the Chinese emperor and sent as tribute slaves and bolts of specially designed cloth. In return, the emperor bestowed upon her the title, "Queen of Wa Friendly to Wei."[3]

The Kojiki

The Japanese version of their own beginnings and early history came some four hundred years later in the writing of the *Kojiki* and the subsequent *Nihongi*, a dynastic project encouraged by various empresses of the seventh and eighth centuries A.D., including Empress Suiko and Empress Jitō. These official chronicles intertwine the mythological with the semihistorical to support the antiquity and glory of the imperial line. They relate the sagas of Amaterasu Ōmikami and the other gods and goddesses to show their relationship with the semilegendary first emperor of Japan, Jimmu, whose dynasty began, according to tradition, in 660 B.C.

A tale popular with Japanese women purports that Hiyeda-no-Are, a woman *kataribe*, a member of the guild of oral story-tellers to which women often belonged in early Japan, played a central role in giving life to the *Kojiki*.[4] When Empress Gemmyō commanded Ōno Yasumaro in 711 to "select and record the old works," he turned for assistance to the aged Hiyeda-no-Are, who had memorized all the old poems, myths, and stories. Word by word, as she recited the oral traditions, he wrote them down and produced the *Kojiki*.[5]

One of the outstanding figures emerging from this account of the misty early years is Empress Jingō (200–269 A.D.) whose posthumous name shows that she is revered as a woman second only to Amaterasu

Gods and goddesses dance and offer enticements to lure the Sun Goddess Amaterasu Ōmikami from the cave in which she hid when her brother brought violence into the world. Artist: Itō Ryūgai. Photo courtesy of the Mayor of Ise.

Queen Himiko, third-century ruler of western Japan, is portrayed in regal attire, wearing a necklace with the curved jewel (*magatama*), one of the three sacred emblems of the imperial family. Artist: Yasuda Yukihiko. Photo couresty of Yasuda Kenichi.

Modern women dressed in holiday finery enjoy the poem card game that is traditionally played during New Year's festivities. The first of the one hundred poems of the game was composed by Empress Jitō. Photo courtesy of the Embassy of Japan.

in greatness. Her dynamism is revealed in reports about how she rode to Kyūshū with her husband at the head of elaborately clad warriors to quell a rebellion. Deciding that the uprising was fomented by Korea, she—now alone, for her husband had died—disguised herself as a man and led the Japanese forces against the Koreans. The story goes that she rode on the prow of a battleship assisted by "great fishes of the ocean" and a miraculous wave across the sea to subjugate the enemy. This conquest opened the door to cultural influences from the Korean peninsula.[6]

Epoch of the Queens

During the remarkable two hundred years spanning the Asuka (A.D. 552–710) and Nara (A.D. 710–784) periods, by which time recognizable history overtakes earlier conjecture, one-half of the Japanese rulers were women. It might well be called the Epoch of the Queens. They were women of command, merry and stout of heart. They set standards for the culture, religion, and mood of their times. They provided a matriarchal continuity for the imperial family as power struggles swirled around the throne. A few highlights can illustrate the political, intellectual, and human strengths for which these women are remembered.

Empress Suiko (592–628) is regarded as the first woman in historical times to ascend the throne of Japan. She presided during a time of intellectual ferment and change in social and governmental organization; she encouraged the channeling of Chinese civilization into many facets of Japanese life. Ruling with her nephew, the incomparable Prince Shōtoku, she helped establish Buddhism as a major religion in Japan and supported the creation of many of Buddhism's finest arts.[7]

Empress Jitō (687–697) was a strong-willed, intelligent beauty, renowned for her political astuteness. She supported the compilation of the great Japanese fundamental laws, culminating in the Taihō Code of 701. Under this revamped tax and land system, it must be noted, women received only two-thirds of the allotments in land redistribution available to men. Interestingly, Japanese women suffragists of the 1940s maintained that such inequity in the code was based on Chinese customs and that changes from the older traditional family system of giving a good deal of equality to women were only skin deep. Apart from her ruling capacities, Empress Jitō is widely remembered for the light-hearted *tanka* she wrote when she moved her capital to Fujiwara. Many modern Japanese can quote it as the first poem of the card game "100-persons-each-one-poem" (*Hyaku-nin-isshu*) traditionally played at New Year's celebrations:

> Spring has passed away
>   And summer is come;
> Look where white clothes are spread in the sun
>   On the heavenly hill of Kagu![8]

It was Empress Gemmyō (707–715), a patron of classical learning, as shown in her role in the preparation of the *Kojiki*, who established in Nara in 710 the first permanent capital of her kingdom, making possible a less casually organized and more centralized structure of government.

Another great beauty and skilled calligrapher, Empress Kōmyō (729–749), consort of Emperor Shōmu, must be mentioned even though she was not a ruling empress because she is remembered by women as the first volunteer social worker in her country. A devout Buddhist, she zealously propagated her faith. She constructed temples for worship and commissioned sculpture to enhance them, including the huge Buddha of Tōdaiji Temple in Nara. Her deep religious sense prompted her to help the sick, orphaned, and needy, tasks that usually fell to the monks and others within religious orders. This reputation for charitable services gave rise to a now famous legend. It seems that one day a leprous beggar came to her and asked that she cleanse his sores with her mouth. Although she was repelled, her religious fervor pushed her to comply. Amazingly, the beggar turned into a Buddha before her eyes. He told her that he had appealed for this demeaning care to test her faith. As might be imagined, the Empress Kōmyō's charitable endeavors were not generally understood by the people, and she was severely criticized. Yet in due course, her good works won her the posthumous name of the "Empress who shines brightly."

Unfortunately, the daughter of Empress Kōmyō, a woman of equally great enthusiasm, managed to bring to an end this period of the queens through her propensity for love affairs. Empress Shōtoku (764–770), or Empress Kōken (749–758), for as she was empress twice she had two names, like her predecessors warmly supported Buddhism and the arts. When her military forces suppressed a civil war in 764, she gave thanks by printing 1 million religious charms. The few existing today are examples of the earliest printing in the world. More important, she served as a catalyst in the compilation of some three hundred and fifty years of native Japanese poetry, which, in straightforward, natural, and sometimes earthy style, had been composed by emperors and empresses, courtiers, soldiers of the frontier, young lovers, and common people alike. Portraying a cross-section of the emotions and longing of the people of early Japan, this collection, *Manyōshū*, or *Collection of Myriad Leaves*, is still cherished as part of the great traditional culture of the Japanese.

Despite her accomplishments, Shōtoku's amorous involvements with the Buddhist priest Dōkyo precipitated a political struggle. He aspired to become emperor with the willing help of his empress. The intrigue aroused the noble cliques at court. Civil war erupted, and the orbit of power swung in a new direction. Except for two figurehead empresses, Meishō and Gosakuramachi, during the Edo period in the seventeenth and eighteenth centuries, Shōtoku was the last of the ruling empresses. Her debacle brought to an end the era of lively female sovereigns. Her passing foreshadowed a major change in the position of women.

Chinese Influences

In all fairness, it should be made clear that factors other than Empress Shōtoku's love life entered into her political difficulties and the subsequent general decline of women's power. Chinese ideas, absorbed for several hundred years under the eager endorsement of the imperial families and the court, were gradually modifying the religious beliefs, governmental structures, social practices, and attitudes toward relationships of the Japanese people.

Buddhism, introduced from Korea in the middle of the sixth century, was fundamental in these changes. It brought new tenets, its own pantheon, and a special kind of mysticism. In time, it became a competitor to Shintō, the animistic native religion with its own deities and semisuperstitious rituals and customs, and precipitated countervailing power struggles in ruling circles and skirmishes over royal succession.

Chinese concepts of centralized political organization helped reorder the structure of government patterns, as seen in Prince Shōtoku's Seventeen-Article Constitution and the court ranking system. Ultimately this new system broke the hold of the age-old hereditary, local, semiautonomous clan ruling groups reminiscent of Queen Himiko's country of Wa.

Confucianism offered a neat catalog of virtues and detailed an orderly and restrained structure of relationships of people to each other and to the natural order of the universe. Its integration into Japanese thinking paved the way for the acceptance of a rigid code of life of hierarchical form and stern moral discipline, subordinating the individual to the family and the state.

For Japanese women the new philosophies presaged less equality with men, more restrictive family relationships, and the loss of power and political authority. In the future they would turn to the indirect methods of leverage for which they are renowned to the present day. They would exert influence through their roles as wives and mothers, as beauties and entertainers, as guardians of the family assets, and as writers.

HEIAN JAPAN—
ARISTOCRATS AND WRITERS

> *. . . Perhaps, she said to herself, even the story of*
> *her own dreary life, set down in a journal, might be*
> *of interest; and it might also answer a question: had*
> *that life been one befitting a well-born lady?*
> —Mother of Michitsuna, *The Gossamer Years,*
> tenth century[9]

The court ladies of the Heian years created the shining hour of Japanese literature.

From within the shadowy, screened confines of the women's quarters of the palaces and great houses of the court, noblewomen of the tenth and eleventh centuries peered out at the comings and goings of their fellow courtiers and shaped for posterity a shimmering world of elegance with their poems, diaries, and novels.

They lived in a golden age of peace and harmony, as the alternate name, Heian-kyō, of their proud capital city of Kyōto spelled out. Kyōto, built in 794 to permit the emperor and his court to escape the over-burdening Buddhist influences developed during the Nara period, became in the Heian years the focal point of this brilliant society. Whereas in the Nara years the native Yamato traditional patterns of religion, life, and government were slowly assimilating the new cultural forms imported from China and Korea, in the Heian years the synthesis produced a thoroughly Japanized civilization. The manuscripts of the noble court ladies sparkle brightly at the pinnacle of this culture.

High-born Heian women, with their heavy gowns of many layers and myriad colors, long, streaming, glossy-black hair, shaved eyebrows, blackened teeth and languid manners, spent their lives hidden from the light and sun behind the silken curtains of their mansions, screened by the heavy drapes of their two-wheeled ox-drawn carriages, or secluded in retreat at a favorite temple. Within this dim world, symbolic in its way of their circumscribed scope of human concern, they looked piercingly around to probe mood and emotion. Unlike the vigorous women leaders of Nara and earlier, Heian women took little interest in politics and government per se. Instead they concentrated on social relationships, the drape of a sleeve, the turn of a poetic phrase, the

Heian ladies are depicted in an elegant secluded home setting, amusing themselves with the popular Japanese game of *go*. Antique screen in author's collection.

beauty of the seasons, the rituals of propitiation, and elaborate ceremonials.

While these women surrounding the imperial court may have, as
Michitsuna's Mother bemoaned in her diary, spent their days in "triv-
ialities,"[10] their perceptive writings about these days—and nights—
depicted the character of one of the great patrician eras in history.
Moreover, because the education given girls did not include adequate
training in Chinese, which had come to be regarded as the intellectual
language and to be reserved for the use of men, the Heian women
wrote in their native Japanese. In so doing, they created the first truly
native Japanese literature—and some of the best of it, at that.

Heian women, at least those of the aristocratic families, enjoyed
certain freedoms and a stature in keeping with their rank. Under the
law they were entitled to hold property. They were educated in the
arts to develop personalities of refinement. Confucian emphases on
family relationships and loyalty prevailed, and Japan was officially a
monogamous society. Moral sensitivities and solid political reasoning,
however, saw no harm in concubinage and the taking of lovers. The
Fujiwara family, to cite the most illustrious example, had built its
supremacy in large measure by providing its daughters to the emperors
as empresses or royal concubines in the imperial household. This policy
insured that future emperors were also Fujiwaras. Alternatively, after
marriage a young wife might continue to live in her family home; the
husband came to visit. This system at least precluded the problems of
adjustment with the new in-laws that so beset Japanese brides of later
times. Only in due time might a new home be set up. The comings
and goings of this kind of marital relationship undoubtedly abetted the
establishment of second houses. Equally, the teasing quality of the
withdrawal of women behind their screens, enticing only with the
display of a sleeve or the sending of a poem attached to a flower, led
to countless more fleeting romantic encounters. The flavor of life was
imbued with the Buddhist sense of impermanence.[11]

Court Diaries

Michitsuna's Mother, acclaimed as one of the three great beauties of
her time, was greatly disturbed by such uncertain conditions of marriage.
(Incidentally, we have no other name for her.) In her diary she lamented
her "irregular" position or, at another point, her "ill-defined position,"[12]
for she was not the first wife of Fujiwara Kaneie. She jealously, bitingly
commented on the other eight or nine wives, concubines, and mistresses
with whom he was involved over the years. She sent her most famous
poem, attached to a withered chrysanthemum, to her husband asking

with poignancy and a certain melancholy, "Do you know how slow the dawn can be when you have to wait alone?"[13]

Other renowned diaries and commentaries of the time display different personalities and reveal varied reactions to this "dream path"[14] world. They vividly illustrate that the real women of Japan have not existed in stereotypic personality.

Lady Sei Shōnagon—quick, witty, perhaps even a punster—pictures in her *Pillow-Book* court life as seen from the palace of the Emperor's first wife, Fujiwara Sadako, where she served as a lady-in-waiting. Born into the Kiyohara family, noted for many generations for learning and literary skills, Sei Shōnagon came to the palace for the last decade of the tenth century, and her reminiscences and journal entries cover that period. Sparing neither herself nor those around her, she dissected episodes both pleasing and displeasing, ragged ponderous courtiers, relished the emotional fervor of her periodic religious services, and considered such subjects as "Disagreeable Things," "Amusing Things," "Things That Give Me an Uncomfortable Feeling," and "Children." That her vivacious, sometimes acerbic sense of humor did not always make her popular may be judged from Lady Murasaki's remarks in her diary: "Sei Shōnagon's most marked characteristic is her extraordinary self-satisfaction. . . . Her chief pleasure consists in shocking people; and as each new eccentricity becomes only too painfully familiar, she gets driven on to more and more outrageous methods of attracting notice."[15]

Annoying she may have been, but the world is the richer for Sei Shōnagon's fresh, amusing view of a life normally heavy with perfumed elegances and fastidious manners. She, at least, could criticize her lover on the clumsiness of his early-morning departure from her boudoir:

It is very tiresome when a lover who is leaving one at dawn says that he must look for a fan or a pocket book that he left somewhere about the room last night. As it is still too dark to see anything, he goes fumbling about all over the place, knocking into everything and muttering to himself, "How very odd!" When at last he finds the pocket book he crams it into his dress with a great rustling of the pages; or if it is a fan he has lost, he swishes it open and begins flapping it about, so that when he finally takes his departure, instead of experiencing the feelings of regret proper to such an occasion, one merely feels irritated at his clumsiness.[16]

By contrast, the shy, introspective daughter of a provincial governor in her *Sarashina Diary* yearns for the romance she savors in her reading of the exploits of Lord Genji. She reaches out for only one brief encounter of the heart. It starts on an evening when "there was no starlight and a gentle shower fell in the darkness."[17] She and an almost invisible young man share a conversation that holds promise of future meetings. It ends a year later after one more meeting and an exchange of poems, as she waits in vain for him to come and play his lute and sing to her. "I wanted to hear it and waited for the fit occasion, but there was none, ever,"[18] she gently concludes.

The provocative, impetuous Izumi Shikibu, daughter of another provincial governor, excelled in poetry, since admired as some of the finest ever produced in the Japanese language. She reveled in her emotions and the sequence of romantic entanglements with noble princes. Her diary covers the year or two of her passionate attachment to Prince Tamekaka and exists primarily to offer a setting for the love poems they exchanged. Early in their liaison she portrayed her emotions in these sentiments:

> I am a drop of dew
> Hanging from a leaf
> Yet I am not unrestful
> For on this branch I seem to have existed
> From before the birth of the world.[19]

Despite the gossip that surrounded her, Izumi Shikibu's fame as a poet prompted Akiko, queen of the Emperor's second household, to add Izumi to her coterie of Lady Murasaki and other ladies-in-waiting. Akiko wished to outshine with literary brilliance the entourage of the first consort, Queen Sadako.

Lady Murasaki

Most famous of all Heian women writers, Murasaki Shikibu[20] supplied still another type of mentality to this amazingly creative group. She was exceedingly bright, critical of mind, and interested in learning, much of which she had gleaned by eavesdropping on her brother's lessons. Of a Fujiwara family, she married another Fujiwara and seems to have had a happy marriage. After the death of her husband from pestilence, she filled her days with the writing of Lord Genji's many adventures and love affairs. *The Tale of Genji*, a piece of realistic fiction and the world's first novel, illuminates the times, attitudes, and life of the court Lady Murasaki knew so well and attests to the astuteness with which she observed the people around her. For example, each of the succession of women Genji loves emerges very much a distinct personality. But their stories also reveal that Murasaki, like Michitsuna's Mother, had few illusions about sexual relationships with men; too

Lady Murasaki, author of *The Tale of Genji*, the world's first novel, sits at her writing table, facing out into her garden. Artist: Kawasaki Shōko. Photo courtesy of the Mayor of Ise.

often they brought uncertainty for women, making them like "bits of driftwood."[21] She was, however, practical in her assessment, rather than wistful, or alternatively, a feminist. With her author's eye she analyzed women and, in the process, offered some advice about how to approach life. At one point, using the voices of her hero and some of his friends, she placed women in categories of merit and distinction in their role as wives. Initially, the gentlemen decide that no one woman can meet absolute standards of perfection. Each must inevitably balance virtue and defect. They consider in turn a "creature of unimagined beauty," "the zealous housewife," "paragons of misused fidelity," and "others who must needs be forever mounting guard over their own and their husband's affections."[22] At last one of the party concludes that in the long run the virtues of "generosity and reasonableness and patience do on the whole seem best."[23]

Lady Murasaki and her aristocratic colleagues of the writing brush left two important legacies to Japan. The first is the well-recognized, incomparable standard of literary merit. The second is that of the powerful role of the social critic who serves as a kind of contemporary public conscience dissecting the events and morals of the time. This latter role survived the passage down the long and tortuous developments of the feudal epochs as a bequest by the Heian women writers to the women of modern Japan—a gift they cherish and utilize to mold the character of their twentieth-century society.

THE MIDDLE YEARS—
WARRIOR HEROINES AND FEUDAL WIVES

> *A woman has no way of independence through life.*
> *When she is young, she obeys her father; when she is*
> *married, she obeys her husband; when she is*
> *widowed, she obeys her son.*
> —Doctrine of the Three Obediences (*Sanjū kun*)[24]

From the twelfth to the nineteenth centuries, during the seven hundred middle years of civil war and feudalism, Japanese women practiced the arts of loyalty and obedience and learned subservience.

As the twelfth century drew to a close, the primacy of the glittering, self-centered Heian court eroded. Fujiwara control, which had maintained a peaceful, orderly land for more than two hundred years, crumbled. Warring Buddhist monks from temples on Mount Hiei outside Kyōto raided the capital. Provincial lords mobilized to protect their local autonomy in face of the weakened imperial system. Heike and Minamoto clans finally swept all before them in their struggles for mastery over the imperial line and, ultimately, over Japan of the Kamakura period. The world of the spartan, rugged, hard-living, hard-dying *bushi* or *samurai* warriors had emerged to dominate Japan. With them came feudalism. Throughout the ensuing years, with seesawing civil wars and with governance divided between symbolic imperial and actual political capitals, this military aristocracy shaped and in turn was shaped by evolving military, governmental, social, and cultural changes.

Women's lives kept pace with these forces of history. The courageous, strong, and devoted samurai woman replaced the aesthetic Heian noblewoman as the aristocratic ideal. Then, decade by decade, the independent-minded samurai heroine of the Kamakura era slipped into the more rigid style of life demanded by Ashikaga and Tokugawa feudalism—a pattern of humbling self-control, obedience exacted by loyalties, and, for most, wearying rounds of work and drudgery at home or in the rice fields. Even the Japanese words for wife, *kanai* and *okusan*, adopted into the language during this era, symbolized her position. They mean "persons in the innermost recesses of the house." She was protected but confined.

Samurai Heroines

Throughout these changes the *bushi* women set the example. Many were trained in the martial arts and achieved skill in archery and the use of the sword. Their virtues, their education, and their housewifely habits were recognized and valued as the norm to be emulated by women of the other classes—the farmers, artisans, and merchants.[25] Stories abound of loyal, devoted, and energetic women of the medieval samurai internecine conflicts. Some take on a romanticized glow. One such woman was Tomoe Gozen, the young provincial heroine who rode with her husband onto the battlefield in the Minamoto-Heike feuds. Even though in jeopardy she insisted on remaining, saying to her husband, "I want to fight with the enemy who is worthy of me and I want to fight the last glorious fight in front of you." This she did.[26] Other heroines from the epic *Tales of Heike* provide the stuff of long-running popularized historical television series in modern Japan.

Most impressive in historical impact, however, is Hōjō Masako (1157–1225), the wife of the first *shōgun*, Minamoto Yoritomo. She is known as the "general in nun's habit." As a young woman in love with Yoritomo, then in exile in eastern Japan, she escaped from an arranged betrothal, running over dangerous mountain paths to find him. "I came to you missing my way in the dark night, enduring a heavy rain." Throughout the years of his wars with the Heike and after he became shōgun, she continued to love him and support him politically. She hated and refused to accept his polygamous arrangements, and various of his mistresses felt her jealous wrath. By contrast, she was sympathetic and helpful to unfortunate women. A popularly cherished example is her befriending the lovely dancing girl Shizuka Gozen, who aroused Yoritomo's ire when she sang of her love for his exiled brother, Yoshitsune, during a command performance at the Hachiman Shrine in Kamakura, which had become the new political capital. After Yoritomo's death in 1199, Hōjō Masako became a Buddhist nun, as was the custom. Far from a recluse, she rallied and bullied the warrior chiefs to stand by the shogunate against pressures from the imperial court. Through many plots and counterplots, she cleverly and ruthlessly fought to sustain the Kamakura *bakufu*, or "tent government." Controlling as regent, very literally from behind a curtained screen, Hōjō Masako employed the determination and courage of her samurai heritage to protect her family's power. It is not inappropriate to call Hōjō Masako the real founder of the Kamakura government.[27]

Loyalty and devotion did not necessarily bring either success or happiness to samurai women. Many daughters and wives, such as those around Oda Nobunaga, Toyotomi Hideyoshi, and Tokugawa Ieyasu, the three great leaders who unified Japan in the late sixteenth and early seventeenth centuries, were used as pawns to secure military and political advantage. In the mélange of double-dealing, perfidy, and changing fortunes, they were frequently sacrificed. Suicide or early death was often their fate. Hosokawa Gracia Tamako, a Christian noblewoman caught in the maelstrom between the forces of Tokugawa Ieyasu and those of the late Toyotomi Hideyoshi at the time of the decisive battle of Sekigahara in 1600, remained in her flaming home rather than be captured and forced to betray her Catholic religion.[28]

This degrading policy of political marriage, political divorce, and hostage marriage, and the espionage involved in all such relationships, led to a general denigration of women. Proverbs warned against possible betrayal by wives whose loyalties might bind them irrevocably to the political needs of their father's house and its chain of feudal obligations. "She may have borne you seven sons, but never trust a woman." Or again, "Even when a husband and wife are alone together, he should never forget his dagger."[29] But no matter which obligation she finally honored, that to her father or that to her husband, the woman knew only too well from her teachings that virtue lay in submissiveness and duty, in obedience.

Buddhism

Inherent in the deteriorating position of women throughout the feudal years were Buddhist and Confucian philosophies. Reshaped through the centuries since their introduction from the Chinese mainland to suit Japanese needs, they carried within them the seeds of male dominance and a class-structured society that reduced women to the lowest classification.

Buddhism appealed to the earlier Nara elite for its offer of the Eightfold Path toward the attainment of enlightenment and salvation and for the emotional satisfaction of esoteric ritual. Despite its support by the empresses of that period, Buddhism had excluded women from the hope of achieving nirvana. It considered them instruments of defilement. Buddhism of the feudal years, adjusting to the social upheaval of war, pestilence, and famine, provided the less sophisticated samurai overlords and their retainers with a simpler faith that gave hope of retribution in the next life. With the broadening appeal through new sects, doctrines also were modified permitting women to seek Buddhahood. Even so, they were greatly handicapped, and sermons warned against them.

Shinran, the thirteenth-century priest who founded the most important of the Pure Land sects, taught, "Women by nature are covetous and sinful. Therefore they must always think of this fact and exert themselves to cleanse themselves of this sinful nature. Without this effort, they cannot be received into the world of Buddha."[30] Such teachings did not keep Shinran himself from the marriage bed and the sin of association with women.

Nichiren, on the other hand, influenced by his affection for his mother, argued against the concept of the sinfulness of women. "Man is pillar and woman is frame; man is wing and woman is body; if the wing is separated from the body, how can it fly?" But he and the Zen sect stood alone on this point.[31]

Abutsuni, a thirteenth-century court lady best remembered for her travel diary, gave some indication of women's view of Buddhism of this time in a letter to her daughter: "The spring flowers and autumn maples you may enjoy or not, but do not forget to contemplate the frostbitten plants of winter. . . . Our life is but a short-lived dream. Study carefully the Buddhist doctrine, and let not worldly pains and troubles torment you."[32] Two centuries later sermonizers continued, "Woman is originally an agent of the six devils and has been born as woman to prevent man from following the way of Buddha."[33] The women themselves were lectured about their husbands: "Even if he seems more lowly than you are, man is the personification of the Buddha and has the sense of reward and punishment as well as that of mercy. . . . You must bear in mind that you have married a Buddhist saint."[34]

In the second quarter of the seventeenth century, Shōgun Iemitsu decreed that every household must register with some Buddhist temple. The move was prompted in part to combat Christianity and foreign influences, and the edict made Buddhism a national religion, allied to the government. The registration process, probably inadvertently, increased the hazards faced by young women. As the father determined whose name should be included in the registry, he at the same time determined who would be eligible for family rights. Too often the decision was used to the detriment of brides, who faced the ambiguous situation of *naien*, or nonregistration in the family, until after the birth of their first boy baby or even later. This custom prevailed until the acceptance of the Constitution of 1946.

In her mid-1930s autobiography, *Facing Two Ways*, Katō (Ishimoto) Shidzue reflected on the centuries-long impact of pessimistic and fatalistic Buddhism on the Japanese people. It brought, she felt, an emphasis on the "negative virtues, such as endurance, self-repression, restraint" and

This woodblock print portrays an old couple prepared to sweep the sandy shore under the big pine trees of Takasago. Based on a tenth-century poem, the legend of *Takasago-an* achieved popularity in the late Tokugawa period as a symbol of longevity and happy married life and was used at weddings. Woodblock in author's collection.

produced "a code of resignation and subjection which offers nothing but sadness for the soul."[35]

Confucian Teachings

Confucian teaching about women and their intellectual inadequacies buttressed the depressed view expounded by the Buddhist religion. The *yin*, the soft, dark, passive, and negative quality attributed to women under this philosophy, contrasted with the *yang*, the active, sunlit spirit of the male. Although complementary in concept, this dualistic principle resulted in a diminishing of women's position. Confucianism, combined with the feudalistic path of loyalty of the man to his lord utilized by Ieyasu to achieve a stable Tokugawa society, left little place for woman except as a vessel to insure posterity. None of the time-honored chivalrous attitudes about women that marked the knights of medieval Europe existed in the Japanese version of feudalism. Marriage had nothing to do with love and affection. For a man that might be found elsewhere. A wife's role was to be that of "a belly borrowed to bear sons."[36] The three obediences, cited at the head of this chapter on the middle years, laid the foundation. Books of morals, such as *Hinekagami* [Ladies' mirror] of Nakamura Tekisai and *Fujin oshiyegusa* [Teachings for women] of Fujii Ransai, contained the multiple rules that established the code of behavior and attitudes essential for her to fulfill her role in the family and society.

Most influential of such books is the *Onna daigaku* [Greater learning for women], prepared in 1672 by Kaibara Ekken, a neo-Confucian moralist. Because there were few books available for well-brought-up young girls to read, his text, written for popular use, became the standard primer and graced every samurai girl's trousseau box.

The enduring authority of this household morality was evident in the hundred or more personal interviews conducted for this book with Japanese women of all ages. Only those born and educated completely in the postwar period reacted to the mention of the *Onna daigaku* with an impersonal schoolroom remembrance. Their elders all know it as a personal moral catechism, drilled into them by their mothers and grandmothers. One social and political leader remembers that her grandfather willed her a manuscript of these teachings, copied in beautifully written Chinese ideograph and tied up with a purple silk cord. She angrily remarked that it was the "epitome" of all she had struggled against.[37] The ideas of the *Onna daigaku* still linger consciously or unconsciously in the attitudes and behavior of most of the mature women of Japan.

What then does the *Onna daigaku* teach? It starts out with its premise:

> Seeing that it is a girl's destiny, on reaching womanhood, to go to a new home, and live in submission to her father-in-law, it is even more incumbent upon her than it is on a boy to receive with all reverence her parents' instructions. Should her parents, through their tenderness, allow her to grow up self-willed, she will infallibly show herself capricious in her husband's house, and thus alienate his affection; while, if her father-in-law be a man of correct principles, the girl will find the yoke of these principles intolerable.

She is admonished, therefore, to develop a "virtuous heart" and to strive for "the only qualities that befit a woman," which are "gentle obedience, chastity, mercy, and quietness." She must observe the rules of decorum about maintaining physical distance between men and women, including her husband and her brothers. She "must form no friendship and no intimacy except when ordered to do so by her parents" or by a go-between who will arrange her marriage. "She must find no fault with her husband." Indeed, in keeping with feudal ethics, she must remember that "she must look to her husband as her lord, and must serve him with all worship and reverence, not despising or thinking lightly of him."[38]

Seven reasons are given for divorce if she should fail in her husband's house: disobedience, sterility, lewdness, jealousy, leprosy and "foul disease," "talking overmuch and prattling disrespectfully," and stealing. She must honor and serve her father-in-law and mother-in-law, and she must never "be angry with them, and murmur not." She must arise early, go to bed late, "not drink overmuch" of wine and tea. She must "go but sparingly" to theatricals and even the temple until she has reached the age of forty. "Without her husband's permission, she must go nowhere." No matter how many servants she may have, she must not "shirk the trouble of attending to everything herself." She must steel her heart to correct her subordinates' weaknesses.

She must guard against the "five worst infirmities" that afflict the female: "indocility, discontent, slander, jealousy and silliness." This silliness may be regarded as stupidity, and the *Onna daigaku* enjoins, "Such is the stupidity of her character that it is incumbent on her, in every particular, to distrust herself and to obey her husband." It should be noted that the limited education given girls strengthened this vicious cycle of "stupidity." She was trained for the domestic duties of weaving, washing, sewing, and cooking, and in some special arts, such as incense burning, flower arranging, and the tea ceremony. As the late eighteenth century shogunate policymaker Matsudaira Sadanobu maintained, "It is well that women should be unlettered. To cultivate women's skills would be harmful."[39]

With such precepts drummed into a little girl from babyhood, it is a wonder that she developed any distinctive personality. The most abiding human relationship in her life was that of mother and son. All others—with parents, brothers and sisters, husband, and in-laws—were inconstant or they were sustained with duty as the first criterion. Her most reliable channel of influence was also that of her sons, preferably the oldest. He, in turn, was required, by duty at least, to care for her. To the present day this mother-son relationship provides a psychological key to understanding many issues, problems, and sociological trends in Japan.

The Confucian ideal forced Japanese women to be strong in order to be weak and subservient. In a perverse way, this discipline forced women to acquire the "inner culture and freedom of mind"[40] that has made them the stabilizing backbone of Japanese society.

Codes and Laws

A final major factor in determining the position of Japanese women in these middle years of male-oriented Japanese society is found in the various codes and laws that ordered their political and legal status. The Formulary of the Jōei era of 1232, a digest of laws to be followed in the shōgun's court, essentially expressed the views of Minamoto Yoritomo and, it is probably safe to add, those of his wife, Hōjō Masako. These laws were fairly liberal toward women. They provided rights in marriage, equal inheritance with brothers, equal rights to dispose of and bequeath property, power to control the peasants, and certain rights in divorce.

Slowly, however, women lost these rights. The changing framework of society and constant strife depressed women to an inferior legal and social status regularized in the "house laws" issued by the *daimyō* (the great landowners), beginning in the fifteenth century, to supplement the earlier Jōei and Ashikaga codes. They were to hold until the Meiji era. By the time the Tokugawa reasserted centralized dictatorship in the seventeenth century, father and husband had become completely dominant. Shogunate justice held them responsible for the actions of their family members. From this situation comes the old saying that there were four things to be feared in feudal Japan: "earthquake, thunder, fire, and father."[41] Primogeniture became the rule. Marriage was strictly controlled. Only a man could demand a divorce, and notification of divorce could be given by presentation of the famous three-and-one-half-line letter simply stating the fact. For their part, women's only escape from an unbearable marriage was to take refuge in one of the very few Buddhist "temples of divorce." For women, adultery was punishable by death.

It should be made clear that men's lives were also fully regulated. The difference came in the fact that they held the ranking positions in this vertical social system. Farmers were tied to the land; *daimyō* were tied to a rigidly circumscribed pattern of life, rotating their time of service at the shogunate court in Edo (now Tōkyō) with time back in their domains. It is interesting that guards at the checkpoints along the route watched the travelers carefully, and especially scrutinized for guns entering Edo and for women leaving, lest such movement herald impending revolt. Dress was prescribed; houses reflected the status of the dweller. Everyone knew exactly how he or she related to everyone else and where obligations and duty started and stopped.[42]

Urban Life

Only in the burgeoning urban centers, such as Ōsaka and Edo, where the merchants, artists, and entertainers tampered with the code, could one find the flexibility and lively qualities of more individualistic life. As the English diplomat and historian George Sansom concluded, "The samurai still had their dignity, the consciousness of high social standing;

New Year's in the Yoshiwara entertainment district of Edo, showing courtesans behind the lattice-caged windows of the brothels. Artist: Miyagawa Issho. From the collection of the Idemitsu Museum. Photo courtesy of Shuei-sha.

but the commoners had most of the money and most of the fun."[43] Many merchant women shared this awakened sense of independence— and the love of money. The great Mitsui financial house, for instance, founded its fortunes on the hard work and commercial ability of the early-seventeenth-century wife and mother who inspired the growth of a small *sake* and pawnbroker family business in Matsuzaka. In time this enterprise expanded into a merchandising and financial giant of Edo and, later, of modern Japan and the world.

In the cities, however, some women entered a newly institutionalized form of bondage, that of organized prostitution, into which impoverished farmers sold their daughters and sometimes their wives. The Yoshiwara entertainment district, often called the Nightless City of Edo,[44] and its courtesans and entertainers are known to many outside of Japan in rather glamorized fashion through the world-famous woodblock prints of the *Ukiyoe* artists who sketched this "floating world." The women, whom one playwright called "the cherries of the night which blossom luxuriantly,"[45] were displayed behind the latticed, caged windows of the brothels to excite the senses of the onlookers. They themselves looked forward to the day when their freedom might be purchased and won. The professionally trained *geisha*, not prostitutes although also in bondage, with their skills of conversation, singing, dancing, and playing of the *samisen* and *koto* epitomized the arts of the time. In amusement quarters where these elaborately dressed women held sway, both samurai and merchant found release from the prescribed social rigidities of home and the tensions of formal society. The charm, style, and talents of the Tokugawa geisha and courtesans helped create an image of the Japanese woman that has made lasting impact on the world's awareness of this culture. By contrast, prostitution, whether of Yoshiwara or illegal modern versions in Turkish baths or in hot spring resorts, has been a prime target of reform-minded Japanese women.

Tokugawa Japan, for almost three hundred years enclosed in its isolated islands and stabilized by its loyally executed codes of ethics and conformity, consolidated customs, a style of life, and a disciplined mentality to forge the traditional way of the Japanese people. Although constrained and hierarchical, this premodern era, as indeed the earlier feudal years, in contrasting fashion nourished the cultural, societal, and political creativity that gave rise to the modernism of Meiji. For Japanese women, however, the constraint side of the ledger weighed heavy; one hundred years after the Meiji Restoration, they still struggle to free themselves from deeply ingrained, restraining habits of mind, emotion, and action imposed by the traditional way.[46]

CHAPTER 2
THE WAY OF MODERNIZATION

ENLIGHTENMENT OF WOMEN—
EDUCATORS AND SPINNING GIRLS

> *Our women are yet in the very beginnings. They have only a low position in society, but little influence, and only a scant education. There is an infinite degree of difference between education and progress for the men and that of our Japanese women. They have not yet begun to take up any work. It is the period of formation rather than organization.*
>
> —Tsuda Umeko, "Letter to an American Friend," 1897[1]

Japanese women took pioneering steps toward emancipation as their country industrialized and moved to a modernized way of life in the Meiji half-century of enlightened rule, the brief period of Taishō democracy, and the early years of Shōwa.

In the mid-nineteenth century Japan stirred from the fetters of Tokugawa Confucianist and feudal controls and from international isolationism as a result of pressures of internal social, intellectual, and economic ferment. These pressures were intensified by the shock of Commodore Perry's Black Ships in Tōkyō Bay in 1853 and proddings by the naval diplomacy of the United States and European countries. In 1868 the last Tokugawa shōgun surrendered his powers, and young Emperor Meiji resumed the rights of monarchical rule. The era of "civilization and enlightenment," as the young modernist elite, made up of such people as Fukuzawa Yukichi and Mori Arinori, labeled it,[2] was under way.

The Charter Oath of 1868, mirrored in the Constitution, outlined five principles—in reality, hopes—to guide the new regime: (1) provision

31

for "deliberative assemblies" and "public discussion"; (2) a plea for national unity; (3) the promise of ending feudal class restrictions, with each person permitted to "pursue his own calling"; (4) the ending of "evil customs of the past," with life to be based on the "just laws of nature"—in effect a corollary of the third point; and (5) encouragement of seeking knowledge "throughout the world so as to strengthen the foundations of Imperial rule."

The fifth article was peculiarly pertinent to the future of Japanese women, for it fostered education and encounters with Western women and customs. The earlier way of tradition was established primarily by women of the nobility. From the Meiji period onward, the story increasingly involved women from the middle and working classes.

Westernization and Imperialism

The first two decades of Meiji rule featured new educational opportunities and an easing of the social structure. The dispatch in 1871 of five young girls, including Tsuda Umeko, to study in the United States set one such important precedent. For a few years in the 1880s Westernizing enthusiasts created another in the unique social scene at the Rokumeikan, or Hall of the Crying Deer, in Tōkyō. The Foreign Ministry conceived of the setting as a "place for international com-

In this woodblock triptych Empress Haruko and her ladies-in-waiting roll Red Cross bandages for the soldiers during the Sino-Japanese War. Kunioki woodblock in author's collection.

munication," borrowing the concept from an old Chinese banqueting poem that praised "the harmonious social intercourse of persons of all nationalities."[3] Here in an elaborate, chandeliered Western setting, elite Japanese women studied Western arts or, dressed in bustles and full-skirted Victorian gowns, joined in parties and Western-style dancing with foreign diplomats. The Rokumeikan, symbolic of an era and of the overly rapid emulation of the West, ended its activities as renewed conservatism reemphasized traditionalism.

The Imperial Rescript of Education, issued in 1890, most readily epitomized the new mood. It proclaimed the principle of universal education but reasserted the primacy of Confucian ethics and filial devotion. It revived the Shintō virtue of loyalty to the emperor. Read regularly in awesome, almost religious ceremony like a creed of faith in the schools from then until the end of World War II, this document became the polestar of nationalist teaching and moral authority. No personal recollection of school life during that fifty-five-year span of history seems complete without remembrance of a somber-voiced principal reading the rescript from the scroll he held in white-gloved hands, usually in front of photographs of the Emperor and Empress, revered as sacred. This mystical indoctrination helped marshal the people for imperial glory.

Successful wars with China in 1894–1895 and with Russia in 1904–1905, as well as the annexation of Korea in 1910, provided fulfillment of the Meiji concept of *risshin shusse*—succeeding in life—which aimed at advancement among the nations of the world. At home the wars excited jingoistic nationalism—an emotion arousable in part because of ever more widespread public education, and in part because of general military conscription, which in 1873 opened to all men the opportunity of bearing arms, a privilege formerly restricted to the aristocratic samurai class.

Aristocratic women rallied other patriotic women to social welfare, to relief work for war veterans or their widows and orphans, and to an enlarged consciousness of national duty. The old samurai heritage reemerged. A few went so far as to perform ritual suicide so as to follow their soldier-husbands in death.[4] Empress Haruko provided the leadership for her women subjects in this era. She encouraged with conscientious patronage the newly developing charity, education, and welfare projects and organizations, such as the Tōkyō Charity Hospital, started in 1887 by high-born ladies organized in the Benevolent Society (Jizen kai). The spirit of Empress Kōmyō, remembered for more than a thousand years for her Buddhistic charities, provided an example.

Newly established organizations, set up with government supervision, became centers of women's patriotic activities. One was the Patriotic Women's Society (Aikoku fujinkai), established in 1901 by Okumura Ioko (1845–1907), a Buddhist missionary to Korea and China at the time of the brewing of the Russo-Japanese War. The organization, its members neatly garbed in distinctive khaki uniforms, grew to three million by the time of the Manchurian Incident in the 1930s.

Another group, strengthened by Yamamuro Kieko (1874–1915), had a Christian base. Yamamuro, inspired by the evangelical zeal of her conversion to Christianity and by devotion to her family heritage, which extended back to the Nara era, felt she must somehow serve her country by "consoling soldiers and sailors." These emotions led her to the Salvation Army; she eventually married one of its second lieutenants. Together they forged this normally internationally concerned, philanthropic organization into a vehicle in Japan not simply for pioneering social welfare programs, such as the building of a tuberculosis sanitorium and rescue homes for prostitutes, but also for nationalistic, imperialistic support.[5]

A lonely female voice raised in challenge to such war efforts was the poet Yosano Akiko (1878–1942). A passionate realist, she struggled throughout her life to seek individual liberty and awareness of herself as a woman. She married the poet to whom she went for guidance, taking him from his wife. She bore him eleven children and finally

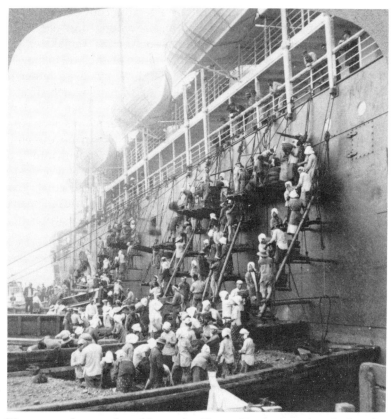

Women workers coal a ship at the Nagasaki naval station during the Russo-Japanese War. Photo courtesy of the Library of Congress.

became more famous for her poetry than he. This rebel was one of Japan's early feminists. She joined with the "new women" of the early twentieth century in their struggles for emancipation. She railed against the discrimination of her time and her position in society. Her much quoted *tanka*, "Black Butterfly," by which she meant the "black world," portrays this feeling:

> These scraps of paper
> Scribbled with poems
> In which I cursed and raved,
> I press down hard
> On a black butterfly!

Today, as then, her fighting spirit and liberated convictions, revealed in her poetry and personal life-style, inspire young and old women, both liberal and conservative. Proletarian social critic Yamakawa Kikue considered Yosano's love poems as inspiration in her own life. They sing, Yamakawa said, of a "self-initiated and happy love" rather than of the "miserable, forsaken love" typical of women writers from the Heian to Edo eras. Contemporary college women, when asked what Japanese woman, living or dead, they most admire, often select Yosano. In the summer of 1972 an Ōsaka woman, eager to expand the antiwar movement, dyed parts of Yosano's famous antiwar poem into a dark blue *noren* (a door-top curtain used in Japanese homes and shops) and distributed her handiwork around the world. This poem, which Yosano wrote for her brother, who was in the Russian war, caused many to castigate her as a traitor and some even to throw stones at her house. Its opening lines read:

> Oh, my brother! I weep for you,
>   Don't die.
> You are the youngest,
>   Most loved by our parents.
> Did they teach you
>   To kill a man with a knife!
> Did they watch you grow up to twenty-four,
>   Only to kill yourself after killing a man?[6]

Industrialization

Industrialization became a prime goal of the Meiji reformers as they acted to make Japan a modern state. Early developments in steel, electricity, transportation, and so on under government sponsorship moved more swiftly by the turn of the century when, in response to government policy, private individual entrepreneurs assumed control. The business cliques, known as *zaibatsu*, began to take form. Mitsui, expanding from its feudal-period matriarchal origins in the merchant class, became with Mitsubishi, Sumitomo, and Yasuda great financial and industrial empires.

Initially, it was in the cotton and silk spinning industries that industrial progress gained momentum. From the first they depended primarily on female labor. By the end of the century, textile mills employed almost 250,000 people, or 63 percent of Japan's factory workers. By 1920 there were three times that number of mill women, weaving and spinning cotton and wool.[7]

Empress Haruko and the Empress Mother visit the new Tomioka Spinning Factory in June 1873. Artist: Arai Kanpō. From the collection of Meiji Shrine, Shōtoku Memorial Hall. Photo courtesy of Tōkyō Bijitsu, K.K.

The first spinning factory in Tomioka, Gunma Prefecture, built in 1872 with the guidance of a French engineer, employed some 400 women. Mostly daughters of the now-defunct samurai class, their carry-over status gave dignity to the mission of developing this new technology imported from abroad. Only later did women from the farms and fishing villages take their place. Conditions in the factories deteriorated. By 1892, 56 girls had died at the Tomioka factory from the unhealthy sweatshop life, the youngest aged nine years and ten months. Brought into spinning centers like Ōsaka from their simple homes and housed in dormitories, the girls—teenagers or less—lived in conditions of semislavery. They sang pitiful little songs to express their unhappiness: "Working in the factory is nothing less than being cast into a prison, without being bound with a chain," or "Boarding life is more painful than that of a caged bird or a prisoner."[8]

Factory laws of 1911 and 1923 provided some amelioration, with improved regulations for child labor, night work, length of shifts, maternity leave, and the like, but these new regulations did not apply to small firms. Factory girls also enjoyed some benefits from Taishō-era democratization. When the workers' mutual aid organization, called the Yūai kai (Friendly Society) in honor of the Friendly Societies of Great Britain, swelled with new members, it established a Women's Division. This provided counseling, special lectures for cultural improvement, part-time work for housewives, entertainment, and a monthly magazine, *Friendship Women* (*Yūai fujin*), for its members to read after their twelve-hour workdays. Ichikawa Fusae was briefly responsible for the publication in 1919. Her endeavors on behalf of the Japanese working girl impelled Hiratsuka Raichō to invite her to join in the movement that became the New Women's Association (Shin fujin kyōkai). In this way the liberal forces for women's rights, in the fields of both labor and political emancipation, moved closer together.

By 1920 the Yūai kai's Women's Division numbered 3,000 members. When the Yūai kai became the Great Japan Labor Federation (Dai Nippon rōdō sōdōmei), the Women's Division took the name Working Women (Rōdō fujin).

Out of the pre–World War II labor pattern of the factory girls emerged the commonly accepted dogma that the facile hands of Japanese girls, working as teenagers for a limited period of time before marriage, should constitute a basic element in Japan's economic capacity to produce and to compete internationally.

By the end of World War I, Allied demands for ships and textiles had turned Japan into a world creditor nation and brought about an economic boom at home, which, in turn, created an erratic domestic price situation. Labor union activity increased; labor unrest grew. Rice

Girls line up for their teachers, having taken off their *zoris* (sandals), at a school in Yokohama at the turn of the twentieth century. Photo courtesy of the Library of Congress.

riots erupted. Women of Toyama still proudly tell how the fishermen's wives of their prefecture started it all when they demonstrated before town officials to complain about the rice speculators who were causing rising prices and shortages. From Toyama the phenomenon spread. Troops had to be called out; ten thousand people were arrested; and finally the cabinet fell. For many rural women these protests served as their chance to exert independence and to challenge traditional authority. For them the riots were comparable to the educated urban women's emancipation campaigns. Their techniques were an early and unstructured manifestation—part of a mass movement (*taishu undō*)—of civic action (*shimin undō*), which, in the contemporary period, erupts over consumer and pollution issues.[9]

Public Education

Promotion of education was a major thrust of the Meiji policy of enlightenment. It built on a remarkably strong base of late Tokugawa literacy and the long heritage of samurai attention to the dual injunction summarized in "learning on the left, and arms on the right."[10] For women, as already seen, this took on the meaning of training for womanliness and the vocation of marriage.

By the opening of the Meiji era, about 40 percent of boys and 10 percent of girls attended some kind of elementary school. Many went to the temple or parish *terakoya* schools that had grown up during the Tokugawa period. It is likely that about 50 percent of the elite samurai women, who were usually educated at home, were literate; the proportion was probably even higher among women of merchant families living in the urban centers of Edo and Ōsaka. The percentage for country and lower-class women—this peasant group, male and female, represented close to 90 percent of the population—was much lower. Confucian concepts militated against too much education for women outside the home. Interestingly, geisha were among the well educated. Their profession required that they be trained conversationalists and knowledgeable about issues of interest to their patrons.

Early Meiji educators planned the new modern public schooling system to give boys and girls equal elementary education, initially three to four years. By the end of the Meiji era, the Ministry of Education extended basic schooling through six years. The success of this dream is written in the statistics: By 1897 the rate of elementary school attendance was more than 50 percent for girls and more than 80 percent for boys; by the end of the Meiji era in 1912 the rate was 98 percent for girls and 99 percent for boys. Today, a century after the founding of the Ministry of Education, Japan takes for granted a basic literacy rate of almost 100 percent.

Equality at middle school and university levels, however, was not part of the general scheme. In 1894, for instance, only thirteen public middle schools for girls, with about 2,000 students, were operating. Slowly, the needs of the expanding Japanese economy and of mobilization for the wars with China and Russia nudged the government to provide better-educated girls for the factories and for white-collar jobs. In 1899 the Higher Girls' School Law called for one middle school in each prefecture. By 1920 more than 11 percent of girl elementary school graduates went on to secondary school; by 1940 the figure had doubled. Comparable figures for boys were almost 14 percent and 28 percent. Unfortunately, textbooks for girls were deliberately written with lower-quality content; public school education automatically built in superiority of boys over girls with the same number of years of schooling.

Government-sponsored higher education for women lagged even further behind. Most government attention went to teacher training in the two higher normal schools in Tōkyō and Nara and to specialized professional and technical training in dentistry, pharmacy, domestic science, and so on. The first real medical school for women, established by Dr. Yoshioka Yayoi in Tōkyō in 1900, was set up only after much official opposition and many tribulations. Of the forty-eight higher educational institutions for women in 1938, just six were government sponsored. When Waseda University, one of the leading private institutions, opened its doors to women in 1938, a lengthy editorial in the *Japan Advertiser* commended the "progressive action." It lamented, however, that it seemed to have required the exigencies of the war in China to make this step palatable and possible.[11] Girls had to wait until the reforms of the U.S. Occupation before they could compete equally for entrance into the prestigious government universities considered, in Japan's vertically organized society, to be the launching pad for professional success.

Conflicting Educational Philosophies

From the Meiji era to World War II the education of women continued to be a controversial issue. Steeped in centuries of Confucian ideals, educators and parents pondered what the impact of new training and new ideas would be on the precisely arranged life of girls and their established roles in the home. Even a missionary, getting ready to devote her life to the education of Japanese girls, asked, "Ought we try to change the Japanese women by education? Can these admirable traits be kept and still give them a broader outlook?"[12]

Despite the preamble to the school code that cautioned that any guardian who failed to send his young girl to primary school was "negligent of his duty,"[13] as late as the beginning of the twentieth century, farm girls and those of poor families were often believed to be needed more in the home and fields or earning money in the factories. They were, in effect, nominal students. As Fukuzawa Yukichi lamented, "Stone houses and iron bridges are easy enough to build, but the spirits of men change slowly."[14]

Fukuzawa, known as "the Great Enlightener," educator and founder of Keiō University, was one of the creative influences of the Meiji modernizing spirit and an advocate of emancipating women's education. Having traveled to America and Europe just after Commodore Perry's visit, he became an exponent of Western ideas and methods. He believed in the equality of all human beings—men and women, peasants,

merchants, artisans, and the high born. "A man," he argued, "will have
rank only by dint of his talents, virtues and accomplishments"—hence
the importance of learning.[15] He inveighed against the moralistic Confucian ideas on the subjugation of women, and he opposed polygamy.

In 1898 he wrote his answer to the *Onna daigaku* in his *Shin onna
daigaku* [New women's higher learning] and *Onna daigaku hyōron* [Com-
ments on the *Onna daigaku*]. As this was the year the new Civil Code
was enacted, ordering great changes in Japanese social and legal relationships, Fukuzawa thought it timely to establish a new set of ethics
between men and women. "Men are different from women in sex, but
there is no difference between them in status or in value." He urged
that women first study physics as the basis of practical science, as even
cooks and maids must understand the physics of heat transfer if they
are to deal properly with pots and cookstoves.[16] After this beginning,
women should turn to special subjects, including economics and law,
which they should use as "the dagger of the civilized woman" in the
same way that a feudal samurai woman relied on the dagger, worn in
her bodice, as protection against any threat to her chastity. He did not
ignore preparation for marriage, housekeeping, child care, and more
conservative values; on them rested women's maternal responsibility
in the society. His ultimate desire was to give women a sense of self-
respect.[17]

So progressive were these views that his *Shin onna daigaku* was
promptly banned in some girls' schools. Many were uncertain about
the extent to which women should adhere to the concepts of the "old"
or the "new" *Onna daigaku*. A marvelous, perhaps apocryphal, story is
told of the Shintō priest who presented copies of both books to the
bride so as to let her choose her careful path between the two.[18]

Fukuzawa was not alone; other educators and leaders entered the
fray. As early as 1876 Doi Kōka, inspired as were many other feminist
advocates by John Stuart Mill's essays, helped launch the argument
with his *Great Civilized Learning for Women* (*Bunmeiron onna daigaku*).
By the 1880s, during the liberal Rokumeikan era, a spate of books of
feminist theory and studies of women's education appeared. When Mori
Arinori, himself educated mostly in England and the United States,
became minister of education (1885–1889), he turned to David Murray
of Rutgers College for advice on women's educational standards. One
result was the founding in 1885 of Women's Normal School, which
later became Ochanomizu Women's University.

Mori's assassination by an ultra-nationalist in 1889 and the Imperial
Rescript on Education a year later stemmed the liberalizing tide. Government education of women, guided by principles of Confucianism
and nationalism, resorted to the motto "good wives and wise mothers"

(*ryōsai kembo*), which an educational historian affirmed really meant "obedient wives and militant mothers."[19] This philosophy emphasized practical womanly subjects, such as sewing, painting, flower arranging, and the tea ceremony, as well as Japanese, Chinese classics, and arithmetic. Atomi Girls School in Tōkyō, established in 1875 by Atomi Kakei (1840–1926), daughter of a samurai, exemplified this educational approach. The similarly minded Shimoda Utako (1854–1936), who helped establish the Peeress School for nobly born girls, explained that education given by the state should create a "perfect woman." She meant one who was "perfect for the nation," with qualities of patriotism and national morality and with a splendid physique.[20]

Even during the time of Taishō democracy, when novels popularized the modernized woman and city girls with Clara Bow haircuts flocked to the silent films, national educational policies had not been liberalized. The onset of the war years required only an intensification of patriotism and the pursuit of the "way of great duty" in order to serve the "way of the Empire" as the morals textbooks of the schools exhorted. Adult education programs for women, instituted to fill gaps in earlier education, stressed child care and the wife-mother relationships. "The duty of the woman of our Empire begins with the valuable life of mother. For that purpose . . . cultivate self-confidence and develop your potential to meet any difficulties as a substitute for men being in the battlefield."[21] The majority of Japanese girls and women faithfully followed these instructions. In so doing, ironically, they also helped prepare themselves to cope with the responsibilities and opportunities of the reforms and new rights to come after the war.

Overseas Education

While general public education from Meiji on was creating a fully literate population, two other educational factors were at work. The first was overseas education of girls, a policy started under the famous Article Five of the Charter Oath. The second was education of girls from kindergarten to college in Christian schools, usually built and maintained by foreign missionaries. In both instances, the dominant influence was American.

Spurred on by his Western-oriented advisers, the Emperor Meiji became a proponent of including women in the search for knowledge overseas. In a special rescript in 1871, acknowledging that the formal schooling system for girls had not yet been set up, he directed his aristocracy, when traveling abroad, to take with them their wives, daughters, and sisters so that they might learn how women receive education and bring up children in other countries.

That very year, in company with a Western observation trip headed by court noble Iwakura Tomomi, five girls of good families, ranging in age from seven to fifteen, were selected to go to the United States to study. One feminist writer has commented that "it was the first time that equal opportunity for education was opened for Japanese women."²² The five were Yoshimasu Ryoko, Ueda Sadako, Yamakawa Sutematsu, Nagai Shigeko, and Tsuda Umeko. In keeping with the spirit of the time, Empress Haruko honored them with an audience before departure. From behind her secluding screen, she encouraged them to become "models" for their countrywomen upon completion of their study abroad.²³

Yamakawa Sutematsu and Nagai Shigeko went on from preparatory school to Vassar College. In time, the former married General Ōyama Iwao and became a leader in women's patriotic work during the war with China in 1894–1895. The latter, who married Admiral Uryū Sotokichi, was trained as a teacher of piano and helped introduce Western musical education into Japan. But, of course, it is the youngest of the group, Tsuda Umeko, who is best known. Little could that small, seven-year-old child, dressed in formal, long-sleeved kimono with a scarlet shawl around her shoulders as she waited for the side-wheeler ship to sail from Yokohama port, have realized how momentous her experience in the United States would be for the future of women's higher education in her country.

Tsuda's father had gone to the United States on a special mission for the Tokugawa shogunate. Himself a pacesetter, he sent his daughter off for an unprecedented eleven-year stint of education in the United States. Young Umeko flourished under the care of Mr. and Mrs. Charles Lanman in Washington, D.C., where Charles Lanman was the American Secretary at the Japanese Legation. They educated her at the best schools and molded her character to self-respect and personal dignity. She became a Christian at age eleven, the only one of the five who took this step.

Returning to Japan almost a stranger in her own society, Tsuda Umeko could barely speak Japanese. She began to teach English in girls' schools and then in the Peeress School. Although successful and popular, for she was brilliant and charming, she chafed under the conservative educational policies. The puppetlike responses of her students—well born, often Paris-garbed, maid-attended, and well disciplined—frustrated her. In 1889 she went again to the United States and studied biology at Bryn Mawr College for three years. Here she made her decision to work for higher education for women in Japan,²⁴ concentrating on middle-class girls who would have more freedom to make use of their education. Friends in Philadelphia established a

Departure ceremonies for Ambassador Iwakura and his mission as they prepare to leave for the United States on December 23, 1871. Tsuda Umeko and the other girls preparing to study in the United States are seen in boat, lower right. Artist: Yamaguchi Hōshun. From the collection of Meiji Shōtoku Memorial Hall. Photo courtesy of Tōkyō Bijitsu, K.K.

Tsuda Umeko (right) and friend studying in the dormitory at Bryn Mawr College sometime between 1889 and 1892. Photo courtesy of Bryn Mawr Archival Collection.

scholarship for study in the United States. This was the beginning of a chain reaction that has brought many Tsuda College girls to the United States, and especially to Bryn Mawr College, so that they might, on their return, contribute their educated talents to the education and improvement of Japanese women.

In 1900 Tsuda Umeko opened the first private college for girls in Japan. That first class of ten students, studying in an ordinary *tatami*-matted Japanese house in Tōkyō, started the Tsuda College tradition of educating girls to develop their individual personalities and to become financially emancipated and independent working women. Usually fluent in English and trained to a high standard of academic excellence, they were prepared to avoid "helpless economic dependence on men," as one graduate described Tsuda Umeko's purposes.[25]

This emancipating goal has proved a continuing inspiration to the graduates. One such is Mishima Sumie. A Tsuda College student during World War I, she subsequently graduated with honors from Wellesley College and became an educator and author. Her two vivid autobio-

Japanese and Chinese students dressed for roles in a Japanese play, "Princess Radiant," performed as a benefit for Tsuda College at Wellesley College in 1924. Mishima Sumie on left. Photo courtesy of Wellesley College Archives.

graphies serve as a history of the struggles and adjustments of an educated Japanese woman who was a "grand returner from the West."[26] Contemporary Tsuda graduate students equally emphasize the importance of economic independence achieved as a result of their education. As one young woman explained, her economic independence gives her "spiritual independence from her family."[27] The success of Tsuda Umeko's goal is continuously evident in the scores of graduates who lead in community life and education throughout Japan.

During this time, Tsuda's American friends continued to encourage and support her. Alice Mabel Bacon was such a friend. Her family had opened their home to one of the original five girls who went to the United States. In the 1880s she was invited to Japan to teach English at the Peeress School. Once again she came to Japan, at Tsuda's urging, to help and to teach when the new little private college was opened. However, it was Tsuda Umeko who had to take the actual steps of innovation. The task she set for herself was far from easy; it took not only ability but courage of conviction. Ultimately her life proved pivotal because she pioneered one of the new ways to modernize Japanese women.

Cultural Interaction

The whole process of going abroad, engaging in an alien culture, and competing academically in a difficult foreign language required intelligence, determination, and stamina. The Americans or Canadians and others who received these girls may have been kind and helpful, but adjustment and survival took sheer guts.

Newspaperwoman Shiraishi Tsugi recalled in an interview that it took her a year to get used to her new college life in Toronto. In her second year she overcame her self-consciousness, typified in her memory by people who came back in the trolley cars to stare at her. By her fourth year she felt so much like a Canadian that she got a part-time job in a department store and enjoyed the fact that because she was a "curiosity, everyone came and bought from me." Her roommate, who became a lifelong friend, served as her faithful cultural "go-between, explaining Western life to me and my Japanese ways to those around me."[28]

Others who returned from the adventure of receiving an education abroad related comparable emotions and experiences. Mishima Sumie detailed some of her reactions during her first days at Dana Hall in Massachusetts in her autobiography:

> My Japanese training, requiring every physical movement to be elegant and every word uttered to be according to etiquette, made me extremely sensitive and self-conscious in this environment, where I was completely blind, socially speaking. . . . I felt myself a being fallen from some other planet with senses and feelings that had no use in this world.[29]

Even in the jet age, when international exchange involves thousands of students, the hazards of cultural shock exist. Earlier, going abroad to study was an unprecedented personal challenge—an unknown world waiting to be explored. It should be remembered that if Meiji girls wanted a higher education, their only chance lay in going abroad for it. Obviously those who made this decision passed through a crucible of mind and spirit.

The return home to Japan demanded another reorientation. The simpler aspects were those of readaptation to the physical patterns of living and, sometimes, to the Japanese language. Legs grown accustomed to Western chairs suffered the aches of retraining muscles to be comfortable kneeling on the *tatami*. Some never made it! The mother of Tsuda Umeko's protégée Nishida (née Yamada) Koto, fearing her daughter would look out of place, brought a kimono, *obi, zori,* and *tabi* to the ship in Yokohama when welcoming her back in 1916 after her seven years in the United States. Greeting long-time Tsuda College friends, she was too busy in ensuing days to switch back to Japanese-style clothes. However, when the neighbors at her home in Kofu, peering at her standing in the yard beside the chicken coop in a white, Western-style summer dress asked, "Is she a nurse for hens?" she finally reverted to the kimono.[30]

More complex were the tasks of trying to bridge the gap due to the change in Japanese life and thought that had occurred during the absence. Mishima Sumie said she felt so conservative when she returned from the United States in 1927 because so many people around her were radicals and communist sympathizers.[31] Five years' absence during the vigorous Taishō period caused a major attitudinal chasm.

In fact, for the prewar girl, any overseas living experience—Manchuria, Korea, China, Europe, the United States, or even frontier Hokkaidō— was likely to make her sufficiently different from her Japan-based peers to give her the awareness and willingness to experiment and assume a role of leadership. Having escaped from the homeland "box" of Confucian constraints, as a Japanese phrase describes it, long enough to lose some characteristic inhibitions and shyness, she was able in later life to take courage in hand to negotiate with male authority in government or community affairs. Her own eyes had seen that there was more than one way of organizing family relations and society. Collections of biographies of national and regional women pioneers of the last century, issued to commemorate the centenary of the Meiji Restoration, show that more than 50 percent of these women leaders held in common the early experience of having studied, traveled, or lived abroad.[32]

Christian-Sponsored Education

For the educational horizons of larger numbers of girls of the Meiji and Taishō eras, study at missionary or Christian-sponsored schools in Japan served as a variation on going overseas to live and study. The opportunities these schools provided must, in the words of the president of a prominent women's college, be publicized to the world in "large and flaming letters."[33] These schools gave the girls access to democratic and higher-level education. Contact with foreign teachers enabled them to meet and observe real Western people and to be exposed to Western ideas in the heart of Japan. Sometimes such missionary schooling paved the way for the brightest and most able to continue on to higher education in the United States and Canada. Many Japanese girls may have been permitted to go to missionary schools because their families felt their education was not important enough to oppose it. Equally, however, many samurai and middle-class families proudly asserted their appreciation of modern ways by having their daughters attend such Westernized schools.

U.S. missionaries arrived in Japan in 1859 shortly after the commercial treaty with Japan was negotiated by U.S. representative Townsend Harris. Education for women soon became one focus of their work. Vermont-born Mary Eddy Kidder established Ferris School in Yokohama in 1870. Other schools, such as Aoyama and Tōyō Eiwa in Tōkyō, Kassui Girls School in Nagasaki, Kōbe College, and Hiroshima Girls School, followed. They offered education to the poor and underprivileged as well as to those of good families. Because of the government's indifference to girls' middle and higher education and despite periodic difficulties from zealous Buddhists and antiforeign moods, these mission schools were able to proceed with greater freedom, being less controlled by the national policies that by the 1890s emphasized chauvinism.[34]

The curriculum, conducted in English and modeled on institutions like Mt. Holyoke Seminary in Massachusetts, established high standards. It also included studies in the Japanese language of Japanese and Chinese literature. The English the girls learned opened to them vistas of Western literature and the ability to communicate better with people of Western cultures. Their music studies popularized the organ and the piano. These schools introduced Western domestic science, promoted physical education, and maintained strict and puritanical discipline in nineteenth-century U.S. fashion. By 1885, there were more than fifty missionary high schools for girls, more than the government established until after the turn of the century.

Christians or Christian influence also created the first higher educational institutions for women. Tsuda Umeko was a Christian. Both Japan Women's University, established in 1901, and Tōkyō Women's Christian college, founded in a cooperative interdenominational effort in 1918, had Christian origins. All received staunch support from Japanese and U.S. male educators who espoused advancement of women as an integral element of the modernization of Japanese society.

Dr. Naruse Jinzo, who founded Japan Women's University, offers an excellent illustration of the powerful results of these convictions. Converted to Christianity in 1877, he subsequently went to the United States to study women's education. His motivation came from concerns aroused by the contrast, as he saw it, between the ideal expressed in the passage in the Book of Proverbs of the Bible that begins "Who can find a virtuous woman? For her price is far above rubies" and Japanese women as he observed them. He held them to be "foolish" and incapable of playing a constructive role in the modernizing society. He determined, therefore, to change them, and he established Japan Women's University to put into practice his theories as set forth in his book *Women's Education* (*Joshi kyōiku*).

Naruse felt it was necessary to educate girls first as human beings, second as women, and third as citizens. He provided a curriculum of intellectual training that would make his students capable of solving problems, of moral training that would inspire them to community service, and of physical training that would strengthen their bodies to carry out these functions. The university taught practical ethics.

Because he asked the assistance and financial support of many prominent people of the era—Prime Minister Itō Hirobumi, Minister of Education Saionji Kinmochi, the Sumitomos, the Mitsuis—his university, when established, publicized the virtues of women's higher education. Among progressive thinkers, he was, in the words of the statesman Count Ōkuma at the opening ceremonies, "setting up a double standard," because the nation would be twice as strong if its women were well educated.[35] Certainly, many students who went to Naruse's college did become creative activists and have fulfilled his dream by making their mark working for improved social conditions—and for Japanese women.

Organizations Rooted in the West

For many Japanese girls and women, particularly those no longer of formal school age, the Western-rooted organizations provided an opportunity for ongoing education and offered support to help them rise from their semifeudal existence. Historically, the Anglo-Saxon peoples have used voluntary associations to express public opinion and perform societal functions not provided for by services available from government. At the turn of the century in Britain and the United States, these popular organizations and their adherents also glowed with Christian evangelism. Japan, with rising social problems related to its accelerating industrialization, became a natural theater in which the socially concerned of both cultures could work to serve society and God via the Christian tradition of "good works."

The Salvation Army, for example, concentrated on "rescue" programs. It battled, often together with Western missionaries and similarly minded groups such as the Women's Christian Temperance Union, those exploiting elements that made money out of prostitution and human oppression.

Hani Motoko, known as the first newspaperwoman in Japan, with her husband Yoshikazu, focused their organizing efforts on housewives. Their dedication to Christian ideals of love and freedom pointed the way. Guided by the tenets of "thinking, living, praying," they enunciated the principle that wholesome family life led to righteous community life. Their program never advocated demands for women's rights nor proposals for revision of the social and civil system. The Hanis carried out their goals through a monthly magazine, *Fujin no tomo* [Woman's friend], which in an earlier form dated back to 1903; through education; and through the Tomo no kai (Friends Association), started in 1930. By the 1970s the magazine and the organization, with a membership of more than 25,000, had fanned out from Japan to advise Japanese housewives meeting together as far away as Argentina, Brazil, and the United States.

The Japanese Women's Christian Temperance Union (WCTU) (Kyō-fukai), with its aim of "purity, peace, and temperance" was established in 1886 and is, therefore, the oldest women's organization in Japan. It came into being when Mary C. Leavitt of the Women's Temperance Society of America visited Japan in 1882 and moved the spirit of Yajima Kaji, a converted Christian and school principal, who had suffered long years of marital bondage to a drunken, impoverishing husband. In the next fifty years, Yajima led her dedicated followers, whose prewar numbers grew to more than 10,000, in many crusades of social consciousness.

As early as 1890, at the first session of the Japanese Diet, Yajima appealed for a law to make plural marriage a crime—the "one man–one woman" law. Later she petitioned against the discriminatory sections of Article Five of the Peace Preservation Law. She made a thorough study of parliamentary law, regarded as so pertinent to effective organizational activity that a WCTU leader recommended such education for all Japanese women to the Occupation authorities. This was typical of her innovative approach to techniques of action. Over the years, prostitution, legislative protection of women and children, war work with the wounded and the widowed with children, earthquake relief, and pleas for peace all received attention. Her conviction that social ills, especially abuses of prostitution, required reform legislation led the WCTU to become a staunch proponent of women's suffrage.

The universality of WCTU concerns and its ties with sister organizations in the United States, Britain, and Europe early awakened Yajima and the organization to a recognition of the need for women to help create better international policies. Twice Yajima called on U.S. presidents on behalf of peace. The first time was in 1906 when, in the United States at an international WCTU convention, she personally thanked President Theodore Roosevelt for his help in concluding the Treaty of Portsmouth to end the war with Russia. He later commented that she was one of the two most interesting Japanese he had ever met. The second time, at age ninety, while attending the Washington Conference on limitation of armaments, she presented to President Warren Harding a petition signed by more than 10,000 of her countrywomen supporting the idea of the conference and concepts of peace.

Yajima's successors, equally devoted to peace, have shown the stout courage of veteran fighters for difficult causes. In the mid-1930s, in the face of militant authority, they opposed big budgets for the army and navy and the publications that inflamed sentiments for war. In the 1960s they took up the cudgels against the war in Vietnam, repeatedly petitioning the U.S. government to end its action there.[36]

The Young Women's Christian Association (YWCA) (Nihon Kirisu-tokyō joshi seinenkai), founded in 1905, also owes its origins to the. internationalism of Meiji-era Christian evangelism. Its history is replete with the rewards of intermingling the talents of Americans, Australians, British, Canadians, and other foreigners with those of educated Japanese men and women to nurture a creative instrument of education and social amelioration. Carolyn MacDonald, a Canadian sent by the World YWCA, worked for three years with a few Japanese women who had been educated abroad to lay the foundations of the Japan YWCA. She was followed by, among others, her compatriot Emma Kaufman, who from 1909 to her death more than sixty years later spent her personal fortune and energies to improve the Japan YWCA. Kawai Michi and Katō Taka assumed responsibilities as first general secretaries of the National and Tōkyō YWCAs. They aimed activities at college students and young working girls and encouraged them, in the words of later secretary Watanabe Matsuko, "to a democratic way of thinking which gave freedom within a feudalistic society where women were regarded as subordinate to men."

Secretarial vocational programs, leadership training, group activities, and social welfare provided the practical base for living in accordance with these ideas. Physical education and recreational programs, regarded by most pre–World War I Japanese as simple gymnastics and unnecessary leisure, extended into an annual educational summer camp project on the shores of beautiful Lake Nojiri and a full three-year physical education course in Tōkyō. Home economics and English departments were opened to girls eager for training beyond high school. These trailblazing projects produced professional women and willing volunteers. A visiting American in 1921 was told that vigorous social service work had become women's principal public activity in Japan and that the work was largely the result of the "transplanted line of endeavor" of the YWCA. The YWCA called it "freedom in service." For most of its history before the forties, the strength of the YWCA rested in training women for democratic living—in effect for the role needed in the Japan of the postwar period.[37]

The education provided Japanese girls after the Meiji Restoration by the public school system or by the tradition-heavy private schools turned out carbon-copy young women suited to fulfill the unremarkable role their elders thought appropriate for them. Most worked in the home and on the farm, as confined as ever. For growing numbers there was merely the variant of a more impersonalized and encaging factory setting. They were allowed no voice in public-policy making except as the influence of the bedroom prevailed.

Girls who escaped from such stereotypic anonymity to implement the promises of the Charter Oath very often found their way made possible by varying combinations of Christian-sponsored education, overseas schooling, and the friendly interest of the internationally minded and internationally organized. The dynamics of their preparation for leadership issued from the timing and unique circumstances of Meiji modernization, which coincided with the educational outreach of turn-of-the-century conscientious Christianity. Such education created not only thinking women, but women of a special persuasion of societal responsibility, a situation that was not to be duplicated by the forces of history.

STRUGGLE FOR EMANCIPATION—
"NEW WOMEN" AND ICONOCLASTS

> *Away with shyness, timidity and slavish servility! Cut the chains which bind the whole feminine population of Japan to the old feudal system! Through such courage alone will the women of Japan be able to fashion life and labor in harmony with women's needs, and advance into the future hand in hand with men.*
>
> —Ishimoto Shidzue, *Facing Two Ways*, 1935[38]

Winds of social change, once freed, may veer at unforeseen strengths in directions hardly anticipated. Even the carefully controlled Meiji revolutionizing ran this risk, and the enlightened women who sought emancipation provided some of the surprises. Many of their social, economic, and political struggles proceeded in concert from the late Meiji period to World War II.

Modernization

For the large majority of women, change came slowly, especially before the opening of the twentieth century, and modernization was concentrated in urban centers. Rural areas suffered from the growing tenancy problem, revision of common land provisions, declining population due to out-migration, and falling productivity. Women shared in the daily hard labor of growing rice, of harvesting the catch of the sea, and of survival. At times, poverty forced women, particularly married women, to work in the mines—a practice greatly condemned by liberated social welfare partisans in the Taishō period. Fishing village and farm girls, as they grew up, took their turns as bond-laborers in the factories. Some served as domestics or baby-tenders in prosperous homes in the cities. In good homes they gained a schooling for marriage. Normally, the girls returned home after a few years to marry and carry on the usual village and family traditions. Older villagers were wont to complain that the girls brought back unconventional ideas that were disruptive to their rural society. In some ways these simple country girls, although economically depressed, had greater personal freedom in their youth organizations, marriage arrangements, and community life than did their higher-born urban counterparts.

In the cities girls inched their way into jobs newly created by the needs of modernization. With increased education, they became telephone operators, railroad ticket sellers, trolley conductors, typesetters, and office and clerical workers. It was hailed as a sign of the times when the Ministry of Communications in 1907 made its female employees eligible for promotion, a right formerly restricted to men. Even then the ministry's motive was suspect—a device to retain diligent girls rather than a move for women's emancipation.[39] Young women typists who could work in English or another foreign language were among the best paid—a practice that still prevails. Generally, however, wages were low. Some, as a *Yomiuri shimbun* study in the early Taishō period showed, became trapped in the age-old dilemma of choosing between job and chastity. Many more faced the scorn of the narrow-minded who depreciated the reality of economic need and tossed off the girls' entrance into the labor force as "a matter of the lower class." Said one school principal, "It is not good to discuss the question of women going out to work; there is only one way for women to live and that is to make a good family."[40]

Nonetheless, educated women too began to take their place in professional fields such as teaching, medicine, journalism, and the arts. Higuchi Ichiyō, with her novel *Take kurabe* [Comparing heights] about the Yoshiwara, reestablished the tradition of women as great novelists. Artists such as actress Matsui Sumako and soprano Miura Tamaki, who was internationally famous for her portrayal of Puccini's Madam Butterfly, brought recognition to women in the performing arts.

By 1919 about 13 percent of women worked outside the home, and of these, three-quarters were classified as manual laborers in agriculture, industry, and mining. The census of 1930 reported an increase to about 33 percent. Agriculture still claimed the largest number, followed in order by commerce, the manufacturing industries, domestic service, and the professions.[41]

Taking jobs out of the home setting gave women a greater sense of personal independence and self-confidence. Liberalizing Western influences, gleaned from the mass media, also encouraged this development. Movies, very popular, projected first-hand impressions of Western life, its cultural patterns, and attitudes of freedom. Books and magazines brought worldly information; they served as forums for discussion of problems of interest to women. In 1927, *Fujin no tomo*, one of some twenty magazines for women published at that time, carried in its April issue comments on the ten new problems facing women: world peace, suffrage, "new education," free love, birth control, protection of children, "women and international labor," factory girls, women in agriculture, and "professional women and the modern girl."[42]

The first quarter of the century had brought enough progress to carry many urban women from semifeudalism to the era of the "flapper" or, as it was called, *moga*, a Japanese-language elision of *modan garu*, or modern girl. The male counterpart was, of course, *mobo*. Although reactionary forces resurfaced in the 1930s, for the average urban woman the transition had already been made.

Marriage and Divorce

One result of jobs, education, and Taishō-era self-emboldenment was delayed marriage for women. A famous woman social critic in 1926 observed that Japanese girls, who in olden times praised "getting married as if marriage were almighty," were deferring taking the step "not because there is nobody to marry, but because there are few they care to marry."[43]

In early Meiji the average age of marriage for girls was fifteen or sixteen. Those unmarried at twenty were regarded, as the saying went, "as wares left over" and at twenty-five, a disgrace to themselves and their families. By the 1920s, the age of marriage had increased to the twenty-to-twenty-five range, while for men the age remained between twenty-five and thirty. Women completing higher education for the professions often delayed so long, i.e., until after age twenty-five, that they came to be known as *"orudo missu"* ("old miss"), a typically Japanese way of using a foreign-language phrase to ridicule an unfortunate innovation.

Many who went to universities overseas never married—a highly unusual situation in Japanese society. One foreign-educated spinster explained: "Before I left, I was too busy for a *'miai'* [arranged meeting for purposes of marriage]. After I returned, it was difficult to meet a suitable man, for I needed someone with an advanced concept of women."[44] Traditionalists pointed to such choosiness as evidence of the impropriety of overeducating women.

Interestingly, a declining divorce rate during Taishō kept pace with the increasing marriage age. One divorce in three marriages was the peak rate from 1879 to 1897, when a man or his family could readily dispose of an unwanted wife, but the rate had dropped to one in ten by 1926. Concubinage, justified to insure perpetuation of the family line but officially abolished by the criminal code of 1880, also decreased.[45]

Despite such trends apparently indicating a softening of feudal dictatorial family attitudes, women legally had very few rights. The Civil Code of 1902, put together piecemeal in typical Meiji fashion with the help of continental European jurists, based its family relations laws foursquare on patriarchal power and respect for the family line. Primogeniture ruled inheritance arrangements; a wife had no rights to share in her husband's family property. She had no rights over her children. Registration of marriage at the husband's option placed her and the legitimacy of her children in legal jeopardy. After marriage a woman lost all her own property unless it was protected by the marriage contract. The woman was regarded as legally "incompetent" along with three other classifications: minors, the physically abnormal, and the mentally deficient. She needed her husband's permission to receive or use funds, make contracts, deal in real estate, and so on. With no domestic courts, women had no redress except in regular law courts. These were both too expensive and too publicly exposed for most women, who were shy and inexperienced in such affairs. The Civil Code did little more than neatly legalize the concepts of the *Onna daigaku*, binding women within the dominating patriarchal power.

A nobleman's daughter, wretched in her two unhappy, family-arranged marriages, gave voice to the sufferings created by this legal code in a poem published about 1915 under her pen name Byakuren, or White Lotus:

> The law of this world that mortals share
>   Is hard to bear;
> Yet only in my dreams I dare to pray
>   For my own way.[46]

Modernization of the Civil Code became one of the goals of both suffragist women and a few sympathetic men like Diet member Katayama Tetsu of the Social Mass party, but little happened until the postwar Civil Code was promulgated.

Pursuit of Social Freedoms: Bluestocking Women

In the forefront of feminist modernization were the "new women." This appellation achieved prominence in two different stages of Japanese women's pursuit of social and political freedoms. Initially, it applied to the Bluestocking women of late Meiji. At that time it carried a tone of public opprobrium. The notoriety arose from the publicity attending the articles the women wrote for *Seitō* [Bluestocking magazine], founded in 1911 by Hiratsuka Raichō and named in honor of the Bluestocking Movement in England, about the portrayal by the actress Matsui Sumako of Nora, a new woman, in the production of Ibsen's *A Doll's House* in 1912. Later, after World War I, the suffragists picked up the "new women" expression in feisty fashion as a name for their organization, the New Women's Association (Shin fujin kyōkai), which they established to fight for greater political rights.[47]

The "awakened and moving" women, as the poet Yosano Akiko described her Bluestocking colleagues,[48] devolved from modernizing educators and Christian humanitarians. They emerged when liberal trends were on the upswing and became inspirational harbingers of the modern woman rather than effectuators of actual change. They projected an atmosphere of feminine defiance that stimulated other women of ideas and courage to act.

As the "women libbers" of their era, the Bluestocking women shook the moral code. Their dissentient improprieties excited outraged cries from the conservative and orthodox. Dr. Yoshioka Yayoi, founder of Japan Women's Medical School, sternly criticized them. While Tsuda Umeko viewed their "spirit of unrest and rebellion" as good because it aimed at the freedom of women, she felt sorry for "this new type" of woman. She finally concluded that their opinion was "lawless and immoral" and their influence, "bad."[49] Kawai Michi, Bryn Mawr graduate, Christian worker, and professor at Tsuda College, bewailed their misbegotten ways with, "Oh God, please save these poor girls from Satan." She joined in 1913 with Shimoda Utako of the Peeress School and others to help Miyazaki Mitsuko start a countercampaign, whose purpose was to "uphold humanity" against "brutal liberation" of mind, manners, and the flesh.[50]

What was the credo of the Bluestocking women that so irritated their peers and late Meiji society in general? Hiratsuka Raichō, as their philosopher and founder, provided the poetic interpretation:

> I am a new woman.
> Daily I wish to be and try to become a true new woman. What is truly and forever new is the sun. I am the sun.
> A new woman does not live "yesterday." . . . is no longer satisfied with the old life where women were forced to remain ignorant slaves used for man's selfishness. . . .
> A new woman, not only wishes to break the old morals and codes of men's egoism, she wishes also to create in herself a kingdom of new religion, new virtues, and new laws . . . [and] fulfill her own divine mission.[51]

Hiratsuka, who was eulogized in a *Mainichi Daily News* editorial at the time of her death in 1971 as "a true 'one and only,' " breathed life into the feminist movement of modern Japan.[52] Like Tsuda Umeko, she was a pivotal figure. Born in 1886, fifteen years after little Umeko left on her famous voyage to the United States, Hiratsuka was a child of the next generation. Her inspirational leadership benefited from the improved capacity given by emerging opportunities for higher education for women.

Hiratsuka Haruko—she later took the pen name of Raichō, meaning "snow grouse," in remembrance of days spent watching these birds in the snowy Japan Alps while recovering from a love affair—grew up in an intellectual and Westernized but conservative home. Her father, a government official in the Ministry of Finance, tried to rear his daughter in traditional samurai ways. He resisted her efforts to enter college. Aided and abetted by her mother, Haruko followed her studious bent. She went not only to Japan Women's University but also to Tsuda College and Seibi Girls' School to learn English. She studied shorthand, Chinese, and Zen Buddhism. Romantic and beautiful, she had an unfortunate love affair with the young but married novelist Morita Sōhei. Her reputation for the Bohemian and offbeat was established.

It was Hiratsuka's interest in writing and literature that finally led her, with a few friends—also well-educated girls of good middle-class families—to found in 1911 Seitō to further the development of women's literary and intellectual talents. Her mother assisted with the money reserved for Hiratsuka's dowry. Hiratsuka hoped the magazine would help uncover the "hidden sun," as she labeled the "genius" of Japanese women. The Bluestocking Society (Seitō sha) took shape shortly thereafter.

The magazine and the society attracted the participation and mustered the support of many outstanding women leaders, journalists, authors, and poets of the time: Yosano Akiko, Nogami Yaeko, Jodai Tano, and Kamichika Ichiko, to name a few. By 1913 the literary venture had evolved into advocacy of women's liberation. Lecture meetings were held on Ibsen and on the popular Swedish feminist author Ellen Key, who proposed in her book Love and Marriage that educational and political equality would better prepare women for their roles as mothers. Round-table discussions on the status of Japanese women drew large audiences. Many were said to have come just to look at the beauty of Hiratsuka. For others, she was the spiritual leader of the women's movement and, as such, "an object of adoration."[53]

Meanwhile, newspaper reporters seized every lead to write up the activities of the Bluestocking members as risqué and spectacular. Over-blown episodes such as a visit to inspect the Yoshiwara brothel district and the sipping of an exotic "five-colored liqueur" created stories with a sensational twist. The daring and fleeting affairs of the heart of some of the members added a further aura of scandal. Hiratsuka entered into a free-love, common law marriage with the artist Okumura Hiroshi to demonstrate her opposition to what she called "feudalistic marriage." This devoted relationship, later regularized because of the children, lasted until his death in 1964. Society, as might be expected, frowned and retaliated. For example, Kamichika Ichiko, who much later, after World War II, was elected to the Diet, was fired from her teaching position in a girls' high school after her Bluestocking affiliation became known.

Gradually the group began to crumble. Members' attention waned because of the personal demands of marriage and babies. They split on whether their focus should be on literature or women's problems. The government banned some issues of the magazine, such as the one carrying Fukuda Hideko's article calling for liberation of both men and women through a communized society. Reluctantly, a tired and disconsolate Hiratsuka let her young protégée, Itō Noe, take over the editorship of *Seitō* in 1914. She, in turn, ran it for two more years, carrying on fiery debates on chastity, abortion, and the abolition of licensed prostitution. Finally, financial troubles, a diminished response, and the changing mood of the World War I years ended *Seitō* and the first manifestation of the "new women" phenomenon.[54]

One highly rational contemporary woman leader admitted to being uneasy about Hiratsuka's concept of the "hidden genius" of the Japanese woman and as a result did not become a Bluestocking member. She commented a few years after *Seitō* folded that the members "seemed to roam about in a dreamland of love and liberty, oblivious of actual life," but that somehow they "succeeded to touch the young heart and kindle there the aspirations for liberty and independence."[55]

Reflecting on the actions of her life shortly before her death in 1971, Hiratsuka assessed the Bluestocking Society with the hindsight of her eighty-five years:

> I still think it was right that we started the movement as an expression of inward desire. It was a spiritual women's movement; it was an explosion of women's ego which had been so suppressed that they could not even breathe. . . . women were not prepared for a social and political movement. . . . Some said, in those days, that we should work first for women's suffrage, but I thought we should reform women's consciousness first. And I still think I was right.[56]

The many young Japanese women who had welcomed *Seitō* as a "window" through which their hearts' yearnings (*kokoro no mado*, they called it) might escape to freedom agreed.

The stage was now set for the larger, more dynamic emancipation drive that followed during the propitious years of late Taishō after World War I.

Pursuit of Political Rights

New governmental and institutional forms gradually evolved after the Restoration, with political leaders following models based on patterns in Great Britain, the United States, Germany, and France. In 1889 the Emperor Meiji handed down the first written constitution, a beginning in parliamentary democracy. Political parties slowly took shape. The Upper House, which consisted of new hereditary nobility and imperial appointees, held more power than the Lower House, whose members were elected by a voting system giving suffrage to about 1 percent of the population—i.e., males twenty-five years or older who were substantial taxpayers. Rights of citizens included freedom of speech, writing, association, and religion—all with limits set by law; duties were taxes and military service.

The first quarter of the twentieth century, now considered in retrospect as a golden period, brought further liberalization of male enfranchisement and broadened the political base of power. Under legislation in 1919 and 1925, all male citizens twenty-five years or over became eligible to vote.

At the close of World War I in 1918, women had gained the right to vote in only four countries: Sweden, New Zealand, Australia, and the United Kingdom. The United States followed in 1920. Optimism spread; the time seemed ripe for the franchise to come to women of other countries as well. Japanese women who traveled abroad to make connections with the international suffrage movement learned with some astonishment that this Western progress resulted from almost a century of struggle, culminating in its final activist stages in the English suffragists' torchlight parades in Trafalgar Square and American suffragettes chaining themselves to the White House fence.

In Japan, too, there was a slender thread of emancipationist activity extending back into the nineteenth century. Early in the Meiji era, Kishida Toshiko (1863–1901), while still in her teens, was invited to Tōkyō from her home in Kyōto to lecture on Chinese literature to the empress. She soon espoused the popular rights movement. These interests not only brought her arrest but also turned her into a feminist. She reacted with vigor. "You men want to reform and revitalize this society but you leave out one question. This is the question of women. Why do you follow this obsolete custom?" She criticized despotic men as being "cunning like foxes, vicious like monsters, and bad as burglars." She spoke with passionate eloquence at many political meetings, elaborating on "the way of women." As the only woman lecturer, barely twenty, brilliant and beautiful, she enchanted her audiences.[57] Her oratory at a gathering in Okayama in 1881 inspired seventeen-year-old

Fukuda (née Kageyama) Hideko (1865–1927), already inflamed by the story of Joan of Arc, to a life of feminist and political activism. Fukuda Hideko has been called the Susan B. Anthony of Japan. While greatly different in personal life-styles, these two women were alike in their fighting spirit and dedication to the improvement of women's rights.

Shortly after the Kishida meeting, Fukuda organized her first women's social group to work for the abolition of the "traditional disabilities." Almost immediately the group ran into trouble with the law when members publicly made speeches extolling freedom—incredibly, on a boat in the middle of a river. Irate, Fukuda determined to combat such "injustice," an emotion that spurred her to leave home and go to Tōkyō, where she studied in a mission school. With a friend, she founded the Society for the Liberation of Women (Fujutsui kaisha) to teach self-reliance. Her political zeal led to her association with the "movement for freedom and people's right" (*jiyū minken undō*) and the Liberal party, a predecessor of the current conservative Liberal Democratic party. These connections brought arrest and a jail sentence when, in 1885, she took part in an international escapade of the Liberal party involving gun-running to Korea. Her trial as a political offender excited public attention, making her a celebrity and building her reputation as a fighter for freedom. In time, entangled in successive love affairs with her political confreres, she became disillusioned. She angrily charged that these political men used women members lightly as tools or as temporary love objects—a complaint often made by contemporary young activists about their experience in the university radical student movement.[58]

After the death of her husband, impoverished and with obligations to support her children, Fukuda made contact with intellectual Christian converts, many of whom in seeking parliamentary reforms had espoused socialism. Poor herself, she undertook programs designed to help the needy, including the training of deprived girls to give them economic independence. "Are not women also human beings?" she asked. ". . . it is as human beings that women have their divinely-given rights and liberty. . . . What reason is there for regarding politics as outside the sphere of woman and resting indifferent to man's monopoly of it?"[59]

Peace Preservation Laws

Ahead of their time in their endorsement of women's political equality, Kishida and Fukuda undoubtedly contributed to the conservative backlash that produced the Peace Preservation Law of 1887. This law was designed to control the Westernized democratic forces grown so dynamic in the first two decades of Meiji and especially those associated with the budding Liberal party. Amended from time to time over the years, the

Peace Preservation Laws served through World War II as the legal basis for police controls of social, economic, and political opposition to the government.

Article Five specifically dealt with women. It prohibited women and minors from (1) joining political organizations, (2) holding and attending meetings where political speeches or lectures on what might be construed as political subjects were given, and (3) initiating such meetings. Its promulgation brought to a halt the small, rather scattered stirrings of the early feminist movement. The pamphlet *Japanese Women*, prepared a few years later in 1893 by a group of Japanese women for distribution at the Chicago World's Columbian Exposition, set forth the prevailing attitudes of these formative years of modernizing while this law was in effect and indicated why average women were so reluctant to assume an active role in public affairs. It read: " 'Customs and circumstances' weigh against women taking an interest in political affairs. [Only] household cares and such public affairs as appertain to the minor charities and female education are well suited to the feminine nature, while unbecoming to the stronger sex."[60]

From 1887 to 1922 the law forbade the consideration of even academic-style study of political subjects in public groups and places—a seriously inhibiting condition not faced by Western women. As a result, the newly developing women leaders paid little heed to studies of political science. Because the field was ignored in educational programs, successive generations of Japanese women also had no adequate schooling in routine civic education.[61] It was only in 1951 that the advanced Tsuda College introduced into its curriculum an elective course in general politics and only in 1968, an international relations program.

The performance of Japanese women in public affairs reflected these restrictions. Women's groups concentrated on studies of family and domestic problems or the pursuit of literary interests and writing. The latter often led emotionally to discontent over equality and social justice, as demonstrated by the Bluestocking Society. Some individuals, such as Itō Noe, stepped over the line into areas that were considered radical and that involved punishable political action. Itō moved from the Bluestocking Society to the anarchism of Emma Goldman and finally to political activities that caused her peremptory execution in the police purge after the Kantō earthquake of 1923.

Generally, however, the ubiquitous information-gathering study group remained acceptable and was widely used. The American teacher at Tsuda College, Alice Mabel Bacon, writing in 1902, pointed out that women's "mutual improvement clubs" were, along with legislation, education, and the press, the major vehicles for bringing advancement to Japanese women.[62] In the 1920s, women's suffrage received quiet support among middle-class women and wives of prominent men, whose family connections permitted only the most inconspicuous endorsement, in the study-group setting.[63] For most women this officially tolerated approach was preferable to more direct political methods for correcting societal ills.

Although the effect of the Peace Preservation Laws should not be exaggerated, their long-imposed psychological influence on patterns of public behavior in a tradition-laden society like Japan must not be underestimated. It is hardly surprising that women who desired political emancipation set as a primary goal the revision of the inhibiting Article Five.

Fukuda Hideko joined with several hundred other socialist women in 1905 to wage an early campaign to obtain such change. Their petition to allow women to join political parties received a favorable vote in the Lower House of the Diet in 1908, but it was rejected by the more traditionalist Upper House. Thus it failed. This became a familiar sequence in the siege against Article Five. This early drive ended in 1911 when the government took vigorous restraining measures against all socialists as a result of a plot to assassinate the emperor. Any so-called social agitation was thereafter regarded as suspect.

The "New Women" and Article Five

Not until the New Women's Association went into action in 1920 was any change in Article Five effected. For this second and formally organized appearance of the "new women," Hiratsuka Raichō shared starring roles with Ichikawa Fusae and Oku Mumeo, who provided leadership to Japanese women in political and public affairs for much of the next half century.

Hiratsuka, in the years since the cessation of *Seitō*, had withdrawn from public activities and devoted herself to her husband and children and to dealing with the constraints of a tight family budget. Her attitudes mellowed. Japan, too, was adjusting to the ramifications of World War I and events of its aftermath, such as the Russian Revolution. Talk of self-determination, with its democratic concepts, and of internationalism and pacifism enlivened the discussions of intellectuals. New currents flowed in this postwar democratic era. Startling news of the rice riots started by the women of Toyama in 1918 aroused Hiratsuka from her familial hibernation to fresh concerns about the social conditions of her countrywomen. Her awareness of suffrage developments in Western countries, observation visits to textile factories where so many girls worked, and conversations with socially alert friends consolidated into her conclusion that an "organized movement to obtain women's rights"[64] was now needed.

She recruited newspaperwoman Ichikawa Fusae and Oku Mumeo, her former classmate at Japan Women's University. The latter agreed to help only reluctantly because her husband insisted that it was "a good thing to work with an outstanding woman like Hiratsuka."[65] Together they undertook fund-raising and sketched out the purposes, organization, and program for a new Japanese feminism. Seeking the cooperation of a cross-section of women, they planned a national federation that would reach out to local organizations. Their objective was equal rights for all men and women, taking into account the functional differences of the sexes and the need for women to develop their own "innate potentialities." Specifically they would work to realize (1) a higher standard of education for women, (2) coeducation in primary schools, (3) women's suffrage, (4) revision of laws unfavorable to women, and (5) protection of motherhood. They would undertake research, set up meetings and conferences, put out a publication, and offer personal consultation for women with problems. They would establish an office, a public meeting hall, boarding accommodations for women, a library, and recreation facilities.

When invited to be a guest speaker at what promised to be a well-attended women's conference sponsored by the newspaper *Asahi* in Ōsaka in November 1919, Hiratsuka seized the moment to announce the New Women's Association. The organization was formally inaugurated at the well-known restaurant Seiyoken on the edge of Tōkyō's Ueno Park on March 28, 1920. Hiratsuka explained to the some seventy men and women present that:

> The time has come for women to unite for the sake of all women to fulfil our natural obligations, and attain our natural rights. . . . we must cooperate with the men, and participate in the actual movement of postwar social reconstruction. If women do not stand fast at this time, the future will be no different—women will again be excluded from society which will remain the monopoly of men. If this occurs, it will be a great catastrophe for the world, for mankind.[66]

Membership soon numbered more than 200; the rush was on for "emancipation of women from traditional means of treatment," as Ichikawa phrased it.[67] By July the leaders had submitted to the Diet a petition, signed by more than 1,500 women of "light and leading in the Empire,"[68] to amend part of Article Five to permit women to organize and attend political meetings. A second petition, more to Hiratsuka's liking than to Ichikawa's, called for proscription of marriage for men with venereal disease and provision for divorce for such cause. This second appeal was rejected at once. The proposal, the women were told, did not "accord with the standard of Japanese custom which gave predominance to men over women."[69] Day and night Hiratsuka, Ichikawa, and others petitioned Diet members for support of the amendment to Article Five. Aided by a few sympathetic Diet men and advisers, such as Ishiyama Kenkichi, they learned how to lobby by doing it. Association members attended Diet sessions hoping to exert influence on the legislators by their presence and by the persistency with which they submitted entreaties written on their name cards. Oku recalled:

> We had our opinion printed on pieces of pink and lavender paper and distributed them on each parliamentary seat. Looking down from the gallery, we could clearly see who was absent and did not read the leaflet. We noted this information on a seat chart. . . . Women's seats were in a corner of the gallery, the rest were for men. The gallery was covered with wire netting. We listened to the Diet men quietly like tiny animals in a cage.[70]

The arrest of Ichikawa and Hiratsuka for violation of Article Five at a meeting at the YMCA increased the suffragists' zeal to overcome the obstacle to their right of assembly. Several times their Article Five petitions passed the Lower House but failed in the Upper House. Meanwhile, the association published a bulletin, *Women's Federation* (*Josei dōmei*), got its research committees functioning, arranged for endorsement of candidates favorable to their petitions during the 1920 election, put on a music festival, and pushed ahead with other aspects of the association's program.

Abruptly in 1921, probably because of repeated disappointment, extreme fatigue, and personal incompatibilities between the pragmatic, no-nonsense Ichikawa and the softer, more emotional Hiratsuka, both these leaders withdrew. The former went to the United States to study. The latter, who was ill, secluded herself with her family and only rarely thereafter came forth to support the peace movement or women's activities. She had, it was said, "lost her passion."[71]

The final and successful thrust for the revision of the Peace Preservation Law fell to the third of the leadership trio, Oku Mumeo. Kimono-clad, with her small son strapped, Japanese-style, to her back, she became the familiar and principal figure enjoining support for their petitions. According to a well-known story, it was her sweetly maternal shushing of her baby during a crucial petitioning visit to opponent Baron Fujimura Yoshiro that turned the tables and persuaded him that Japanese women could both maintain feminine qualities and sustain interest in public affairs. His observations of Western suffragists on trips abroad had made him dubious! His conversion, plus the liberal mood engendered by labor's strikes for its rights, made the difference. In a cliff-hanger session of the Upper House, racing the clock to closing, the petition was finally approved on February 25, 1922. Women had won legal freedom to organize and take part in political meetings.

Women promptly acted on their new prerogative, and political meetings proliferated throughout the country. Often what the women tried to say and do lacked finesse. Their gaucherie brought criticism and rebuff, and inevitably there was some disillusionment. They needed time to find their way, a theme that still prevails among women leaders who seek improved performance in public affairs.[72]

Oku, alone at the helm of the New Women's Association, began to lose interest in politics as a viable approach to feminism. After the revision of Article Five, she spoke in many parts of Japan, coming to realize that only women with free time could take part in meetings and engage in politics. These organizations had become "fashionable" rather than hard-working and effective. Women with children, like herself, needed a different avenue. She withdrew from the association and the suffrage movement. Groping for some other solution, she tried her hand at settlement house and child-care-center work before discovering that her forte lay in the consumer movement, the career for which she is most famous.[73]

In 1922 the New Women's Association dissolved. Ichikawa subsequently ascribed the collapse to impure motives and weakness and, like Oku, to the plethora of women's organizations taking up the cudgels for suffrage.[74] Hiratsuka commented, "I regret to say that we women today do not possess in our hearts a quality necessary for unity."[75]

The New Women's Association, although short-lived, played a crucial role in focusing the efforts of Japanese women's leadership. It was the link between the Bluestocking movement and the more practical emancipation programs of the middle and late 1920s. Hiratsuka herself provided an integrating force. The unfolding of her own convictions exemplified the maturing of the women's emancipation movement. From romantic idealism it progressed to a recognized, albeit not completely respectable, position in Japanese life. Individual leaders still were occasionally criticized as unwomanly or called "new women" with a "mixture of disdain and curiosity."[76] Ichikawa, looking back, said that the task of elevating women's status was difficult because there was not enough cooperation from either women or men.

Nevertheless, the New Women's Association channeled the energies and refined the concepts of those associated with its program, such as writer Yamada Waka, artist Naganuma Chieko, and, importantly, Ichikawa and Oku. Never before had members of literary groups, labor groups, and socially minded groups and plain housewives come together in one cause. It established political emancipation as an issue capable of uniting women and their organized endeavors.

Even the press, which had spoofed the Bluestocking adherents, now supported and encouraged women's suffrage. Said the *Ōsaka Mainichi:* "Politically speaking, Japan maltreats and insults her woman to a graver extent than any other country of the globe. If the old saying, that the standard of civilization of a country can be judged by the social position of its women is true, then Japan's position among the Five Great Powers is doubtful."[77] The expanded social consciousness and intellectual ferment of the time had managed to establish a somewhat more receptive public mood to the issues of women's rights.

Proletarian Women

Interestingly, women leaders of the proletarian movement had, during the early 1920s, shied away from a focus on women's political emancipation. They criticized the New Women's Association as bourgeois in attitude, impractical, and lacking in attention to the fundamental needs of the poor and the workers and the class war. For such purposes, they argued, revision of Article Five had little value: Socialism must come before suffrage.

Yamakawa Kikue, the intellectual socialist, maintained that "such a change has no important bearing upon the proletarian women because, whether they have any legal right or not, they can never imagine enjoying freedom of speech or association in the same way as their men-folk." She was impatient because even when women joined with men for a cause, as in the labor unions, they did not know what to do with themselves and remained inactive. She believed they needed special training and motivation rather than a separate movement. She worried, however, that women, unlike men, never had any time to educate themselves, for after a day's work in the factory or office, they faced household burdens.[78]

Yamakawa, together with Itō Noe of earlier *Seitō* fame and Magara (née Sakai) Kondo, organized in April 1921 the first socialist women's organization, the Red Wave Society (Sekirankai), which was principally for the wives of socialists. Within the larger socialist-labor movement, it tried to raise the level of women's socialist education and get them to take part in May Day rallies and other activist programs. Magara amusingly recalls that she sometimes borrowed a baby to wear on her back when she took to the streets to distribute leaflets, believing this show of motherhood would forestall arrest. Close police surveillance

Yamakawa Kikue, Itō Noe, and Magara Sakai, leaders of the Sekirankai, at the time of a lecture-meeting, July 15, 1921, at the Kanda Young Men's Hall. Photo courtesy of Yamakawa Kikue.

discouraged membership; the leaders were arrested. The society went underground in 1922 and was finally disbanded in 1925,[79] no doubt suffering from the conservative mood that produced in 1925 the new Peace Preservation Law (*Chian ijihō*), prohibiting groups that harbored dangerous thoughts or might advocate a change in Japanese political forms or the private property system.

Throughout the 1920s the proletarian political parties continued to take a stand in favor of women's suffrage, and their women finally came around to support this point of view.

The Great Earthquake

In 1923, with the New Women's Association disbanded and with the fervor of the leading women flagging as concerted action seemed to be fading away, it was, incredibly, the great Kantō earthquake on September 1 that reinvigorated the women's movement. The earthquake provoked the crisis atmosphere of necessity. This cracking open of a flaw in the earth's surface also revealed to many the flaws and imperfections in society. For the women, the earthquake's devastation

YWCA members and workers outside the temporary headquarters of the YWCA of Japan in Tōkyō after the earthquake of 1923. The "relief hut" was built with lumber given by the government. The woman on the extreme right is an American YWCA volunteer who assisted the Japanese organization after the earthquake. Photo courtesy of the National Board YWCA Archives.

became a challenge to their ability to restore order. They were spurred by the plight of the hungry, the homeless, and the destitute and the agonizing deaths of a hundred thousand, including the indentured prostitutes of Yoshiwara, too confused and afraid to flee their burning quarters.

Without waiting for men or the imperial call to action, women assumed responsibilities that presaged roles for them in social reconstruction in the years ahead. Women leaders mobilized their efforts under a newly formed umbrella operation, the Federation of Women's Associations of Tōkyō. They started with basics, with milk distribution. By November, forty-two different organizations were working under this aegis. Familiar figures such as Kawai Michi and Dr. Yoshioka Yayoi gave leadership. Mary R. Beard, famed as a pioneer in the writing of women's history who came to Japan with her historian husband, Charles A. Beard, who was advising on urban reconstruction, helped shape the federation and its work.

With the crisis over, the ongoing program of the federation turned to concentrate on longer-range women's issues—the ending of licensed prostitution, achievement of economic independence and property rights for women, improvement of working conditions for women and girls, and securing a voice in the government. A new era opened.

In the long chronicle of Japanese history, the earthquake is a landmark for its women. It propelled them into leadership in ways accepted by society, thus giving impetus and credibility to their efforts. Furthermore, women's early recognition of need and prompt action, prior even to official mobilization, was a portent in this most unusual situation of what would become after World War II a natural pattern of their serving as societal forecasters—noting and taking steps through their organizations to remedy practical problems of living or to make social adjustments well before official policymakers awakened to any national exigency. As one of the hard workers of that early time commented, the Japanese woman "found herself." The leaders showed themselves in truth to be the new women, the modernized women, of Japan.[80]

International Cooperation

Throughout the years since the Charter Oath of 1868, personal and institutional connections between Japan and friendly cohorts in the West had contributed to improvement in Japanese women's situation and to international understanding. Japan's participation in World War I stimulated in more dramatic fashion a general consciousness of the outside world and what its people were doing. In the postwar era the flapper became one cultural manifestation of this awareness. But the time also produced two projects of organized benevolence that involved large numbers of women in unprecedented acts of international friendship.

The initial effort was the raising of funds for Belgian war relief in 1915—a step that Tsuda Umeko hailed as the first charity undertaken by Japanese women to help people outside their own country. Almost 2,000 women's organizations, including the very large, semigovernmental Patriotic Women's Society, raised ¥50,000 (then $25,000) for the Belgian program. Yamakawa Kikue organized the second drive to aid the victims of the Russian famine of 1920 and 1921. She hoped it would broaden public appreciation of the Russian Revolution. Campaign workers came from beyond the small socialist circles to include Yosano Akiko, the poet Fukao Sumako, Katō (Ishimoto) Shidzue, and even—surreptitiously because of the watchful conservative eye of President Yoshioka Yayoi— some of the students of the Women's Medical School. The organizers were happily surprised when their national lecture series and sale of picture postcards of Russian farm women at three for ten sen brought in almost ¥8,000.[81] Both ventures encouraged the women.

But it continued to be, after as before World War I, the more modest comings and goings of individual Japanese women to the United States and Europe and of Western women to Japan that strengthened relationships between the Japanese women's movement and the internationally organized women and social leaders. Birth control and women's suffrage, two issues of significance in both pre– and post–World War II Japan, benefited greatly from these relationships.

The Birth Control Movement

Katō (Ishimoto) Shidzue's friendship with the American Margaret Sanger served as the fountainhead of the Japanese birth control movement. Born in 1892, young Shidzue was educated at the Peeress School and reared according to the most exacting traditions of a feudalistic samurai family. Soon after marriage to her first husband, Baron Ishimoto Keikichi, she encountered the poor in a coal-mining community in Kyūshū and discovered the stark realities of life outside the high protecting walls of noble birth and family wealth. She acquired personal self-confidence and discovered ways to undertake social action during her years of study in the United States in 1919–1920. One afternoon at tea, YWCA friends arranged for her to meet with Margaret Sanger. The magnetism of the charming and delicate American woman and the birth control cause for which she crusaded won for Japanese women that day an unflagging advocate for their right to family planning.

Katō (Ishimoto) Shidzue has devoted her life to the belief that birth control can protect motherhood and serve as an "agency for women's emancipation." Not only a feminist but also a humanitarian, she stressed that birth control, along with improved living conditions, would ultimately achieve "true progress and harmony for mankind," thus serving the cause of world peace.[82]

Japan, by mid-Taishō, had doubled its population since the Meiji era began. Government policy called for a "rich and strong Japan" and, naturally, for sturdy workers and soldiers to meet the requirements of industrialization and nationalism. Families took pride in having many children who would, according to Confucian heritage, carry on the family name. The 1930 census showed Japan's population to be nearly 64.5 million, up from almost 56 million a decade earlier. By 1940, it was more than 73 million, a 30 percent increase between the world wars.

In a country the size of California the large population intensified social and economic problems.[83] As early as 1902, some intellectuals had pondered the merits of birth control for humanitarian reasons but were overwhelmed by the chauvinism rampant during the Russo-

Margaret Sanger meets with Baron and Baroness Ishimoto during her visit to Japan, 1922. Photo courtesy of the Sophia Smith Collection.

Japanese War. Official policy condoned population growth; population limitation smacked of socialistic ideas.

Under the circumstances, the prospect in 1922 that Margaret Sanger would undertake a lecture tour in Japan at the invitation of the magazine *Kaizō* [Reconstruction] provoked unease in the government. Official Japan first tried to forestall her visit by refusing her an entrance visa. Then, when her steamer arrived at the shores of Japan, they forbade her to land. The government finally relented, in the face of public uproar, after getting her to agree that she would not discuss birth control in public meetings. Her arrival, described as "the invasion of Sangerism," seemed comparable in Katō (Ishimoto) Shidzue's mind to the excitement aroused by the first appearance of Commodore Perry and his Black Ships. Japanese humor prompted the police to call their visitor "Sangai-san," which may be translated as "destructive to production." While obeying the police prohibition of public speeches, Sanger, in private sessions in homes, with Katō standing guard at the door lest the thought police descend, answered questions on her birth control ideas. She discussed such issues as the neo-Malthusian doctrine, whose implications excited contention among liberal and Marxist groups. The official opposition, press coverage, and resulting public furor over her visit undoubtedly publicized the birth control cause far more than would have a routine visiting lecture series.

By May 1922 the enthusiastic baroness and her husband, with laborite politician Matsuoka Komakichi, medical doctor Kaji Tokijiro, and others under the leadership of Professor Abe Isō of Waseda University, organized the Japan Birth Control Institute. It stressed that "the right practice of birth control principles should not be an act of immorality; it should be in harmony with social morality."[84] The uphill battle of public education got under way. The society, under the directorship of Dr. Kaji, soon established a research medical clinic at the People's Hospital, while the baroness continued her educational efforts with high-born and laboring groups equally.

In 1932, inspired by the International Birth Control Convention in the Netherlands, the Women's Birth Control League of Japan was organized, with Katō as president and women leaders like Hiratsuka Raichō, Yamamoto Sugiko, and Yamataka Shigeri joining with male officers. Meantime, the Proletarian Birth Control League also got under way to spread information among the poorer women, who were most in need of advice, adding a bourgeois-proletarian political seesaw to this already sensitive issue.

In 1934, after Katō's further studies at Margaret Sanger's Birth Control Research Institute in New York and in Europe, her dream of a medically scientific birth control clinic became a reality. Starting with funds raised in the United States, she consulted with women two days a week in a private doctor's office. Case histories revealed that the women wanted smaller families so they could afford to give their children a better education. This motive still predominates in modern, affluent Japan, where the successful birth control program has stabilized the formerly expanding Japanese population. Margaret Sanger returned to Japan again in the late summer of 1937 to lecture and to visit the clinic, now under the aegis of the Women's Birth Control League of Japan. But the tide was running out for any social reform activities not in keeping with government policy.

Katō (Ishimoto) Shidzue was briefly imprisoned in December 1937 for her "dangerous thoughts" and for connections with the labor movement, officially labeled as communism after the Japanese anticommunist pact with Germany and Italy. Her Japanese and American friends, including Japanese Ambassador to the United States, Saitō Hiroshi, Margaret Sanger, the U.S. publishers of Katō's autobiography, and the women she met at the International Congress of Women Conference in Chicago in 1933, successfully bombarded the Japanese government with pleas for her release. Katō's international reputation supported her in this difficult time.[85]

In January 1938, "in order to conform with the national policy now followed by the government," Katō was compelled to close her birth control clinic. The well-publicized slogan, remembered clearly by all women of childbearing age of that time, of "*Umeyo fuyaseyo*"—"Produce more babies and increase the population"—expressed the exigencies of the time. To lend support to this policy, the Ministry of Welfare in September 1939 announced special monetary awards to honor 25,000 families who had ten or more children over six years of age. Patriotic Japanese did not seem to take umbrage at what seems the irrationality of urging colonialization in Manchuria and emigration overseas to ease the population pressure while promoting big families at home.[86] Until the coming of the Americans in the Occupation, Katō (Ishimoto) Shidzue reflected in later years, "All I could do was to keep silence. That was all I could do. That was my silent resistance."[87]

The Suffrage Movement

The women's suffrage movement in Japan gathered momentum from the drive for universal male suffrage. Women anticipated that the forces at work in Japan that successfully pushed through legislation in 1919 and 1925 to give all men the vote would carry the day for them also. The slogan, making a play on words that in Japanese sound the same but are written differently, was "from *fusen* to *fusen*" or "from universal suffrage to women's franchise." It is now axiomatic among feminists that improvements for them often coattail the progress of other groups suffering discrimination, but the strategy in Japan in the 1920s was mainly hope, hunch, and hard work. Sadly, neither the axiom nor the devoted effort bore the expected results.

Communication with their Western counterparts widened the social base of the suffragists, increasing their respectability. Visits to Europe and America provided on-site training and improved campaign and organizational methods. The human encounter gave reassurance. Amusingly, Japanese and Western women each noted with surprise how decorous was the other. Japanese feminists, regarded as progressive, even radical, within their own society, were judged by Western observers as "scarcely . . . belligerent, not exactly militant" although "panoplied for war," or just plain "quiet and wren-like." Japanese manners often compelled these gentle fighters to bow gracefully, although feeling, in the words of one, "fire within, calm without."[88] Japanese, in turn, were struck by the feminine, ladylike qualities of the Westerner, expecting more gruff, tough individuals, given their political accomplishments.

Gauntlett Tsune years later recalled her amazement when she attended with WCTU President Yajima Kaji the Eighth Conference of the International Women's Suffrage Alliance in Geneva in 1920:

> I shall never forget my surprise at the beautiful picture that the platform presented. The president of the I.W.S.A., Mrs. [Carrie Chapman] Catt, occupied the centre seat, with the officers of the organization on either side, Mrs. Corbett Ashby (English), our present president, the late Dr. Streit (German), the late Dr. Jacobs (Danish). . . . But the one whose presence most impressed me was Mrs. Catt, sitting there on the platform with such a sweet, dignified, and motherly look. I could hardly take my eyes off her. . . . I listened with bated breath to (her) every word. . . . I made up my mind that I would not rest until I saw an organized women's suffrage movement started in my own country.[89]

Within a year, Gauntlett's new conviction helped bring a vote by the Japanese WCTU national convention to espouse the cause of women's suffrage. The organization became the core of middle-class and Christian humanist support.

However, it was Ichikawa Fusae who towered above Japanese women suffragist and political leaders in prewar and postwar Japan. Born in 1893 in Aichi Prefecture of a large and poor farm family, she felt that her father's harsh treatment of her illiterate mother led her to a lifetime of dedication to "gain equality between men and women so that women should not suffer like my mother did." Her mother resignedly told her that it "was unfortunate that she was born a woman because women had to endure hardship."[90] Ichikawa in her career faced much hardship, but not the type her mother believed fated for all women—submission to an unhappy marriage and home. Her hardships came from her unceasing struggle for the independence and dignity of women in a society dominated by men.

Her father, recognizing that lack of education caused many of the family's afflictions, encouraged all the children in their schooling. Accordingly, the young Ichikawa attended normal school in Okasaki City and became a teacher. Moving to Nagoya, she became angry when she realized that she, as a woman, was paid less than the men teachers and that she was also expected to wash the teacups and curtains. She became a Christian and joined with the intellectuals who were instrumental in crystallizing her interest in labor problems and women's emancipation.

Liberal Yamada Waka and her professor husband brought Ichikawa to the attention of the famed Hiratsuka. Thus was fashioned the team that with Oku Mumeo, organized the notable New Women's Association.

For Ichikawa it was a formative time during which she tested organizational fundamentals, concepts of leadership, schemes of coordination, and tactics of lobbying that characterized her activities in the women's movement throughout her life. Her childhood lessons of poverty evolved into a sense of frugality and disdain for money that became another lifelong ethic. While working for the New Women's Association, she had to pawn her belongings to survive. Later, she gave up a high-paying job with the Tōkyō International Labour Organisation (ILO) Office to concentrate full-time on the Women's Suffrage League. Fifty years later, as a Diet member, she still ignored the trappings of affluence, refusing to accept salary increases she felt were unnecessarily voted by fellow Diet members. Until her death, she lived in spartan style at the Fusen kaikan (Women's Suffrage Hall) in Shinjuku in Tōkyō, routinely dressing in unadorned plain-colored suits and dresses, an Ichikawa trademark uniform. Her work was her pleasure and achievement, her reward.

After the break-up in 1921 of the leadership trio of the New Women's Association, Ichikawa spent two and one-half years in the United States, where her eldest brother and younger sister lived. Typical of her modest approach, she worked for room and board while studying, starting by improving her English in a Seattle third-grade class! Later, at Hull House in Chicago, she met Jane Addams and learned about her federation of women for peace and freedom. She discussed labor problems with women trade union leaders. She took extension courses at Columbia University. She established a lifelong friendship with Alice Paul, who led the radical wing of the U.S. suffrage movement and set up the National Women's party. She followed the work of Carrie Chapman Catt, who reorganized the middle-ground suffrage movement into the League of Women Voters of the U.S.A. and also developed a women's movement for war prevention. In retrospect, all these encounters influenced Ichikawa during her long career. The suffrage, peace, and social reform programs of these women harmonized with her own aspirations.

When Ichikawa returned to Japan in 1924, optimism about universal suffrage flowed strongly. That December a group of women's organizations banded together to form the Women's Suffrage League (Fusen kakutoku dōmei). Ichikawa became director for business activities; a Christian leader and niece of Yajima Kaji, Kubushiro Ochimi, also just returned from studying women's suffrage in the United States and Europe, became general secretary. The League's manifesto was clear:

> The foundation of New Japan has been laid. As was expected, the universal suffrage bill was passed by the fiftieth session of the Imperial Diet. And yet the women, who form one-half of the entire population of the country,

have been left entirely outside the field of political activity, classed along with a small number of males of less than 25 years of age and "those who are in receipt of relief or aid from State or private organizations." We women feel ourselves no longer inclined to state the reason why it is at once natural and necessary for us, who are both human beings and citizens, to participate in the administration of our country. We must concentrate our endeavors on realizing our participation in politics, having in mind the actual results of the movement for woman suffrage in foreign countries, [and] cooperating with each other regardless of anything else, such as differences of feeling, religion and opinion.[91]

The league initiated a nationwide campaign, using Western techniques of education. Members struggled to convince both women and men of the advantages for Japan of political citizenship for women. Leaders often grumbled that women themselves lacked interest. A poll conducted by an influential Tōkyō magazine, *Woman's Review*, showed that women ranked suffrage fourth in the list of priorities they would act on, if they could, in the Diet. Ahead of suffrage came abolition of licensed prostitution, prohibition of alcohol, and drastic curtailment of the military.[92] Yet, recollection of their historical rights of equality and of early strong women rulers like Hōjō Masako, the nun-shōgun, spurred confidence.[93] At times the Federation of Women's Associations in Tōkyō (the group formed after the earthquake), the All-Kansai federation, and the Ōsaka *Asahi shimbun* women's group joined the league in lobbying at the Diet. By 1926 the proletarian and labor-party women occasionally cooperated. The question of granting the vote to women came up perennially, but the government procrastinated.

Whenever possible, the suffragists sought the backing of women abroad. "Eager to hear, eager to discuss, eager to learn, and ready to give, all in the spirit of friendliness and cooperation" rang forth the voice of Kansai educator, Ide Kikue, at the first Pan Pacific Women's Conference in 1928 in Honolulu.[94] This was the first international meeting with a full delegation of Japanese women rather than merely an observer or two. Ichikawa Fusae presented a resolution for conference approval, requesting "cooperation and sympathy and guidance."[95]

In 1930 the suffragists tried a new approach. They proposed that, as a beginning, the six large cities grant citizenship rights to women to take part in local government. They collected many signatures of endorsement on petitions for presentation to the Home Ministry. Katō (Ishimoto) Shidzue told of an early-morning visit to Home Minister Mochizuki Keisuke. Because he was known to have many geisha friends, the suffragists expected he would "have a good understanding of women." Not of this kind, it turned out. He jokingly turned the petitioning

Minister of Imperial Railways Gotaro Ogawa, an ardent supporter of women's suffrage, gave women railroad employees equal voting rights during his administration, 1940–1941. He oversees balloting in this scene in the Tōkyō railroad office. Photo courtesy of the Library of Congress.

group away with, "Oh you women, how could you leave your house so early in the morning. You should go back home immediately and wash baby clothes." But others, like Minister Adachi Kenzō, helped, and the campaign gained adherents. By the early 1930s, the membership of the supporting organizations numbered more than 3 million.[96]

Descent to War

After the Manchurian incident in September 1931, however, emancipation hopes gradually dimmed. Democratizing goodwill and ebullience gave way, step by step, to what some Japanese have called the "dark valley" (kuroi tanima) of the 1930s. Strident nationalism, authoritarian control, and militaristic domination took over. The resurgence of conservative attitudes could be seen from the vote of 800 to 3 against women's suffrage by women primary school teachers in their convention in 1934.[97] The reformers began to look to the Diet more for improved protective legislation for mothers and children than for political rights.

In 1937, with the outbreak of the Chinese war, government-authorized "spiritual mobilization" programs assumed priority. Women were galvanized by sloganizing that importuned "A United Front" and "Fortitude and Endurance." That September the suffragist and liberalized women's groups formed the League of Japanese Women's Organizations, with Gauntlett Tsune as president. The seven member organizations were the YWCA, WCTU, Japan Women Doctors' Association, Fujin dōshikai (a suffrage group composed of wives of prominent business and social leaders of Ōsaka and Tōkyō), Friendship Society, Japan Women Consumers' League, and Women's Suffrage League of Japan. "The League," they said, "is not specially engaged in so-called wartime activities, but it aims to cope with the situation created by the national crisis and prepare for the reconstruction work necessary at the conclusion of the Incident."[98]

In February 1938, thirty national figures—of whom ten were women, including Dr. Yoshioka and Ichikawa—recommended thirteen practices that all organizations should encourage among their members. Greatly diverse, these recommendations covered worship of the Shrine of Ise, the imperial family, and Buddhism; family budgeting; wearing apparel; ceremonies of marriage and death; fire prevention; nutrition and child discipline; exercise; abstinence from alcohol; neighborliness; and even the "undesirable habit" of sleeping late.[99]

The May 1940 issue of *Japanese Women*, a bulletin in English started January 1938 by the Women's Suffrage League to maintain ties with women's movements in other countries, carried a rather poignant exchange of letters between Ichikawa and La Baronne Pol Boël, president of the International Council of Women in Brussels. They dealt with Japan's lack of response to the international organization for the previous two years. Ichikawa tried to explain that it had been impossible to set up a coordinated, representative Japanese committee because of fundamental differences between the two groupings of Japanese women's organizations. On the one hand, there was the League of Japanese Women's Organizations, made up of privately sponsored organizations; on the other, there were the four large government-sponsored "patriotic" associations run by male officials from governmental ministries: the Patriotic Women's Society, under the protection of the Ministry of Home Affairs and Welfare Ministry; the Women's National Defense Association, superintended by the War Ministry;[100] and the Federation of Young Women's Societies and the Federation of Women's Societies, under the control of the Education Ministry. Ichikawa explained that the "free" independents were much smaller but were "proud of their superior educational and intellectual standard." Essentially incompatible, the two groups were unable to form a committee to represent Japan in the

International Council, to say nothing, Ichikawa expostulated, of the patriotic associations' "utter indifference" to any international body. The discord between the women's associations showed that the struggle of ideas about the education and role of women that had run throughout the fabric of Japanese society since the opening of the Meiji era of enlightenment was still very real. Ichikawa's letter, expressing the desire in this time of delicate international relations for cooperation "towards the end of establishing a better world order," closed with a plea for understanding.[101]

Very soon the private league was disbanded. All women were organized in 1942 under the Great Japan Women's Organization (Dai Nihon fujin kai). The war leaders demanded patriotic unity. Reflected Ichikawa in January 1973, when she received the *Asahi* newspaper prize for her lifelong services dedicated to improving the status of women and to giving political education to voters, "The professional soldiers, whom women hate, had their own way and the suffrage movement was forced to keep quiet."[102]

The Home Front

The war years demanded the utmost in sacrifice and hard labor. Proudly, sadly, numbly, Japanese women met these demands.[103] By 1939, as able-bodied men were called into military service, increasing numbers of laborers in the factories were women. In 1944 it became necessary to draft youth from high school age up.[104] Kawai Michi in her autobiography told about her Keisen School girls and their work in a laundry for soldiers' clothing, a felt factory, with the Fuel Section of the army, and the like. When one of the schoolgirls died of tuberculosis exacerbated by hard work and overexposure, Dr. Kagawa Toyohiko, a world-famous Christian evangelist, preached at her funeral. He extolled not only the little dead Reiko but all her classmates for their devoted labors carried on with the cheer imbued by their Christian heritage:

Day in and day out, in rain, sleet and even in snow, you girls came to the laundry building, carrying very light lunch boxes in your chapped hands, laughing, singing and ever defying death which was stalking you all the time. Rickety were the ladders along the side of the dilapidated storehouse, leading to the temporary drying place on the roof, with poles at the four corners. It was there you young girls used to hang the heavy, wet blankets in the morning on ropes strung from side to side, and take them down toward sunset. It would have been a heavy task, even for full-fledged laboring men to do on cold winter days. How could you sing so gaily whether on the roof or in the splashy washing room, where no

hot water could be had and the cement floor was slippery with ice!. . .
[I pray that you can] forgive this land of your birth.[105]

Except for the religious flavor of this story, its basic picture is typical
of the physical hardship of the time. Women's fortitude and amazing
capacity to suppress personal sorrow could equally well be attributed
to the ennobling traditions of the samurai spirit. Such commendation
was paid to all Japanese women by a professor at Kyōto Imperial
University on the occasion of the fall of Saipan in early 1945, when
the women followed their husbands in death rather than be taken by
the enemy. No matter what the ideology, men extolled the valor of
their women and their fidelity to Japan.[106]

For housewives in cities, finding food for the family became a daily
struggle of major proportions. Elegant kimonos brought into marriage
as dowry and family treasures and heirlooms slowly went as barter for
food—or were lost in the fires of the bombing raids. The traditional
farm woman's *mompe*, a kind of full, puffy pantaloon, replaced the
slim, less practical kimono. Women's enrollment in the gigantic, nationwide Great Japan Women's Organization, which served under the
Imperial Rule Assistance Association (Taisei yokusankai), mobilized them
into the governmental network. In the last year of the war, defense
reservists even trained women in the "bamboo spear" units designed
to help repel the anticipated U.S. invasion of the home islands. Primarily,
however, these government-led organizations, functioning in neighborhood groups (*tonari gumi*), became the focus of daily relationships for
rationing and for communicating to the population. Many families were
finally forced to split up, with children and frailer people evacuated to
the country for greater safety. Doubling up on housing meant that rich
and poor, high-born and laborer were thrown together in community
survival.[107] Democratization was under way through the leveling agents
of destruction and need. Countless autobiographical remembrances of
that time include the despairing question, "When will it all end?"

It was natural for Japanese women to mourn the defeat of their
country. The poignancy of their sadness is symbolized in the simple
story told by a Tsuda College graduate. She remembers, as a little girl
on the day the Emperor announced the end of the war, watching her
mother polishing the wooden hall floors of their home, unmindfully
rubbing in her flowing tears as she worked.

It was equally natural for the women to look to rebuilding their lives
now that the fighting and bombing had ended. With most men in Japan
in a state of shock and more than 3 million in the military overseas,
women carried the burden of the home front when the Occupation

began. As in the Kantō earthquake experience, emergency made women strong. The traumatic social and physical disarray created a setting ripe for a break with the past.

It remained to be seen whether the war had brought any closer the classically Japanese majority of women who found security in the semifeudalistic, Confucian-based "wise-mother-good-wife" heritage and the probing, slender advance party of intelligentsia, rebels, and passionately motivated feminists—and how the liberating reforms of the Occupation years would be handled by the traditional women and those held to be "new and awakened."

EQUALITY UNDER THE OCCUPATION—
NEW VOTERS AND DEMOCRATIC ORGANIZERS

> *"What would have been our status,"* Japanese women
> say thoughtfully to each other, *"if our militarists had
> won the war and continued to rule the country with
> their brutal force?"* This is a candid confession of
> Japanese women's sincere appreciation of the
> Occupation. And whatever reaction may set in in the
> future, the time will never come again when Japanese
> wives, as semi-minors, will be put back under the
> legal guardianship of their husbands and forced to
> surrender all their possessions and their labor to the
> control of the husband and parents-in-law.
> —Mishima Sumie, The Broader Way, 1953[108]

**U.S. Occupation policies opened to the Japanese women the opportunities
of constitutional, civil, and educational equality and gave them the institutional
freedoms to pursue a modern way of life.**

In General Douglas A. MacArthur Japanese women had a powerful
friend. He believed that, once emancipated, they would prove a responsible democratic instrument for building a peaceful and stable Japan.
They would serve as the "most effective single barrier" against "future
jingoism."[109] During his seven-hour flight on August 30, 1945, from
Manila to Atsugi Airfield, MacArthur, corncob pipe in hand and striding
up and down the length of his unarmed C-54, talked of his hopes and
plans for the Allied Occupation of Japan. Enfranchisement of Japanese
women had high priority "to bring to Japanese politics the spiritual
influence of the Japanese home."[110] Like a traditional Japanese, he
valued the home and the woman as the core of society. Unlike a
traditional Japanese, he espoused complete involvement of the home
and the woman in social and political democracy.

Without delay, on October 11 he announced the basic reforms to be
implemented as rapidly as possible to correct the "traditional social
order" to which the "Japanese people for centuries have been subju-
gated." First on the list was "the emancipation of the women of Japan
through their enfranchisement—that, being members of the body politic,
they may bring to Japan a new concept of government directly subservient
to the well being of the home." Only after that did he list reforms to
achieve unionization of labor, a liberal educational system, abolition of

inquisition and abuse by the police system, and democratization of economic institutions.[111]

MacArthur was to face criticism for his policy on Japanese women from Americans, Allied cohorts, and Japanese. These adversaries maintained, he wrote in his memoirs, "that Japanese women were too steeped in the tradition of subservience to their husbands to act with any degree of political independence." But he also had defenders. He cited the hearty approval of President Harry S Truman, Secretary of State James Byrnes, former President Herbert Hoover, and scholar-historian Mary R. Beard. She hailed his enlisting the "force of women on the side of democracy."

By his power of command MacArthur effected greater and quicker change for Japanese women than they had been able to win for themselves in decades of persuasion and agitation. Of all accomplishments of the Occupation, he held none "more heartwarming" than the metamorphosis in the status of women.[112]

Induced Revolution

The Allied (in practice U.S.) Occupation of Japan lasted from August 1945 to the signing of the peace treaty in San Francisco on September 8, 1952. Extending for a longer period than anticipated because of internationally destabilizing events in East Asia, the Occupation went through three stages. It concentrated first on basic reforms and democratization, second on economic reinforcement, and third on building security. Policies were based on the Potsdam Declaration of July 26, 1945, and the Presidential Policy Statement on Japan sent to the supreme commander on September 6, 1945. MacArthur's remarkable execution of these policies and deft handling of the Japanese people, from the emperor to the ordinary citizen, brought about an "induced revolution."[113]

He lost little time in getting this revolution under way. Directives issued by Occupation Headquarters, known as SCAP (Supreme Commander for the Allied Powers), initiated the reforms. In time, the essential features were duly voted into law by the Japanese Diet and carried out by the appropriate Japanese governmental agencies. They thus became law by Japanese action. The legal base was the new Shōwa Constitution, promulgated on November 3, 1946, and the revised Civil Code.

Enfranchisement of Women

For Japanese women, the voting polls and ballot box on April 10, 1946, became their first important chance to demonstrate their willingness to assume democratic responsibility. Revision of the Election Law in

December 1945 had legislated equal rights to vote and to run for electoral office, goals long craved by prewar suffragists. The world watched to see whether the inhibitions of centuries would prove greater than the attraction of the new freedom. In the postwar period women in many countries were preparing to assume rights of enfranchisement for the first time. Japanese women became one more object lesson to those who feared repercussions from so many women's going to the polls for the first time. Women's suffrage will "retard the progress of Japanese politics," grumbled wartime Prime Minister Konoye Fumimaro. "Too soon, too soon," murmured political party figures and traditionalist educators.[114]

Despite the alacrity with which SCAP announced women's enfranchisement, ardent Japanese suffragists had jumped to petition this right even earlier. After reading the Potsdam Declaration (Article X), which promised that suffrage would come with the peace, women renewed their prewar initiatives to stake a Japanese claim to leadership in the field.[115] On August 25, 1945, ten days after the emperor in his first radio broadcast asked his people to pave the way for peace by "enduring the unendurable and suffering what is insufferable," Ichikawa Fusae, Yamataka Shigeri, Kawasaki Natsu, and Akamatsu Tsuneko organized the Women's Committee on Postwar Countermeasures (Sengo taisaku fujin iinkai) to work for suffrage as the first step in the postwar women's movement. They proceeded with a spirit of independence. They maintained that "suffrage is not something to be granted, but something to be attained by the hands of women themselves." Holding its first political meeting on September 24 at Tokiwa House in the relatively undamaged downtown Marunouchi district of Tōkyō, the organizing committee agreed to petition the government, both houses of the Diet, and each political party as follows: that (1) women over the age of twenty be granted suffrage and those over age twenty-five be allowed to run for office; (2) women be given eligibility to run for the House of Peers; (3) the governmental system on the prefectural and municipal levels be changed; (4) women be granted civil rights; (5) the Peace Preservation Laws be revised; (6) women be allowed to take part in political organizations; and (7) the civil service system be reorganized to permit participation of women in each administration institution.

Akamatsu Tsuneko argued that "the people's way of life during the war—which was really a movement in itself—compelled women to come in direct contact with political matters which eventually drew them into a political maelstrom." Therefore, it should be perfectly normal for women to take part in politics. Furthermore, "brightness" might be "introduced into politics by the voices of young women—young women who have fought hard during the war either in farming villages or in factories." On November 3, Ichikawa Fusae followed up by organizing the more specialized League of Women of New Japan (Shin Nihon fujin dōmei), which later became the League of Women Voters of Japan (Nihon fujin yūkensha dōmei). Its purpose was the rallying of kindred spirits to promote the participation of women "who are the apostles of peace in the law-making and administrative functions of the Japanese Government."[116]

Ichikawa very much wanted Japanese women to realize that they were getting political emancipation primarily because the earlier efforts of U.S. and English suffragists, indeed of Japanese suffragists, too, had made this a right recognized as legitimate throughout the world. MacArthur was not just giving it to them; they themselves had earned it honorably. Therefore, it behooved women more than ever to perform well in the first election. To help them carry out this new obligation, Ichikawa traveled up and down the land. She lectured, advised, and stimulated intelligent electoral action. She explained the meaning of democracy. In her usual practical fashion, she cautioned against voting in favor of "mere eloquence" or the good looks of a candidate.[117]

Incredibly, when it was time for Ichikawa herself to prepare to run in the first House of Councillors election in 1947, her candidacy was disallowed. The month before the election, she was purged by Occupation authorities from public life. The reasons cited were her role during the war in the Patriotic Press Association (Genron hōkoku kai) and her trip to China in 1940, when she spoke in support of the Japanese government's policies, particularly the Konoye Declaration on Greater East Asia Co-prosperity. In shock and surprise she resigned as chairman of the League of Women Voters and retired to her native village in Aichi Prefecture to maintain her livelihood by farming. Many pleaded her cause with the obdurate authorities, calling it a travesty of justice. A petition signed by more than 160,000 men and women supported reversal of the ban, but to no avail. Not until November 1950 did she return to active life. In 1953 she was elected to the House of Councillors and, except for one defeat in 1971, served until her death in 1981.

Ichikawa's purge is certainly one of the ironies of history. This woman, who more than any other single person symbolized at the outset of the Occupation the spirit of Japanese women's emancipation, was penalized and removed from an active public role at the moment her long-sought goals were achieving reality. Before the invasion of China in 1937, she and others in the Woman's Suffrage Federation had protested Japanese military action. They were watched by the police, and their publication was sometimes banned because they criticized the government and the military. After 1937, they had no freedom of speech— nor as Ichikawa noted—the power to vote. "Even men of culture could not stop the war. I had been a leader of women and I could not retire abruptly from them. I decided to go with the people, not to encourage the war, but to take care of the people made unhappy by the war." It was then that the League of Japanese Women's Organizations came briefly into existence. After the league was disbanded in 1940, the women could not use the phrase "women's suffrage." In time-honored fashion, however, and to get around the restrictions of Article Five of the Peace Preservation Law, they convened a study group, the Women's Current Topics Study Group (Fujin jikyōku kenkyū kai) in which they could continue to ponder women's suffrage.

Ichikawa admitted to becoming a director of the Patriotic Press Association but said she did so mainly to use it to obtain information about the war "since newspapers didn't tell us the truth." Although named as one of 200 councillors of the Great Japan Women's Organization, she quarreled with their policies and was, apparently, the only one not reappointed for a second two-year term. Concluded Ichikawa in assessing this phase of her life:

> At any rate I cooperated with the war. So, when I was purged I would have been reconciled to it if it had been done in that sense. However, the Occupation Forces mainly purged those who had led Japan to the aggressive war and who hindered Japan's democratization. So I was unhappy. The Japanese knew me and they didn't want to purge me, but the Occupation Forces purged me as a "memorandum case." There were complications. As a Japanese citizen I was not ashamed of having cooperated with the war. There were some who retired and kept quiet during the war, eating good food from the black market. When the war was over, they said they didn't cooperate with the war. I think they were mean and cowardly. First of all we had to strive to stop the war. In Japan it was useless to oppose the war during the wartime. . . . To oppose was only to get arrested and to die in prison. Opposition to war was different in Japan from in the United States and other countries.[118]

In Japan there is a saying that the reed that grows taller than the rest will be the first to be cut off. Ichikawa was such a reed. It is sad that the pruners were the very ones most eager to cultivate sturdy individualists of the democratic fiber of Ichikawa Fusae.

Getting Out the Vote

Fully aware that Japanese women had to be trained in the habits of political democracy, Occupation authorities, principally Civil Information and Education Section (CIE) officers both in Tōkyō and other parts of the country, launched programs to encourage them. Newspapers carried information about voting and urged participation. "Your vote is the brick without which the solid foundation of democracy cannot be completely and securely laid," lectured the *Mainichi*.[119] Magazine articles clamored for political education, although often the writers themselves did not know what it was.[120] Egami Fuji, then a young producer at the important Japan Broadcasting Corporation (NHK), recalled how the "Woman's Hour" program, previously aired once every month or so, became a regular feature. It demonstrated the "real meaning of democracy." Women brought into the studio by the hundreds learned to express themselves. Concluded Egami, "It was good training for women to get ready to vote because they would have to think for themselves at the time of election."[121]

Exhibits flowed out of SCAP headquarters pointing up the "hows and whys" of the new system. One widely disseminated poster, portraying a hand slipping into a ballot box, warned against corruption. It emphasized in bold letters:

> Women: Don't forget to vote.
> Vote according to what you believe.
> Voting is your responsibility.[122]

Most important in SCAP's program was the task of CIE's women's affairs information officer, Lieutenant Ethel B. Weed of the Women's Army Corps. She arrived in Tōkyō in October 1945 to concentrate on teaching democracy to Japanese women. A reporter on the *Cleveland Plain Dealer* before enlisting, she had worked her way up through the ranks. She had attended Military Government School with a specialization in Far Eastern Affairs before being selected for this SCAP assignment. Her programs with Japanese women continued for seven years, the last few as a civilian. She is still cherished by many who remember her as a friend who worked with them during those early years of trying to make democracy come to life.

With elections scheduled for April, Ethel Weed's first important task, in League of Women Voters terminology, was "to get out the vote!" She called women leaders, such as Ichikawa Fusae, Katō (Ishimoto) Shidzue, and Yamakawa Kikue, into SCAP Headquarters to consult on how to proceed. Katō Shidzue, the former Baroness Ishimoto whose second husband was Katō Kanju, a prominent Socialist, recalled her excitement when, arriving home from the countryside with rucksack on her back filled with potatoes, she found a jeep waiting to take her to SCAP Headquarters for her first consultation. Weed also talked to political party leaders to see what they were doing to bring women into party activities, and Women's Divisions were set up with well-

WAC Lieutenant Ethel B. Weed, CIE's women's affairs information officer, discusses the importance of the vote with farm women in Aota village, outside Tōkyō, in March 1946. Photo courtesy of Ethel B. Weed.

Open-air campaigning by members of the New Japan Women's League to encourage women to vote in the first postwar election, April 1946. Photo courtesy of Ethel B. Weed.

known women, such as Yoshioka Yayoi (Liberal party), Muraoka Hanako (Progressive party), and Akamatsu Tsuneko (Socialist party), assigned as directors.

Weed encouraged political education, with *kami shibai*, or paper picture-story shows, becoming one popular method of training. She traveled extensively, trying to make the women comprehend the great opportunity the election offered. She answered their questions. The magnitude of the task can be illustrated by the fact that in rural areas women sometimes thought "suffrage" was a new ration item.[123] While many women obviously wanted the vote, Lieutenant Weed and some women leaders feared that the daily excursions of urban women into the countryside to seek food, dealing in and with the black market, or simply the sheer toil of survival would keep them from voting. She tried to make them realize that, in a democracy, women ought to be represented, that the very things they were having trouble with were problems of government, and that, therefore, they should help administer it by casting their ballots.[124]

Getting women to run for office was another hurdle. One woman from Hokkaidō, exhorting her peers to action in support of their striking miner husbands, shouted, "You cannot be onlookers. Do something!" She followed her own advice, ran for office, and was elected.[125]

Murashima Kiyo of Niigata, respected because of her Tsuda College education and her role as educator in the local girls' finishing school, agreed to run for a seat because a women's committee urged her to seek office to represent women in the Diet. Successful, she commented later that they persuaded her by saying that if "I ran for office, women would realize that they too had the right to vote."[126]

Katō (Ishimoto) Shidzue recounted that, on one of her frequent visits to SCAP Headquarters to discuss women's activities, General Van Dyke prodded her into thinking about running. "You were so very active earlier in the women's movement in this country and now you have a chance, why don't you run a campaign?" A novice politically, she was financially and tactically befriended by a businessman whom she had helped in prewar days. Her constituency covered half of Tōkyō, and as the only transportation was crowded street cars, she suffered endless delays in going from one meeting to another. "I just had to run and run . . . and at night there were no lights so it was dark on the streets . . . and it was a terrible thing." Because of a shortage of paper for posters and publicity, the "voice," haranguing on street corners and in meetings, carried the brunt of campaigning. Katō remembered that she stressed practical issues. "Now that war is finished, we shall not engage in any kind of war whatsoever. . . . We need many things, food, clothing, and we must ask General MacArthur for them . . . and also to bring home our many Japanese soldiers now scattered in China and other places."[127]

One hotly discussed issue was whether the women's vote would swing the country to conservative or liberal dominance. Opinion supporting the former prevailed even though the conservative elements gave least support to women's role in government, worrying that family life would be imperiled or that women's liberty would decay into license. Women themselves admitted that they were ignorant of politics and public economics, but, as Hani Setsuko of the progressive Hani family and the Jiyū gakuen (School of Freedom) commented, "Give them freedom and they will begin to learn."[128] Even magazine cartoons picked up the theme. One showed a young wife in the kitchen absorbed in a newspaper, while a rice kettle belched smoke. Her husband, peering in to investigate, shakes his head and says, "Judging from the fact that the rice is always scorched ever since my wife has begun to take an interest in political matters, it is certainly true that 'Politics is directly connected with the kitchen.' "[129]

Another issue concerned women's independence in voting. Would they continue centuries-old traditions of obeying orders of men or make critical decisions for themselves? The same people who said the women would not vote prophesied they would heed the head of the house.

Japanese mothers line up to enter the polls to vote in their first election, April 10, 1946, while their children play in a chair-nursery. Photo courtesy Ethel B. Weed.

Woman with baby on her back casts her ballot for the House of Representatives, April 26, 1947, in a schoolhouse in Tōkyō. Photo courtesy of Ethel B. Weed.

Ethel Weed, in a speech in the United States ten years later, told a story that substantiated her faith in their electoral integrity at the first election. While she was visiting a polling place with a reporter from one of the big U.S. wire services,

> he stopped a tiny, bent old lady in dark kimono and somber *obi*. "Did you vote?" he asked. "*Mochiron*—of course," she answered.
>
> "How did you vote?" "It is a secret ballot," she replied and peered up at him with bright shrewd eyes, glad, I am sure, to give back the information that the nation's radio for two or three months had been dinning into her ears from 6 a.m. to 12 p.m.
>
> I laughed. He laughed and patted her on the back. "You're all right," he said. "But tell me this. How did you make your decision?" His interpreter went off into paragraphs of explanation during which I caught the words "husband" and "eldest son" and I knew that he was asking the old lady who had told her how to vote.
>
> She appreciated the point and paused a moment as if to savor it. "Well," she finally said, "I listened to my husband. I listened to my eldest son. I listened to the ward officials. I went to the meetings and I listened. And then I thought it all over and voted the way I thought was best. It is a secret ballot." That disposed of the matter.[130]

Election Results

When votes were counted after the April 10 election, thirty-nine of seventy-nine women candidates for office had been elected out of a House of Representatives with a total of 466 members. Political party affiliations were: Progressives, 8; Liberals, 8; Social Democrats, 8; Communist, 1; independent, 14. The only all-women's party, the New Japan Women's Party (Shin Nippon fujin tō), elected one candidate. Yamazaki Michiko, Social Democrat from Shizuoka Prefecture, led all the women candidates, winning 191,293 votes, not much lower than the 211,146 garnered by the male candidate with the largest number of votes. Sixty-seven percent of the eligible women—more than 13 million—voted, compared with almost 74 percent of the eligible males. In all, 73 percent of the electorate had voted—an excellent turnout even for seasoned democracies.

Everyone was surprised, the voters and those elected. The unexpectedly large number of women voting, often with babies on their backs or with toddlers in an election-day child care center, confounded the mass media and many observers. As late as two days before the election, Ichikawa had pessimistically forecast in the Ōsaka *Mainichi* that 90 percent of the women would probably not vote. The most optimistic political observers predicted a turnout of between 30 to 60 percent. *Life* magazine, having decided that the women would not turn out, had to scrub its prewritten story. The election was heralded as "a vindication of the women's sense of political responsibility."[131]

MacArthur applauded the election, pleased that democracy had "demonstrated a healthy forward advance," as shown by the large vote and diverse political affiliations of those elected. He recorded one amusing reminiscence of this historic event. The day after the election results were announced, he received, upon urgent request, an "extremely dignified but obviously distraught" Japanese legislative leader and Harvard Law School graduate. His caller

immediately launched into the subject that was touching him so deeply. "I regret to say that something terrible has happened. A prostitute, Your Excellency, has been elected to the House of Representatives."

I asked him, "How many votes did she receive?" The Japanese legislator sighed, and said, "256,000."

I said, as solemnly as I could, "Then I should say there must have been more supporters than her dubious occupation involved."

He burst into a gale of laughter. "You soldiers!" he exclaimed, and dropped the subject. He probably thought I was a lunatic.[132]

April 10, 1946, was indeed a memorable date in the history of Japanese women, and they have continued ever since 1947 to celebrate the anniversary of the Day of Women's Rights in special ceremonies and programs organized by the Women's and Minors' Bureau.[133]

In the four elections of April 1947, when all local and national offices were at stake, women candidates did not fare as well as the previous April, but for the first time in history they did run for office at every level of government. Twenty-three were elected to metropolitan and prefectural councils and seventy-seven to city, ward, town, and village councils. Only fifteen out of eighty-four made it to the Diet, twelve being incumbents. One of these beat out her husband, who had recently returned from war duty in Indonesia with his Indonesian second wife and children.

Oku Mumeo, remembered as one of the three leaders of the New Women's Association, won a seat in the House of Councillors. For six months before the election she had headed up the Women's Division of the Kyōdō tō political party, which soon merged with the Socialists. She ran reluctantly, having preferred to try for a local office; her campaign was a family affair. She sent postcards for support to all alumnae of her Japan Women's University. She made speeches on street corners, assisted by her son and daughter, who stood beside her holding up flags and homemade placards bearing her name. This son, now an adult, was the baby on his mother's back who helped turn the tide in the petitioning against Article Five in 1922. Oku was to serve three six-year terms in the Diet until failing health forced her retirement in 1965.[134]

Explanations for the smaller number of women elected to the Diet, despite another full year of persistent political education by the press and CIE officers, were many and varied. The voting rates of women had not changed appreciably. Throughout the Occupation period and afterwards, their voting rates remained high, with greater interest invariably shown in the Lower House elections. Political redistricting in 1947 and the single ballot, as opposed to the plural ballot, undoubtedly contributed to fewer victories by women. The *Ōsaka shimbun* of April 14 blamed the lack of women's organizations—wartime neighborhood groups had been abolished, and nothing adequate had taken their place. Some conjectured that in the first election women had been embarrassed to write the names of men and so, whenever possible, wrote names of women on the ballots. Others said that, with increased political knowhow, women were voting with better judgment on the merits of the candidates and not simply for their own sex.

Many women in the first Diet were bewildered in that strange world of male politicians. "A fish on the land" was the way one described her feeling. Only a few, like Katō (Ishimoto) Shidzue, Koro Mitsu, and Murashima Kiyo, had had much public affairs experience outside the traditional sphere of women. In 1946 male Diet members tried at first to isolate the women members, even to the point of wanting them to sit separately. The Diet's parliamentary system made it difficult to get the floor, especially for independents. The press and others scrutinized the women's actions closely, regarded them almost as "curiosities,"[135] and assumed that they would work primarily on issues considered women's affairs. A Diet Women's Club (Fujin giin kurabu) was established, mostly to deal with these outside pressures.[136]

MacArthur tried to bolster integrated action. On June 20, 1946, the thirty-nine women in the Diet, at their request, visited him in his office at the Dai Ichi Sēgo Building. They did not then realize that this remarkable discussion meeting was the first he had granted to any group of Japanese.[137] With Katō (Ishimoto) Shidzue as spokeswoman, the women thanked him for granting suffrage and told him of their support of the peace clause of the Constitution and of their desire for civil liberties. They urged that more food be imported. He expressed confidence in them and their influence for bringing stability and wisdom to the legislative process. However, he admonished them to function not as a women's bloc, but rather as equal legislators sharing full responsibility for finding solutions for the nation's problems.[138]

It gradually became clear that, in truth, all women in the Diet did not always see eye-to-eye. They faced in the legislature hazards inherent in centuries of inequalities of experience, education, and psychological attitude. As many editorials suggested, the important consideration now was the "quality, rather than the quantity of women in public life."[139] They soon had a chance to display this quality in the debates and decisions about the new Constitution, the revision of the Civil Code, and the supplementary legislation required to breathe life into the Occupation reforms.

Social Equality

The Constitution of November 1946 established democratic and parliamentary governing institutions, foreswore irresponsible militarism in its historic renunciation of war, and again laid the base for a democratic society. The Constitution called for respect for individuals and equality before the law, with no discrimination in political, economic, or social relations. Together with the revised Civil and Criminal Codes, it established the legal framework of equality for the women of Japan.

"Marriage," the Constitution reads, "shall be based on mutual consent," and "maintained through mutual cooperation, with the equal rights of husband and wife as a basis." In effect, the conjugal family replaced the traditional multigeneration "house" under patriarchal control. These rights in marriage, mixed with awareness of freedom for the individual, led to some exaggerated practices of wifely independence. The media enjoyed a heyday with stories, true and apocryphal, that appealed to the humor of common people. One cartoon depicted two women rocking away on their porch while a perspiring husband struggles in the background with a bucket in his hand. His wife advised her guest, "You should get married as soon as possible. You can smoke a double ration, and your better half will do all the work!"[140]

The Constitution also opened up the Pandora's box of choice about marriage. Should the postwar young woman follow individual preference and marry for love, or should she, with the guidance of the go-between in the time-honored meeting at a *miai*, or "looking-meeting," enter into a family-arranged marriage? Within ten years, excesses resulting from enthusiasm for individual choice, with a resultant drift toward family instability, led to an unsuccessful movement in the Liberal Democratic party and among conservatives to amend this feature of Occupation reform.

Legal equality in inheritance rights and in divorce swept away previous indignities that had bound women so helplessly to concepts of the three obediences. The end of primogeniture and of women's legal incompetence per se permitted families to determine for themselves how land and resources should be divided. To this day, however, women, especially in rural areas, are ignorant of their full legal rights. Adultery was no longer a crime. Old laws subjected only an errant wife to punishment. Now constitutional equality required that an erring husband must be equally liable and that illicit intercourse no longer be defined as a criminal act. This delicate issue precipitated vigorous debate in the mass media and in the Diet before it was resolved that adultery would constitute legal grounds for divorce by either party. Since then the provision has been widely used, especially by women. One immediate result of the new Civil Code was a jump in the number of people seeking divorce. From 49,705 in 1943, the number of divorces rose to 79,551 in 1947 and to 83,689 in 1950. After that there was a decline. Husbands initiated 20 percent of the divorces, while wives accounted for 79 percent, with less than 1 percent by mutual consent.[141] The strains of long war separations and the stresses of a society in flux created much of the incompatibility, and for the first time in history, Japanese women could opt for and obtain marital freedom.

Constitutional provisions for free compulsory education, with opportunity commensurate with ability, established the base for equal coeducation from elementary school through the university. Rescinding the Imperial Rescript on Education pulled down the psychological hurdles to democratic education, and women acquired the tool with which they could achieve equality of opportunity.

New labor standards provided for equal pay for equal work, at the same time insuring certain protections for women. The licensing of prostitution ended in 1946, but antiprostitution legislation did not pass the Diet until 1956. It came from unrelenting effort by women leaders of organizations and legislators who had introduced the measure for vote in the Diet four times since 1948.

This monumental restructuring of society affected the public obligations and personal lives of every man, woman, and child in Japan. The reworking of the old Civil Code alone took three years and required revision of some three hundred laws, primarily within the area of family relationships. Women lawyers, such as Wada Yoshiko, Watanabe Michiko, and Kume Ai, helped with technicalities, guarding against limitations on women's status. Women in the Diet and prominent women leaders studied with specialists from Tōkyō University so they could lecture on the complexities of the Code and serve as legislative watchdogs. Ordinary women watched closely as these decisions so important to their personal well-being were made; more than half the correspondence sent to the Women's Hour Section of the Japan Broadcasting Corporation from January to March 1947 discussed revisions in the family system.

The name of the Women's Hour Section programs on the Civil Code, incidentally, was "For Happiness Sake"—a theme to which women seemed very much attuned.

In some instances, the Occupation staff managed to inject more progressive provisions into the new Japanese system than existed in the United States. Equal pay for equal work legislation, for one, did not become law in the United States until 1963. Some reforms read like excerpts from the purposes and petitions of the new women of the 1920s and the crusading segments of the more widely based pre–World War II Japanese women's movement. Some policies also achieved reforms long and futilely advocated by the prewar socialist, proletarian, and anti-establishment political parties, which often had stood closer to the liberal suffragist women than had the conservatives.

As a result of the prewar reformist agitation and the rather elaborate public consultation during the Occupation while the new Civil and Criminal Codes were taking shape, the people were intellectually neither unprepared nor unwilling to accept the drastic changes in life-style that swept over them. *Mainichi*'s national public opinion poll revealed that 58 percent of the people favored Civil Code reforms of the "house" system and equality of the sexes, 37 percent did not, and 5 percent were undecided.[142]

Nonetheless, theory and practice are two different things. The social history of the Japanese people since the Occupation is the story of their balancing of old and new habits of mind and of their adjustment to simultaneous change in every aspect of national life.

Exploring Democracy

Occupation authorities realized that legislation of reforms was only the beginning. Unless accepted into the consciousness and daily routine of the people, they would never provide more than hollow freedoms. A civil law expert warned, "If women lack pluck and men lack tolerance, any new system will remain only a scheme drawn on paper."[143] The reforms MacArthur had called for in labor, agriculture, education, and economic institutions and the purges to eliminate the influence of the leaders responsible for the war were all designed to remove the legal restrictions and human barriers impeding the creation of a democratic society. Now, training in democratic concepts and their application became the central thrust of the mission of CIE at SCAP.

The ending of the war left the Japanese people in an ideological vacuum: Old theories had brought the nation to devastation and defeat; a new social order had not yet arisen from the rubble, but a free atmosphere prevailed. Once before in the last hundred years, authority had ordered the people to root out old traditions, study Westernized philosophies, and practice new ways. And they had responded. The focus this time was on demilitarization and democratization.

Although Japan's parliamentary tradition dates back to the Meiji Constitution of 1889, with a base gradually widening to universal male suffrage in 1925, the concepts and practice of direct democracy were not understood by Japanese in 1945, certainly not by most women.[144] Anyone who has tried to explain the meaning of democracy or describe how one lives a democratic-style life to those with little or no background or first-hand experience with such ideas knows what a tough job this can be. In addition, the Japanese language compounds the conceptual and cultural difficulties.

The word "democracy" in Japanese may be said either as *demokurashii* or *minshūshugi*. The former is written in *katakana*, the phonetic syllabary used for foreign words, the later in the *kanji* ideograph with inherited Chinese meanings. Technically there should be no difference in meaning. Yet repeated conversations with young college-educated Japanese not specializing in political science revealed that quite different nuances exist both in the noun and the adjectival forms. The mood ranges from recollections of the Occupation, to a balancing of obligations, to school-room bookishness, to politically "leftist feeling."

"Freedom," too—in Japanese *jiyū*—is a coined word in Japanese. It was created during the early Meiji era, when this idea had to be introduced, out of a pair of Chinese ideographs. It means "self action" or "obeying oneself" and has a sense of unconstrained individual freedom, possibly tending toward anarchy. There is no special word for "liberty." Contemporary women's liberationists, for instance, have used the transliteration *"ūman ribu"* in emulation of the Westernized concept to avoid other connotations.

Further, there is no exact equivalent of the word "community" for grassroots democracy in public affairs, a concept that proved basic to women's political action beginning in the 1960s. Even the democratic obligations implied in the word "citizen" get lost. "Citizen" and *shimin* both literally mean "city dweller," but in Japan the concept of the staunch city freeholder did not exist. The broader "people," or *jimmin*, came to have a leftist connotation, having been co-opted after the war by the communists to mean proletariat. How then to get across the idea for the concept of "community of spirit" needed for democratic citizen action![145]

One officer recalls that the CIE did not use the term "democracy" a great deal, but rather "equality," relating that to practical opportunities open to each person. For a people imbued with notions of hierarchical inequality that was a valid starting point.

Sometimes, however, the equalities of the new Constitution and revised Civil Code were taken as invitations to unfettered freedoms. Stories abound—some funny, some sad, some serious—about how people grasped at these rights and interpreted them to suit their individual desires: Labor union members locked out their bosses to demonstrate their own business acumen; landowners found their tenants demanding land because they had occupied and cultivated it for generations; students began to question teachers; irate housewives accused vendors of unscrupulous practices. Many understood democracy as "people's decision," but there was inadequate appreciation of an orderly way to determine and implement a majority decision.[146] Problems developed, as they sometimes still do, when the democratic mix did not balance freedom and responsibility.

A further complication arose when Communist leaders, feeling vindicated by the defeat of Japanese imperialism and enjoying respectability with the reinstatement of their party in the early years of the Occupation, pursued a policy of cooperation with the authorities to establish a democratic "peaceful revolution." Nozaka Sanzo, titular head of the party on returning from exile in 1947, maintained that Japanese "first must be taught democracy before they will be ready for communism." In this way communism would have time to become "lovable." Organizers fanned out to penetrate labor unions, schools, organizations, and situations in which, in the words of one woman trade unionist, "a tiny group can lead a big number of foolish people." By 1948, however, Communist party adherents, becoming increasingly aggressive, moved to an anti-American position. Occupation policy hardened against them and cracked down. The ideological cold war swept over Japan just as it did over the rest of the world, but at a moment in its development when this bewildering dichotomy of international politics complicated the adjustment to democratic practices in Japan's national and domestic affairs.[147]

Democracy, GI Style

Meanwhile, the practice of democracy benefited in an unexpected and very human way from the presence of so many ordinary American GIs and, in time, their families. These young Americans were in small towns and the countryside as well as in the big cities and were everywhere visible and closely observed. The Japanese people, particularly the women, who had been warned to expect ill-treatment and rape, found instead amiable giants who enjoyed fraternization despite regulations against it.

Women with prewar Western contacts had reassured others that the GIs would be well-mannered and disciplined. Their views were, on the whole, borne out. Soon after the first landings, the GIs' friendliness showed in their relaxed rapport with Japanese, to whom they brought gifts of food and candy for the children. Their general respect for women and the aged, witnessed daily by giving up their own seats on crowded trains and making Japanese men do likewise, invited intercultural comparisons. Even the liaisons with Japanese young women, which sometimes engendered the problems of mixed-blood babies, were characterized by kindliness and generosity. When marriages resulted, the American wives in Japan often helped prepare the young brides for life in the United States with English lessons and discussion of American ways so as to "build a bridge of understanding between Japanese wives of our GI's and their home families."[148]

Japanese reactions ranged from perturbation to outright approval of the coming together of the GIs and Japanese women. Friendship with the GIs, some declared, would help women's adaptability and participation in politics.[149] In any event, fraternization contributed importantly to the standard of living of these young women and their families, whether they were street "pan pan girls" or more respectable young ladies.

Japanese men, already humiliated by capture and defeat, could hardly view this situation with indifference. One artist, writing for a national magazine, deplored first the loss of beauty because so many young girls wore "crude western-style dresses." Then he really warmed up to the unhappy changes of the time:

> The defeat of war has brought discredit upon the male sex. The cries of Liberty! Freedom! and Women's Suffrage! have caused to fly away even those womanly virtues which were the last refuge of the male sex. It is only natural for girls to prefer kind and stylish GI's to Japanese men who have become shabby dirty. Speaking frankly, men are all sick and tired of life.

He suggested the men might need a Potsdam Declaration to give them some rights, too.[150]

Never before had an alien invading army penetrated the reaches of the Japanese countryside. Never before had uncontrolled new ideas and influences infused the society. Happily for Japanese-U.S. relations, this meeting of so many ordinary Americans with the Japanese people has resulted in a long-range general liking for Americans among the Japanese.[151]

Democratic Organization

SCAP, of course, undertook more formal adult education to facilitate understanding of democracy among Japanese women. The first programs on suffrage saw immediate results at the polls and in the Diet. A broader-gauged approach to general democratic public affairs took more time. CIE's women's affairs policy centered this effort on the organizing and running of nongovernmental or voluntary organizations.[152] Tsuda Umeko's interest in organizations as educational vehicles was recalled. Leaders like Gauntlett Tsune urged this method of democratic education and considered related training in parliamentary procedures to be basic to women's civic action. Within their own organizations, it was propounded, women would develop initiative, strength, and self-reliance and learn to solve problems through group effort. New leaders would arise. The organizations would give the women mechanisms by which to insert their ideas into public policy. It was recognized that except for the smaller, sometimes internationally affiliated suffrage and feminist organizations, the massive women's organizations in pre-Occupation Japan had all been directed by men, often retired military men. They had kept women in their "rightfully" subordinate position, firmly channeling their attention to the support of government policy. SCAP abolished these government-controlled organizations; it encouraged instead those that were democratically constituted.

CIE prepared two manuals, *Democratic Organizations* and *Committees and Programs for Democratic Organizations,* and distributed them in Japanese-language versions to provide new standards. Tens of thousands of copies of *Roberts' Rules of Order* went out from the Ministry of Education to the women. To appeal to traditional Japanese poetic interpretation, the *watake,* a young bamboo, fresh and green, which grows straight and increases every year, was made the symbol of the democratic organizational training. As with the elections, the "Women's Hour" on radio, exhibits, press articles, and the informational components of SCAP assisted the program. Upon request, U.S. organizations, such as the YWCA, General Federation of Women's Clubs, League of Women Voters, Business and Professional Women, and the American Association of University Women, as well as the Department of Labor's Women's Bureau, sent publications for Japanese adaptation.

From time to time U.S. women leaders visited to supplement the speeches and training sessions regularly conducted by Lieutenant Weed and the regionally based education and women's officers. Repeatedly, Japanese women who took part in these programs recount their excited embarrassment when coeducational square-dancing was included during the recreation periods. "Never before," octogenarian Katō Taka, a devoted

Youth leaders enjoy outdoor dancing during training programs of the CIE. Photo courtesy of Katō Taka.

YWCA worker, commented a bit breathlessly even many years later, "had I touched the hand of a man."[153] Western-educated Japanese women leaders, such as Tsuda Professor Fujita Taki and YWCA enthusiast Shiraishi Tsugi, joined the educational campaign. Others supported it with their bilingual and bicultural capabilities.

Most Japanese women eagerly reached out for this new knowledge despite their time-consuming household duties. Some walked for six or seven hours over mountainous roads with rucksacks of food and babies on their backs to attend a meeting or, equally patiently, waited until after midnight for speakers delayed by the difficult travel. They learned confidence and freedom of speech by speaking up in these meetings and by asking questions. CIE stressed, sloganistically, that questions should come from those "even in the back row." Often they did, and not necessarily on the subject at hand. One American visitor recalled, with some chuckles, trying to elicit questions after a serious speech on women's rights and having a bright-eyed woman in the back finally break the silence to ask what kind of underwear she wore under her Western dress. One meeting in 1947 in Yokohama with four thousand participants produced literally bushel baskets of questions. A round-table meeting in Ōsaka the same year concentrated on political action, the "purification movement" (prostitution and venereal disease), and price reduction. Other small local groups getting started were variously named the "Wednesday Club of Daimaru Department Store," the "Newly-Born Women's Club," and the "Mothers Club." The Ōsaka report commented that the women

> expressed bravely what they thought. Not any meeting seems to have had such an active discussion by women. In the meeting their daily life was connected liberally to politics. I felt that Japanese women's weak point was they could not concentrate on one problem and then another. . . . And business transaction was very slow. Indeed, it took nearly four hours to close the meeting.[154]

Linking family interests with public affairs, SCAP promoted a democratically reoriented Parent-Teachers Association (PTA) so that education would become the responsibility of the parents and not just of the state and the teachers. An agricultural extension service was started to work with farm women in some 6 million farm families. Dr. Lulu H. Holmes, advisor at SCAP on women's higher education, helped revitalize college women into the new Japanese Association of University Women. International YWCA officers, after a conference in China, attended the first postwar Japan YWCA Conference to join hands once again in peaceful cooperation.

One new, Japan-based nationwide organization was the Women's Democratic Club (Fujin minshū kurabu), founded in 1946 with the blessing and advice of SCAP for the "democratization of women so that never again could women be led to war blindly." Experienced leaders of many points of view and with varying backgrounds in social and political reforms, such as Akamatsu Tsuneko, Hani Setsuko, Katō (Ishimoto) Shidzue, Miyamoto Yuriko, Yamamoto Sugi, and Yamamuro Tamiko, attracted membership with their appeal "A new Japan is about to be born. The time has finally come in which we can think, choose, and act of our own accord for our happiness." The differences between the status of women in prewar and postwar Japan would enable women to take responsible action to achieve "happiness and peace." It epitomized in organization and purpose the new ideal.

Yet within two years, internal personal strife and arguments about the real meaning of equality and whether true democracy was that of the Western heritage or that recently coming out of mainland China shattered the organization's harmony. Adherents of the socialist and communist factions split. Confrontation "red-guard" tactics to compel conformity led to a breakup of the original leadership. Akamatsu, Katō, Yamamuro, and those rejecting the authoritarian communist version of democracy resigned. Matsuoka Yoko, the unknown young Swarthmore-educated interpreter who had worked with SCAP officials, became the first president. Democratic procedures became more *pro forma* than real. The organization, using the vocabulary of democracy, moved into the camp of left-wing sympathizers and communist supporters, whose policies it has advocated ever since.[155]

The history of this organization, caught in the cold war, points up the hazards of intermeshing philosophical political semantics and practical policies. The naive, the uninformed, or the unaware, emotionally magnetized by idealistic goals, may unwittingly lend support to policies at variance with their desired purposes. The not-so-naive and the informed will know the difference. In either case, under the new Constitution, responsibility of choice, which leads to decision, inexorably fell equally on the shoulders of women along with the men, and their organizations were another venue in which they faced this obligation.

Economic Opportunity

Closely related to the political aspiration of Japanese women were the newly opened doors of economic opportunity. Whenever women of earlier periods had sought greater personal freedom, they soon decided that economic independence was essential. The Constitution and the Labor Standards Law of 1947 at least eliminated the legal barriers to inequality. The law provided regulations about equal pay, working hours, night work, menstruation leave, maternity leave, holidays, employment of minors, dangerous work, restrictions on underground work, and so on. It was both advanced in concept and protective, so protective that the regulations in time worked against the principle of equality.

The Women's and Minors' Bureau, set up in the reorganized Ministry of Labor when the Socialist Katayama government assumed office in 1947, prepared to serve as guardian of Japanese women, especially in the area of the employment of women and children. Leading women had organized a committee and struggled to bring the bureau into existence. They consulted with Ethel B. Weed and counseled with knowledgeable labor authorities like Golda Stander and Frieda Miller of the U.S. Department of Labor. They sought public support in speeches explaining its importance to groups in many parts of Japan. Because it was a project endorsed by the Social Democratic party, Katō (Ishimoto) Shidzue sponsored the needed legislation for its formation in the House of Representatives and Akamatsu Tsuneko, in the House of Councillors. Some difficulties arose in a jurisdictional conflict with the Ministry of Welfare, but these were resolved. For the women who worked for acceptance of the bureau, the experiences of banding together for a

Girls working in a wool factory
near Kōbe, September 1947.
Photo courtesy of Martha Tway
Mills.

common goal, developing favorable public opinion, and winning the
cooperation of men in government were valuable lessons in democratic
government procedures and leadership responsibility.[156]

Yamakawa Kikue, a Tsuda College graduate remembered for her
activism in the proletarian women's movement, agreed to serve as the
first director of the bureau. She had for years read the materials sent
her from the U.S. Women's Bureau. Judging that agency to be "doing
a good job," she thought "Japan should also have such an office." So
she took the post to become the first woman to hold the high position
of a bureau chief in a Japanese government ministry.[157]

Yamakawa's prominence as a social reformer and author lent prestige
to the new venture. She promptly undertook the large task of explaining
to Japanese women what their rights were under the Labor Standards
Law. She urged proper training as a way of insuring competence on
the job, thereby contributing to an attitude of confidence, a stance badly
needed by simple working girls cowed by unsympathetic male super-
visors. She spoke to the problems of combining home responsibilities
with those of the job. The majority of women—54 percent—as a 1948
Tōkyō area survey showed, worked to support or supplement the family
income.[158] To help reach and care for the women workers, Yamakawa
began to set up regional offices in each of the prefectures. In the
Women's and Minors' Bureau, the women of Japan now had their own
governmental channel to authority and someone to champion their
position.

Most women during the Occupation were unpaid family workers in family shops and farms. The others, principally employed in factories, sales jobs, and offices, were under twenty-five and unmarried and quickly rotated out after about three years on the job. Their salaries were consistently in the lower brackets.

With the encouragement of trade unions as part of the Occupation policy of promoting democracy, the percentage of employed women workers enrolling in unions rose to a peak of 51 percent in 1949, by comparison with 1 percent at the height of the democratic boom after World War I. By 1950 their union membership had dropped to 30 percent. Women were not comfortable with strikes, unionist political intrigues, and communist agitation. Despite their union affiliations, they were not aggressive about securing their job rights or seeking promotions. The few who showed such interest were typically called "eccentric" and perhaps laughed at—a terribly humiliating situation for any Japanese.[159] Women also faced the greater hazards of just plain unemployment when the men returned to civilian life and civilian jobs.

By the end of the Occupation, society no longer regarded the average girl or woman who worked outside the home "with contempt," which had been the prewar attitude; the factory girl of the Taishō era had been looked down on as a *"shokugyō fujin,"* or "occupational woman." The needs of the war and immediate postwar years and the reforms of the Occupation had combined to establish for her a position of respectability.[160]

Further, in the postwar spurt of optimism and opportunity, outstanding women did move into positions of responsibility. SCAP Headquarters fostered this breakthrough. But women in the Diet like Kora Tomiko also insistently prodded ministerial officials about the "who" and "when" of women's appointments to government positions so that others followed Yamakawa into administrative positions of prominence in the central government. Yamamoto (née Omori) Matsuyo, for example, a 1937 graduate of the University of Washington, was promoted from a job in education to chief of the Reform of Living Section of the Agriculture and Forestry Ministry, a post she held until becoming a consultant to the United Nations Food and Agriculture Organization in 1965. Yamamoto Sugi and Hori Hidō advanced into the Welfare Ministry. Kondō Tsuruyo received appointment as parliamentary secretary in the Foreign Office.

In the unusual years of the 1940s, many capable young women established careers that subsequently took them to top positions in business, public relations, mass media, government, and academia. In wartime, they had moved diligently ahead because the absence of men had provided rare opportunities. Often a little knowledge of English made all the difference in the boost that the Occupation circumstances offered.

Ariga Michiko, educated before the war in law at Tōhoku Imperial University, which at that time did admit some women, was one such woman. Widowed, with four children to support, she started her climb by working at the Finance Ministry on antitrust measures. She later served as the first woman commissioner of the Fair Trade Commission and represented her country at Organisation of Economic Co-operation and Development (OECD) conferences, in time achieving an international reputation in her field. Nakagome Fumi, who became president of the International Inspection Company, began an eminent business career by serving as an English interpreter in a postwar Bible class, which led to liaison work between Japanese and foreign trading groups. Shoji Masako, retired professor of education at Hiroshima University and the first woman chairperson of a graduate department at a Japanese national university, admitted that she became the first woman assistant in the humanities division because the men were in the army. The atomic bomb brought her first promotion, and later the purge by the Occupation authorities decimated the normal male teaching staff. She proved herself worthy of such advancement by working two or three times harder than the men around her.

Capable though these women were, they themselves doubt that they could have achieved such distinguished positions without the Occupation interlude of opportunity. As Saisho Yuriko, honorary Board of Director's chair of Nippo Marketing and Advertising, said, "The postwar confusion gave opportunity to many Japanese women who otherwise would have followed more routine paths."[161]

Travel in the West

During the late 1930s and the war years, Japan had cut off its people from normal channels of communication with the outside world. To fill the gap, MacArthur advised that they "seek a healthy blend" of the best of their culture and life with the best of that of the West. In the tradition of Emperor Meiji's Charter Oath, he encouraged overseas travel. He hoped to show the Japanese that no "people or country was sufficient unto itself."[162]

For MacArthur, this policy applied to Japanese women just as much as to men. In fact, the first passport issued to any Japanese after the cease-fire was to a woman—Uemura Tamaki, president of the National YWCA and an ordained minister, who left for the United States in May 1946 on the invitation of the women of the Presbyterian Church, USA. Returning a year later, she carried a gift of a beautifully bound Bible for the Empress from American women. As a result, at imperial request, she gave instruction for a time to the Empress about Christianity and taught her hymns.[163]

For the most part, however, women educators and leaders had to wait for GARIOA (Government and Relief in Occupied Areas) grants, which started in 1948, until the initial tide of important male professors and political figures had made the ocean crossing. Shoji Masako thanked U.S. educator Dr. Verna Carley for sponsoring her first trip to the United States in 1951. How much clearer a democratic style of life becomes when seen, felt, and absorbed through the pores in contrast with the sterility of the lecture room and instruction book. Shoji vividly remembered her impressions of

> so many wonderful American women in so many fields: principals, on Boards of Education. . . . At that time my ideas about democracy were not so clear, but I saw in America that each one could express himself. In Japan, especially women could not speak out what you feel or what you want; we had to press our ideas inside. In America everyone could speak out frankly. This was very different.[164]

Tōkyō women leaders were less hesitant. Having learned that ten members of the Diet, all men, had been chosen to visit the United States, a delegation of women complained to Ethel Weed, who referred them to the more powerful Government Section of SCAP. Their apppeal was immediately effective. Cutting through red tape, General Courtney Whitney, chief of the Government Section and devoted deputy to MacArthur, promptly called Ethel Weed to his office. Pacing up and down, he asked how soon she could select a cross-section of ten women leaders and get them ready to leave. He proposed that she and an interpreter accompany them. They were to take three months to study the political, economic, and social activities of U.S. women. The members of the delegation were Akamatsu Tsuneko, House of Councillors; Egami Fuji, NHK; Gotō Shun, Democratic Liberal party; Kume Ai, Conciliation Committee of the Family Court; Marusawa Michiyo, National Railway Workers' Union; Nomura Katsuko, Consumers Union League; Yamamoto (Omori) Matsuyo, Ministry of Agriculture and Forestry; Tanino Setsu and Takahashi (Tomita) Nobuko, Women's and Minors' Bureau; and Togano Satoko, House of Representatives.

The accomplishments of these ten women during the next thirty years thoroughly justified their selection. They absorbed deeply the experiences of their brief tour. On return, they generously gave of their impressions and special training to those at home in endless radio appearances, press conferences, meetings, and articles.[165] This pattern

Eleanor Roosevelt and U.S. women's organization leaders entertain the Japanese women leaders during their visit to the United States in 1950. Photo courtesy of Ethel B. Weed.

of passing on the benefits of their educational travel by women leaders granted such a privilege has become a modern tradition in Japan, multiplying many times the impact of each trip. Just before these women sailed for the United States in March 1950, General MacArthur received them in his SCAP Headquarters office. Whitney recorded that MacArthur, in greeting them, praised the women of Japan. They

> fully justified my faith in the part Japanese women were destined to play in the transformation of a completely regimented society into one composed of individuals, each of whom of right is free, by demonstrating their capacity to assume coequal responsibilities of citizenship in a democratic state. . . . The rapid development of women's influence in community affairs without sacrifice to their position in the home is . . . one of the truly momentous developments in Japan's history. . . . the women of Japan now share equally with men the sovereign responsibility of political direction. Never in history has there been a more far-reaching and dramatic transformation.

The impact, MacArthur said, would "be found in the character, the wisdom and the vision of Japan's future leaders."[166]

In the long history of Japan, the Occupation was but a brief interlude. For Japanese women, however, it accelerated dramatically their natural evolutionary progress toward equal rights, so long sought by the handful of dedicated reformers, educators, and liberalizing women, and it precipitated them into a status with rights greater than those of women in many other countries. There is reason for the knowing smile that so often accompanies the remark that the Constitution and its companion codes are their *"omiage,"* or souvenir of the Occupation.

Second-guessing—with the advantage of hindsight—seems fitting for this segment of history, because the reforms were so purposefully designed and implemented. Should the Occupation have ignored the traditional segregation of men and women and autocratically included women in all projects and agencies rather than encouraged specialized organizations and programs geared specifically to women? Having torn up the old patterns anyway, might the authorities have insisted on integration, eliminating, for instance, purely women's sections in labor unions or in political parties? Theoretically, the span between men and women was bridged in the legal and constitutional overhaul. Yet implementation required that women themselves, in cooperation with men, take the necessary steps to cross the bridge. For this move, fraught with emotion and dependent for success on greater training of women, better transitional gains, undoubtedly, came from the less risky separated approach. Despite the postwar mass media banality that "women and nylon stockings are stronger," the truth was that women at long last had more equality than strength.

The concentrated abruptness of the Occupation's program triggered issues and problems that, in their own way, the Japanese are still dealing with. It did, however, remarkably advance the democratic modernization started by Emperor Meiji and his enlightened advisers. It did place the future of Japan in the hands of its people, the men *and* the women.

PART 2
THE FABRIC OF
CONTEMPORARY TIMES

Traditionally, Japanese women have been thought of by other people as very humble and self-effacing with no real will of their own. That's quite different now. They are thinking very hard and they are facing up to all kinds of problems with their minds. So there is a great diversity of women in Japan, not just one image. They are also great sources of energy which, if well developed, might work not only for the good of Japan but for the good of the world too.

—Psychiatrist and educator, Kōbe, Fall 1972

Contemporary Japan, everywhere recognized as a miracle-maker of development, has simultaneously refashioned its societal patterns to adjust to the quiet revolution of its women. The combination of economic growth and social change to this degree is unique to Japan in the postwar world and entails invigorating tensions—some difficult, some pleasurable.

A passing observer immediately, if superficially, sees modernization in the flashing multicolored neon signs of the Ginza and the Shinjuku section of Tōkyō, in smoothly speeding blue and white "bullet" trains linking Tōkyō with Ōsaka and points southwest, or in the pollution-clouded skies over urban industrial centers. Less apparent as social revolutionists are the women engaged in their normal activities a quarter century after the Occupation's end: housewives of the many suburban apartment complexes, or *danchi*, do housewifely, motherly, and community chores on schedules fixed by school and commuting routines. Determined mothers petition municipal authorities or campaign on street corners for improved environmental conditions. Young office women, eager to spend their salaries, crowd stylish boutiques on Saturday afternoons and Sundays to finger racks of brightly hued skirts and blouses or piles of matching sweaters. Grandmother-aged, kimono-clad, slightly aggressive theater-goers attend traditional *kabuki* plays or modern elaborately staged, swift-moving music and dance extravaganzas of Kōbe's Takarazuka or Asakusa's Kokusai Gekijo and enjoy their outing while happily munching the ubiquitous *osembei* rice crackers, tangerines, or boxed rice *obentō* lunches. Serious women of all ages cooperate to

---

Photo opposite: Loyal supporters of Ichikawa Fusae (seated center) celebrate at the Fusen Kaikan her election victory to the House of Councillors on June 23, 1980 with shouts of *banzai* and raised arms. The sign proclaims that "Victory is based on ideal elections." Photo courtesy Kyodo Photo Service.

organize international conferences and welcome delegates from overseas. Themes in the earlier Meiji, Taishō, and Occupation eras dealt with personal educational advancement and the struggle for rights and legal reforms needed to bring Japanese women into the "way of modernization." Post-Occupation women, released from the time-honored doll's glass case of prewar traditionalism, are concerned with using this revised status and value system, not just for themselves or for women alone, but more broadly for the nation and its international relations.

CHAPTER 3
SOCIAL PATTERNS

UNFOLDING LIFE-STYLES—
EVOLUTIONISTS AND NEW FEMINISTS

> *Femininity is neither obedience nor self-sacrifice for which Japanese women have had a reputation. True femininity is both weakness and strength that was common to women in the past, is now, and will be.*
> —Tohya Yumiko, Women of Japan, 1969[1]

Scientific advancement and economic affluence propel Japanese women into modern life-styles increasingly similar to those of women in the United States.

The nature of their personal experiences, particularly the trauma of war, and nostalgia for Confucian teachings tend to differentiate women by age blocs and influence the ease with which they understand and utilize these new factors of contemporary life. Differences stem not simply from the ordinary generation gap, but more from the type of education received and from how they are living and dealing with others. Women thus fall into three general groupings: those born prior to World War I, those born between the two wars, and those born during and after World War II.

Meiji Matriarchs

Women who were born in the Meiji–early Taishō eras and grew up and received all their education before World War II are one of two types. Some adhere to the past and reject change while others, in contrast, stand forth as leaders in politics, volunteer organizations, and community life. The latter welcome the challenges of a society and world undergoing rapid development. Both types possess personal assurance, whether in adhering to traditional beliefs or in rising to the demands of the present—assurance rooted in the firm dogma that surrounded them in their formative years before shattering Asian wars made everything in life uncertain.

For this age group higher education was a rarity. Those who received it—either in the few women's institutions of prewar Japan or even more rarely overseas—project progressive ideas. Such leaders are eagerly followed by others less fortunate. Education level divides leaders and followers in this group much more than among younger groups, probably because those with higher education are such a small minority. Listen to the self-confidence of Sakanishi Shio, Wheaton College and University of Michigan graduate. Before the war she served for more than ten years as head of the Japanese Section of the U.S. Library of Congress. After the war, until her death in 1977, she was a luminary among Japanese—men and women—as a social critic, lecturer, and responsible citizen serving on national government commissions ranging from review of the Japanese Constitution to security matters:

> Even before my American sojourn, I was determined to take life as it was. Independence and equality are not given one by the society in which one happens to live, but rather they are qualities one builds up in oneself, and no outside forces can take them away. In this sense I found Japan also "a land of feminine emancipation" just as America was.[2]

The bulk of women in this group are so-called Meiji women, those born during the reign of the Emperor Meiji. There is a kind of rugged individualism about them that is not egocentric. Their composure and inner strength, amid whatever vicissitudes of hard labor or tragedy life has brought, appear to carry them through and, if need be, their families also.

The stolid cigarette vendor in the suburbs of Kyōto, who in 1971 at age sixty-one was one of nine Japanese outside the imperial family honored by having her poem read at the annual imperial poetry-reading party, reflectively gave voice to this capacity in her successful poem. Written on the theme of *ie*, which means both home and family and suggests all the deepest emotion of ancestral heritage and the "house" system, the few lines tell simply and poetically the facts of her life:

> Beside the Wakasa Highway,
> Now turned into a mere byway,
> I have kept our family going
> By selling cigarettes.

She commented later that "for a woman born in the Meiji period, the *'ie'* of bygone days seems to be better than *'ie'* of today."[3]

There can be a wistfulness in remembering how honored was the position achieved by having lived to age sixty. In Confucian-influenced cultures, it was at sixty that a person was released from responsibility and entered a second childhood. Younger members of the family cherished and revered the aged one accordingly. Alice Mabel Bacon, writing in 1902, for instance, noted that

> the woman of thirty-five is just at the point when she has bid good-bye to her youth, and, having little to hope for in her middle life, is doing her work faithfully, and looking forward to an old age of privilege and authority, the mistress of her son's house, and ruler of the little domain of home.[4]

In contrast, in contemporary Japan the psychological distress of those advanced years can be critical. For women such difficulties are likely to be more severe than for men, for they have been caught up in the repercussions of the modernizing life cycle during a time of transition.

First, women live longer—79.13 years compared with 73.79 years for men by 1981. Also, the population sixty-five and over has risen steadily: In 1970 it was almost 9 percent of the total population, and it was expected to reach almost 15 percent by the end of the century. The steadily climbing longevity patterns increase the likelihood that women will be widowed soon after age forty because women marry at an earlier age than men. Almost half reaching sixty-five are without husbands.

Second, in good Japanese tradition a mother's closest emotional tie is normally with her son. As the younger generation establishes more separate nuclear households, this umbilical tie is loosened. The massive population migration into cities from 1950 on—usually into inadequately small housing—has hastened this separation. A family usually has no space for the mother-in-law even if the daughter-in-law is willing to include her.[5] For the older woman, who as a young bride suffered humiliation under the tyranny of her mother-in-law and now yearns, however subconsciously, for her turn, this prerogative of age is gone.

Many older women brood over the injustices and indifference that modern life seems to have brought them. Some 3.5 percent of men and women of sixty and over flee their homes as runaways, a shocking national police report of the mid-1970s highlighted. Each year the Respect for the Aged national holiday on September 15 is greeted by a flurry of suicides by those protesting their plight. Their misery can be measured in the suicide rate of Japanese women over sixty-five. In

1975, it was the second highest in the world after Hungary, and the highest among Japanese women since 1947, except for 1967–1971, when young women between fifteen and twenty-four had an even higher rate.[6] The elderly desire a *"pokkuri"* death, named after the Buddhist deity enshrined in Nagoya, who brings a quick and painless death, one causing minimal disruption to the family. All advanced countries must cope with this sociological problem of the aging—the "greying" of society—but it is encumbered with special problems and even guilt in Japan, with its patriarchal—and matriarchal—heritage.

Alternatives to moroseness for the older woman are available. She can enjoy her newly gained modern leisure, made more pleasurable by economic well-being. Bevies of outing-bound women, seen on every side, show the popularity of group trips. Others, dispossessed of traditional rights of pampering grandchildren and lording it over the daughter-in-law, turn vigorous energy to minding the needs of the community through women's organizations, religious groups, and social education classes.

Midway Generation

Japanese in the middle age-span are called *"senchūha,"* or "mid-war generation." They grew up and were educated in part under the old system and came to adulthood during the lengthy China and Pacific wars and their aftermath.

A social critic, who is himself a *senchūha,* commented in 1965 that men of this age group "stubbornly, self-reflectively," and sometimes "bitterly" ponder the results of having given their youth to the cause of war. He affirmed that the typical *senchūha* was likely during the Occupation to have joined the Communist party and thrown flame bottles in subversive activities.[7]

Women, too, have tended to find life a "melting pot of contradictions."[8] Sufferers from the malnutrition, diminished educational opportunities, and emotional hazards of the war during their formative years, they have been confronted with unique responsibilities as the first generation to put democracy into action in the family as well as the community. They have hovered somewhat precariously between two systems, uncertain about doing many things for the first time.

Particularly confusing for this group of women has been the task of bringing equality into the family system. They have borne the brunt of managing the transition from the hierarchical "house" system to the democratic nuclear family. Many of them know at first hand the multigeneration, under-one-roof living pattern. In 1949 a Women's and Minors' Bureau survey reported that 42 percent of the women said that

The author, during a visit to a rural section of western Japan in June 1965, asks how many of the farm women live in homes with three generations of the family. Photo courtesy of USIS/Japan.

this traditional custom interfered with the improvement of their life standards.[9] A quarter century or more later, going out of the home to work, "new fashion," they still may have to submit to the demands of a resident mother-in-law, "old fashion." A Tōhoku urban professional woman tells of getting up two hours early every morning to prepare breakfast rice on a charcoal fire rather than in a fast electric rice cooker. She does this, she says, because her mother-in-law insists that only the old-time method produces the good taste she likes. This midway generation is often caught in the middle of quarrels between the old family grandmother and her son's wife, who is likely to hold differing viewpoints on issues ranging from kitchen sanitation to Buddhistic rituals to childbirth.

This generation of women decided it was wisest to stay married despite erring or absent husbands. After all, said one when asked why she did not divorce the husband she had apparently never liked even after three children and twenty-five years of marriage, "We all walk a lonely road, *deshō?* Is it not so?" Others have tried divorce to find, in the early tests of making the new Civil Code work, that gaps in social welfare protection and lag in social custom made it almost impossible to bind the husband to court-ordered child support and alimony. Divorced women also found to their horror that this step ultimately punished primarily the children: Sons, who when ready to seek entrance into the company that would provide a lifetime job, or daughters, when negotiating for a husband, would encounter unexpected handicaps because they came from a broken family and were, therefore, not quite perfect. The divorce rate, given such attitudes, continues low by comparison with other industrialized nations.[10]

This age bracket includes many women who, because of the war, either lost their husbands or the opportunity to get married—both types are misfits in society. In a culture where most women consider children and home—not their husbands[11]—to be the reason for their being, the unmarried and childless are isolated from this most fundamental raison d'être. Some single women, of course, are professionally successful and occasionally envied by others who are tied into humdrum, orthodox living. A Social Welfare survey in the mid-1970s, however, found that about one-half of the women without spouses lived alone with no one to depend on, existed on a subsistence level, and looked into the future with "strong apprehensions."[12] They, like some of the aged, feel as if they have been cast adrift by a society emerging from its patriarchal system.

Birth Control Par Excellence. This same midway generation, after the postwar baby boom of 1947 to 1949, carried out what has been called by population experts "a demographic revolution unprecedented in international society."[13] Straitened economic conditions, scarcity of food, low morale about the future, and reaction against the government's wartime policy of promoting large families provided incentives.

CIE's Ethel B. Weed remembered that upon her arrival in Japan in 1945 the first question asked of her in a meeting was about birth control, so eager were the women for help in this matter. She was not permitted to answer. MacArthur adamantly forbade Occupation interference in this sensitive social policy, which, he felt, the Japanese must resolve by themselves.[14]

The Occupation, obviously, did permit and encourage discussion of the population issue by the Japanese. Katō (Ishimoto) Shidzue, writing in 1947 a history of the birth control movement in Japan, described the "thrilling experience" of participating in a large public forum with high governmental officials and a psychiatrist, of answering "many enthusiastic questions" from men and women in the audience, and of having this event broadcast all over Japan. To a supporter of Margaret Sanger before the war, it seemed "an unbelievable dream for a person who has had to undergo persecution, in the past, by the authorities" for calling public attention to this issue.[15]

Such discussions led in 1948 to passage by the Japanese Diet of its Eugenic Protection Law, which legalized contraception, sterilization, and abortion in cases in which childbirth might endanger the health of the mother. The next year the law was broadened to permit abortion when the mother's health might be endangered "for economic reasons." This legislation was enhanced in 1952 by a national education program about family planning techniques, a step taken to insure that women knew of alternatives to what had become the widespread use of illegally induced abortion. The overall result was that highly motivated women of all social classes brought down the birthrate from the immediate postwar high of 34 births per 1,000 population to 28.1 in 1950 and 17.2 in 1970; by 1980 it was down to 13.7, giving Japan one of the lowest birthrates in the world.

This unique "demographic revolution" was made possible by the use of inexpensive abortions, in effect, in place of contraceptives. In the early postwar years an estimated 70 percent of fertility control depended on this method, which had a cultural acceptability going back to the Tokugawa period. Abortions were estimated to be as high as 2 million annually, but the number has now declined. Among contraceptives, the condom method is preferred, followed by the rhythm method. Intrauterine devices are not much used, having been legally authorized only in 1974 and later questioned on grounds of safety. The controversial pill was finally made available on prescription, but many women are not aware of it.

Japanese women's deftness at artificial birth control is demonstrated in the drop in the birthrate in a single year, from 1965 to 1966, of almost one-third. Incentive came from the Confucian calendar, for 1966 was the Year of the Fiery Horse, which occurs every sixty years. Superstition holds that girl babies born in such a year may possibly kill their husbands; hence they grow up to become poor marriage prospects. An amusing sociological footnote reveals that some intellectuals, by comparison, decided that 1966 was an ideal year to have a baby: Competition in 1984 university examinations would be much less severe!

The principal reasons that mothers gave for abortions in the 1970s were to provide good education for the children and to protect the mother's health. "Economic reasons" in this society of increasing affluence slipped to fifth place and became controversial as a reason for legal abortion when revision of the Abortion Law was again debated. The sizable number of abortions and the ease of obtaining them, for good or for ill, has long given Japan internationally the nickname of "Abortion Paradise."

Success in family planning by this mid-war generation helped make feasible the nuclear family, for parents established in the minds of their daughters the "two child" family concept that is now considered the norm. The willingness of Japanese women to practice birth control has set them free from the burden of excessive childbearing and long years of child-rearing; they have thereby acquired personal time to work outside the home or partake of other aspects of a liberated life.

Side Effects of Modernization. This middle-generation also coped with the societal stresses that puzzled a population moving rapidly from postwar devastation through reindustrialization into a postindustrial technocratic and wealthy society. Often unaware of the complex socio-economic impact of the industrialization process, women assumed that their postwar exercise of new individual rights, instead of classic selfless devotion to family, caused contemporary social maladjustments. They worried that they were the primary culprits for problems of the "key children" (children left alone in the home after school until their parents return from work), juvenile delinquency, unsettled attitudes of human morality, and even environmental pollution. Those more aware of the negative side effects of modernization increasingly felt impelled to undertake corrective political action and citizen protests.

This middle generation of married women, for instance, was the first to break classic social and economic patterns and take jobs outside the home to contribute to the support of their households. At the same time—as working mothers they had to stint on energies they could give their family—they had to contend with conservative attitudes and labor practices that discouraged their being in the job world in the first place.

In the mid-1960s, this middle-generation group in rural areas of Japan was the mainstay of more than 76 percent of the farms because so many of the men were lured to work in the cities, on major construction jobs, such as the 1964 Olympics, the world's fair (Expo 70), and the highway systems, or in industry. This led to the prevalence of "sanchan-nōgyō," or the "three *chan* agriculture" (*chan* is an intimate diminutive appellation), meaning that farm work was done by the grandfather, grandmother, and mother. By 1971, with a further decline in the agricultural labor force, the farm-mothers also began to go out to earn money while still managing the family enterprise. Although farm house-wives continue to be the main farming work force, there is a trend toward *ichan-nōgyō*, i.e., agriculture by one *chan*—the grandfather or grandmother.

In consequence, although farm women are assuming greater authority and responsibility in their communities, they are occasionally reduced to appealing in newspapers for wives for their sons to continue the farm. Contemporary girls of marriageable age want an easier life. One searching farm-mother plaintively publicized the attractions of beautiful, mountainous Nagano Prefecture: "Farm work here has been totally mechanized, and the system of management is totally new. There is no suffocating crust of conventionalism. There is no environmental pollution. Won't anybody volunteer to be their brides?"[16]

"Rationalized" Homemaking. On the plus side, this midway group is the first to enjoy the gifts of technology and prosperity to the home. Newspaperwoman Shiraishi Tsugi called it the "Westernized or rather Americanized way of living" and concluded that, more than the Constitution, it had liberated housewives "physically and spiritually."[17]

The real liberators then are electric gadgets that have simplified housekeeping and smaller houses or *danchi* apartments adequate for the nuclear family of four. By 1970 urban worker families in overwhelming numbers owned such electric time-savers as refrigerators, electric washers, and vacuum cleaners. Later in the decade, microwave ovens and air conditioners joined the list of desirables. Farm families owned only slightly fewer. Florence Powdermaker, a psychiatrist brought in to advise during the Occupation, had recommended neighborhood laundromats if women were to have time for civic responsibilities.[18] Few Japanese women could have imagined how soon the electric rice-cooker and home washing machine would be almost universal and that "rationalization," the ubiquitous Japanese term for modern efficiency, would become the natural way in the Japanese home. The resulting blessings of added leisure time brought by science and affluence were soon popularized, with characteristic Japanese humor, in the widely heard cliché that marriage today for a woman has become "a job with three meals, TV, and an afternoon nap."

That job includes controlling the household budget. By the mid-1970s, Japanese urban housewives managed 97 percent of the family purse and those in rural areas, 66 percent. The projection for the 1980s is that nationwide, women will control 80 percent of consumer spending.[19] This situation underlies the recurrent witticism about how Japanese women really dominate their *"hyakuyen teishu"* husbands, which means doling out daily allowances of ¥100 for lunch and cigarettes. Inflation may have created "¥500 husbands," but this budget-management duty emphasizes that the home is woman's "business." One upshot of the women's banker role is their ever-mounting anger about rising prices. Incensed, they have become determined to stop soaring prices and to receive assurances that full value and quality are received—in short, they have turned to consumerism.

Their husbands, recovered from postwar dejection, have settled into their work- and business-oriented lives, taking their women for granted and, in so doing, shutting them out of the mainstream of men-made events. Especially for white-collar management families, the lives of men and women cross rather superficially, almost in a hotel-valet kind

Mothers watch as their children, wearing their "dress-up" school uniforms, line up for the ceremonies of their first day in primary school. Photo courtesy of the Embassy of Japan.

of arrangement. The wife has one set of friends; the husband, another. Communication is limited to basics and the well-being of the children, who encounter their father mostly in passing, with an occasional Sunday given to a family outing. Personal interchange on such a limited scale brews the disturbing "discontinuity between generations" and hastens the decline of parental authority.[20]

Education Mama. A by-product of Japanese women's new life cycle is the phenomenon of *"kyōiku mama,"* a commonly used term for a mother suffering from a mania about pushing her children, especially sons, upward in their education. The goal is often not acquisition of knowledge, but a diploma from the most illustrious institution possible.

Cut off from many other emotional outlets in the nuclear family with the husband often absent, middle-generation mothers, as household burdens lessened with the gifts of modernization, in the late 1950s turned their energies more and more to the educational accomplishments of their children. In the vertical society of Japan the reputation of the school and the level of educational attainment predetermine chances of success in industry, government, and academia. It became a social imperative, discussed in PTAs and in the media, for mothers to see to the tutoring of their children to pass examinations to enter the best kindergarten possible; then more tutoring and more examinations to enter the best primary and middle schools, until finally the goal of admittance into a prestigious university might be achieved. Quizzed in opinion polls about what they most wanted of their children, mothers cried, "Study more!" Home discipline was secondary, leaving character formation to the schools. Many are concerned that this undeviating concentration on educational attainment teaches self-absorption and selfishness. It can also interfere with conjugal togetherness—for example, how can the child study if the father is home in the evening looking at a noisy television in a small apartment?

The situation has contributed to the creation of a national health problem of fat children who have insufficient time for exercise but are coaxed by their mothers in their studying with hot chocolate, snacks, and extra goodies. In big cities, 75 percent of preteens are enrolled in *juku* cram schools, and all teenagers worry about "examination hells." This situation has helped maintain a high teenage suicide rate of 17.6 per 100,000 (compared to about 13 per 100,000 in the United States), despite freer and more relaxed life-styles. This pressure has been one underlying reason for disillusionment among university students. They have found, after eighteen years of anticipation, that admission almost guarantees graduation, and university life is not as challenging as expected. Employers make job offers to juniors or even sophomores, which gives little incentive for further study. Students gave vent to their boredom and disillusionment in the 1960s in unrest and violence on the campuses. The shock to the parents from such rebellion and the reflection on the values of the system have now started to slow down the harrowing stampede toward educational mecca. The lower percentage of entrance applications to prestigious national universities is evidence of more pragmatic aspirations. The fact that the autobiography—*Madogiwa no totto-chan* [The little girl who looked out of the window]—of television personality Kuroyanagi Tetsuko, which seriously questions the cog-machine aspects of Japanese education, became in 1981–1982 the biggest bestseller in postwar Japan indicates the ambivalence of current attitudes.

University-trained younger mothers, although realizing the risks, feel caught up in the "education mama" syndrome. If they do not promote their child's future, they might diminish his future chances, thereby bringing disgrace upon themselves. The subliminal tradition of "good wives, wise mother" lingers—but in modern style.[21]

"Housewife's Blues". Middle-generation women have been called a "shy generation," but many are just glad, in more recent years, to enjoy the absence of struggle. Many, as in the "Housewife's Blues," a song popular in the Kansai women's organizations in the early 1970s, frequently wonder what life has been all about:

When I was most beautiful,
I married an ordinary man
As arranged by my parents
Although I was adoring somebody else.

My newly married life, which should have been happy,
Was during the war.
My husband was sent to an unknown southern island,
And I was weeping with *mompe* on.

Soon a child was born.
I devoted myself to the care of the baby,
But my mother-in-law began to interfere
And mother-in-law and daughter-in-law were on bad terms.

When I discovered that my husband was unfaithful to me,
Naive as I was, I was disturbed in mind.
Were it not for my child,
I would have got divorced then.

I will soon be an old woman.
My pretty pleasures at present are
"Tabiji" in the morning and "Kokinji" in the evening.
    [Popular TV programs]
TV is what I live for now.

(Chorus)
Now I ask myself
"Have I lived as I should have?
Is being a housewife the only way of life for a woman?
Have I lived a real life?"

Despite this lament, it is fair to conclude that the talents of this middle group of Japanese women have been fully utilized, as they have gone into stabilizing the quiet revolution of social change. They have unfolded a new life-style, which the younger generation, the modernists, may one day appreciate and enjoy.

Young Modernists

Girls and young women born during and after the war are products of the postwar system. They are geared to the present world. They are taller and more shapely, legatees of an improved diet and less time spent kneeling on the leg-numbing *tatami* mat. They share with their peers in other modernized societies the joys and problems of the late twentieth century; but they also face the distinctive realities of being Japanese.

January 15 is Coming-of-Age Day in Japan. Young men and women who have reached the age of twenty-one (nineteen or twenty by Western count) are honored privately and publicly in ceremonies saluting their adulthood. Girls dress up in festive light-colored kimonos, the "uniform" for such occasions, yet soberly realize that they have arrived at a major crossroad in life.

Most young women look back on their growing-up years as a happy time.[22] They were not spoiled quite as much as their brothers, but they were not forced to study as assiduously either. A contemporary expression of filial piety is the hope that they will "not make their parents worry," "will understand their parents' feelings," and will, at the right time, marry and build a "good family life." They will assist their parents if financial need appears, but only if it is not too burdensome to their own families. Family for them, as for their mothers and grandmothers, is the core of organized life, but it is arranged independently and with minimal responsibilities to their ancestors.

As with their grandmothers, the amount of education creates a gulf between those who are university trained and those who reached only junior or senior high school. The university groups (by 1980, one in every three women high school graduates advanced to higher education) are independent in spirit and psychologically on their own when they plan marriage and future. Because so many more have a college background than do their mothers, the generation gap surfaces with the youthful cry, "Do they know what I am worrying about and what I wish to do?"[23] They usually still need financial support from their parents, but their goals are set at economic independence to match their psychic independence.

The twenty-year-old expects to marry. Cognizant of the complications of confronting the dominant social pattern of *kekkon tekireiki* (the years of a girl's life considered suitable for marriage), a university-educated young woman who passes twenty-five with no prospects of a husband—perhaps because she had refused a traditional *miai* meeting—may become disquieted or even neurotic. Those dubious about marital happiness or those dedicated to self-expression and a career still feel that marriage is essential, providing a social status that will enable them to do other things they may want to do.[24]

Most young modernists in the 1970s seemed not to expect a life of great personal happiness—an attitude at variance with the optimism of twenty-year-olds a decade earlier. Often there was a morbid feeling of "emptiness" for the present and the future, as evidenced by the immediate nationwide appeal in 1971 of the published diary of a Kyōto-area university student who committed suicide despite a seemingly normal set of college experiences. Her introspections, written at various times in the six months before her death, evoked empathy:

> Today is my birthday. I am twenty years old. I am now allowed to smoke and drink. I feel uneasy that I am a grown-up while I am still immature. . . . I don't want to be a tame human; I want to be a creative one. I want to be Takano Etsuko herself. TV, newspapers, magazines and all try to make tame people. I want to be a person who does what one decides to do, struggles with all the problems, sings songs, paints pictures, cries, laughs, and weeps. . . . I joined the *demo*. How happy I am! I wanted to sing the poem, "I am alive, I am alive. Yes, I am alive in this belly of the barricade.". . . I will never be defeated by the things outside of me. However, I don't know what to do with myself when I feel that the inward thing that supports me is uncertain. . . . I want to sleep.[25]

Many others regarded the bravura and arousal of the *demo* (parading protest) and barricades as their most invigorating and satisfying moments. They found Takano's life and death symbolic of their own. "We must not let her suicide be a useless death," declared a recent Kyūshū University graduate when asked about the future of Japanese young women.[26] Rather the young must find their own purpose to give design and dimension to their future.

This sense of independence extends to job behavior. Like some young men, some modernist young women switch from one job to another—a procedure unheard of until recent years. One middle-aged woman personnel manager regards young women as not "dependable" and poorly motivated. She blames their attitudes on "lack of basic knowledge" and the "rigid thinking" resulting from the rote studying required to pass entrance examinations, a process that turns all knowledge into clear-cut choices of "right" and "wrong" answers with no allowance for subtlety of ideas. She feels that the small family and lack of grandmotherly influence have led to "poor home training" with evident results, an evaluation typical of older people who observe or employ the young.[27]

Dispirited by this vague hollowness of soul, perhaps a lack of spirituality, perhaps just plain boredom or frustration, many look primarily to transient pleasures: shopping, visiting coffee houses, fashionable English lessons. One goal that excites a positive reaction—as with their elders—is travel, both overseas and within Japan, which may also reflect the desire to run away from a lackluster and stultifying routine. Overall, their experience has shown that although affluence can provide some physical satisfactions, gratification of the spirit may be elusive.

Despite this apparent malaise, there is among those in their twenties a basic motivation of, "I've got to do something! . . . and do something constructive!" As with youth in most countries, the problem usually comes down to finding out what this "something" is.

A bright-eyed Sacred Heart University student won the coveted first place in the competitive Intercollegiate English Oratorical Contest in 1969 with her thesis that "a woman can make a great contribution, whether it be at her husband's side, or as an independent career woman" by keeping "up with the changing time" and becoming "fully involved in helping to shape a better world."[28] True, but it is easier to say than to get accepted in a job where one can fulfill these desires and support such an undertaking. Usually, such ambitions are brushed aside by elders as momentary inclinations that will give way to the permanent business of getting married and assuming housewifely duties.

Girls who firmly reject such counsel and opt for the unusual, such as the Japanese version of the Peace Corps (the Japan Overseas Cooperation Volunteers), Alpine-style mountain-climbing, or serious professional endeavor, find themselves isolated from others of their own age. They may finally forego marriage because they slide past the "best age" or because they are too strong-minded or too unorthodox.

Many college-educated women of recent years have determined to marry first and work afterwards.[29] Thus, they satisfy their aspiration of using their education, but on their own revised time schedule. Such innovations increasingly call for adjustments in traditional labor patterns to receive women over thirty back into the work force. Some already married, living often without clear goals, in tiny undemanding apartments with small families, try to find their way by studying, sometimes by themselves. Already well educated, some are generating purposeful political and community activities. Their modest momentum shows signs of building a new wave of feminine energy in public affairs.

New Feminists

Outspoken in their pursuit of a raison d'être, particularly of sexual equality, are Japan's new feminists. Only a handful, perhaps two or three thousand, they are often individuals spun off from radical student movements, disillusioned with being used only as a "female" in the revolution "doing cooking and cleaning of lavatory" or "supporting the men-revolutionists with mother's tolerance and prostitute's coquetry."[30] Some were members of the peace movement, believing that war-makers use women and their bodies to supply the human energies and human instruments of armies. They are also just ordinary young women— married, unmarried, divorced. They share personal dissatisfaction with their existence and an active egocentric search for some deeper meaning in life.

Pioneering philosopher and acclaimed poetess of the movement is Tanaka Mitsu. Slight of build, with great black eyes in a well-shaped head almost too large for her body, she speaks of her ideas and plans with intelligent purpose, emphasizing her points with a graceful wave of a hand. She seems too fragile for the power of her emotions. She is both shy and confident in the same moment. Her autobiography, *To My Spiritual Sisters* (*Inochi no onna tachi e*), published in 1972, established her as the philosophical standard-bearer for Japan's new radical feminists. In it she tells how the buffeting of growing up—involving rape at age eight, a broken family, and attachment to the university radical communes, to Vietnam relief, and to other causes—brought her to despair that all humanity is negative. She feared she existed in a "world of darkness." Sheer anger at her state then lifted her to the "light." With renewal of self came her conversion to the women's movement.

Officially, Tanaka started her movement in 1970 when she was twenty-seven. Late that summer, she distributed leaflets to call together spiritual sisters. A few months later, she fostered an outdoor demonstration that led to a debate on "Indictment of Discrimination" and subsequently to more meetings. Workshops in Nagano and Hokkaidō of young women from all over Japan followed in 1971 and 1972, with an intervening conference in Tōkyō attended by more than 1,000 feminists. They maintained regular communication (*comi*) through their own "mini-*comi*" as opposed to "mass-*comi*." A small "Women's Lib Center" (Ūman ribu senta) in Shinjuku in Tōkyō served as the office. It should be noted that the term "women's lib" was regularly used by the younger activist women until late in the 1970s. To them it had not acquired the Western derogatory connotation. They started raising funds for their own building to house the center, where women might consult compassionate gynecologists, arrange abortions, receive financial help, and study. Tanaka envisioned that these studies would help break the "vertical relations" (*tate kankei*) of Japanese society and establish her goal of "horizontal relationships" (*yoko kankei*). She was making long-range plans, thinking in units of ten years. Like the pre–World War II feminists, Tanaka has called economic independence the goal of women's liberation, commenting that most of her group are ordinary working women, who dropped out because of the "bitter frustration of their jobs," which they considered beneath their skills.

The young feminist philosophers, among whom Tanaka is at her best, tried to create their own distinctive feminist philosophy worthy of discussion and activities on the international level. With this purpose she and others traveled to Mexico City to the International Women's Year Tribune. U.S. feminists visited Japan to take part in the dialogue. The best-known commentator on the movement, Higuchi Keiko, regularly travels abroad to attend women's conferences and to consult with feminist leaders. Older Japanese feminists, such as the late Ichikawa Fusae, feminist historian-philosopher Morosawa Yoko, and some labor union officials, encouraged the contemporary movement with moral support as it unfolded.

The new feminists have been greatly splintered. In personal interchange, talking becomes a catharsis, with much self-analyzing and agonizing over present status and future potential. Newsletters abound to foster intercommunication. One of the early ones, the *Neo Lib*, recruited Ono Yoko, famous through her relation to Beatle John Lennon, to contribute a fiery poem storming against "one thousand years of male society."[31] At least two small groups, one called Red June (red in this instance signifying women's vigorous talk, from the Japanese expression *akai kien*, and June, the month of founding), and the other, Hotmo kai, or Heart Open Together Association, concentrated on issues of "middle age women's lib" (*chūnen ribu*), recruiting members thirty years of age or·more. They asked, "How can women be truly liberated if they cannot contemplate the realization of having arrived at middle age?" Even "PTA libbers" (a Japanese term for PTA members and groups that focused on feminist issues) entered the feminist ranks.

Other groups like "Womanpower Taikai (rally)," organized by former Fulbright student and University of Tōkyō graduate Kageyama Hiroko, a blunt-speaking labor specialist and writer, acted to train women to improve their capabilities and gain full equality in the labor field. Tanaka and her colleagues rejected this concept of "womanpower" as simply working within the establishment. They rebuked it as the polishing of "gems," or women of ability, rather than the ordinary "stone."

Stormier activists of the movement took more highly publicized steps. The Pink Helmet brigade of Chūpiren, appropriately wearing pink and blue helmets and waving pink flags, engaged in *demos* for legalization of birth control pills and against proposed restrictions in the Eugenic Protection Law that would eliminate the economic justification for legal abortion. In the latter, incidentally, these younger feminists were joined by the now well-established Planned Parenthood Association of Japan. They also picketed wayward husbands or those delinquent in alimony or child support. Expanding their field of action, Enoki Misako, trained pharmacist and Chūpiren founder, organized in mid-1977 a Japan Women's party to seek to give women a better voice in the Diet. She ran for a seat in the June 1977 House of Councillors election, announcing that, if defeated, she would withdraw from feminist activism and become a good wife and wise mother. She lost and kept her promise. The media siezed on this as evidence that the new feminist movement was dead.

Women's liberationists have been criticized by Japanese men, who insist that since the Occupation "there is little from which women of Japan need to be liberated. This has been, in fact, an age of 'female supremacy' and if anyone needs liberation, it is the downtrodden, browbeaten men of Japan." Author Mishima Yukio's dramatic ritual suicide was even cited as endorsement of this point of view, for he "died to restore masculinity for Japanese men."[32]

New liberationists have also been criticized by other women: "Women's status in Japan is stabilized and better than in the United States so we don't have to think about women's rights," said a Kyūshū working mother.[33] Catholic-educated Sono Ayako's phenomenal best-seller, *Love for Whom?* (*Dare no tame ni ai suruka*), upbraided their "liberation of sex" and recommended devoted wifeliness and motherhood. Mishima Sumie in her quick, fluent English succinctly labeled it "Cheap show!"

Only time will tell whether this modern version of feminist agitation will prove to be merely a passing cloud from the West, a transitory feminine follow-up in the 1970s of the student rebellions of the 1960s, or a longer-range contribution to the Japanese women's movement. Nakane Chie, an anthropologist at Tōkyō University, has advised that the feminist spirit is a foreign import and alien to Japanese traditional culture. Nonetheless, it is reminiscent of Hiratsuka Raichō and her Bluestocking movement of the pre-World War I era. It, too, was small in scope and greatly scorned, but the Bluestockings stirred the souls of the women suffragists and activists who followed. Tanaka Satoko of Chifuren felt by 1976 that this radical, emotionally charged version of women's liberation had become inundated in the much larger rising tide of interest in sexual equality. The organization in 1977 of the All Japan Feminist Association (Zen Nihon feminisuto kyokai) (AJFA), looking to "human liberation through women," suggested this type of maturing. Certainly, the wide-ranging mainstream attention, both official and private, to insuring progress under the impetus of the International Women's Decade, bears out the longer-range assessment of Tanaka Satoko.

If contemporary young women, however, continue to need some passion to lift them from their "emptiness," the voice, if not the role, of Tanaka Mitsu might make them take heart: "Libbers are not simply cross with the general 'man' society. What I want is not a man or a child. I want to have a stronger soul with which I can burn myself out either in heartlessness or in tenderness. Yes, I want a stronger soul."[34]

The Determinant of Education

If electrified, modernized homemaking and the practice of birth control have given both leisure time and unused energy to Japanese women, it is their education level that determines their use of these benefits in the work force and in the community.

Criticism of the training of women's minds plagued the women's movements of the Taishō period. It was an issue in 1946 when women first voted, a time when only 23 percent went beyond the sixth grade. The less well-educated of the current older and middle generations are sensitive about their alleged lack of rationally trained minds. They mention it repeatedly in personal conversation when invited to try some previously untested venture. This attitude, reinforced by the traditional Japanese virtue of *tsutsumashii,* which enjoins everyone to appear humble and belies any suggestion of self-confidence, accounts for much of the timidity of women in assuming leadership roles.

Appropriately, Japanese women are enthusiastic about self-improvement and wish "to study humbly." Social education, as adult or continuing education is usually called in Japan, is carried on for women by the Ministries of Education and of Agriculture, local governments, the mass media, women's organizations, and private schools of all kinds.

Expanding beyond family matters, the postwar Ministry of Education's social education programs have been revamped to address women's roles as workers and as citizens, including, in recent years, the changes inherent in material affluence, leisure, and the information explosion. The needs of different age groups are recognized in varied projects. There is, for example, an annual "Grandmother College" for those over sixty-five in Kitakyūshū; ideas about constructive use of leisure are directed at the middle-aged; classes on "community-mindedness" for young mothers support that age group. Overseas observation trips for organization and education leaders add an international dimension.

In the fall of 1977 the National Women's Education Center, associated with the Ministry of Education and located outside Tōkyō in a beautiful campus setting, opened with plaudits from Prime Minister Fukuda Takeo. A national and international exchange, research, and training center for enhancement of women's education, its superb facilities symbolize the educational achievement of Japanese women and of their organizations

Table 3.1. Percentage of Girls and Boys Attending
           Senior High School, 1955-1980

	1955	1965	1975	1980
Girls	47	70	93	95
Boys	56	72	91	93

Source: Japanese Ministry of Education publications.

since the late 1960s. Its first director, Nuita Yoko, journalist, educator, and experienced official, represents the best of such women.

Many women's organizations tie in their programs with official social education emphases. Local women's halls serve as centers for study programs and for consumer activities and sponsor classes in the tea ceremony, flower arranging, crafts, and cooking. Occasionally cocktail mixing is taught to modernize the women's skills. Rural women learn about civic matters, nutrition, home management, farming health, and the use of the latest insecticides.

Starting with the Occupation, educational reform policies instituted coeducation and equality of opportunity from the elementary grades through the university. Girls have made the most of this situation with the result that they now receive more schooling than do boys, and their competitive powers at the higher level are escalating.

Postwar education became compulsory for the first nine years, divided on a track of six, three, three, i.e., elementary, junior high, and non-compulsory senior high school. Attendance for both boys and girls is almost 100 percent at the compulsory level. The proportions of those going on to senior high school, for which entrance examinations must be passed, reveal dramatic growth, with the percentage of girls exceeding that of boys by 1970 (see Table 3.1).

The increased participation of women in higher education is similarly impressive. Although the percentage gap between men and women at the four-year university is still wide, with 12 percent of women and 39 percent of men high school graduates entering in 1980, there has been a fourfold gain for women since 1955. In addition, the two-year junior college is very popular with women. The 1980 data show that 41 percent of men and 33 percent of women go on beyond high school, more than six times the percentage of women in 1955. In 1970, 1 percent of women in the appropriate age group were in postgraduate studies, compared with almost 5 percent of men. The percentage of women graduate students had not increased by 1975.

Women students in the quadrangle of Tōkyō Women's College in the early 1970s. Photo courtesy of the Embassy of Japan.

Through senior high school, the curriculum is essentially the same for boys and girls. In higher education, women converge on the literature, home economics, and teacher-training departments, although a composite faculty called law, politics, economics, and industrial management draws more women than home economics in universities. These concentrations, achieved by competing successfully with men in grueling entrance examinations, has tended to push men out of the literature and education fields even in prestigious universities like Tōkyō, Keiō, and Waseda.

Rumblings by university professors against this "female invasion," which it was predicted would lead to the "decline of the country," came to a climax in 1966 when the president of government-supported Kumamoto University in Kyūshū announced an anti-woman admissions policy, in contravention of laws about equal educational opportunity. He argued that, because women were entering the university but not going on in sufficient numbers to graduate school or getting jobs, there would soon be a shortage of qualified faculty members. Others tried to analyze the dilemma of how educated women can "refund" their education to society if they do not proceed into the traditional male

Table 3.2. Percentage of University-Educated Women
           and Men Finding Jobs, 1959-1979

	1959	1970	1979
Women	57	60	63
Men	--	83	77

Source: Japanese Ministry of Education publications.

professions. Involved were attitudinal complications about employment opportunity for college-educated women and their marriageability.

It is true that a literature major without graduate school specialization leaves women with no functional training and temporarily, at least, blurs their aims when they are ready for employment.[35] Those trained as teachers know they can get jobs, and more and more have been going after them. The home economics major, the choice of almost 40 percent of the junior college students, is very often little more than glorified preparation for marriage and modern homemaking—but most go to junior college for precisely that reason.

While the controversy raged, young women, unmindful, increasingly competed successfully to enter the coeducational, highly rated universities because there they could get "more serious studies." Furthermore, the overall number of university-educated women finding employment continued to increase[36] (see Table 3.2).

Education as an instigator of change takes time, like the hand-looming of a beautifully designed length of fabric. So gradual is the process that the emergence for the first time of a whole generation of women educated equally with men leaves society unprepared for the provocative impact of their trained presence. How this fresh, creative force meshes into Japanese life is a story just beginning to unfold.

If one asks whether Japanese men's lives have changed as much as those of their women since the end of the war, the immediate answer is no. Women have been more affected than men by the modernization impulses of the postwar world.

First, the drastic reforms of the Occupation era modified women's legal standing and opportunities to a greater degree than it did those of men. Second, the barrage of scientific and economic transformers— greater longevity, effective birth control, mechanization in the home, economic well-being with time to take advantage of it—imposed beneficial changes peculiarly fundamental to the well-being and traditional roles of women. As a result of the new, modernized life cycle, women find themselves by age forty or so with their children in school, leisure time because of easier housekeeping, educated minds, and the long stretch of another thirty or thirty-five years of active life ahead with which to do something—a life pattern occurring for the first time in the second half of the twentieth century.

Japanese women are probably unique among national groups of women in recent decades in adapting their lives to both of these revolutionary influences simultaneously. They have shared the first set of adjustments to constitutional equalities primarily with women of the newly independent and developing nations whose cultures still await the impact of advanced industrialization. They have experienced adaptation to the modernized life cycle with women of the United States and a few other technologically advanced nations who have already had a generation or more of practice with equal citizenship.

Japanese women leaders in the 1920s and 1930s bemoaned the lack of response of women to their own progress. Queried in 1949 about what they should do to better their status, women overwhelmingly replied that they must promote a "positive attitude" and improve their "self-consciousness," a Japanese turn of phrase for knowledge of and confidence in themselves.[37] All the other desires they expressed at that time, with the possible exception of having their men understand them better—perhaps a universal problem—have now come to pass. As they continue conscientiously to develop this self-consciousness, setting their own modernized standards for performance in society, they create the image of the modern Japanese woman, which they wish to portray.

142

LEISURE TIME—
TELEVISION VIEWERS AND VOLUNTEERS

> The significance of women's political participation
> does not rest simply in the number of women in
> elected and high positions. What is just as important
> is how women work for the betterment of everyday
> life and community as productive members in society,
> as opinion-makers, as "welfare bearers" of society and
> culture.[38]
> —Tanino Setsu, Director, Women's and
> Minors' Bureau, Tōkyō, 1964

Endowed with the largess of free time by the good fortune of their prosperity, Japanese probe the perplexities of what to do with it. Is it to be an outlet for selfish pursuits or a boon for larger purposes?

Japanese women, for almost two decades, have been experimenting with various ideas about the use of nonhousehold time. By comparison, the incipient five-day week is only beginning to offer increasing leisure to men. While men want it, they still face the problem of knowing what to do with it. Said one Mitsubishi steelworker, "Maybe I'll just sleep."[39]

The prospect of the shorter workweek for husbands does not necessarily please their wives. They fear that the men will be burdensome, demanding lots of extra attention and service of food or beverage while they watch television. Their presence would interfere with the Saturday household routine and might even deprive the women of outings of their own. Admittedly, leisure is a mixed blessing at best.[40]

Factor of Time

There are two factors that have increased leisure time in Japanese women's lives. First, in this mechanized era ordinary housewives spend an average of seven and one-half hours per day on housekeeping and child-tending in comparison with more than ten hours before the war, a gain of three hours spare time per day, if they do not have full-time work outside the home.[41] However, the nonobligated hours are often cut up into small chunks by schedules of children who come home for lunch or need care on a clock-regulated basis. Hence, leisure without nursery or child-care facilities is circumscribed in usability. The leisure hours of the young unmarried, with work force schedules and compulsory group functions, are similarly hedged.

The second factor is increased longevity, the result of medical progress. This dramatic change since the war has opened up the leisure potential of a space of thirty healthy years after basic family responsibilities are diminished. Confucian wisdom had admonished women not to go out of the home very often to the theater or even to the temple until they reached age forty. Two hundred years after Kaibara Ekken's *Onna daigaku*, modern medicine and household technology enable Japanese women to embrace these teachings on life-style with gusto.

Philosophy of Time

While the existence of free time is now apparent, women, especially of the middle generation, still seem a bit surprised at their good fortune. They are unsure, both philosophically and practically, how to deal with it. Most respond, when asked if they have free time, only with the wonderfully expressive and noncommittal Japanese phrase of uncertainty, "*mā mā*."[42]

In Japan, being "busy" is a virtue. Routine conversation starts more often with "I know you are busy, but . . ." than with "How are you?" Busyness lends importance, and in this atmosphere, for instance, men contribute endless overtime as a gesture of loyalty to their employers, making Japanese labor famous for its tireless toil and productivity. A conscientious woman, therefore, may not wish to admit to having hours of nonbusyness.

For one not busily engaged in responsible chores, the most acceptable use of free time is study. "Free time is not for rest," said a hardworking resort-area innkeeper's wife, "but for self-improvement." Young women before marriage busily study flower arrangement, the tea ceremony, or cooking. As an Ōsaka organizational leader explained in the mid-1960s, middle-aged housewives aroused no husbandly objections when they left home and its duties during the day provided it was to study at the local women's hall. If perchance they made some pin money with their handicrafts, true to the business-oriented Kansai mentality, it was all the better.[43]

At a conference in 1968 in the azalea-covered mountainous area of hot springs near Nagasaki, women leaders from all over Kyūshū, discussing rest and leisure as a human right, had difficulty differentiating their personal rights from their role within the family. Said one, "Leisure is not just play. Baking cookies or caring for my garden means leisure to me. Isn't being happy the same as having leisure?" An older woman held that "time with the family is not free time, but duty." Leisure for her came when her mind was free. A farm woman explained that the farm machinery that saved her hours of physical labor in the fields cost so much that she had to allow her children to become "key children" in order to go out selling insurance to pay for the tractor. A Sasebo leader less charitably expressed another viewpoint: "Times have changed. Some women have plenty of time; some are much busier. I am trying to get women to take part in civic activities, but they lack social consciousness. They just watch TV from morning to night."[44]

Leisure Boom

Television viewing or other forms of rest, recreation, and amusement can hardly be begrudged the normally hardworking Japanese. Television, for instance, regularly reaches about 98 percent of the people, and most families have multiple sets. It offers an easy, immediate contact with the world outside the home and becomes a natural way to escape the confinement of small housing quarters and to divert the mind—and possibly the spirit. The average housewife watches almost five hours a day, recreation made further permissible because it is compatible with sewing, ironing, cleaning, and the like.

Affluence is the key to leisure outside the home. The rate of spending on leisure activities doubled between 1967 and 1972, and it continued to rise as wage-based incomes increased 15 to 20 percent annually in line with the booming economy. Not unrelated is the fact that the cost of buying land to build a house is so exorbitant that many people regard home ownership as patently impossible. They turn spending to the possible: more recreation and leisure to escape from confining rented housing.

Caught up in delightful possession of more free time *and* bulging purses, Japanese women of all ages plan pleasurable events. They group with alumnae friends or working colleagues to take trips, overseas if possible, or short vacations within Japan to hot spas or sightseeing spots. Club members organize outings to view blossoming iris, azalea, or cherry trees or brightly colored autumn leaves. Typical farm women of Northern Honshū contribute to a fund all year to go off as a village group for a couple of days to the man-made resort of Tōhoku's Joban Hawaiian Center. Urban women have luncheon parties at fashionable restaurants or drive to the countryside to savor the delicacies of a local seasonal fish. They play Mah Jong and pachinko—but not as much as the men. Younger ones engage in athletics, ranging from bowling to badminton to skiing. All join hobby clubs in droves. On weekends and holidays, crowds surging off for recreational pastimes are so great, and often so careless of life and limb, that a major newspaper finally lamented what it termed the "kamikaze leisure."[45]

The "leisure boom" is a reality for women. Its enjoyment shows how far the women have come from the time of the Tokugawa shogunate, when it was recommended that wives "who idle away their time simply swigging tea, and who are always out making sightseeing tours, should be promptly divorced."[46]

Alien Concepts

Quietly, in the midst of lemming-like pursuit of *nouveau riche* leisure, women have gradually expanded their volunteer and social service work—also carried out during spare hours. Such attention to civic endeavor becomes an ever-strengthening manifestation of their social consciousness which, in the de Tocqueville tradition, is a partner of democracy in action.

It is essential to understand that, historically, community volunteerism and impersonal service have been alien cultural and philosophical concepts not only in Japan but in much of the rest of Asia, where concerns embrace family, but not unknown neighbors, and where the fatalistic spirit of traditional Buddhism may well inhibit social outreach. Assistance to a relative or institution to which binding ties exist is part of the obligatory give-and-take within a delimited unit of society, perceived as living up to the highest expectations of duty. This dedication is not required or expected outside the established circle. There is no "Good Samaritan" ethic, no casual involvement. Quite the contrary. Just reaching out with a sense of social responsibility, as required in a humanistic democratic society, an arouse suspicion: "What does this person want in exchange?" It may call into play the opprobrious words for meddler (*ossekai*), intruder (*deshabari*), and meddlesome (*sewayaki*). "Why do you have to go to other people and meddle in women's affairs?" protested the eighty-year old mother-in-law of a socially conscious lecturer, educator, and social service volunteer not too many years ago.

The older woman bespoke the traditional reluctance about involvement in the troubles of others. She was echoing the sentiments of the long-held proverb, "The god won't bring evil to you if you don't touch him"—a Japanese variation on "let sleeping dogs lie." In the Tokugawa era people sagely commented, "The pheasant would not be shot but for its cries." One volunteer enthusiast in Ōsaka, explaining the difficulties of volunteer recruitment, cited the "passive character of the Japanese people," which truly "reflects this background of three hundred years of Tokugawa feudalism."[47]

Early would-be volunteers discovered that opportunities for service were difficult to find and organize. Those attempting to serve learned that their helping hands and altrusim were not much wanted. Stories are repeated of hospitals and similar institutions in which the nurses and other personnel objected to "meddlers" interfering in their jobs and domain—in their closed shop. How can people volunteer if the recipients reject those who would help because to accept personal kindness obligates them to return the favor? Once rebuffed, the women were likely to retreat into their comforting women's halls, not to try again. Not only did the prospective volunteer workers require proper training to make them confident and useful, but those receiving them also needed broadening of attitude.

In 1963, in an attempt to arouse a sense of general charitableness toward fellow human beings, the highly respected Kaya Seiji of Tōkyō University, Jodai Tano, then president of Japan Women's University, Sakanishi Shio, and others organized the Small Kindness Association. The Japanese people proudly and self-consciously were then preparing for the influx of foreign guests who would soon come to the summer Olympic Games in Tōkyō. Everyone wanted these visitors to think well of the Japanese and their country. It proved a powerful incentive. By the end of 1964, the association had awarded 20,000 "medals of practice" (jikkōshō) for meritorious "small kindnesses." Since then the movement has been introduced to 130 countries through The Rotarian, and the more than 700,000 Japanese members concentrate their efforts on school children. Unburdened by older traditions, the young may pursue the path of kindness simply because of friendly human rapport, a sentiment characterized in the association's theme song as "fresh air in the society."

The geometrically increasing but still relatively poor record of giving in the annual Red Feather Campaign—the Japanese version of the Community Chest—reflects the slowly changing attitudes. Funds channeled through religious groups or philanthropic foundations are still relatively insignificant.

Japanese women have long been intrigued by the nature and extent of voluntary community efforts and with the large-scale U.S. participation by young and old, by well-to-do, and by people of average income. U.S. visitors have been questioned about hospital volunteering, social service, church-sponsored endeavors with the blind or aging, or youth-support activities. Weather beaten farm women with hands red-roughened and arthritic from hard labors in the northern cold of the Tōhoku, kneeling crowded on tatami mats; earnest-faced regional educators and club leaders gathered around the edges of a U-shaped conference table; dignified, elegant kimonoed "top ladies," as the wives of prominent businessmen and officials are called, gathered for afternoon coffee in a

U.S. diplomat's home have all been equally curious about the what, how, and why of U.S. volunteer civic programs. Upon hearing the answers to their questions, they would nod their heads knowingly, often ascribing the humanitarian drive to the virtues of Christianity. Others, who knew more about U.S. history, cited the motivation of frontier life, which demanded that everyone cooperate or perish.

During the 1960s, as in scattered instances earlier, women were frequently willing to follow a locally resident foreign woman who showed the way in community projects and thus freed them from making decisions or overtures. Her presence imbued the hours spent in planning and volunteering with the sophistication of international friendship, and some English-language practice, along with goodwill. A hospital library and visitation program in Nagoya, an orphanage project in Nagasaki, a foundling home in Shizuoka, and charity fund-raising and child adoption services in Tōkyō exemplify such pioneer experiments to improve community conditions through volunteering.

After a lecture-discussion meeting in Fukuoka in 1966 with former U.S. ambassador to the United Nations Marietta Tree, who talked about her own work in hospital welfare, civil rights, and politics, a young matron who earned money by teaching English to pay for her babysitter wrote:

> Being a busy housewife and a mother of three young children, I need to make quite an effort and sacrifice to leave the young ones and the household chores with a helper. Today, I am greatly encouraged . . . that my colleagues share the same problem on the other side of the Pacific Ocean. . . . I came home all enlightened with firm determination to . . . do my small share in contributing to society.[48]

Underground Water

Fewer family obligations, more education, improved economic well-being, and ever-increasing contact with Western habits have gradually helped social consciousness combat feudalistic inwardness. In 1963, when the Japan Broadcasting Corporation surveyed how people spend their time, there was not even a category for voluntary community action endeavor. Ten years later another survey indicated that less than 1 percent of the women—mostly urban, higher-income, in the fifty-to-fifty-five age group—spent free time on social service and civic action, although this poll may have been biased on the low side. By 1976 the figure had jumped to 20 percent participation by women in public activities of which 11 percent were social-welfare-oriented—a quantum leap to be sure.[49]

More often than women admit, their activities in organizations include substantial volunteer, community support service, whatever it may be labeled in surveys. An observant social critic has called this the "underground water" of social progress in Japan. How else to designate serving as Family Court councillors, visiting old peoples' homes, assisting at day care centers, or working with children and youth to forestall juvenile delinquency—cheered on in one Wakayama town by the motto "A little word of love makes our world like heaven above."

Determined women have set the pace of change. One Ōsaka leader felt that "nothing was ever born from the chatter by the well" and that for her volunteer service filled "the gap between the individual and society." It was the program of Makino Fusako, an Ōsaka gynecologist of the middle generation, that lured this Ōsaka woman from the well. After a trip to the United States in 1959 to study voluteerism as a guest of the Department of State Exchange Program, Dr. Makino worked for similar activities in Japan. As both physician and housewife, she believed she was a good bridge between hospitals and lay volunteers. Her program aimed at training women in nursing techniques, assisting short-handed hospital staff, and bringing women out to learn the "spirit of mutual help." Dr. Makino urged, "Japanese women need to learn that 'another's child is also my child.'"

At first medical colleagues and women's organizations dragged their feet. It was too soon. "We have to wait for the time when we can, like the Americans, lock the door behind us and just go out where we need to in our own cars." In 1962 two young hairdressers offered to do the hair of hospitalized children and so became her first volunteers. Excuses of others eroded. Dr. Makino's patience and persuasion got her first program started at the Yodogawa Christian Hospital in Ōsaka. As other hospitals followed, she slowly linked up twenty-six hospital volunteer groups in scattered areas of the Kansai, Nagoya, Yokohama, Niigata, and Tōkyō. Wearing white-and-blue-checked uniforms with a special badge, the Yodogawa housewives, volunteering about three hours a week, made beds, delivered meals, read books to children, and rolled bandages. Girl Scouts and students did their part on weekends. They assisted a traveling library, a Red Cross Nursery, and blood drives.

By the early 1970s, Dr. Makino's volunteers numbered about 1,000, a proud operation that had overcome both practical and cultural resistance to volunteer "meddling." In recognition, the Japan Women Doctors Association in 1970 awarded her the first esteemed Yoshioka Yayoi Prize, named for the indomitable Meiji physician and educator. She forthwith donated the ¥300,000 prize money to support communication among the many groups she had nurtured into life.[50]

Members of the Women's Association of Asahi-mura in Niigata Prefecture entertain the elderly in an afternoon of folkdance and other activities. Photo courtesy of Niigata Prefecture Social Education Program.

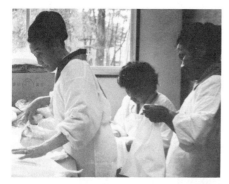

Women sew in volunteer service for the old people's home in Akita. Photo courtesy of Karen Marston.

Outdoor playtime at the orphanage in Shizuoka, supported by volunteer help and funds raised through the leadership of a long-time Western resident, Mrs. Duncan MacKenzie, and Japanese women active in community work. Photo courtesy of the author.

Government Stimulation

Important to the future of community participation is the social education program of the Ministry of Education. Building slowly since 1960, it has indoctrinated and helped train selected educators and organization leaders through annual overseas observation trips to the United States, Europe, and elsewhere in Asia. In 1970 the Social Education Council endorsed the nationwide implementation of the program to enlist "women volunteers who will work to build up a sense of solidarity within their respective communities" and thereby overcome the disturbing phenomenon of "human alienation."

Ten pilot projects were undertaken. Each approached the volunteer concept from a different angle. Fukushima Prefecture, for instance, included attention to welfare of the aged, Tochigi Prefecture to youth and cultural facilities, Niigata Prefecture to training and administration. Aichi Prefecture's program in Nagoya expanded the already pioneered hospital program. Its development was apparent. The nursing matron welcomed them, hoping they would "appreciate the pleasure of social service." The volunteers found that they were learning and stretching their minds. Said one, "My experiences have made me think of the whole present complicated medical system." As hoped, they, like their volunteering sisters elsewhere, were gaining new perspectives and looking beyond their immediate efforts to the broader social problems of modern Japan.

The Prime Minister's Office and the Ministry of Welfare, among other official agencies, also encouraged the concept and stimulated "Volunteer Corners" and "activities based on goodwill." With the nod of governmental approval, traditional attitudes about "meddling" crumbled more swiftly. Volunteerism has increasingly proved to be an acceptable way of spending leisure time—and, simultaneously, of taking part in nonpolitical, democratic activism.

The Organization Woman

Organizations serve as the principal conduit for the "underground water" activities of Japanese women and as the institutional channel for their public affairs activities.

Group action has a long history in Japan, going back before Meiji into Confucian-inspired collective responsibility, *daimyō* loyalty patterns, the "five-man-unit system" (*gonin-gumi*) of local government, and the young men's and young women's village associations that organized social life and marriage arrangements and maintained their code of ethics. The first modern special-purpose organization with Western ties, it will be recalled, was the Women's Christian Temperance Union founded in 1886. In 1915 Tsuda Umeko estimated that there were 2,000 women's organizations devoted primarily to charity, self-education, and socializing.[51] The heyday of the women's movement in the 1920s brought new experiments with activities before the totalitarianized war years mobilized all women under one huge organizational banner. After World War II, many women, left to their own initiative, felt any organized life after the regimented war years was too much; they wanted to be left alone. Nonetheless, many organizations that are now prominent began to take shape. By 1978 the number of women's organizations had multiplied to almost 37,000. About one-quarter of the eligible women voters were members of one or more women's organizations, cutting widely across the social fabric of Japanese society.[52]

Organizations of national scope are relatively few, probably between fifty and seventy-five. The largest is the National Federation of Regional Women's Organizations (Zenkoku chiiki fujin dantai rengo kyōgikai), generally known by its abbreviated name of Chifuren. In 1979 it alone had more than 6.5 million members and accounted for some 60 percent of all women in organizations.

Chifuren is significant not only because of its size but also because it is thoroughly Japanese in spirit and organization. The only U.S. organization with which it is at all comparable is the loose-knit General Federation of Women's Clubs. Chifuren became a national organization when women's regional and neighborhood groups were gathered under this umbrella in 1952. "Since olden times women's groups were attached to local places because they did not have any big issue or big objective," explained Chifuren's devoted president, Yamataka Shigeri, a pioneering newspaperwoman and suffragist. After Occupation authorities broke up the wartime national organizations, new community groups arose for adult education and training. Often the same former "top ladies" of the community once more came to the fore. Japanese, when asked by SCAP officials for recommendations for organizing leaders, knew only such people to name. As a result, Chifuren is still associated with the mainstream conservative political groups and, through subsidies for its programs and women's halls, with the government at all levels, particularly the Ministry of Education.

Nevertheless, Chifuren pursues its own interests, which are broad. It covers the "whole domain of living," from the status of women to world peace. Given this latitude, the women, as Fukuoka Prefecture Chifuren President Uchino Umeko explained, are "in a free position" to take up any problem that locally, prefecturally, or nationally is deemed most in need of attention.

Over the years, the Chifuren movement has cooperated with other organizations or pushed campaigns on its own against prostitution, sensational magazines, stimulant drugs, and atomic bomb testing and for clean election procedures, consumerism, and the return of Okinawa and the Northern Islands. Its community power varies prefecture by prefecture, but its interest is appreciated by electioneering politicians in need of support and votes. Members of its own local, prefectural, and national leadership have often served in elective offices and in the Diet.

Chifuren is usually the central force in building, maintaining, and using the women's halls (*fujin kaikan*) located in every prefecture. Their facilities, varying from spartan to luxurious depending on the age of the building, offer dormitory accommodations for visitors and conference-goers; meals; Shintō wedding rooms and associated photography studios, bridal outfit rentals, dressing rooms, and hairdressing assistance for the complicated traditional hairstyles (usually wigs nowadays) to reduce wedding costs; classrooms for cooking, tea ceremony, flower arranging, doll-making, lectures, and discussion studies; conference rooms and auditorium space; and, increasingly, testing laboratories and displays for consumer programs. These clubhouse-like halls exemplify the physical emergence of women from their homes into the community and serve as a base of operations for their diverse activities. Whether this format will appeal to a younger generation of more liberated women may determine the future of Chifuren itself.

In addition to this huge regionally organized federation, there are a variety of special-purpose national organizations, ranging from the University Women, the Widow's Association, and housewives concerned with consumer issues to groups that affiliate by professions and business. These smaller national associations average well under 10,000 members and mostly under 5,000; the chapters are usually in urban centers. Some with Western heritage or affiliation provide a focus for organizational international-mindedness. On the prefectural and local levels, unaffiliated women's groups proliferate, sometimes with a focus on common professional, educational, social, or community interests.

Major male organizations, such as the organized fishermen, labor unions, Rotary, the Lions, and the political parties, often have women's auxiliary sections. That of the Agricultural Cooperatives is second in size only to Chifuren; it has a membership of about 3 million. It concentrates on modernization of agricultural methods, business procedures, and the practical matters of being a farming woman at a time when responsibility falls more and more directly on her shoulders. There are also mixed-membership groups, especially those ad hoc citizen action or *shimin undō* groups established to take care of a special problem.

The Parent-Teachers Association, which includes both men and women, is fundamental in the grassroots life of Japan. It is almost compulsory for both parents and teachers to join; mothers feel particular pressure to support its activities lest they be regarded as less than properly solicitous about the education of their children. In consequence, almost 40 percent of women belonging to any organization are members of the PTA.

The PTA was started during the Occupation to help democratize education, adding new purposes to a less popular prewar school-related parent organization. With the early postwar emphasis on rebuilding the physical needs of schools, the new PTA slowly became a financing adjunct to public funding for schooling needs, an aspect that grew to controversial proportions.

From its beginning, the PTA provided young mothers with an incomparable training ground for performing as alert citizens. In the 1950s and 1960s, young housewives under PTA aegis petitioned democratically on issues like prostitution and even turned to activist lobbying of various kinds. In recent years, many units of the PTA have espoused other causes unrelated to school issues. Some have become feminist consciousness-raising groups probing contemporary equal rights and philosophies similar to that of the United Nations Decade for Women and Development. An integral element of local life, the PTA can be the adult school, social center, or neighborhood improvement rallying-point for the mothers whose children bind them to it.[53]

Long-established organizations often do not attract younger women. Instead, the latter set up their own organizations or remain aloof, enjoying personal hobbies. If in the work force, they take part in activities sponsored by companies and trade unions. They find that their modern education and interests make them socially incompatible with organization women over fifty years of age, who may act too domineering. New feminist groups, such as the alumnae association of Tōkyō University, illustrate the younger approach. Alert leaders of older organizations, such as the YWCA and the League of Women Voters, as well as the very knowledgeable social education officials, recognize the generation gap. They appreciate that "because the world is moving," as one said, organizations must make necessary transitions to entice young members. The alternative is a moribund organization with an aged membership. This generational challenge is worldwide, not Japanese alone.

Foibles of Cooperation

Japanese like to come together and do things as a group. Gregariousness protects each person with a multiple, faceless front. The postwar democratic emphasis on the individual has not erased, even in the younger generation, the security of happy assemblage. The binding tie can be as trivial as sporting a distinctively colored cap or blazer for a group climbing Mount Fuji during the summer holidays or as devastating as the undeviating cohesiveness demanded of members of the extremist radical student groups.

One well-educated young matron, returning to Japan in the late 1960s after living abroad with her husband, an executive for an international trading company, decided not to reinvolve herself actively in any organization. She knew that if she did the resulting relationships would tend to dictate her circle of friends, use of spare time, and mode of activities. For women faced with this dilemma, an ardent exponent of the democratic process, Sakanishi Shio, advised that individual development and group cooperation are not mutually exclusive. The individual must maintain her own judgment in a group, she counseled, and not lose her identity or fail to question or understand her own role by blindly accepting the instructions of her leaders.[54]

Such advice can be very difficult to put into practice in Japan. Insistence on consensus prevents acknowledgment of minority opinion. A thought-provoking member may seem too individualistic for the harmony of the group. Others are likely to criticize her as "egoistic." Jealousies may be inflamed; schism may result. This kind of interplay helps explain the fragmenting of groups seen in the peace and consumers' movements and among feminists. It is a basic reason also for the innumerable, usually rather small, one-of-a-kind groups in which satellite members hover around an energetic central leader, her dicta, and the program she devises as the best to speed a solution to the problem that motivated this leader and her group in the first place. Before the war, the leadership of Hiratsuka Raichō exemplified this individual-centered group process. Similarly, many a postwar woman depends upon her supporters and the loyal members of her organization to march as one with her to attain civic goals and, sometimes, political office.

Given such propensities, ongoing intergroup cooperation has frequently been a chancy business. A YWCA report prepared in 1938 noted that women's organizations work as if they are "in shells." They concentrate "so hard on their own problems that they do not see the others or fail to touch the more fundamental or underlying problems."[55]

Social critic Sakanishi Shio and the author discuss issues of democratic action and community affairs highlighted at the Kyūshū-Yamaguchi International Women's Conference on Community Affairs, May 18–19, 1964 (photo of conference in the background), for the Women's News program of RKB television in Fukuoka. Photo courtesy of USIS/Japan.

Late in the Occupation era, the Women's and Minors' Bureau, equally aware of this problem, promoted concepts of cooperation in civic action as the theme for its national Women's Week. A visiting U.S. specialist on organizational affairs agreed that cooperation was greatly needed but found the women's reactions rather baffling. Many were reluctant to cooperate, individually or by groups. They explained that during the war they had been regimented to work together, and for them cooperation held disquieting memories. By contrast, the visitor found, other women seized on blind cooperation on simplistic platitudes, no matter how or with whom. An ebullient Kansai-area president, intelligent and influential, purportedly declared that "all women of all kinds should work together regardless of which country they come from. As long as they work for the betterment of women and children—and let the men bother about politics—what did it matter!" Communist agitation at that time was grave, and the American was disturbed, in large measure because the mood to cooperate seemed just as euphoric as the reasons for not cooperating seemed childish. Emotion rather than logic shaped the decisions.[56]

Since then, Japanese women have gradually matured in their appreciation of organizational cooperation. They have learned that without united strength the spearhead of reform is blunted; the crusades they espouse suffer.

During the 1960s one could visit anywhere in Japan and find that most local organizations were agitated about the same few social problems: the impact on children of television, especially its portrayal of violence; the causes and cures of juvenile delinquency; the application of democratic principles in home situations; and the problems of the working mother. Despite identical worries, they were either unaware that other groups were similarly concerned or uncertain about how to rally to cooperate. It took an outstanding leader, someone greatly admired or recognized as superior, to coax them from their "shells" into combined effort. The unparalleled Ichikawa Fusae, for instance, could do this on a national level when forming in 1957 the National Committee for United Nations Non-Governmental Organizations of Women, composed of eight major national women's organizations.[57] It took the Tsuda College–educated, humanitarian Tokunaga Kikuko to crystallize the Black Feather miners' relief program in Kyūshū in 1959 and 1960. Sometimes the impartiality of a foreign expert, such as those brought in under the sponsorship of an American Cultural Center, could encourage cooperation on studies of obviously mutual interest: environmental issues, international friendship, or lifelong education.

Leadership

Leadership is a complex matter in Japanese society, much written about in sociological and anthropological studies. As noted, the societal dynamics of the culture rarely produce towering national leaders—male or female—whose individual charisma sways historic events and major trends. Society moves forward through a series of accommodations by ordinary people to consensus-determined stimuli and pressures from fairly well-calculated domestic policies. International events, as a result, may come with surprise or even as "shocks," as with some of President Nixon's economic or geopolitical policy moves.

Normally in women's organizations, the titular leader possesses certain ideal characteristics that endow her with the necessary image of respectability and responsibility and bestow upon her the mantle of authority by which she negotiates agreement among subleaders. There are four essential traits. First, the proper age, usually at least forty for prefectural or national organizations. Second, prominence, either held

Hirose Katsuyo, president of Hyōgo Prefecture Chifuren, views parading local officers at festivities celebrating their organization's twentieth anniversary in Kōbe, June 5, 1965. Photo courtesy of USIS/Japan.

by reason of family heritage, explained at times as the benefits of "parental prestige lighting the child's way with seven lights" (*Oya no hikari wa nana hikari*), or acquired through writing, television appearances, or mass media attention. As one critic, herself in constant demand, said, "There is the mistaken notion that anyone who has become well-known enough within society must be a good leader"[58]—meaning, in fact, must have influence. Third, good education, which quickly limits the choice of potential leaders among the older women who had been educated before the war. Fourth, married rather than single—although single women with very great ability are much in demand.

Practicing physician Kawanobe Shizu of Shizuoka, long-time leader in women's activities and social welfare projects in her prefecture and former Diet member, stressed that a president must be healthy and well-to-do. Organizational jobs are not salaried, and her family must provide her with whatever financial support is needed. Her tasks can keep her running to meetings, planning, and consulting many more hours per week than those put in by the average job-holder. In fulfilling her presidential role, Kawanobe advocated that a woman "should listen to and understand the other officers and members, efface herself, yet still give the last decision." For such decisions, Uchino Umeko of Fukuoka would add, the leader "must have good judgment about what is worth doing on behalf of all the members."[59]

This array of requirements can produce an acceptable leader who is neither a dynamic personality nor a good administrator. Her leadership is personal. Nevertheless, she gives stability to her group; it will not function in her absence.

Such a unifying personality is well illustrated in the pageantry of the field day scheduled for many years during the annual conference of Hyōgo Prefecture's Chifuren, of necessity held in Kōbe's large baseball stadium. Ten thousand local Chifuren presidents, wearing dark purple kimonos to represent the oneness of the group, each tied with a different yellow *obi* chosen by the wearer to represent democratic diversity, paraded before the grandstand filled with celebrities and honored guests and the reviewing patrician figure of their prefectural president, Hirose Katsuyo, who had been decorated by the Emperor. She gave focus to the huge membership and their programs.

Once elected, a leader often continues in her position for many years. Exceptions are organizations, such as Pilots and the Society of Japanese Women in Radio and Television, in which women of all ages with Western higher education or experience have rotating elected officers. One advantage of continuity is that all the other organizations get accustomed to this representative leader. Consensus on interorganizational matters is achieved more easily among groups with long-term leaders. Quickly rotating leaders disturb the balance of rapport and require the reshuffling and establishing of new personal relationships each time a change is made.

Furthermore, continuity helps dispel any unease between men and women that can arise when leaders must consult and sit together on joint committees. Men find rational exchange with women on levels of equality awkward. Women leaders who successfully cross the bridge and are well received by men are recognized by women and men alike as the best qualified. Newcomers are only disconcerting. One perennial woman leader, a Meiji modernist, merely laughed when asked about her adroit relaxed ability to work with men, replying, "Oh, I have many boyfriends, and I have good techniques to make men understand by showing them the work which women can do best."

One result of these leadership patterns is to preclude the flexibility that women might otherwise achieve. Their democratic choices reflect the larger needs of good relations with the government, mass media, and community organizations, all male dominated. Another result is that a successful leader may find herself the president of many organizations, sitting on innumerable joint organizational committees, and occasionally, a member of an elective popular assembly as well. The indefatigable Kawanobe has been an example of just such a woman.

These practices equally complicate opportunities of younger women to assume leading roles. The middle generation has, by and large, been skipped over because of the increased longevity of the older group and the exigencies of implementing the postwar changes, which absorbed much of their energies. Strong leadership seems inevitably to fall now to the younger women. The organizations in which they congregate, such as the PTA and the Red Cross, have provided them with experience at an early age, and in their own new special organizations they are turning to different procedures to find and support their leaders. Meantime, older leaders continue in office in most organizations with some of the strong "personal" leaders training younger women as their aides and successors. Nonetheless, the accession to leadership power, according to Kamiya Mieko, is often "left as a matter of chance as it were."

Platitudes or Issues

For nearly a century, Japanese women characteristically joined organizations for two reasons: first, to be a sociable part of the group, usually the local women's association; and second, to follow a hierarchical or status-giving leader, whether it be the empress for high-born ladies or for the lesser born, the mayor's wife or a revered teacher. In neither instance was the solution of particular issues the compelling motive.

In the postwar years, when women were bringing new organizations into being, they naturally wrote noncontroversial statements of purpose for their groups that reflected their current interests. Even organizations of widely diverse political coloring, size, and power shared the aims of improving women's status, providing more adult education, protecting and giving happiness to children, and promoting world peace. As program lines of organizations were developed with only the broadest of purposes, members were left to select their own emphases. Said Chifuren's Yamataka, "At first we did not have definite objectives, we just got together. Anything and everything is connected with the daily life of housewives."[60]

Their first concern was for the woman as wife and mother in the family; their second, for her concomitant obligations. Adult education agencies, like NHK and the Social Education Program of the Ministry of Education, were supportive. Older women identified with such a good traditional focus. The midway generation, for example, could not be stopped by old-fashioned mothers-in-law from going to the PTA, to the Life Improvement Sections (Japan's home extension program), or to the neighborhood women's groups for such purposes. Discussion of family subjects did not require difficult conceptualization beyond what their education had made feasible. More education was required before they could cope with analysis of more complex issues like political and international affairs.

For instance, in 1955, when 2,000 women from all over Japan gathered at the First National Congress of Mothers, in a therapeutic release of their feelings they discussed such issues as mothers-in-law, children with incurable diseases, and family sadnesses over the wartime death of husbands and fathers. They were responding to the founding slogan, "Mothers who give birth to new life wish to have life protected." That conference became known as the "Congress of Tears." The members were caught up in passions of sentiment that propagandists have found advantageous when using such emotionally enveloped situations and organizations for ideological ends. The motto "If mothers change, society will change," which was repeated faithfully by an officer of the congress for many years, undoubtedly has deep meaning.[61] Rarely, however, does such a motto produce concrete results that influence policy.

Proceeding at this family level of concern, organizations and their members drifted in the 1950s and 1960s through seasons of study classes and vaguely relevant activities. Egami Fuji, of NHK fame, having witnessed her country proceed blindfolded with only official news and information provided by the wartime government, declared that they were enjoying "the right to know," the cherished prerogative of democracy.[62] Further, they were "talking up" in discussions in their local groups where they felt secure, and sometimes outside as well. This new "virtue," according to U.S.-trained political scientist Kubota Kinuko, was a U.S. contribution to Japanese grassroots society. Tsuda College President Fujita Taki, reminiscing about the progress of women, affirmed with pleasure, "Now at least they are *all* talking, which they never did in the past."

In the earlier stages, also, women limited themselves to action by indirection. They drafted resolutions that noted situations needing correction and then simply referred implementation to local or prefectural governments or the appropriate national ministry. They were adhering to the old traditional wisdom that recommends, "Rely on a big tree" (*Yoraba taiji no kage*). Typically, the All-Hokkaidō Chifuren Conference in the mid-1960s, attended by some 2,000 housewives in subdued-colored kimonos who conferred just as earnestly in the big school complex as if they were still in school themselves, "took action" in this way on more than twenty items covering many of the economic and social aspects of life. They were complaining to government rather than lobbying for proposed solutions.

Such tactics, perforce, kept women in their shell-secluded impotence, outside the mainstream of public affairs, and isolated from the hard-hitting power structure. Authority could receive them with due courtesy, commend their conscientious interest, and send them back to their discussions. At election times the cordiality of relationships would be refreshed.

Women additionally hampered their activities by their cautiousness about money and budgets—a housewifely virtue. Dues assessments were usually a mere pittance, a fact repeatedly cited with pride by prefectural and local presidents. Substantial projects could not be undertaken unless subsidized by government or some impersonal institution or industry. Custom decreed that women who devoted time to projects, either as organization members or as outside volunteers, must be given an *obentō* box lunch and thanked with small gifts and their efforts courteously acknowledged with small sums to pay bus fare. Such genteel customs use up budgets and curtail activities. Raising money for activities presented more a psychological and cultural problem than a true lack of resources.

Bit by bit, however, as the 1960s unrolled, women began to take action on small, specific, practical problems: a children's recreation program in the precincts of a Buddhist temple in Northern Kyūshū to combat juvenile delinquency; a survey of the needs of old people in Niigata to try to ease their cares; a commodity-testing program in Sapporo to assist disgruntled housewives; a weights-and-measures check among fish dealers in local Tōkyō wards to protect the consumer. Each successful foray gave courage for another. Issues such as prostitution reform in 1956, widowed mother and child welfare in 1964, and consumer protection in 1968 became dominant enough that the national leadership could excite women to the necessary cooperation and support to push legislation through the Diet.

As Mishima Sumie has pointed out, women were getting to know more about Japan's day-in, day-out social problems and standard-of-living economics than most men.[63] In dealing with contemporary issues, not platitudes, they applied with increasing confidence the techniques of citizen action they had been testing from the earliest PTA days. Armed with righteousness as mothers and secure in their understanding of family welfare, they confronted awesome authority figures in government or public life and demanded attention. When necessary, they reinforced less dramatic petitioning with placard-carrying demonstrations.

The success story of many *shimin undō* and consumerism movements since the late 1960s give testimony to women's ability to use what they view as women's natural interests to penetrate the sanctums of establishment policy decision. After more than thirty years of democracy, the halo of motherhood still gives them great confidence, more perhaps than their basic political rights as citizens, but their civic effectiveness improves as they tie the two together.

Tokunaga Kikuko has visualized women in community, volunteer, and public affairs activities to be in three concentric circles, each resting on the solidness of the inner layer. First, and at the core, is the individual and her education and training. Then, she continued, "their own personal situation in society" gives them social awareness and contact with community affairs. Finally, expressing her hopes for the future, "I'll try to get them to open their eyes to the outside world." Too many, she feared, are still in the first two stages.[64]

CHAPTER 4
ECONOMIC ENTERPRISE

WOMEN AS PRODUCERS—
"OFFICE FLOWERS" AND FIGHTING LITIGANTS

> *In the past, women workers were regarded as "flowers" in the office and such miscellaneous work as serving tea was allotted to them. I would like to believe that such a feudalistic way of thinking no longer exists in our offices. Although we are physically weaker than men workers, we work together with them on equal standards, struggling in the severe realities of society.*
>
> —Twenty-three-year-old office worker,
> Tōkyō, 1965[1]

Japanese women workers are the unacknowledged heroines of their country's dynamic pursuit of economic and industrial growth and its spectacular advance into foreign markets.

Before and since the war, their facile hands have shaped the manifold products of the assembly line and loom. Exploitation of women in a time-honored labor system, imbedded in social attitudes as well as economic planning, has buttressed the competitive capacity of Japan's export trade.

The Economic Miracle

By way of background, it is useful to consider a few facts and the implications of what world-renowned economists have variously called "Japan's economic miracle," "*le defi japonaise*," and even the "Japanese century." In the short span of one generation, Japan changed from a poor nation, shattered by a disastrous war, into the world's third-largest national economy. A combination of fortuitous external circumstances plus dogged hard work made it possible. The needs of the Korean War stimulated Japan's economy with demands for production that was then supported by massive foreign loan capital. The ill fortune of its neighbor gave impetus to Japan's literal rise from the ashes. During the 1950s and 1960s, building on the inflow of technology incorporating the newest industrial and scientific know-how, the emphasis of production changed from labor-intensive light industry to high-technology, capital-intensive industry. This shift brought results. Never before in world history has a major economy achieved such a substantial growth—a doubling of gross national product (GNP) every four or five years, reaching a GNP level exceeded in the early 1980s only by the United States and comparable to that of the Soviet Union.

A number of factors in domestic life account for Japan's great economic accomplishments. One is the nature of its work force, male and female. Universal literacy established the solid core of competency needed for the highly technical industrial scene. Their work ethic considers long workdays routine and permits only a few days off per month. Vacation time is seldom fully used.[2]

A second factor is the relatively strong control the Japanese have over national finances. Throughout the 1960s Japan invested more than 30 percent of its GNP in private new fixed capital. The Japanese personal savings rate reflects strong motivation for family-arranged security and is the highest in the world. In turn, these funds are channeled by banks, with Finance Ministry "window guidance," into new high-technology industrial plants.

Third, nonproductive employment in Japan was kept much lower in the 1960s and 1970s than in the United States, Italy, and France. Although this phenomenon is related to the system of life-long job security for men—the paternalistic parent-child (oya-bun/ko-bun) tradition—the chief worry of production planners for most of this period was an inadequate labor supply.

Fourth, industrial labor unions, because of nonmobility of employment, are closely woven into company affairs. Many union representatives, for instance, are "promoted" to become company executives. Workers rarely actually stop working during their "strikes." To damage the company's profitability would destroy their own future livelihood.

Fifth, national taxes in Japan drain off less of the national income than in the United States and the United Kingdom, thereby leaving more money available for investment in productivity. Also, defense and welfare do not dominate Japan's national budget.

Finally, there is the national sense of dedication, shared equally by business, government, and labor, that all must cooperate to raise Japan,

Young women work on television assembly lines at the Ibaragi plant of Matsushita Electric Industrial Company. Photo courtesy of the Embassy of Japan.

its institutions, and its people to its international place in the sun. The oft-sung song of the workers of Matsushita, the largest electronics conglomerate in Japan, illustrates this purposeful zeal:

> For the building of a new Japan,
> Let's put our strength and mind together,
> Doing our best to promote production,
> Sending our goods to the people of the world.
> Endlessly and continuously,
> Like water gushing from a fountain.
> Grow, industry, grow, grow, grow!
> Harmony and Sincerity!

This spirit, more than any other of the elements of economic growth, gives rise to the phrase "Japan Incorporated," which evokes envy, despair, or pride, depending on the viewpoint. Working women are part and parcel of this achievement.

Textile workers in the 1970s in their *tatami*-matted dormitory room at the Anjo
Mill of the Kurashiki Spinning Company use their leisure hours to write letters
and lay out kimono patterns. Photo courtesy of the Embassy of Japan.

Work Force Trends

Ever since the symbolic samurai daughters graced the opening years
of Japan's first textile mill in Tomioka, young women have gone forth
from their homes in numbers sufficient to keep the factories humming
and, somewhat later, the offices staffed with clerks.

Until the mid-1960s, the role of the woman in the work force was
taken for granted, and this role traditionally excluded her from the
rights and benefits of the regular employee track. Occupation-era reforms
had expanded the perimeters of opportunity, but she was still taken
for granted. New laws detailed legal rights theoretically equalizing her
work horizons with male workers of comparable education and ability.
Nonetheless, all assumed that large numbers of junior high school girls
would follow the classic work force role: They would inevitably graduate
into the low-labor-cost, high-productivity jobs of Japanese industry,
work a few years, and then retire early for marriage, making way for
a new crop of low-salaried beginning workers. The seemingly sudden
dearth of this supply in the late 1960s provoked surprised consternation.

Farm women of Sanjo City, Niigata Prefecture, study the making and use of compost to improve farming as part of their social education programs, 1966. Photo courtesy of Niigata Prefecture Social Education Program.

A labor emergency loomed. Momentarily, it even prompted proposals for increasing the birthrate to fill the gap, including one such statement—one never repeated—by then Prime Minister Satō!

Government statistics should have forewarned any who took time to study them. Since the late 1950s it had been obvious that the changing life-style of Japanese women would cause a reduced flow of young women into the labor arena. These trends followed, but with a ten-to-fifteen-year lag, the patterns of U.S. women in the work force. Japanese planners should have forecast that just as many women—or even more—would be available but in different age groups and, therefore, with different fringe benefit requirements.

What are the trends in women's changing relation to the work force?

Employed women for decades have constituted about 50 percent of all women and almost 40 percent of the total labor force, many of them in family enterprises. The marked change is the increase in number of those working away from the home and family farm. There was a more than threefold growth from 1953 to 1980—from just over 4 million to 13.5 million paid women employees over the age of fifteen, with a rate of increase double that of men since 1975.

The percentage of women workers employed in family enterprises and farms dropped from 52 percent of the female labor force in 1955 to 22 percent in 1980, while the proportion employed by industry increased from 31 percent to 61 percent in the same period. The service industries, manufacturing, and trade absorbed 70 percent of these new employees. As recently as 1965 self-employed and family workers outnumbered those working for industry and government. With the great migration from farms to the cities, the decrease in agricultural employment has been the most abrupt. Women farm workers now outnumber men. The change has contributed to social and family crises in rural areas.

Changes in age, marital status, and length of service make up the second set of variants in the profile of the modern Japanese working woman. No longer is she inevitably young and unmarried and a short-term worker. The average age of women workers has risen from 23.8 years in 1949, to 29.8 years in 1970, to 34.9 in 1980. Mirroring the lowered birth rate and the surge of boys and girls toward more and more education, the numbers of junior and senior high school graduates seeking employment continue to fall. The percentage of girls of fifteen to nineteen years who work dropped from slightly more than 50 percent in 1955 to less than 20 percent in 1980. The drastic decline in the number of junior high graduates seeking employment prompted industries and the media to label them "golden eggs."

Banks, securities firms, and department stores particularly woo high school women. Slick pamphlets outline benefits. Allurements include a five-day workweek in banks, annual paid vacation of twenty days, provision for leisure-time activities such as skiing and classes in Zen, painting, and field archery. The Sanwa Bank proudly publicized the substantial number of marriages between its employees, for which solemn ceremony it built marriage halls in Tōkyō and Ōsaka. Sometimes even these inducements pale when daily routine loses out to the lure of trying something different. Some young women have turned to better-than-average salaries as electric welders in the shipyards of Kōbe and full-fledged crew members on the world's largest oil tankers. Said one of the first such sailors: "Being a bank clerk, I felt a bit confined and wanted to get out somewhere else." High school girls find themselves in a propitious labor situation—and well they know it.[3]

The median age of women workers has risen as the number of workers over thirty has increased despite the traditional opprobrious social classification of "old" worker. Women in this age group made up 10 percent of women workers in 1950 and 57 percent in 1975. Age distribution follows the "m-curve" seen in other advanced countries, with a so-called hill for the twenty-to-twenty-four-year-old group, slipping to a valley for those twenty-five to thirty-four years, and then a rising hill again at forty to early fifties.

With the increase in the average age of the woman worker has come both a lengthening of the term of service with one employer (3.2 years in 1950 to 6.2 years in 1979 compared with 10.8 for men), and a growing proportion of married women working outside the home. In 1952 only 8 percent of the employed, nonagricultural women were married. By 1979 the figure had skyrocketed to 67 percent, including those widowed or divorced.

Progress in technology and in productivity and the shortage of young workers are causing a third major change in workforce trends, i.e., the upward wage curve. Although the principle of equal pay for equal work was established in 1947, and Japan has ratified International Labour Organisation Convention No. 100 on equal remuneration, significant narrowing of the wage differential started only in 1958. Since then women's wages have risen faster than men's, but the gap is still considerable, with women's wages at 54 percent of men's. Lower wages are attributed to Japan's wage system, which is rigidly based on seniority, women's shorter service periods resulting from marriage and home affairs, and to women's lower status and less onerous duties at work. One may add that many women work in small factories and industries where wages are low and fringe benefits almost nonexistent. The differences will undoubtedly continue until women do indeed remain longer on the seniority wage ladder and until bias against women in responsible positions in large business and industry relaxes. The same attitudinal problems receive attention in any international women's meeting where status and opportunity are items on the agenda.[4]

Viewed as a whole, these trends reveal socioeconomic cause and effect in operation: After women received their emancipation, they gradually sought more rights, better jobs and wages, and access to formerly closed careers. These aspirations were fed by the expanding economy, which created new labor demands and required capacity employment. Shortages of young women workers emerged in spot situations. Tōkyō newspapers in late 1964 carried headlines such as "Demands for Workers Here Rising by Leaps and Bounds." Simultaneously with rising standards of living, more and more families began sending their children, daughters as well as sons, to college, thus delaying their entry into the labor market. More education raised their job aspirations. Both factors created new problems for corporate recruiters.

Other social and economic changes generated still more breaks with the past:

1. Lower-paying industries, such as textiles, lost ground to higher-paying companies, such as transistor radio and television manufacturers, thereby upsetting the normal flow of labor and bidding up salaries.

2. Young women, whether married or not, were wanted longer in the work force, as evidenced by readjusted pension schemes. One typical textile company, popularly known as Kanebō, acted early to offer a pension for three years to women employees who worked for five years or more, a "reward for the strenuous efforts made for the building of a greater Kanebō." Family life-styles began to change to meet the needs of working wives and mothers.

3. Planners in the Ministry of Labor urged management to employ middle-aged and older people. Labor unions went along. By the early 1970s, the concept of compulsory retirement at sixty rather than fifty-five was broadly acknowledged, if not necessarily implemented, as a good policy for men. Women still contend with forced retirement at fifty or fifty-five, or even younger. The Economic Planning Agency's projection in 1969 that by 1975 as many as 60 percent of all workers would be women did not come to pass. However, the agency did pinpoint the shift toward greater dependence on the older woman, bringing closer age comparability with women workers in the United States. The classic portrait of the Japanese woman worker, a young girl, must be redrawn to include in its contemporary version a mature woman companion.

Blossoming Flowers

Appreciation by the Japanese economic machine of the productivity of the ubiquitous working woman in no way presupposes recognition of equal status. Even when recognized, inequities are excused in statements like "The age-old tradition-bound discrimination against women is not easy to eliminate. . . . It has to be a long process." Women's evaluation of their position often carries more emotional overtones.[5]

A feminist who had struggled for more than ten years to achieve professional recognition in television described in her 1973 autobiographical best-seller the contemporary limbo in which women are stranded between actual equality and attitudinal discrimination:

> We seldom hear the phrase, *onna no kuse ni* [being a mere woman]. On the contrary, men have delicate consideration for women, especially for single women, and sometimes even outright admiration. But, beware! It is still a grim reality in the office that men, while flattering women as *shokuba no hana* [a flower in the office] hinder those who want to work for life and selfishly plan to use women as tea servers and sub-workers.[6]

By 1976 another television professional had done more than write about her dissatisfaction. Thirty-nine year old Murakami Setsuko, of

Table 4.1. Paid Women Workers by Occupational Category,
1960-1980 (in millions)

Occupation Category	1960	1970	1980
Office	1.70	3.39	4.43
Skilled and manufacturing	2.40[a]	2.91	3.14
Professional and technical	0.60	1.00	1.76
Service	1.08	1.50	1.74
Sales	0.58	1.12	1.57
Laborers	-- [a]	0.66	0.54
Transport and communication	0.05	0.22	0.14
Managers and officials	0.02	0.05	0.11
Farmers, lumbering, and fishing	0.24	0.10	0.10
Total	6.67	10.96	13.53

Source: Adapted from Japan Institute of Labour, Japanese
Industrial Relations Series, The Problems of Working
Women (Tōkyō, 1981).

[a]Laborers in 1960 were included in the figure for skilled
and manufacturing.

Nippon Television, took her case to court and won when her boss tried to transfer her because "I was no longer pretty and too old to be an announcer. . . . It's the same in all the professions. Japanese men really believe women are inferior. . . . It's getting better, but the number of women willing to fight is still very small." Why, she asked, are not more women willing to fight?[7]

A look at the occupational distribution of paid women workers over the last twenty years offers evidence about why most women are not well located for upward mobility (see Table 4.1). Since 1960, women office workers have come to outrank women manufacturing workers, but these two categories continue to dominate. An encouraging note is the increasing proportion of Japanese women in professional and technical positions, a percentage rising more rapidly than that of men.

Interestingly, in recent years clerical jobs have come to be regarded as positions offering social status—even though they include the "tea girls" who serve the endless cups of tea needed to honor the stream of visitors. Not all take to this duty too happily, and feminist consciousness-raising discussions brought episodes of resistance throughout the 1970s. Prefectural women clerks in Yokohama in 1972 went on strike and refused to carry out this "degrading" service. Some years later feminists in the Tōkyō Metropolitan Sanitation Department protested, carrying placards demanding "equal work opportunities for women" and "down with tea-serving duties." The issue in this frustrating male-female tug-of-war was not simply tea, but women's capacity to do more meaningful work.[8]

Women office workers tend to receive lower wages than factory workers and, despite their gracious smiles and deferential bows, are often bored by their roles. However, clerical status enhances marriage-ability or, as young women may say, the opportunity to be "eternally employed." Young women will sometimes switch from high-paying blue-collar jobs to become "flowers" in an office. There, a better-educated, higher-status mate may be found, and the honored go-between at the wedding ceremony will be able to read out a more respectable dossier connecting the bride with an illustrious Japanese business or industry.

Management, even today, is too prone to regard women secretaries and clerical workers as ineffectual and essentially supplementary. This attitude is mirrored in the comment of the managing director of a big electric machinery manufacturing company that "office girls are just like matches: they are simply expendable."[9]

They may also be compared unfavorably by management with their Western counterparts, even though the office tasks in Japan are not comparable. In business meetings and related ceremonials executives need to be flanked by solicitous junior male subordinates, precluding any real handling of arrangements or note-taking by the female secretary. She is usually left with minimum substantive obligations. If a receptionist, she may simply wait for the next caller, sitting placidly behind a green baize-curtained screen, or if a clerk, at a desk marshaled with others in close rows to save space, as in a schoolroom, hand-copying routine messages or documents.

Bilingual secretaries in Japan have, however, proven essential and efficient to their employers in international and binational offices. They perform comparably to the best of Western secretaries and handle multicultural protocol as well. Such women are very well paid. After ten years' experience, their average monthly salary in the late 1970s was triple that of the average female employee and double that of the average male worker having equivalent seniority. One side effect for these efficient, affluent young women is that they frequently find themselves almost unmarriageable. They have learned at their offices a different approach to human relations and have savored an inde-pendence that breeds distaste for the subservience still expected by even a modern Japanese husband. Equally, they frighten off the suitable young Japanese male who is likely to be earning considerably less.

Successful Careerists

The expanding role of women in the professions is a direct offshoot of their new access to equal higher education in postwar Japan. Their progress illustrates their determination to use their brains and talents.

During the 1960s, college-educated women faced considerable job discrimination. For one thing, they were a "new species"—an unknown quantity. Their education warranted high starting salaries, for academic accomplishment is the established criterion in such matters. But because it was assumed that they would not work their entire adult lives and most probably would not wish to move from place to place in job progression—a normal process in Japan—the employer considered them expensive and a needless luxury. Business and industry invest money in college graduates during their first two years of service, when their time is heavily devoted to training and indoctrination; their productive performance begins to balance such costs only during the third year.

As the normal age of women graduating from college was twenty-two, three years' service was about all employers expected of them. High school graduates, starting at age eighteen and considered equally trainable, were cheaper. All females were pressured, if not forced, to retire at ages twenty-four to twenty-seven to prepare for marriage. If, on the other hand, college women worked too many years, they accumulated seniority and a commensurately higher annual salary, becoming with time costly labor once again. They were also criticized for being less "agreeable" (i.e. less subservient) than high school graduates. Finally, because most college women majored in the same limited fields, they competed heavily with each other for opportunities in prestigious corporations, mass media, education, and government, thus cheapening their own value.

When Japan Broadcasting Corporation, the powerful NHK, let it be known in 1962 that it would hire no more college-educated women, others followed suit. That year the Economic Planning Agency found that 48 percent of the almost 500 companies they surveyed refused to hire college-educated women, 30 percent employed them for specific jobs, and only 4 percent recruited them by the same standards as men.[10]

By 1971 the flood of college graduates, male and female, had produced a glut on the labor market.[11] By that year women had turned to journalism as their first choice in careers, to teaching as second, and then to exotic situations, such as airline and travel agencies, where everyday business deals with the glamour of international travel. Ten years later, government and public service had superseded journalism in first place.

Experienced and mature women with good educations who had persevered through the 1960s were, by the 1970s, more evident in government, public office, including the judicial system, and in technical professions. For such upward mobility, Katō Tomiko, a Tōkyō University graduate and professor of local government, believed that the basic requirements are (1) "to have a husband who can take care of himself and does not feel it inconvenient to live away from his wife, and (2) to have a supervisor who acknowledges a woman's capability and promotes her if she is capable."[12]

Male support is a recognized key to advancement for hardworking, able Japanese women who seek to rise into the upper echelons. Personnel and training specialist Kageyama Hiroko has estimated that male attitude accounts for 70 percent of a woman's chance at promotion.[13] Witness the appointment in 1971 of Tsuda College graduate Nuita Yoko as first woman bureau director in a local government—in this case the large and important Tōkyō Bureau of Social Welfare—by Governor Minobe Ryōkichi. A proponent of "government by the people" and astutely aware that his election successes had depended on the women's vote, Minobe selected a top-notch woman professional to exemplify his beliefs. Similarly, Takahashi Nobuko was appointed Japan's first woman ambassador (to Denmark) by Prime Minister Masayoshi Ohira in 1980 after he observed her experienced excellence during consultation with women leaders on budget questions.

For the long pull, nonetheless, success requires educated intelligence, continuing study, and hard work. Certainly Nuita and Takahashi have paid heed to these demands, and comparable efforts are everywhere apparent among achieving women. A rising professional woman in the Labor Ministry, who combined family, motherhood, and career, reported a nightly regime: After dinner and helping her child with schoolwork, she and her husband study, each in a different room, until 11:30 pm, when they get together for discussion of the ideas learned and the application of these ideas to their jobs. *Asahi* newspaper foreign correspondent Shimomura Mitsuko, of her envied roving assignment in the United States, simply commented, "I'm working my head off."[14]

The rags-to-riches story—albeit these were the postwar rags of a young woman nobly connected—of the competent chair of Nippo Advertising Agency, Saisho Yuriko, explained her ideas about the road to business success:

Sympathetic cooperation of the family members is most necessary. But then we have to work three times harder than ordinary women if we want to succeed. . . . three times harder mentally, and ten times harder physically. Once you start you cannot say I am a housewife, my baby

Young women police officers work in the Traffic Control Center of the Tōkyō Metropolitan Police Department. Photo courtesy of Japan Information Center, New York.

is crying for milk or my husband is waiting for me. Business is no play thing.

She organized her daily life in "five channels": (1) executive of Nippo Advertising Agency; (2) "cute" wife; (3) "good" mother; (4) housewife; and (5) "just" a lady. She advised women with ambition to become qualified by college and after-college training "as your husband may be killed any time in a traffic accident. Then where are you?" "Be internationally minded," she urged. Learn a second language, probably English. "Think of yourself in ten years' time."[15]

For many more average but educated young women, teaching is the route to professional fulfillment. Women teachers, courtesy of Teachers Union (Nikkyōsō) pressure, are likely to get equal pay with men teachers and continue to work after marriage. By 1970 women occupied one-half of the positions in elementary schools, about one-quarter of those in junior high schools, and almost 40 percent of those in junior colleges, but much lower proportions in senior high schools and four-year colleges and universities, a general ratio that prevailed though the 1970s. Women teachers' achievement of a majority in primary schools precipitated a stir throughout the land. Editorials announced that Japan had arrived at "the age of women teachers." "Education mamas" fretted that women teachers would not aggressively push their children through "examination hell" to get into prestigious institutions. Worries about teachers' marriages with absences for honeymoons (which rarely last more than three to five days) and pregnancies in the middle of the school year excited concern. Despite such worries, women teachers are doing a good job. Further, they are needed to fill the classrooms because men have been turning to more lucrative positions, although men in 1981 still held better than 98 percent of the jobs as elementary school principals and 99.8 percent of junior high and 97.5 percent of senior high principalships.[16]

Finally, it is interesting that job tedium has encouraged the adventurous into new occupations. The entrance of junior college women into the police force is a good illustration. Sakanishi Shio, the only woman member of the National Security Council, who specialized in the training of young police officers in the mid-1970s, reported twenty-seven women applicants to one acceptance. Many of the successful concentrate on juvenile and traffic problems and are intrigued by the human contact opportunities as a way to "build their personalities."[17]

Others who seek the unusual include those joining the Women's Army Corps (WACS) in the Self-Defense Forces and those entering metropolitan fire-fighting squads to educate and inspect for fire prevention. In achievements paralleling those of women in the West, women have given fine performances in the Japan Overseas Cooperation Volunteers (JOCV)—the Japanese version of the Peace Corps. They are entering the computer field, for which their reputed "patience" supposedly makes them most suitable.

On all fronts, when given the opportunity, women are demonstrating their capability and productivity. What they continue to need is more such opportunities.

Working Housewives

"Making a job and housework compatible is the biggest problem facing women workers in the next five to ten years." In her straightforward way, Maeda Sumiko, director of the Women's Department of Sōhyō's Zen-nittsu, Japan's Transportation Union, put her finger on the most traumatic contemporary facet of integrating women more fully into the work force, as Table 4.2 shows.[18]

Although from time immemorial married women and mothers have worked in family-owned shops and inns or labored in the patrimonial paddies and fishing operations, going out beyond these confines gives rise to conflicting emotions. Because of the Japanese emphasis on the

Table 4.2.   Percentage of Female Employees
            by Marital Status, 1955-1980

	1955	1960	1970	1980
Single	65.2	63.1	48.2	32.3
Married	20.4	24.4	41.4	57.6
Widowed and divorced	14.3	12.4	10.3	10.1

Source: 1955, 1960, 1970--Statistics Bureau, Office
of the Prime Minister, Population Census; 1980--Office
of the Prime Minister, Labour Force Survey.

precious child as the link to the future family line, the working mother who leaves her progeny in impersonal hands seems somewhat traitorous. Husbands, too, may complain that wives who go out to work do not do their housework as well as they should, even though the husbands welcome the money their wives earn. Business managers, even those favorable to the concept of working mothers, give way to exasperation when the employee leaves on schedule to perform her domestic functions, regardless of office needs.[19]

Wives and mothers are working because Japan needs them, not in a war emergency, but to fulfill the country's long-range goals in terms of its economy and its position in the world. Further, in 1982 more than 86 percent worked to bring in supplements essential to family finances or to make possible higher education for their children. A few work simply because of the challenge or to escape the dulling enclosures of the home—the last an explanation of why young farm wives may from time to time take jobs on road repair or other rough construction work so they can watch the outer world go by.[20]

In the early 1960s the Labor Ministry began to take notice of the growing phenomenon of working housewives; both officials and employers thought of it as temporary—an aberration in the normal labor supply.

Those actually working full-time may be classified by personnel offices as "temporary" workers. This classification denies women the lifetime security and pensions accorded permanent career male workers. Not only are their basic wages lower, but the classification deprives them of routine perquisites, ranging from housing assistance to annual seniority pay raises to semi-annual bonuses that total from four to six months' extra pay. One such "temporary" in a southwest Honshū bottling factory of a nationwide soft drink and beer company had worked fairly steadily for almost twenty years under such interim regulations. As a temporary worker she was, fortunately, not forced to retire by age thirty!

Professionally trained working mothers can find themselves equally disadvantaged. A Berkeley-educated Ph.D. had after eight years not escaped from her "part-time" appointment to International Christian University. She consoled herself that she was "much freer this way" and that her frustrations were less because she enjoyed a happily married life and motherhood. Subsequently, she moved ahead, achieving recognition internationally.

From the women's viewpoint, it is true that working only part of the time is preferable if they are both to fulfill their home duties and to provide supplementary income. But this system has presented both organizational and conceptual difficulties in Japan. Part-time may turn out to be "temporary," short-term, part-year, seasonal, permanent part-time, or cottage industry. The problem is twofold. First comes the practical difference between the Western job-oriented pay system and the Japanese pay system, which is based on age, education, and years of service. A mature worker who has once retired and then returns to the work force is an anomaly to personnel. Where does such a person fit into the hierarchy? The second hazard is the psychological loyalty between employer and employee implicit in the "womb to tomb" job system with its attitudes of disregard-the-clock-come-early-stay-late, which views any time measurement of work input as frivolous or unworthy. Even trade union officials are indifferent to the problems of part-time workers, as part-timers or "temporary" workers are not likely to join the union; they hardly qualify as true workers.

Illustrative of the antagonism directed in the late 1950s and early 1960s toward part-time arrangements was the situation of a group of nurses trained under the Fulbright Program at the university level in the United States for supervisory and highly specialized nursing positions. Most finally abandoned their careers, not because of lack of professional interest, but because hospitals, public health services, and the medical profession refused to permit them, after marriage and motherhood, any variation on the full work load and orthodox schedule that was considered mandatory. Requests for adjustments were turned down. Their special skills, moreover, were a challenge to the old-fashioned, less well-trained head nurses educated exclusively in Japan.

Japanese labor teams and women leaders visiting the United States during the 1960s found the part-time U.S. woman worker of mature years—one who had returned to the labor force—a subject of fascination. They were intrigued with her universality and sought practical data about her hours of work, salary, and efficiency. When they visited U.S. department stores, for example, and found older workers behind the counter, they were astounded; in Japan sales clerks are invariably young and newly out of school. So rare are the exceptions that an encounter with the Daiwa Department Store of Niigata City in 1967 was memorable. Its personnel office maintained an availability registry for women aged twenty-two to forty-eight and used such older women as part-time reserves. The scheme was the brainchild of the thoughtful woman training director, herself over thirty, who found older part-timers both trainable and reliable.

By 1968 there were 650,000 part-timers—two-thirds of them women—defined as those working less than a thirty-five-hour week. Only about half the companies granted them the status of "regular employees," opening to them the important bonuses and fringe benefits. Most had factory jobs or performed unskilled services, such as office cleaning. Many were making it possible for the medium-sized and small enterprises that subcontract to the major industries to cope with the much-publicized "labor bankruptcy," meaning the shortage of low-cost labor. By the beginning of the 1970s, 91 percent of the part-time workers in Tōkyō were women over twenty-five; more than 80 percent were married; and more than 70 percent had school-age children. By 1980 the national total was more than 2.5 million, a four and one-half times increase since 1960; these workers were preponderantly married. They represented almost one-fifth of all women workers. For Japan, women part-timers constitute a labor bargain in boom times and a convenience in times of economic downturn, when they can be laid off.

Public approval of working married women, mature and with children, will continue to grow. Mature married workers are steady and reliable, often more so than young unmarrieds. One patent law office in Tōkyō purposely recruits married personnel for that very reason. After all, if one of the daughters of the Emperor, albeit married to a bank executive, could take a part-time job as a fashion consultant in an exclusive Tōkyō hotel shopping arcade, others can follow with propriety into the double worlds of marriage and employment. Managing this mix harmoniously is the task given equally to employers, to government, and to the women and their families.

Children of Working Mothers

Effective utilization of the housewife and mother in the work force while providing freedom from worry about her children and family is not easy. Similar problems arise in all industrialized countries. Nurseries and child care centers, relatively new to Japanese society, are insufficient and not always well regarded as mother-substitutes. With the trend to nuclear families, grandparents are less and less available as babysitters.

In the 1960s, working mothers in nuclear families started giving their school-age children house keys so they could care for themselves at home after school until a parent returned from work. The house-key substitute for an adult guardian aroused major social anxieties and was blamed for juvenile delinquency and family disruptions. The issue of the *"kagi-ko,"* or the key children, increased social disapproval of mothers' going out of the home to work. It aroused women's organizations to promote more adequate, publicly serviced child care systems.

Inadequate day care facilities, along with growing inflation and the labor shortage, contributed to the revival of cottage industry. By late 1972 almost 2 million women—up 250 percent since 1965—mostly of mature years, did piecework in textiles, on television and automotive parts, ornaments and trinkets, and the like. The number had fallen by 1980 to 1.25 million; but this "home work," called *naishoku* to imply a kind of home sweatshop, continued to pay extremely badly. The women, usually unorganized and isolated despite a protective Cottage Labor Law, unknowingly hamper progress on minimum wage regulations.

Younger mothers also have been coming to grips with the child care problem in some less traditional ways, for many want to work and do not wish to be tied down. In big apartment complexes they sometimes organize informal day care cooperatives. They may also rouse community backing for their needs, moving the question out of the home and school and into the political arena.

To retain its women operators, the Japan Telegraph and Telephone Corporation very early found some answers for the problem of working mothers by adhering closely to the 1947 Labor Standards Law. It has since liberalized paid maternity leave before and after childbirth and provided for nursing periods during the working day. More recent legislation provides other options that are massively supported by workers themselves. The *ikuji kyūgyō,* or child-bearing-child-rearing leave, permits absence without pay from the job for a year or so, but with freedom to return without a decrease in salary. This alternative system, however, needs more employer support.[21]

One innovator in this tangle of motherhood and the labor market has been the relatively new, non-*zaibatsu* company, Sony. In its transistor plant in Atsugi, a suburb of Tōkyō, is found a personnel system designed to meet the needs of working mothers. The company's "philosophy of flexibility" and executive Kobayashi Shigeru's "I love people" attitude led to a personnel program beginning in the early 1960s that built on both these tenets. It begins to approach the lifetime employment practice normal for males.

In the traditional early phase, teenage girls are employed and live in a company dormitory. They are given the opportunity to complete high school and pursue some of the extra finishing touches of tea ceremony, flower arranging, and other Japanese arts that enhance marriageability. Many young workers then take their first retirement to become wives and mothers.

In a second phase, many of these same women return to the plant after a few years, usually in part-time jobs. Some 80 percent of the plant's workers are part-timers, with morning and afternoon shift workers paired off to insure efficient and conscientious operation at each work station. Sony overcomes the difficult commuting with special busing. Mothers may bring their two-to-six-year-olds right along to attend the day care center, located in pleasantly landscaped plant grounds. Worker fees cover approximately half the cost of the day care center, which follows the Montessori educational system. The well-trained and friendly director, known respectfully and fondly as Uchida-*sensei*—*sensei* being a term of address for a revered teacher—became herself an institution inspiring confidence. The result is that mothers work with an easy mind, suffering no worries about timing stops at a neighborhood day care center en route to and from work. Sony may not be promoting many women up the management ladder, but it is solving its own labor needs and those of mothers with small children who must work.[22]

Welfare Versus Opportunity

In July 1972 the new Law Concerning Welfare of Working Women took effect. Its purpose was to elevate the social status of working women and improve their welfare. Its measures concentrated on elimination of discriminatory and illogical employment practices, review of the maternity leave system, and steps to help improve women's vocational abilities through counseling, vocational guidance, and training. This legislation marked a new era in labor relations; it acknowledged the dependence of the Japanese economy on women workers, married and single.

As the legislation developed, shibboleths about special protection for women came under fire. The 1947 Labor Standards Law hinged on "protection of motherhood" and "frailness" of women—vague slogans prated so often that the true meaning of the phrases is lost. At issue were retirement, length of hours, night work, hazardous work, and physiological (menstruation) and maternity leaves. Inevitably related to these issues were equal pay and equal opportunity.

The Tōkyō Chamber of Commerce, seeking solutions to the labor shortage, had recommended in 1970 abrogation of "excessively" protective provisions. It sought easings of the bans on midnight labor, overtime, and handling of dangerous and harmful substances, and clarification of the regulations on menstruation leave. The chairman (himself the father of three daughters) of the chamber committee, which

婦人参政権行使
20
周年記念

第7回
全国婦人の集

主催 第7回全国婦人の

御 入 口

Trade union women, members of the large Japanese Confederation of Labor (Dōmei), leave the Japan Youth Hall in Tōkyō after meetings of the Seventh Women's Conference on April 15, 1966. Photo courtesy of USIS/Tōkyō.

surveyed 2,000 major metropolitan companies, termed the old regulations "obsolete" and excuses for discriminating against women in job advancement. Improved working environments and employee health had eliminated their rationale.

The chamber report led leaders of both the Dōmei (Japanese Confederation of Labor) and Sōhyō (General Council of Trade Unions of Japan), Japan's major trade unions, to fear "manipulation for the worse." They conjectured that capitalistic exploitation was the true motive. They called upon women trade unionists to conduct a letter-writing campaign to influence the Labor Ministry committee studying welfare reforms. Women of both union groups, meeting in their respective annual conventions, in frustration reiterated that even with the Labor Standards Law, they were still "cheap labor." Voice after voice elaborated discriminations. They ranged from a metal machinery manufacturing employee's complaint that women had to report in thirty minutes earlier than men every morning to sweep the office floors, with no allowance for that extra chore, to tales of lack of relief in arduous work conditions during pregnancy, to discriminatory temporary layoffs at times of "rationalization," to multiple problems revolving around marriage and the working woman. In 1971 and 1972 national meetings proposed to solve worker's problems more aggressively at the political and social level rather than by bargaining with government and corporate managements. The change in tactics was illustrated by the Dōmei women's rally slogan in 1972, "Solidarity and Action Toward Women's Independence," compared with the 1968 slogan exhorting, "Let Us Contribute to Making a Richer Tomorrow."[23]

Suspicious of the revised welfare legislation, union leaders discussed other changes. Some wanted the word "sex" inserted along with "nationality, creed and social status" in Article 3 of the law prohibiting discrimination. Article 4 on equal pay, it was proposed, should be extended to include equal treatment. Union officials argued for extension of child-bearing leave from six weeks to eight, extra paid time for breast-feeding periods in addition to the present unpaid thirty minutes per day, and paid sick leave to see doctors when suffering from morning sickness.

As of 1982 there were just over 3.4 million women trade unionists, slightly less than 28 percent of all union members and about one-third of the total work force. For many, union education raises "consciousness" and, importantly, gives a sense of dignity as a worker. The Transportation Union's Maeda Sumiko emphasized, "It is discrimination against women which deprives them of their will to work." Having learned about "equal rights for men and women in their school education," they are prevented by disillusionment from "concentrating on their job as a life-long work."[24]

For some, the union becomes the center of extracurricular activities. It gives purpose, or *ikigai*, and builds fulfillment and satisfaction, attributes especially important with the younger generation. The twinkling smile of a thirty-year-old electrical worker, enthusing about her folk-dance group and its community programs for youth, portrays the merit of such values, which may be realized through union affiliation.[25]

As in the United States, union leadership is primarily male. Often men head the women's departments and sections set up to handle women's problems. The situation breeds ambivalence, for it is left to men to promote the rights of women workers and also to relate to the male structural hierarchy. At contract time an easy, familiar compromise can be based on the expendability of female labor.

The comments of the secretary-general of the National Textile Union (Zenzen Dōmei), which has more women members than any other union, point up that the general emphasis on welfare has depreciated concerns for greater equality in pay and job advancement. In the mid-1960s he opined that the "best way to activize women workers in industry and the unions is to take care of their 'worries.' " By this he referred to dormitory facilities, food, pensions, and welfare regulations covered by the 1947 Labor Standards Law.[26]

Some of the contentious issues affecting women's working status— early age or marriage retirement and menstruation leave—are rooted in Japanese custom. The last welfare measure is a privilege virtually unique to Japan. When foreign visitors ask why it is necessary for average healthy young women, the response is invariably that it is a "protection for motherhood"—a peculiarly Japanese answer combining traditional concern for the family and modern awareness of worker protection. Unfortunately, this leave is a constant reminder of the so-called frailness of women and perpetuates discrimination.

Illustrative of the issue is the row, beginning in 1970, between Keiō University and its women employees. In order to curtail wage costs, the university annulled that aspect of the labor contract providing for paid "feminine" leave. Keiō argued that the women abused the leave privilege, regularly taking it before or after Sundays and holidays; it cited a nurse who tried to take it during pregnancy. The union voted a strike. Finally, in 1972, seventy-four Keiō women employees filed suit for repayment of back wages for lost menstruation leave and cessation of the antileave policy. The suit was supported by many men at Keiō, and the union won in an out-of-court settlement. Several years later, court decisions ruled that such leave must be allowed and not penalized as absentee time but that payment for menstruation leave is a matter for collective bargaining. Invariably, however, the practice of physiological leave, even though declining in use, boomerangs against women, and it does not solve the real welfare issues of adequate sick and vacation leave for everyone.[27]

The courts in recent years have become an effective mechanism for overcoming limitations on women's rights. Early cases dealt with the issue of equal pay. In 1966 Suzuki Setsuko of Fukushima Prefecture won the first of the rulings that mandatory dismissal in case of marriage was unconstitutional. When employed by Sumitomo Cement Company of Tōkyō at age twenty, she had signed a routine, compulsory acceptance of company rules that all female workers must quit when they marry or reach age thirty-five—a not unusual practice. Six years later, with the backing of her labor union and after a court battle of nearly three years, she successfully defied this unwritten law of employment of women.[28] Subsequent judgments have held that marriage cannot be grounds for dismissal whether or not a certificate was signed, and neither can so-called nepotism if created by the marriage of people in the same work place.

Encouraged by Suzuki's success, Shiga Sueko took the Tōkyō Kurogane Kōgyō Company to court in 1967 on their policy of mandatory retirement

Keiō University Hospital nurses in Tōkyō walk out on strike over menstruation leave pay in April 1971. Photo courtesy of Kyodo Photo Service.

for women at age thirty. Dismissed with seven other women workers as part of a rationalization process, she and a small group of supporters passed out handbills at company gates proclaiming, "To hell with this nonsense! I WILL NOT accept the thirty-year-old retirement regulation of the company." She was the first discharged woman to bring action against the limitation on length of service. Six years later she won her case. In the course of the proceedings, the company raised their female retirement age to fifty, although for men the age is fifty-five.

Suenami Kazumi of Ōsaka instigated legal action against Mitsui Zōsen, a leading shipbuilding company, for dismissal after the birth of her first child. Although the management–labor union agreement allowed such dismissals, she argued that her constitutional rights, which guarantee equality of the sexes, had been violated. Upon her marriage she had been transferred from the status of a regular employee to that requiring yearly renewal of contract, and after the birth of her child her contract was terminated. Returning to her job after the favorable court decision in 1971, Suenami vowed to continue to "destroy" the discriminatory system.

Equally determined was Nakamoto Miyo in her case against Nissan Motor Company, a battle over discrimination in retirement age waged in the courts from 1969 to 1981. Dismissed at the age of fifty (by comparison with the male age of fifty-five), Nakamoto challenged the system and sued Nissan. In 1973 the Tōkyō High Court, on appeal from the lower court, ruled that women are physiologically inferior to men as workers. The judge, upholding this employment philosophy, concluded that a fifty-year-old woman's capacity was like that of a man of fifty-two.[29]

The anachronistic decision evoked heated reaction and caused many to consider the issue of whether indeed man or woman is the weaker sex. Kaji Chizuko, writing in the emancipationist *Fusen kaikan* monthly, admitted that even women "sometimes mix sex difference with sex discrimination" and cited welfare provisions concerning motherhood. But, she angrily concluded, "The differential retirement system has nothing to do with the welfare of women. It is sex discrimination banned by the Constitution."[30] Kageyama Hiroko promptly organized a countermeasures group with the support of Ichikawa Fusae and such women's organizations as the Business and Professional Women, the Japan Nursing Association, Chifuren, and the Kindergarten Teachers to fight the verdict. She labeled the group a kind of *kakekomi-dera*, or place of refuge, like the temples of divorce used by women fleeing unhappy marriages in the Tokugawa era.

Interim judicial support in this lengthy struggle came when the Tōkyō High Court, this time with a woman judge playing a role, ruled in

1975 in the Izu Cactus Park case that a compulsory retirement system discriminating against women is unlawful. Two years later, as a result of the Japan Plan of Action for the United Nations Decade for Women, the Labor Ministry announced it would encourage abolition of such discrimination. Finally, in the spring of 1981 the Japanese Supreme Court, acting on yet another appeal from Nissan, declared it illegal. It determined there was no difference in work performance between men and women at least up to age sixty. The perseverance of Nakamoto Miyo and her many supporters had won a benchmark decision in the legal fight for equality. Still ahead was the persisting challenge to actual practice—in 1980 one out of five enterprises continued to set an earlier mandatory retirement age for women.[31]

So long as women workers are limited by discriminatory welfare regulations, they will be tied into second-class situations as workers. As long as they are subject to blanket inhibitions on overtime, prohibition of night work, and enforced early retirement, they will be deprived of an equal chance for promotions into supervisory and executive ranks and for higher salaries.

Takahashi Nobuko, speaking from her lengthy background as director of the Women's and Minors' Bureau, has stated with rightful pride that Japan has "perhaps the most active and effective social welfare system for working women and youth in the entire world." She explained that the biggest difference between U.S. and Japanese working women is their "consensus aims." Americans stress equal employment opportunity; the Japanese desire security more than opportunity. To encourage Japanese to join Americans in an emphasis on equality, Takahashi has looked for ways in which organizations other than the bureau, which has no authority to deal with this problem, can launch test cases and other types of action. A joint United States–Japan governmental two-year study on women in the labor market has encouraged comparative thinking. Japan's National Plan of Action recommends practical steps to encourage a change of policy emphasis.[32]

One last point: If Japanese women are to achieve greater opportunity and upward mobility into management, more and better training is essential. The 1972 women's welfare legislation takes this requisite into account, as does the National Plan of Action. The National Women's Education Center is designed for this purpose. Kageyama Hiroko pioneered in programs with the Japan Management Association to get companies to conduct training for the advancement of their women. This latter approach is vital, for almost all employee training is carried on by companies.

Kageyama's comments in a June 16, 1969 speech at the Tōkyō Womanpower Taikai Conference sum up the continuing basic problem for women. "Computers and women—all the company executives are at a loss to know how to use them. Yet it seems to me that the future of the companies depends upon the use of the two." The computer problem is solved. Now comes the question of women. For them must still be achieved a viable balance between protections and access to full job opportunity.

Despite the slowness of court rulings and managerial hesitations, a progressive mood is pushing along the cause of the Japanese working woman. The pace of advancement accelerated in the 1970s. Initiative for recognition and implementation of their rights comes now from the broad reach of women's organizations, related government agencies, and the mass media.

Advancement is also due to the effects of the changed life-style of women and modernization of family life. Shiraishi Tsugi fretted that too many women—especially those who remember the harsh years of the war and its aftermath—would relax their diligence in the feminist fight because they think that "we never had it so good."[33] Yet, economic independence has become a widespread and normal aspiration. Any young woman who puts her mind to it can secure this freedom. Her economic independence enhances her personal dignity even though it may add to her social adjustment problems.

On the economic front, Japan's dependence on women's services is forcing revisions in the welfare system and the life-employment pattern. It is even influencing consideration of some variation on the Western pay system, which is job-oriented and related to the time worked. Such a system would give flexibility to suit the needs of the working mother or returned mature worker. Japan should not assume that it can rely on an unending supply of cheap, pliable female labor. Production planning and overseas investment policies are beginning to take this factor into account, particularly as Japan enlarges its base in other Asian countries.

In comparative international terms, Japanese working women have demonstrated a rate of progress that can be considered another economic miracle. Before the war, the women worked under conditions similar to those in underdeveloped areas, even though their nation's economy was already highly industrialized. By the United Nations Decade for Women, Japanese women compared well with their sisters in the other highly developed countries of Europe and America. They have joined with them to remove persisting inequalities and to close gaps in the enforcement of regulations and constitutional provisions purporting to give all democratically equal status.[34]

Prosperity is fundamental to the hastening of Japanese women's continued progress. As long as they produce goods and services for democratic Japan instead of large families, their economic worth will continue to escalate. This economic value, in turn, gives them greater leverage in decision making in society. To make the most of this strength, however, they must resist the ever-inhibiting attitude that declares women are not ready for equality. They must cooperate among themselves in giving life to their National Plan of Action. They must, as well, in the process of fulfilling their economic ambitions, neither skimp on their public affairs obligations nor lose the effectiveness of their decision-making power by concentrating primarily on narrow feminine interests.

WOMEN AS CONSUMERS—
STATUS SEEKERS AND RICE-PADDLE PROTESTERS

> *Looking back, I did what I wanted to do within the limit of my ability. . . . A household economics movement, which had been in my mind since I left the political movement in 1922, has been realized bringing improvement of consumers' social conditions. Public opinion is beginning to lend support. I am glad about it. In the future consumers will be the supreme rulers of society.*
> —Oku Mumeo, *Watakushi no rirekisho*, 1958[35]

In their role as guardians of the household budget, Japanese women have come to exert directly on public affairs their strongest and most vociferous influence.

The consumer movement may not involve exclusively women's issues, but women do most of the shopping—and provide most of the activism. They are also able to challenge policies of the corporate establishment with greater impunity than their employee husbands. If they wish, they can take almost all the credit for establishing consumerism as a major movement in Japan—a force that is having significant impact both on the quality of life and on Japan's economic priorities.

The modern movement came into being in the immediate postwar period when production and distribution of life-support essentials were in chaos. Okinawa-born Higa Masako carried a petition to Occupation authorities in Ōsaka urging greater food imports and organized other protests and boycotts, including a particularly successful one on meat. Oku Mumeo and others, such as Nomura Katsuko and Maruoka Hideko, started their efforts in Tōkyō. In time, a centralized liaison office for all regional consumer groups, the Japan Housewives Association (Shufu rengōkai), popularly called Shufuren, came into being with Oku, now a member of the Diet, at its head. Successful actions were taken against a rise in public bath prices and against shoddy safety matches and textile goods. Popularly based consumer education and activism were under way.

Oku became the first member of the Diet to speak up in that august body on behalf of the consumer. She made speeches about the prices of rice, electricity, and milk, among others. Dismayed at this housewifely approach to the governing of the land, some men in the Diet complained,

"Women are like that, wanting to talk about tiny things like vegetables. The Diet is the place to discuss what the country should do." Today, Oku's daughter notes, even the prime minister talks about the price of apples. The groundwork had been laid for the women's mundanely practical, nudging, prodding, democratically organized, market-basket approach to the cost of living and national economic policies.[36]

The Cost of the Economic Miracle

Only because of the great publicity attendant upon the rise of Japan's GNP to a position second in the noncommunist world in 1969 did the Japanese people begin to comprehend that they were no longer a poor country or a poor people. Although in the 1960s Japan was seventh in per capita income among countries with populations of more than 10 million, the Japanese government and press repeatedly publicized a United Nations ranking placing Japan around twentieth, below such countries as the United Arab Emirates, Aruba, and Monaco. That modest place reinforced concepts of national poverty, thereby encouraging energetic production to overcome such a demeaning condition. The Japanese people's surprise when the announcement was made of their newly attained status indicates that their unprecedented economic strides had not been taken without a heavy cost.[37]

For instance, nationally in 1968, there was one dwelling for every four people, but the enclosed space was only 350 square feet per dwelling, and this was three times larger than the average in major cities. In 1971 new housing units averaged 700 square feet, and by 1981 this had become the overall average. The tense faces, usually of housewives, watching the tally boards to see if their number had won them a new home in the public housing lotteries held to select new tenants from the many applicants regularly displayed the anxieties of the housing situation. In the 1970s most older dwellings did not have flush toilets, and they were not serviced by sewer systems. In urban areas more than half the households do not have bath facilities, and by the early 1970s, because of the land boom, even price-controlled public bathhouses were closing down at a worrisome rate. For a people who regard the ritual of the bath not simply as hygiene but as a psychologically healing event, the social friendliness of a public bath is an asset not fully appreciated by most Westerners.

The average wage-earner has rarely been able to buy land to build a house. As the *Japan Stock Journal* editorialized, prices had "moved from the outrageous to the fantastic," the cost of land around urban areas having increased twentyfold from the mid-1950s to the mid-1970s. When possible, grandparents and parents have forfeited the gardens of the paternal house—often formerly in the country but now engulfed in sprawling suburbs—to build new homes for the younger generation or to increase their income by rentals.[38] Although the government in the late 1960s did loosen the money supply for private housing loans, the steps were still inadequate to fill pent-up demand. By 1974 Sōhyō, realizing that wages alone were not a criterion for a good standard of living, announced it would take up the "housing struggle."

Improved wages have brought the status-giving automobile. Between 1960 and 1974 total motor vehicle registrations increased dramatically, from 3.4 million to 26.3 million, and by the end of the 1970s almost half the family households were proud possessors of cars. But infrastructure planning for roads, parking garages, and the predictable auto exhaust pollution were scarcely considered. The narrow streets, friendly and neighborly for pedestrians, bicycles, or the earlier rickshaws, became hazardous.

Social security expenses in 1966 were only 14 percent of the national government budget and cost $50 per capita compared to $430 in Sweden and $250 in the United States. This low figure contributed to a broadening uneasiness over small retirement allowances. Such worries prompted the 1972 annual spring labor offensive to depart from the customary concentration on wage increases to focus on the "life struggle" for improved pensions. They precipitated the 1973 union demand, backed by 3.6 million striking workers, for a more scientific formula for social welfare rates, based on a pay-as-you-go system. In response to these pressures, social security has improved, rising to provide average monthly pensions of $460 in 1980, slightly lower than in West Germany but higher than in other European countries and the United States.[39]

By sacrificing living standards and social benefits in the postwar decades, the Japanese people delayed a higher standard of living for a national economic miracle. They underwrote the cause of the GNP with industrious labor, delay of social security, and deterioration of the natural environment. Only during the 1970s, in a mood of increasing disenchantment, did the realization come that something must be done about spiraling retail prices, congested and substandard living conditions, air and water pollution caused by the factories that were the means of achieving the new affluent society, and automobiles that are the result of it. Meanwhile the palliative is a nationwide shopping spree.

Escalated Living Standards

Nothing marks the escalation of living standards of the Japanese woman more than the gadgets and appliances she aspires to own. The wits of Japan periodically link such items in symbolic triad, the "Three Sacred Treasures of the Home," reminiscent of the "three things" (*sanshū no jinki*) the legendary gods handed down to the imperial family— sacred sword, mirror, and jewel. Having struggled through the destitute 1940s and 1950s when farm women saved cupfuls of rice to barter for kerosene stoves to replace those made of stones and dirt,[40] 1960s housewives who toiled from dawn to dark had goals of "refrigerator, vacuum cleaner, and clothes washer." A decade later, having secured this trio of appliances, plus television and sometimes a long-awaited telephone,[41] housewives were in an upgraded pursuit of the three "Cs" of rocketing affluence: "cooler [air conditioner], cottage, and car."

Enthusiasm for the good material things of life led to an attitude popularly described as "my-homeism," an inner-looking, contented enjoyment of the peaceful well-being of a more affluent life. Apartment-complex or *danchi*-style living isolates married women and bolsters such inward turning, a mood that has worried women leaders who frown on such selfish concentration as a detriment to fuller participation in community affairs.

In snatching at the fulfillment their fattened pocketbooks can buy— and most spending is for cash, not credit—Japanese men and women seek compensation for the hard work and tensions of being "lashed into the race" to push Japan into a ranking world position. That phrase, used originally by Mishima Sumie to characterize the experience of the 1930s to expand military prowess,[42] is no less appropriate for the competitiveness of the post-Occupation economic initiative. Many measure reward for the success of this "race" in acquisitions. Feminist philosopher Morosawa Yoko has called it a remedy for "a continuous feeling of deficiency."[43] Such spending provides release and satisfaction in a society that has moved toward a consumer culture.

Within Japan, affluent jockeying for status may be typified by the "golf boom." Couples often buy multiple resalable golf-club memberships as a hedge against inflation. They can swing the cost of a share of a golf course when they cannot afford land for a house.

Overseas, free-spending Japanese swell the coffers of tourist resorts and prestigious shops. Young couples go abroad to marry because it is cheaper than the social ritual at home, and they can enjoy the éclat of a foreign honeymoon. The custom of bringing souvenirs to family and friends after any trip, no matter how brief, encourages the spending propensity. Young unmarried "office ladies" and shop clerks are among the most uninhibited spenders. Incurring minimal living expenses by living at home, they can and do buy expensive vacations in Europe or the United States, costly fur coats, and designer dresses.

Shopping for vegetables in a local traditional family grocery. Photo courtesy of the Embassy of Japan.

Outmoded and discarded in the excitement is the tradition of restraint. The old proverb "Honorable poverty is the glory of the true samurai" (*Bushi wa kuwande otakayōji*) is a haunting antiquity.

One aspect of the high-moneyed living of Japanese sustains the samurai's ghost. His presence is felt in escalating inflation. The prewar level of average consumer spending was passed in 1954 and has moved steadily upward ever since. Although wages have increased proportionately, inflation when viewed from the kitchen agitates the keeper of the family budget. In the words of a college-educated *danchi* housewife of a Tōkyō suburb, she feels "betrayed."[44]

As early as 1964, in one of the periodic morning meetings Prime Minister Satō held with women leaders, delegates from the League of Women Voters, Shufuren, and other groups took him to task for his government's economic policies on housing and commodity prices. Promising to do his best, he laughingly ended the meeting by asking the women not to shout their opposition too loudly. "We won't shout anything if you keep commodity prices low," was the retort.[45] They did not have to keep their word. The situation of spiraling inflation has driven women into louder consumer protest and into politics. Egami Fuji, then a member of the Rice Price Board and Tōkyō's Council of Social Welfare, said flatly, "The biggest problem we face internally is rooted in the economy and, there, the biggest problem is price. . . . This is the responsibility of the administration as well as that of the people."[46]

It is the imbalance in the total economy brought on by government policy that makes television sets easier to come by than *sukiyaki* beef and cars easier than cottages. The same young matron who talks, almost bemusedly, of owning two golf-club memberships is irked at her bills from the butcher and rice vendor. Tōkyō food prices, including those of staples like milk, sugar, fish, and eggs, are the highest among the world's major cities. Rice, still an absolute fundamental in diet, which is under government subsidy and price control for obsolete reasons of food self-sufficiency, import payment restrictions, and domestic political maneuvering, costs Japanese two to three times the average world price.

Imported products, whether food like oranges, coffee, chocolate, and juices or luxury items of scotch, soap, and woolen goods, carry, along with their aura of sophisticated prestige, prices that are several times the cost at port of entry. To cite one example, coffee, all of which is imported, moves from arrival at dockside through an elaborate distribution chain to sell with a domestic markup of more than 200 percent. Even after the yen revaluation, while prices on some luxuries fell, commodity prices did not. In fact, prices of some commodities, like beef, wheat, maize, and soybeans, went up. Amid the ensuing protests, the Shufuren newspaper expressed the hope that the "dollar shock" would at least teach housewives the importance of learning more about international economics.[47] Their cause—that of the consumer—and that of Japan's trading partners coincided.

Recognizing the negative world and domestic reaction to its economic policies of GNP above all, the Japanese government since 1971 has been shifting its announced policy emphasis. Finance Minister (later Prime Minister) Fukuda Takeo declared in the Diet that year that Japan would aim at "enhancing social well-being through a stable economic expansion." Next year Prime Minister Satō Eisaku told the Diet that the government would "plunge a scalpel" into the distribution system for imported goods so the consumer might share in the yen's upvaluation. In April 1973, the Ministry of International Trade and Industry (MITI) turned to the public and called for a consumer boycott of textiles with inflated prices, such as men's and women's clothing and underwear. The Economic Planning Agency (EPA) announced it would cooperate in such boycotts by providing the latest price information, and its director-general met with representatives of Shufuren, Chifuren, and

"Housewife scientist" Takada Yuri (right), chief of testing and vice-president of Shufuren, appeals to the Emperor on behalf of the consumer as he greets her at the autumn imperial garden party, 1973. Photo courtesy of Kyodo Photo Service.

the Federation of Livelihood Unions (Seikyōren). The skeptical Haruno Tsuruko, the late vice-president of Shufuren who was known for her trouser suits, which recalled the austere war years, demurred at being led by a "government-sponsored" price policy, but she agreed because consumer organizations need such information to function. Chifuren's Tanaka Satoko summed up the remarkable situation as a "most unusual thing for a government office to appeal to the people." It was the first time government agencies had directly urged consumers to boycott goods.[48]

At long last there was some recognition that the life of the "salaryman"—an adapted English term for company wage earners—and the skilled laborer, who together dominate the middle class, had to be made to seem worthwhile by bringing prices of essentials into balance with income.[49] Consumer powers, "grumbling less in the kitchen and more in direct negotiation" in accordance with the wisdom of Oku Mumeo[50] and undergirded by awakened labor union anti-inflation activities and by countrywide despair over environmental disturbances, had forced the government into a new look at objectives based on "public-interest-first principles."[51]

Heroines of the Hearth

Scientifically trained Takada Yuri, chief of testing and vice-president of Shufuren, reportedly surprised the Emperor when, as a guest at the autumn imperial garden party in 1973, she responded to his praise of her consumerism efforts with a fervent appeal on behalf of the budget-conscious housewife and her worries about PCB and mercury-poisoned fish. Her audaciousness brought press attention.[52]

Takada, a prewar graduate of the Kyōritsu College of Pharmacy and a professor there, has brought a new dimension to the consumer movement. In 1950 Oku Mumeo persuaded her to come out from recent retirement to establish the technical product testing necessary for Shufuren's consumer-protection undertakings. Encouraged by her newspaperman husband, she started her career, becoming in time widely known as the "housewife scientist."

Since the only "laboratory" the organization could then offer was a tiny sink in a tearoom attic, she returned to her college laboratory to conduct analyses. First came tests of margarine, then soy sauce and milk. Shufuren's public announcement that the fat content of milk was below standard and that its pasteurization was unevenly controlled riled both producers and the responsible government regulatory agency. The women stood firm, and improvement in milk standards resulted. The concept of scientific testing to validate consumer complaints, benefiting from observation studies by Oku and Takada of consumer testing facilities in Europe and America and encouraged by international leaders like Colston Warne of the International Organization of Consumer Unions, became part and parcel of the movement.

The long hours in the laboratory—since 1956 the sizable, well-equipped top floor of the new Shufuren headquarters building—of Takada and her two fellow-alumnae assistants provided the ammunition necessary for new consumer laws. Oku, an indefatigable Diet member, picked up where Takada's work left off. Reinforced by Shufuren adherents, organized women, and cooperative leaders, the consumerists fought through passage of legislation. It took three years to get a law establishing quality standards in textiles and correction of false labeling of clothing. Then, with the help of the Fair Trade Commission and Minister of International Trade and Industry Satō Eisaku, came legislation requiring correct labels on canned foods. To cite an illustration that was much publicized in this truth-in-labeling struggle: No longer was it legal

Shufuren Vice-President Takada Yuri and her assistant test canned goods products in the laboratory on the top floor of the Shufuren headquarters building in Tōkyō. Photo courtesy of the Ministry of Foreign Affairs, Government of Japan.

to sell canned meat labeled with the picture of a cow, but containing rabbit or horse meat.

In 1964, Takada's new techniques of analysis of juices to determine actual natural fruit juice content received recognition by the Pharmaceutical Society of Japan. She believed that the juice issue provided an important precedent influencing subsequent consumer action.[53] Takada pioneered the scientific basis for consumer complaint and consumer action. Her prototype sink lab of 1950 is now reproduced many times over in modern, mostly government-financed facilities in municipal and prefectural consumer offices from Hokkaidō to the tip of Kyūshū. A visit to any of them shows not only a working lab, but also "before and after" displays of items found faulty, dangerous, or misleading. Plastic tableware, children's toys from which the color can be sucked off, poor-quality stockings, shrunken "washables," and more line the walls of the consumer centers. They constitute a museum of battles undertaken via the scientific method by Japanese consumers.

Oku, who was symbolic of the battling consumers of Japan, personally linked the "new women" of the 1920s, the endeavors in welfare, child care, and women's rights of the 1930s, (which were considered socialistic), and contemporary activism. Garbed in a white "mama-san" apron enveloping her traditional subdued kimono, she ran in front, literally and spiritually, carrying the big rice-paddle-shaped placards (*shamoji*) of the protesting housewife, which became the emblem of Shufuren. Over the years she passed on the rice-paddle burden to others.

Members of the Diet Togano Satoko (Socialist), Nakazawa Itoko (Democratic Socialist), and Tanaka Sumiko (Socialist), for example, battled alongside Oku in the Diet for consumer protection legislation. Unsuccessful in getting the Diet to establish a ministry of consumers, Oku did get a substitute in the Consumers Division of the Economic Planning Agency. Today there are any number of consumer sections in government agencies. Togano played a lead role in passage of the Consumer Protection Basic Law of May 30, 1968, which established a credo for the "positive role" of the consumer as a voice and as an activist. It provided for correct weights and measures, proper standards and labeling, and prices established through "fair and free competition." It set up a conference or office on consumer matters, with the prime minister as chairman, serving with other appointed heads of government agencies. It encouraged education and consultation with administrative bodies; it developed inspection facilities and a system for hearing complaints. More than seventy consumer centers with complaint windows are now established in many parts of the country, often housed in the women's halls, usually under the aegis of the Chifuren.

Led by Oku Mumeo, dressed in a white "mama-san" apron, Shufuren members go forth from their headquarters building in Tōkyō with rice-paddle (*shamoji*) placards to protest the rising cost of living. Photo courtesy of Shufuren.

Oku's consumer legacy on the prefectural level, for instance, activated Fukuoka Prefecture's decorously powerful Chifuren President Uchino Umeko, who said, "Oku connected the kitchen with politics, which I liked. From her I learned how to solve our daily problems as housewives. I did not imitate everything of Oku. I thought her ideas too materialistic, so I added education to my movement."[54]

Locally, Oku's spirit thrusts the movement deeper into the countryside, as seen in the work of Hosokawa Kou. She has followed the motto "Man shall not live by bread alone" and has interlaced her consumer, child care, and political activities in the Tōkyō suburb of Urawa City. She led her nursery school mothers' association into the Shufuren federation in 1958. By the mid-1970s, with a membership of 3,000 women, mostly in their twenties and thirties, this local organization had built a distribution cooperative to hold down the price of milk. Success with milk led to cooperative distribution of other foods to fight inflationary prices. Her organization has employed all the arts of petitioning, advisory services, and education to induce the government to respond to consumer wants. She has preferred not to use the boycott, which she called "group-egoism."

Elected to the City Assembly on the platform, "Government should listen to the voiceless voice," Hosokawa has used what she called "enthusiastic persuasion" with other assembly members to help her causes, which include budgetary provision for the care of handicapped children and nurseries for tots under two, free refrigeration for the Milk Center, and a greatly needed sewage system. She has believed that good leadership is being "free from self." Hosokawa's record shows that she has fulfilled this criterion.[55]

Outstanding in this parade of consumerists who continue to carry the torch of Oku. is Tanaka Satoko of Chifuren. Of the midway generation, she has risen out of the administration of Japan's largest women's organization to achieve leadership status in her own right. Coached in Occupation days by Ikuta Kasei, who had been a member of Seitō, the Bluestocking Society, she found herself, as she said, "just swimming with the stream." Then she met Yamataka Shigeri, with whom she worked in the late 1940s to elect Takeuchi Shigeyo, a pioneer doctor, to the Diet. Encouraged, Tanaka started a career "in real earnest" that gradually brought her to the position of secretary-general of Chifuren in 1963. One of the new generation of leaders and reared within a going organization, Tanaka, unlike many of the prewar leadership, has not felt compelled to rove from one place and role to another to fulfill her ambition for the improvement of women.

Her methods reflect this difference in background and age. Using delicate diplomacy to keep satisfied the thousands of presidents of prefectural and local Chifuren groups, she has been described by one such president as a "cool person." The head of Tōkyō's Nerima Ward Association elaborated:

> In her coolness she has warm feeling. That is why she is loved and trusted by all the presidents throughout the country. She skillfully deals with complex human relationships and the work which is changing. None of the presidents have ever complained about her. I think nobody can imitate her skill.[56]

In democratic fashion, Tanaka has mobilized the force of the huge membership for which she works. She has given administrative direction to rationally planned, educationally based, effective lobbying operations. Tactics are not simply boycott and the endless *"Hantai! Hantai!"* ("We oppose! We object!") of the chanting protest groups. Tanaka has helped Chifuren gain unique stature and power in the way it has brought consumer problems into focus so that average women can exert citizens' (*shimin-teki*) strength on them. Tanaka has simply said that Chifuren has shifted from begging for "protection of the consumer" to a more dignified, self-confident assertion of the "right of the consumer."[57]

"Catching Fire"

During Tanaka Satoko's meeting with enterprise executives at the Japan Productivity Center, to which she was invited in 1973 to discuss the consumer boycott movements, she described consumer action as the "something is strange" (*kore wa okashii*) movement. She tried to make them understand that housewives act from no particular theory or advocacy, undoubtedly to dispel any notions that they are ideologically inspired. Rather, she explained, an issue will "catch fire" when consumers feel that producers and sellers are not giving them straight answers, saying "black is white or five to six times is really two point eight times." She asked for a change of attitude so there could be a real exchange, not just an unresponsive complaint desk. When such warm-hearted understanding and social consciousness is practiced, she prophesied, society would no longer need a consumer movement.[58]

The consumer groups' golden hour, when they brought the powerful electronic industries of Japan to the point of supplication, was their "color TV campaign" from fall 1970 to spring 1971. Chifuren took the lead, rallying the cooperation of Shufuren, the League of Women Voters, the Japanese Consumers Association (Nihon shohisha no kai), and the Japan Federation of Livelihood Cooperatives to carry out a unified initiative. They became known as the "big five." These organizations carried the impact of their combined memberships of 15 million, mostly housewives, and thereby amassed the frightening power that made their boycott devastating. Even Japan's total trade union membership, some 11.5 million at that time, fell short of such numerical strength. News commentators called it the "greatest crisis" in the history of the television industry.[59]

The television incident started in January 1970. One must understand that in Japanese stores all items are price tagged, and to preserve customer confidence that the marked price is fair market value, discounting is often considered a breach of faith. Appliance manufacturers' suggested retail prices are generally respected except by discount stores in urban areas, such as Tōkyō's Akihabara district. Consumers think manufacturers are unethical, if not always illegal, when products are priced anywhere at profit margins higher than such discounters require. Chifuren, at the request of the Fair Trade Commission (FTC), undertook a price survey of some 900 articles, including clothes, soaps and detergents, food, and durable goods, in the greater Tōkyō area. Lawyer

Ariga Michiko, until retirement in 1973 the only woman member of the commission, explained that Chifuren and Shufuren are good for such studies because their memberships have many "eyes" and can give the commission an "overall" view on pricing and packaging conditions. An earlier survey of the price of propane gas by Saitama Prefecture's Chifuren had grown into nationwide action endorsed by the FTC; the success of this project had encouraged the larger double-pricing study. Chifuren's report, released in early August, found that the price discount on color television sets averaged 28 percent and that generally the higher the fixed dealer price, the higher the discount rate.

For some reason, the color television issue caught fire among the members, and a decision was made to boycott color television manu-facturers. The Chifuren federation closed ranks to promote the boycott. Four days later the "big five" consumer campaign was solidified. Within the same ten-day period the U.S. Treasury Department coincidentally announced investigation of alleged dumping of color televisions. In-numerable meetings among the consumers and the Electronics Industries Association, Matsushita (on which the boycott focused), the FTC, and MITI followed. In November, local Chifuren groups and others through-out Japan took to the streets in protest. On December 1, Prime Minister Satō met with the consumer representatives. Meanwhile, the boycotters, unable to get information from the industries on a breakdown of the cost and shipping price of the sets, gained strength of purpose from their anger. Between 1.5 million and 2 million color television sets sat unpurchased, backlogged in stock.

After the turn of the year, Matsushita, the largest consumer electronics firm, gave way; it announced retail price reductions of 15 percent. Sony broke the dam on clarification of factory shipment prices. Other com-panies followed suit. Unsatisfied, consumers continued to push discus-sions on distribution, rebate policy, and pricing. On March 4 the United States declared damage to U.S. industries from the dumping of Japanese television sets. Two days later the Livelihood Co-ops put color televisions on sale at prices considerably lower than the name brands to show that the big companies set their prices too high. Matsushita admitted it had carried out illegal retail price-fixing practices and apologized to the FTC. On April 16, 1971, the longest and largest consumer resistance in Japan's history came to an end.

The campaign held great import for consumers, business, government, and even international relations. For consumers, as Chifuren President Yamataka Shigeri pointed out, the campaign was an "eye-opener," teaching them a "good lesson" in self-confidence. It demonstrated that consumers can work their will, once aroused and willing to stand firm. It revealed that a consumer boycott of a discretionary item of considerable cost has more chance of success than a boycott of food because the consumer can delay purchase and thus bring compliance from the manufacturer. The united front of the "big five" consumer organizations could effectively bring to bear the impact of their prodigiously large memberships, which blanket Japan—once housewives are aroused and united in agreement that "something is strange."

This campaign benefited from the support of certain influential agencies of government, tying the women's efforts into the mainstream of the power structure. This is not always the case—for example, when the urban housewife fights the conservative pricing policies of the Ministry of Agriculture, which is protective of the special interests of the farmers. Because the boycott coincided with the dumping investigation by the United States, women were alerted to the subsidy consumers pay indirectly to Japanese commerce and industry to advance Japan's international trade.

The concerted and sustained color television boycott induced shock in some of the largest industrial companies in Japan. Matsushita's annual report disclosed a decline in profits for that winter because of decreased sales attributed to both the consumer movement and the recession. At a meeting with the representatives of the "big five," President Matsushita Masaharu said, "In answer to your desires, my company will shortly put on sale a series of new products with greatly lowered official cash prices. I beg for your cooperation"—after which he bowed deeply.

The success of this spectacular boycott raised the organized consumer in national esteem.[60]

Other Fires: Cosmetics

During the final phase of the color television campaign, Chifuren planned new boycotts of products of manufacturers who were able to control retail prices of their products through loopholes in the anti-monopoly law. Special exemptions cover five industries—medicine, cosmetics, soap, detergent, and toothpaste—in order to prevent price wars among retailers, insure reasonable profits for the manufacturers, and forestall deterioration in quality because of unduly low pricing. Chifuren called on Shufuren and the National Widows Association of Japan, with which President Yamataka of Chifuren had long been associated, to unite in "joint struggle" to abolish the system.

This time Chifuren modified its techniques. Not only did it proclaim a boycott directed against the leading Japanese cosmetics firm of Shiseido during the three months of July, August, and September of 1971, but it also offered alternative action to the concerned consumer. Chifuren placed on public sale its own Chifure cosmetics line, in which almost all of the items sold for ¥100. Chifuren wanted to show that there is little difference in quality between ¥100 and ¥1,000 cosmetics and that elaborate packaging and advertising cost exorbitant amounts. Their line, packaged in simple but attractive white plastic cases embellished with a neat abstract design and meeting all technical standards and specifications, was offered at major department stores and some supermarkets. For a while, the low-priced cosmetics sold like the proverbial hotcakes. For four years previously, Chifuren had sold its ¥100 cosmetics to its own members and had used the profits to finance its consumer movement. Shufuren and the consumer's cooperatives, as well as labor unions and some political groups, similarly distributed their own brand-name products.

The summer boycott produced a drop in Shiseido's gross sales for June of 0.6 percent from the previous year. Although small, it was the first decline in twelve years. A year after Chifure went on public sale, Chifuren optimistically claimed it had risen to second-best unit seller after Shiseido and that it showed a tiny profit of ¥7.8 million ($21,000). The line expanded into men's hair tonic and aftershave lotion, but by mid-1973, Chifuren's sales had slowed. Despite a "buy one more" promotional campaign, by 1975 rising prices of raw materials and labor had forced a mark-up to ¥150, and the new products were given fancier containers. Chifuren had to contend with the mystique of the dream world of hope and glamour that is sold along with soaps, creams, and powders of the high-priced, elegantly promoted cosmetics. "A woman's heart (seeking charm) cannot be regulated by sheer 'wise consumer' theory," maintained the public relations chief of such a caterer to women's vanity.[61]

Chifuren's Tanaka indicated that the boycott of Shiseido, and thus indirectly of Kanebō, Pola, and Max Factor, which was then the largest foreign-brand seller, was really a boycott against the dealer retail price control system. Ultimate success required a change in the law and its administration. Nakagome Fumi explained the logic of the cosmetics boycott from her business point of view:

> Consumers boycott is the only way to show their opinion, I believe. I don't think it is necessarily the best way, but they have no other way . . . if they want to get attention in the Diet. . . . For me to go to the Diet and ask to make a speech is impossible in Japan. So we have to raise a movement and in this way make an approach to the higher people.[62]

Knowing they needed intermediaries to get their ideas injected into the political mainstream, eight consumer groups, including Chifuren,

Shufuren, the Japan Consumers Association, and the League of Women Voters, submitted a questionnaire on the price control issue to each of the political parties in 1971 to arouse interest and possible support. The first breakthrough came in May 1972 when a Socialist member of the Diet, Nakamura Jūkō, addressed questions to the head of the FTC during a meeting of the House of Representatives Standing Committee on Commerce and Industry. That fall the consumers' organizations joined with four chain stores—Daiei, Seiyu Store, Nagasakiya, and Jasco—to combine a purchase boycott movement with a sales boycott to try to influence the Fair Trade Commission to rule against the retail price maintenance system.

It is difficult to judge progress in such an extended program to change both law and personal habit, but there are some clues. For example, the Annual Ministerial Conference on Consumer Protection, chaired by the prime minister, decided in 1973 to "review the resale system." MITI, after complaints from the Japan Consumers' League and individual consumers, ordered cosmetics companies to restrain their door-to-door sales methods, which have often relied on "importunate" techniques.[63] The trade association of cosmetics companies, under pressure from the Fair Trade Commission, now words advertising slogans to avoid excess claims of beautification lest the consumer level grievances against the companies' integrity. Even so, Shiseido and Pola have paid solatium in consumer-mounted grievance cases. The cosmetics industry is undoubtedly under much closer scrutiny by both consumers and government.[64]

Other Fires: Beef

Sophisticated circles in Japan often criticize the housewife-consumer for naive and rough-hewn techniques of protest and lobbying. Newspaper headlines play up stories that make it natural for "boycott" and "price-conscious housewife" to be paired in word-association response. One economic critic has repeatedly explained that in a time of inflation and general price rises, the price of rice, for instance, must also go up. No shouts of "*Hantai! Hantai!*" can change this economic fact.[65] Ariga Michiko agreed, but further elucidated, "If consumer activists make a petition and it is not successful, they still have a boycott." The latter protest method is usually "not effective in dealing with food price problems because food is a necessity." But, she went on, "even if not so effective, boycotting does make the government think!"[66]

Kansai Shufuren's Higa Masako, remembered as the organizer of the beef boycott during the Occupation, by the 1970s had turned to other methods for achieving her ends. She advocated acting from a producer point of view, explaining, "We don't fight against the producer and the seller regarding prices. We find out why the prices are so high and what are the reasons. We give the government ideas and push them to change policy. Before we oppose, we study and decide which direction we should take."[67] This philosophy moved Higa and her organization, which is not affiliated with Shufuren, to unusual measures to secure inexpensive beef for the Kansai-area housewife.

Japan has become notorious worldwide for the price of its beef. The renowned Kōbe beef is superb. It comes from steers daily fed beer and lovingly massaged with *sake*. In a world of new habits and increasing incomes, Japanese by the early 1970s consumed about three times as much beef as they did in 1955, but consumption was still less than one-twentieth that of the United States on a per capita basis. If desire were the only factor, consumption would undoubtedly go up more rapidly. The problem facing the housewife is that the demand for Japanese beef exceeds the supply, and therefore beef is exorbitantly priced—the best grade of *sukiyaki* sirloin in the late 1970s went for up to $45 per pound.

Domestic production has remained about the same since 1969. With pasture acreage too small for large grazing herds, producers have not moved to expand. The increased supply option, using greater imports of cheap beef from countries like Australia and New Zealand, was routinely forestalled by import quotas to protect the Japanese beef industry. All too often housewives complained they could not find the imported beef that was allowed in. Kansai Shufuren and other consumer groups accused butchers of mixing the imported meat with domestic beef to sell it at the higher prices. Even the Corporation for the Promotion of the Livestock Industry got involved over this malpractice in 1972 and assigned housewives in major cities to inspect for violations.

Amid the beef furor of the early 1970s, Higa determined to attack the archaic, multilayered distribution system to avert high prices. In this she was helped by her own research, her political savvy, and the development of a new institution—the supermarket. A member of the Prime Minister's Committee on Price Stabilization, she had access to power. Going directly to the minister of agriculture, the Diet Committee on Agriculture, and the prime minister himself, she was able to persuade the government to give her and her organization an allotment of the beef import quota and in October 1971 was able to purchase 1,000 tons of beef for Kansai Shufuren for direct sales to retailers, thus skipping two or more steps of the distribution pyramid. She made her own arrangements for butchering and storage. She organized sales at half the going market price through Mitsukoshi department store, knowing it could ensure adequate sales of her allotment because "only the rich shop there," and through Daiei supermarkets and her organization's five cooperative shops in Ōsaka and in Wakayama and Hyogo prefectures because "meat must be given to ordinary people." By late spring of 1972, Higa reported monthly sales of 100 tons. She admitted that neither the government nor the trade unions were very happy about her arrangements, but at least she had cut through the distribution maze to demonstrate to the consumer how prices could be brought down. As with Chifuren's sale of Chifure, Higa expected to finance her ongoing consumer education program with the profits.[68]

Higa helped her cause by negotiating with Daiei supermarkets, Japan's fastest-growing chain store. Its driving president, Nakauchi Isao, whose policy is to sell everything at prices "which the consumer can and will pay," has made his goal possible by excluding the wholesaler and dealing directly with the producer, often selling products under his brand names. As early as 1966 Nakauchi tried this with beef, working both the cheaper import route and a bypass of the regular beef industry with his own breeding-raising-fattening-slaughtering-retailing line. As an entrepreneur devoted to "breaking the system," with the motto "Consumers Made Me!" he became an ideal colleague for Higa and her purposes[69]—as undoubtedly she was for him!

Higa also broke precedent in her beef campaign by dealing directly with the Australian government because of unconfirmed stories about the questionable quality of beef from one Australian producer. The Australians, realizing the importance of the alert consumer in their efforts to increase imports, in 1971 invited Higa to inspect the meat company in question. She found it "good, but small. . . . Australia is clever. Importers and sellers have connections and invite each other to visit, but Australia invited the consumer, directly skipping the importer and the seller. I think it's wonderful!"

A controversial figure among leaders of women's organizations, and undoubtedly in government circles too, Higa nonetheless had gone to the heart of the problem by dealing in imported food at prices the ordinary family could afford and by circumventing the distribution system. Ariga Michiko has pointed out that pressure on the Japanese government to relax import barriers normally comes from other countries. Only with beef, and to some extent with cheese, has the pressure come from within.[70]

"Bamboo Shoots in the Rain"

"Ten years ago no one knew the meaning of 'shōhisha'—consumer. Today, everyone knows."[71] In this succinct statement Itoh Nanako, secretary-general of Shufuren, described the impact of the consumer movement in Japan.

By 1977 consumer organizations had proliferated to more than 2,600, with total membership of about 10 million, preponderantly women. If cooperative associations and the schools teaching home economics are included, the number of organizations runs close to 6,000. Although some of these groups are long-established, with histories going back to prewar days, many have sprung up, to use a familiar Japanese simile, "like bamboo shoots in the rain."

In this heyday of the consumer, organizations of all kinds include consumer study and action as part of their programs. Young women activists—formerly on the barricades with radical student cohorts—join socialistic organizations in a national campaign to study hazardous detergents and to arrange for the production and sale of their own environmentally safe brand. Feminists discuss consumers' issues to raise the consciousness of women and improve their status. Conversely, a Chifuren officer made it clear that their efforts should not be thought of as "'women's lib.' We are just making efforts to change the pattern of our living at home."[72]

Goals of organized consumers are essentially threefold: to hold down rising prices, to insure quality standards, and to conduct education for wiser consumerism. Education establishes the foundation for informed, effective action. It is the most important continuous program of the multiplicity of organizations in the field, and it sometimes causes schism in old organizations and the establishment of new ones.[73] Approaches are many and varied.

Yamamoto Matsuyo built on her years of experience as the director of the Ministry of Agriculture's Rural Home Life Improvement Program to establish the Home-Family-Community-Life Research Institute. Working with illustrious educational advisers like Fujita Taki and with scientists and experts in dietetics, household economics, hygienics, and so on, she sought data to provide a "quality of life index." With this material she developed advisories for consumers about expenditures on items ranging from leather pocketbooks to home study desks for children to overseas traveling that are released in ads in the *Sankei shimbun* and reviewed in a nationwide semi-educational television consumer program, suitably named "Tele-Shop."[74]

Mitsumake Akiko broke away from Shufuren in 1964 to establish the Consumer Science Center (Shōhi kagaku senta). She emphasized study, testing, and cooperative sales rather than "raising a big movement against the administration." She hoped that her Consumers College, organized by consumers, producers, dealers, and scholars, would educate the young people of Japan. Nomura Katsuko, whose influence has been likened to the "salty taste" needed to keep "stored food during the rainy season from going bad and mildewing," went one step beyond to admonish, "While studying, you must put what you have learned into action. . . . consumers must not remain silent."[75]

Social education classes, sponsored by the Ministry of Education nationwide, develop heightened awareness as women study consumer themes based on recommendations of the annual Ministerial Conference on Consumer Protection. Fieldwork supplements such class study: Teams of women leaders have gone to the United States and Europe under the Ministry's Overseas Education Program to meet foreign leaders in the consumer movement and inspect their testing, research, and education facilities.

From Meiji days, Japanese consumer and cooperative leadership has maintained close international ties to support its development. Nomura Katsuko has translated U.S. reports and journal articles into Japanese for her colleagues. Some, such as Gotō Masa of Hokkaidō, exchange publications and information with local U.S. consumers' unions. She, like Nomura, has visited the United States repeatedly to learn the newest techniques of education and action. That consumer leaders are internationally aware is obvious in the promptness with which they echo U.S. consumer or Food and Drug Administration (FDA) action—witness the immediate banning of cyclamate sweeteners in 1969 following action in Washington. Their international hero worship was demonstrated in the almost hysterical welcome given Ralph Nader during his triumphal visit in 1971.

The result of all this education is that the Japanese consumer advocate has become increasingly tough-minded. The 1973 petroleum protein issue well illustrates the dramatic results of such snowballing momentum. The episode also points up how the sins of the past can bear fruit, with emotion tending to confuse the merits of the issue.

Some Tōkyō housewives joined together in the Tōkyō Consumer Liaison Council (Tōshoren) in late 1972 to launch an anti–synthetic protein drive. The Ministry of Health and Welfare, after three years' study by its Food Sanitation Study Council, had released data indicating that protein made biologically from petroleum was safe as livestock feed. The new year brought protests to the minister and demands for him to ban such feed. Even though he insisted that the Food Sanitation Law did not cover such animal feed, when faced with stronger and stronger consumer reaction, the minister backed down. The two major chemical companies, Dainippon Ink and Chemicals and Kanegafuchi Chemical Industry, which had spent close to $12 million to demonstrate the quality and safety of the oil protein product, canceled plans for manufacture. Other companies expecting to enter the market also withdrew. Said the president of Dainippon: "We are confident of the harmlessness [of oil protein] but we will not steamroll customers' misgivings. We cannot risk the loss of society's confidence in us any more than a decline of our company's image by launching production."[76]

Interestingly, this product, developed by the British in 1963 and now produced in a variety of countries, is regarded as a useful, inexpensive animal feed to lower costs of chicken, pork, and beef, always an important issue with housewives. However, the consumers' lack of trust, both in the Ministry of Health and Welfare and in the Kanegafuchi Chemical Industry, aroused their fears. They remembered only too well the black record of the ministry in the arsenic-poisoning episode of Morinaga dry milk. They held Kanegafuchi Chemical responsible for the PCB *kanemi* oil disease that occurred when cooking oil was accidentally contaminated by a customer company. The housewives' appeal was more a matter of distrust of institutions rather than one of scientifically based knowledge of costs and benefits. The horror stories of the environmental diseases of recent years and the sensitivity of government and of industry have made it impossible for any responsible Japanese institution not to heed the clamor of the people aroused to protect their safety.

Successful consumerism in the 1970s reached into management offices of industry and business throughout Japan. In a brief ten-year period the timid housewife has turned into a dragon whose fire these companies now wish to avoid. Milkmen resist producers' proposals of a price hike in fear of encouraging more milk cooperatives. Farmers and fresh food distributors join with consumer cooperatives to restrain prices and simplify distribution. Major corporations, such as Toshiba, Shiseido, Ajinomoto, and Nihon Ham, have set up consumer divisions. Keidanren, Japan's most powerful organization of industrialists, in a complete reversal of policy now talks with consumer advocates and seeks ways of fulfilling the "social responsibilities of enterprises."[77] Oku's dream has become reality.

The consumers' movement is classically middle class. The poor have no time and often no knowledge to pay heed; the rich need not worry. Japanese women have turned their traditional role of paying attention to small household tasks into a major movement encompassing a broad cross-section of the population increasingly caught up in middle-class mores. Their concerns, which leapt from the kitchen into the middle of the public square, have affected three main currents in Japanese life.

First, their interest in a higher standard of living has brought them to a position in which time and again their goals confront the governmental and industrial drive to generate an ever-larger GNP. Long before the outer world took notice of the results, the women pleaded for some siphoning-off of this energy to improve public welfare. An overflow of this original family welfare–consumer focus was their follow-up to correct environmental problems that they believed pollute both the moral and physical qualities of life.

Second, the anger and frustration of the aroused housewives, long given a casual reception by government and industry, pushed them to use political machinery to accomplish their aims. The deeply personal causes of their homes turned them into politicians, so long considered a man's role, more readily than did years of study about democratic responsibility.

Third, consumerism has provided for the women an understandable link between themselves and the policy their country pursues in international economic relations. For them the subject is extremely complicated, but in the prices of imported foods and household items, they find a bond to events in the foreign world they had not previously noticed.

CHAPTER 5
POLITICAL PROCESS

IDEALS AND INCLINATIONS—
SEMINARISTS AND CLEAN ELECTIONISTS

> *When I talk to Japanese women about democracy, I explain that historically liberalism did not grow in Japan, and the individuality of each person has unfortunately not been fully realized. Japan remains a vertical society, and democracy requires a horizontal society. I am sometimes afraid that true democracy will never mature. As this vertical society emanates from the character of the Japanese people which flows from their history and geography, it is very difficult to change it.*
>
> Ichikawa Fusae, Tōkyō, 1973[1]

Ambivalence best describes the feelings of Japanese women about practical politics or theories of government. Distaste for the assumed unsavoriness of the one and unease about the imponderables of the other color their attitudes. Muted performances, seen in public opinion polls as the often expressed "I don't know," or in attachment to the "clean" election process that bypasses grubby politics, reflect an uncertainty about their role in Japan's political processes.

Since the end of the war—and since the beginning of women's suffrage—the conservatives have dominated national political affairs. Only briefly in 1947–1948 did two liberal coalition groups assume leadership, under Katayama Tetsu and Ashida Hitoshi. Continuity, not only of the conservative groups but also of single figures—Yoshida Shigeru, Ikeda Hayato, Kishi Nobusuke and his brother, Satō Eisaku—through repeated elections to the premiership, provided a stability that softened other exceedingly rapid economic and social changes and

213

minimized the public disorder that frequently accompanies such transitions in other societies.

As in other countries, the addition of the voice of women to the election process did nothing to alter national political trends. Women themselves, however, have proceeded through three stages of political maturing: (1) apprenticeship during the Occupation; (2) retreat during the 1950s and 1960s to wrestle with social change, economic development, and reassessment of values; and (3) reassertion in the 1970s through civic movements and local elections.

Conversations with women about public affairs invariably result in musings about the nature of democracy and human values as practiced in their society. Because universal democracy was thrust on the Japanese suddenly, it came to include for them endless nuances of philosophy, ethics, religious precepts, social relations, customs, manners, and educational principles. It caused a reexamination of the entire spectrum of differences between oriental and occidental ways. For this reason, its contemporary interpretation by women is significant for an appreciation of their predisposition in public affairs.

Value Systems

In late 1964, almost 400 Japanese women, coming from a broad variety of organizational and educational backgrounds in the urban complex of Ōsaka, Kōbe, and Kyōto, met with a sprinkling of representatives from other countries to determine a set of values that would provide a philosophical base for community action. They agreed that the following six elements expressed a code to which all should adhere:

1. Faith in and respect for the individual and the individual personality, including one's own individuality and personality
2. Honesty and integrity
3. Helpfulness and cooperation
4. Neighborliness, especially as seen in the relationship of the individual to her society
5. Sense of responsibility to self and to society
6. Awareness of the stream of history so one may fit oneself and one's society and its problems into this stream[2]

This late autumn day of analysis was unusual only because of the size of the gathering and its international exchange, the latter important because it tied these Japanese standards—in reality well recognized—to those also espoused by public-spirited women from other parts of the world.

Haru Reischauer, wife of the U.S. ambassador to Japan, speaks at the international meeting in Ōsaka in 1964 on the importance of international understanding and participation in community activities. Photo courtesy of USIS/Japan.

Uncertainty about how to work within their democratic framework to carry out responsible civic action has plagued Japanese women since the shift from the authoritarian society after the war. Feudal doctrines offered the well-understood and judicious method of the vertical society, defined as "yielding to power" (*nagaimono ni wa makerero*). The ready pace of Meiji modernization and later the relatively easy acceptance of the U.S. occupiers was possible because Japanese accepted the orders of their modernizers and conquerors just as they had those of the pre-Meiji shōgun. Free to make their own decisions after the Occupation, women in the 1950s and 1960s tried to sort it all out when respite from the onerous chores of daily life provided time and energy.

Overall expectation required fulfilling democratic performance, first, in political and citizenship responsibilities, essentially equated with voting. It required, second, revised practices in family life so that each now had individual freedoms that modified old-fashioned patriarchal, vertical authority. One woman in the mid-1960s exemplified the contradictory anxieties this engendered in her quizzing of a Western visitor about the extent of her right to curtail her young son's freedom by insisting he turn off the television when she thought it detrimental to his study time or health.

Third, there was the economic element, which feminine idealists, eager for improved job opportunities and broader economic equalities, have long emphasized. Finally, there was the struggle to define the inner moral principles and value patterns of a democratic people. Even long-time practitioners from the United States, Britain, or France find it difficult to explain these niceties in precise terms. They may resort to proclaiming "liberty, equality, fraternity," or "life, liberty, and the pursuit of happiness," but every word of each rallying cry needs definition. Some cite bills of rights, such as the Magna Charta or the first ten amendments to the U.S. Constitution. Moreover, Westerners usually rely on their feel of the thing—a gut reaction, an inner sense not quickly cultivated.

It is appropriate to note that adapting to the new democracy in postwar Japan was rather easier for men. As loyal workers within their companies or the government, they adhered to the guidance of their primarily vertical organizations. Women, by comparison, were required to adapt not simply to the new Japanese norms, but also to the expectations of their new equalized status and increasingly modernized life-style—all complex adjustments.

Democratic Attitudes: The Women's View

How do women leaders, a quarter century or more later, view values in their modern, democratically constituted society? As with the old story about the group of blind people meeting an elephant for the first time, they answer in keeping with the depth and nature of their "touching" of the democratic system.[3]

"Democratic ideals," psychiatrist and educator Kamiya Mieko made plain,

> were achieved in Western countries step by step by people really thinking about them very hard. Winning them step by step is hard work. Here in Japan democracy arrived in a sudden switch. Freedom and democratic ideas were placed on the people, not just spontaneously, but through the American Occupation process with the result that it was rather unnatural, I think.

This frequently expressed view does an injustice to the devoted activities of prewar suffragists and other liberals, even though some admit that success on their own would have required many more decades. The grant of "democracy from above after the war" is also deprecated by some with anti-establishment policies. The Women's Democratic Club, which during the Occupation was involved in controversial takeover from its Western-oriented, democratic leadership, espouses this philosophy. Kyūshū-based young women of the "new left" persuasion declared that they worked in this club in their post-university, radical *demo* life to strengthen democracy at the local level in order to overcome the problems that arose from the way democracy was given to Japan after the war.

Matsuoka Yoko, an intense, seasoned radical and author, claimed it was the Constitution promulgated under the Occupation that moved her to the left. She was disappointed in the giver for having brought only a document to provide "bourgeois democracy." Educated before the war at Swarthmore College under a Tsuda scholarship and after the war at the Fletcher School of Law and Diplomacy, she was critical of what she considered the gap between democracy as she studied it and the way it was practiced under the Occupation in Japan and in the postwar United States. Her disillusionment turned her into a leading advocate of the "new left" and its causes. She embraced the peoples' democracy of the People's Republic of China, North Korea, and Vietnam, in which the "masses of people have a sense of values."[4]

Hirose Hamako, a Christian educator long associated with Hiroshima Women's University, regarded the spiritual foundation as more pertinent than political history:

> Even in the base of Japanese democracy, by comparison with American, there is the difference of the influence of Christian beliefs. Western democracy builds on Christian humanism and recognition of the dignity of man. By and large, lack of this Christian concept and naive reliance on under-cultivated religions, even animism, hampers the growth of Japanese democracy.

Old-time YWCA worker Katō Taka worried that only the skeleton of democracy is practiced, not the sense or the heart of it. Katō (Ishimoto) Shidzue, conscious of her own traditionally based training, explained this "skeleton" syndrome as a product of the sheer formality of Shintō and Buddhism. These religions require "no religious thinking, no profound philosophy of life." Their influence, she believed, is one of centuries of assiduous attention to ritualism and purity of form. Their influence makes it possible for many Japanese to equate tokenism with accomplishment. Katō warned that the advantages of democracy, if not fully assimilated, could lose Japanese the advantages of their traditional discipline.[5]

Kawanobe Shizu lamented that Japanese are selfish in their practice of democracy, lacking knowledge of the responsibility needed for its practice. In these charges she has been joined by many others. Parenthetically, the words "selfishness" and "egoism" are widely and interchangeably used to describe freedom or license exercised to the detriment of other citizens. Seki Fumiko, active as an Education Board member in Sapporo, blamed postwar schooling for teaching such "false democracy." She believed it makes young people forget the "soul, mind, and thoughtfulness of others, social service, and self-sacrifice." Instead they pay attention to "egoism, rationalism, and materialism designed to impress the surface of things." Sōma Yukika, with the heritage of the Ozeki family and a famous father who defied totalitarianism all his life, warned that lack of such moral principles leads to action "on an expediency basis."

As a corrective, Kawanobe recommended that mothers, as teachers and upholders of recognized mores, must themselves have a true appreciation of democracy and teach their children in the home (*katei-gakkyū*). How well they are doing with this responsibility fitfully enters discussion among women. The more pessimistic despair that mothers are no longer interested or are too busy with their outside jobs and have simply given it over to the schools.

For many, democracy is a system of live values that determines human relationships. One such is Kihira Teiko of the League of Women Voters. "Democracy for me is to have a real understanding of others; to have my heart refined and polished; and to be considerate of others and to put myself in others' places." Ichibangase Yasuko, viewing the issue as an educator, confirmed that "in recent years people begin to consider democracy a philosophy and one way of living. Making this happen is the hardest part of education." Yet, she noted, many come to an understanding of democracy through practical implementation because after the war democracy was "mainly a guiding principle of political methods, of voting, and of decision by the majority." Ichikawa Fusae, too, adhered to making democracy come alive through actual practice and advised that

> all people concerned in a question should come to a decision in which each is equal . . . this is a method which if applied in the home means the democratization of the family. If it is applied in politics, it is parliamentary democracy. Each person in such practice should be full-fledged and independent. Otherwise democracy becomes mobocracy.

She advocated that one of the best ways to give democracy strength is to get good people to come out and run for election, especially on the local level. Bito Shizuko of Hiroshima, locally active but unwilling to run for office, characterized her approach as achieving harmony through the give-and-take of true discussion. She set her hopes on the young generation to give strength to this way.

Of this younger generation in whom Bito has faith is Taguchi Sachiko, a modern university product and political activist. She has maintained that people must exercise democracy through the use of democratic machinery. She has been concerned lest people forget that in democracy the "majority will must be accepted at the same time the minority must be respected. It is like males and females. There is power in the minority status. Out of the respect of the majority for the minority as a good partner will come a better society." As a hard-working member of the Social Democratic party, which has always struggled as a minority in the political life of Japan, she has been keenly aware that the minority position assumes particular significance.

Equally conscious from her own experience with the preciousness of majority-minority balance is Shufuren leader Hosokawa Kou, who is not affiliated with a party. Depreciatingly, she likened democracy in Japan to a "wrinkled three-year-old child. . . . People think they have mastered democracy and are fully grown up, but they are actually very childish and immature." To illustrate, she criticized journalism as too much interested in "scooping and fault-finding, spoilt with commercialism"; she decried some of her younger fellow City Assembly members who indulged in loud shouts of *"baka"* (stupid) to express opposition to the views of another speaker. Such "egoistic" disregard for the opinion of others makes cooler heads "fear that democracy in Japan is getting weaker—or may not be true democracy at all."

Democracy is still a short-lived adventure in a country in which traditions lean on centuries of habit. Interpretation may have been clouded by the policies of the Ministry of Education since the end of the Occupation. Some worried about the doctrinaire proclivities of teachers, who as intellectuals and members of the teachers' union, Nikkyōsō, often favored the ideology of the left to counteract the mind-control of previous authoritarianism. As a result, the ministry decided it was undesirable to use the term "democracy" in class discussions about family matters, preferring such phrases as "human relationships between family members." Under this policy, "democracy" describes only the political form and does not extend to the community-mindedness of citizens (*rentai-ishiki*).[6]

That at least some of the women of the middle generation enjoy discussion of these issues was evident at the 1967 Niigata Conference, at which Kubota Kinuko urged that "political ceremony" was not enough. Some 500 women energetically argued over Japanese terminology of "citizenship" in a question-and-answer period that dominated the meeting. They sought not semantic answers but understanding of their civic responsibilities. The intellectual furor brought praise from both Kubota and the press.[7]

Foreign observers pass through Japan and, with their hurried Western sense of time or with the impatience of Third World critics, look unsuccessfully for dramatic upsurges of democratic self-assertion among Japanese women. After a superficial scan, they sweep on to the next country, reaffirming the cliché that Japanese women still wear the badge of "second-class citizens."

Yamamoto Matsuyo, experienced in Western concepts and living, thoughtfully pondering the often confusing and contradictory elements intertwined in democratic attitudes today, summed up with a typically Japanese reading. "Democracy was a drastic change and it takes time . . . it takes time." Younger women, trade unionists and educated after the war, simply said, "We have been living for a long time in a democratic way. We don't need to think about it again. Democracy is a matter of everyday life."

Political Training: Partisan and Nonpartisan

In 1972, on the tenth anniversary of the political education courses given at the Women's Suffrage Hall in Tōkyō, the *Asahi* newspaper heralded their work with the headline, "Remarkable Housewives Study at Fever Pitch." During the decade since 1962, 23,000 women had enrolled for a day each week of lectures and discussion on politics, the history of social philosophy, classics, psychology, and the law. Carrying their lunch boxes, they regularly converged on the secluded Shinjuku women's center from all parts of Tōkyō and its suburbs. The story reported that something over half the housewife seminarists were in their forties, had graduated from senior high school, and were "nonpolitical," i.e., not partisan. They were "eager . . . to study humbly."[8]

Civic education has never really been taught in schools in Japan. For one thing, it is not a prerequisite for those all-important examinations en route to higher education. Social education, which has successfully drawn thousands of adult women to classes, dwells on generalized social and political consciousness-raising. An illustration from Honshū's Tōhoku area shows how inspirational such programs can be. At the end of two days of one prefectural gathering held in the beautiful, almost snowbound spa of Hanamaki, a farm woman, with cheeks and hands weatherworn from working the family land in that area's harsh climate, encouraged her classmates: "Let's keep our eyes wide open for the changing world so that we, Iwate people, may not be left behind.

We will be the nucleus of Iwate women to . . . influence the policy makers. Let's be the torch to light up the future of Iwate."[9] One highly visible result of such classes is that since the mid-1960s more women than men have gone to the polls. This lesson in citizenship they have fully learned—and practice![10]

Social education officers handling adult education tread gingerly to avoid political ideological pitfalls. They themselves tend to be more conservative than classroom teachers and undoubtedly choose more restrictive interpretations in offering courses in practical citizenship. Each prefecture's program is drawn up "by democratic methods," Ōsaka's Toda Satsuki explained. The final offerings cautiously take into account the broad policies of the Ministry of Education, prefectural needs, and ideas from major women's organizations. Planners know that women hesitate to talk politics and are aware that training in how-to-do-it can inadvertently turn into indoctrination for support of one party or another.[11] The result is that adult education, like school courses, provides limited, nonpartisan citizen training to enable the ordinary individual to use the political system—including the mechanism of political parties— to achieve solutions to public problems. This policy of aloofness from the political scene helps explain why aroused citizens or groups who want to correct community problems or express grievances turn to petitions, demonstrations, and the increasingly popular *shimin undō*, a kind of civic action. These are the processes available to those outside the core political-governmental structure when they want to make themselves heard.

An exception that proves the rule was the two-year program of Tadotsu City, highlighted at the Kagawa Prefecture annual spring conference in Takamatsu in the mid-1960s. Combining classroom lectures and independent discussion with observation of local assembly meetings, the women's educational experiment became, in the words of the mayor, "the window to the town." He emphasized that there had been no criticism that the program had become political. Moreover, the participants felt, most importantly, that they understood town problems better, that they understood more fully the problems of the Assembly members, and that each was better able to contribute to conversation within her family. Said one panelist, "Now when I meet an assembly member, I don't just bow. I also think of that member's views and problems."[12]

Politically partisan groups also provide women's political education through classes or programs of special groups or full-blown organizations. Their purpose, as Kawakami Sueko announced in 1967 when the Social Democratic Women decided to form a Study Group on Women's Problems, is to establish a "main gate" through which to encourage women to enter the party fold.[13]

Advocates of democratic education and training in political processes—Kubota Kinuko, Sōma Yukika, and Katō (Ishimoto) Shidzue, 1967. Photo courtesy of USIS/Japan.

Starting on the left, the Communists have the New Japan's Women Organization (Shin nihon fujin no kai). It was reorganized in 1962 out of an earlier version with the support of leaders of the women's movement, notably Hiratsuka Raichō of Bluestocking fame. Twelve years later it claimed a membership of 300,000. Although party leaders indicate that this is only one of twenty-one women's organizations acting in concert with them, they rely on this organization as the major influence and about half their women party members belong. It is, according to the leaders, a "reservoir of potential new female members, and future party influence expansion depends on women."[14] The Communist party also recruits working women through small study and hobby groups at their working places, educating them about the indignities of their inequalities. Some of the legal cases discussed in previous sections on Japanese working women had their roots in such activities.[15]

The Socialist party has its Japan's Women's Council (Nihon fujin kaigi). Popular Upper House member Tanaka Sumiko, who in 1980 became the first woman elected deputy of her party, was one of the council's founders in 1962 and became its leader in the late 1960s. She has placed emphasis on bread and butter projects such as improvement of medical services and the health of women. More important is the connection between the Socialist party and the Sōhyō trade unions, of which Tanaka has also been a bureau chief.

Former Socialist Diet member Katō (Ishimoto) Shidzue has tended to scoff at the national power of the Socialist party women. The seesawing policies of the party itself, which result in fluctuating results in national elections, may account for her opinion. On balance, local Socialist-leaning groups, which consistently work for practical improvements, often of an anti-establishment nature, offer greater continuity and resultingly greater strength in local affairs. The Seikatsu Club in Tōkyō, for example, was founded in 1965 by the wife of a long-time Socialist who had learned in the bitter experience of electoral defeat that voters "cast their ballots not for mere theory or ideology, but for what politicians can do for them." The club, as a result, works to help housewives to a better life via a milk cooperative, thereby meshing the teaching of "capitalism's pitfalls" and women's interests.[16]

Organizing on a smaller, less effective scale, the Democratic Socialist party (DSP) has the Japan Democratic Women's Association (Nihon minshū fujin no kai), and although it is independent, works closely with the Dōmei-affiliated trade unions.

Kōmeitō, or the Clean Government party, relies on the religious network of Sōka gakkai. Converted women in endless telephoning recruit—or hound, depending on the point of view—individuals to join their small local groups and take part in discussions. There are two women's organizations—Shufu dōmei and Hataraku fujin no kai. The zealous spirit of the organizers of both Kōmeitō and Sōka gakkai can leave little doubt in the minds of any individual attracted that she is part of a huge religious-political force. Some 30 percent of those attending Kōmeitō's political school classes are women. The discipline of the members of the Sōka gakkai and of Kōmeitō has been compared to that of the Communists. Kōmeitō has been very selective about the timing and place of offering candidates, and pressures on members at election time depend upon whether Kōmeitō candidates are running. It is a movement of total devotion that carries along many men and women, particularly the less educated and those of lower incomes.

Comparable to the organizations cited above for the Liberal Democratic party (LDP) are Zen Nihon fujin renmei (All Japan Women's Federation) and Zen Nihon fujin bunka renmei (All Japan Women's Cultural Federation). An interesting variation is Fujin semina (Women's Seminar). LDP stalwarts Sōma Yukika and Hashiguchi Toshiko and others organized Fujin semina in 1970. They aim as much at education of wives of the LDP leaders as at conversion of the uninitiated. Said Hashiguchi: "On the average, Japanese read two newspapers a day. As a result they know something about politics. . . . but they don't understand the meaning. If they understand, they understand through their daily life experiences, not through fundamentals." Through Fujin semina she has tried to develop understanding as well as knowledge of events. The organization publishes a newspaper, has meetings with speakers, and takes up issues of the day, ranging from foreign policy to self-defense to vocational training in the United States. International exchange programs and leisure interests are part of the regime.

Hashiguchi, herself a continuous student and vigorous talker, commented on the study phenomenon. "In Japan, we say that women become talkative and noisy when they study." This belief led some of her male LDP friends in the Diet to resist her efforts to get their wives to the Fujin semina meetings. "I don't want her [my wife] to study," these men say. "I want her to be quiet."[17]

Some study groups, although not linked to any of the above parties, get entangled with party ideologies. By and large those of the "new left" point of view or the dissatisfied, such as radical feminists, follow the pipers of one or another of the anti-establishment political parties. Matsuoka Yoko, to illustrate, associated her followers with the Asian Women's Conference to Fight Against Aggression and Discrimination. On international issues, she encouraged support for the "line" of the people's democracies and, domestically, of proletariat improvement programs tied to removal of discrimination against women, particularly in the labor field. She has carefully made a distinction between this philosophy and feminist doctrines. Young working women gather in Matsuoka's tiny organizational headquarters in the top of a narrow building in the Tōkyō Ginza area to discuss, for instance, how to choose lawyers in discrimination cases and how to improve themselves. Said Matsuoka, "I know I am in a minority—very much so—and I do enjoy it. In a world wide sense, I feel I am in the majority. That is why this work is so hopeful." She believed that Japanese women are beginning to think for themselves, which she hailed as a good sign.[18]

The political power of such splinter groups is almost nonexistent within the legislative political framework. They manifest themselves when they join with others in special campaigns or take to the streets for massive rallies and demonstrations.

Ever since the Meiji-Taishō era's Peace Preservation Laws, women have used the ever-popular study-group route to organize themselves to influence political decisions. Now, with legal emancipation, many women, especially the more sophisticated, are still cautious lest through the wrong study-group connection they fall into political ideological traps. The situation results in political neutralism and a desire to be independent of party affiliation.

Long and Short Noodles

The difference between politically concerned women who run for political office and those who do not, said Kobayashi Hiro, is the difference between "long noodles, which stay on the chopsticks, and short ones, which slip off." Herself a persevering "long noodle" with a formidable record of pioneering electoral service in Nagasaki, Kobayashi lamented in this homely metaphor that there are many fewer long noodles than short. She and her family were in Nagasaki when the atomic bomb fell in 1945. The subsequent problems and consumers' difficulties of the postwar period led her to conclude that women had been politically irresponsible. Deciding she "wouldn't leave everything to the politicians," she ran and served in local and prefectural political offices for much of the next twenty years.[19]

The explanation for so many short noodles follows the logic of tradition and culture. Historically women were ostracized in the world of politics. Although legally permitted after the war, interest in politics has been considered unusual for women. They are "still shy," explained a fortyish Sōka gakkai organizer who believed young leadership, with encouragement, would react differently.[20] Supporting husband-candidates has seemed more natural—a practice followed abroad and in Japan since prewar times. Even so, an attitude of reluctance to put oneself forward is thoroughly Japanese. When questioned about running for office, prominent women answer that they need to know more before it is appropriate to take on the concomitant responsibilities. Jealousies between leaders add hindering complications. Women voters, especially in the middle-generation group, often feel men are more "appropriate" candidates.[21]

Certainly some of the women best trained in political science—and there are relatively few—might seem likely possibilities. Not so. Ogata Sadako, professor of international relations at Sophia University, after serving as the first woman minister in the Diplomatic Corps, responded when asked about running:

> I can't stand the idea of electioneering. . . . I can't get simple answers to the questions. I simply don't have the right kind of mind. I think good politicians see all this and can hook it on to something very simple in order to relay it to the public and to the constituents. I simply don't have the right style.[22]

Taguchi Sachiko of the DSP International Department declared that she would rather work hard behind the scenes to put someone else in the Diet. This, she explained, is the organizational way of activists. Matsuoka

Yoko, another likely candidate from the ranks of political scientists, has been afraid that if she ran under a party label she would simply be manipulated by the machine.

Others, politically minded if not academically politically trained, believe that sitting in the Diet takes away their freedom of action. Higa Masako of the Kansai Shufuren asserted that she had more power by not being in the Diet and preferred to use her strength for straightforward lobbying on issues vital to her and her group. There is serious question among many community and nationally prominent figures whether, given the political procedures within the Diet, a switch from "doing their own thing" into the political arena is worth the burden of personal limitations and rigid party adherence. Mincing no words, one Kyūshū community persuader spoke for those of this negative point of view: "I would have to be a 'fool' to run."

Those who do become candidates under political party sponsorship may be long-time political activists. Katō (Ishimoto) Shidzue of the Socialist party, whose husband was also a member of the Diet, sat in the Upper House almost continuously from the time women first could run until she was defeated in 1974. She candidly admitted that party affiliation gave her access to power within the Diet that she would not otherwise have had. Because she was a party member, she was able to sit on Diet committees and exert greater influence through these mechanisms.

Nakajima Nobue, a faithful Kōmeitō worker and official, ran for office, when asked, as a party service. She was defeated. She acknowledged that she was nominated in a situation in which she was not likely to be successful, a technique of political parties in more than one country to obtain token representation of women in politics without making real changes in the political power structure.

The lure for Kawanobe Shizu of the LDP was the argument that the government needed a change and that the time for social welfare had come. Her backing in Shizuoka Prefecture rested securely on support cutting across sex lines, which is essential for national-level campaigning. Male support Kawanobe welcomed as "that pinch of salt which makes a sweet cake sweeter." The decisive impetus pushing her toward candidacy, she claimed, were the detractors who said, "What can a woman do?" Hardly one to be intimidated, she regarded this view as a slur on all women. At the peak of her professional and volunteer power, Kawanobe decided that her age (64) made it a now-or-never gamble. Her sweeping election to the Diet in 1971 became the culmination of her many years of public service in Shizuoka.[23]

Candidacy as an independent has served the purposes of many a famous figure in Japan's women's movement. In the late 1940s most women had no official political affiliation, and parties reached out to them to obtain the female representation encouraged by Occupation authorities. Many were pushed into running because of their prominence in women's organizations. Oku Mumeo, for one, resisted party encumbrances, the better to pursue her own unorthodox interest in consumer affairs. She became one of the founders in 1947 of the Green Wind Society (Ryokufukai),[24] which was organized in the new Diet to symbolize the fresh start of democracy, steering a moderate course between right and left. Yamataka Shigeri held that her political party resided in the constituencies of the huge Chifuren and the Widows Association, which in the postwar decade was a powerful force. Even in 1977, Enoki Misako's organizing of the Japan Women's party, an offshoot of her feminist Chūpiren, was a contemporary expression of women's approach to the legislative arena as independent contenders.

In 1963, when the number of women in the Diet had declined to seven from a high of thirty-nine in 1946, many, such as Socialist Yamaguchi Shizue and Democratic Socialist Motojima Yurika, argued that such nonparty politics caused the decline in female representation. They pointed out that lack of party affiliation deprives the candidate of practical training, party organizational support, and financial assistance.[25] Lack of money has been a chronic complaint of women who seek to accomplish their purposes in public affairs. On the other hand, women within party ranks face the uphill battle of overcoming discriminatory in-house tactics.

Perennial Diet member Ichikawa Fusae, elected to the Upper House once again in 1980 at the age of eighty-seven, was perhaps the classic and certainly the most persistent example of the independent in Japanese national political life. She was her own woman. She stood alone. Not simply aloof from normal political party affiliation, she confronted the establishment. She represented the voice of morality in politics. A champion of women's rights, she always ran on the basis of a political process known throughout Japan as "clean elections." This should not be confused with the Clean Government party (Kōmeitō).

Ideal Campaigning

The ideal or "clean" election concept in Japan started with Tazawa Yoshiharu in 1924, the year he established the Dai Nihon seinen dan (Greater Japan Youth Group). When his young followers urged him to run for office, he agreed and used the slogan of *"Risō senkyo,"* or ideal election or campaign. From this episode emerged the philosophy and technique so intimately associated with Ichikawa Fusae and many of the women's organizations.

Electioneering in Japan is nominally regulated by highly restrictive laws. The time span allowed for campaigning is only three weeks. Photo picture displays of limited size should be only on shared billboards, giving equal space to portraits of all candidates. These and other regulations are largely ignored by aggressive candidates, who spread largess around liberally and hire squads of sound trucks to blare out the candidate's name in endless repetition.

Basically, a fair campaign requires that the candidate (1) observe the Election Law, (2) not use more money than is designated by law, and (3) rely on volunteer campaign promotion by ordinary voters. This means precise observance of the official dates for public announcement of the candidacy, not starting early to promote the person. Only the legal number of posters are to be pasted up and the legal number of promotional postcards mailed out. As the candidate may not use his own money, supporting voters must contribute funds. They also raise small sums from many others—the so-called 100-yen method. They bring their own *obento* box lunch when helping with the campaign. In this day of expensive campaigning and lavish use of funds, as well as frequent reliance on candidates who are mass media personalities, the ideal campaign with its low-key electioneering style becomes largely an act of faith. The clean election group calls such campaigning a protest against the misused power of the political party and money.[26]

Support for clean elections has been a basic tenet of the Japanese League of Women Voters since its founding in the Occupation years. Chifuren endorsed the principle at its inaugural general assembly in 1952. Other women's organizations joined in a call for people to keep their eyes open for illegal pre-election campaigning. Chifuren in 1954 petitioned each political party for a more detailed election law to sustain this view. It printed a pamphlet distributed nationwide, "Twelve Don'ts in Regard to Election," and promoted a clean election song. The movement disseminated a picture-story play done up as a coloring book for mothers and members of the women's associations to fill in and then dramatize the story of "Haru and One Vote."[27]

In 1960, at the instigation of Ichikawa Fusae, a citizen's Ideal Election Campaign Association was founded at a meeting of more than 200 men and women in the House of Councillors' Club in Tōkyō. It has helped select and nominate candidates to run for the Diet on the principles of this ideal ever since. The voice of Ichikawa and this group undoubtedly influenced Governor Minobe of Tōkyō to announce at the time of his first candidacy that he, too, wished to conduct a fair campaign. This declaration heightened his attractiveness to women voters, with whose support he swept to victory.

Table 5.1. Number of Women Elected to Local Office by
Party Affiliation, 1951-1979

Affiliation	1951	1960	1971	1975	1979
Liberal Democratic Party (LDP)	54	82	55	39	41
Japan Socialist Party (JCP)	22	39	85	101	109
Democratic Socialist Party (DSP)	11	11	16	13	11
Kōmeitō	--	--	10	24	27
Communist party	17	15	126	264	330
Independent	905	429	308	275	272
Others	11	--	--	--	3
Total	1,020	576	600	716	793

The ideal candidate is one who is hesitant to run for office and yet is considered perfectly suited by the voters. Candidates should be drafted by those who believe in them and volunteer to work on the candidate's behalf. This is a congenial method for women, who typically hang back and need to be pushed by group consensus to stand apart and above in the candidate's spotlight.

Ichikawa and the election of 1953 provided an early example of the fair election in action. Having just returned from the United States, she was invited by the League of Women Voters to stand for the House of Councillors. She refused to respond until a number of prominent women's organizations cooperatively rallied the consensus voice to draft her. At that point she relented. She accepted with the proviso that she would run only "if I can go on not only clean and clear but also with an ideal election. . . . I shall not use sound trucks and will do no street speaking. I shall not plead with people—just make public speeches and put up the legal number of posters and [send out the legal number of] recommendation cards."[28] She did just that, and although she spent less than 10 percent of normal campaign costs, she was elected.

On the local level, women candidates running clean election campaigns on independent tickets until the late 1970s did better than those of any party affiliation. Then in 1979, with an overall elected total of 793 women, one short of that of the first local election in 1946, the Communist candidates moved ahead, accounting for most of the increase of 77 seats since 1975 (see Table 5.1).

The League of Women Voters thinks both local candidates and those aspiring to the House of Councillors will get more votes if they eschew party connections. Even independents, however, may have a loose, personal party affiliation evidenced more by the ideology the candidates express than by direct party involvement. The clean election–independent position allows candidates to disassociate themselves from long-established graft or power patterns, local party in-fighting, and ward-heeling. They are free to stress issues dear to women and to practical community development.

Ōta Hiroko of Saitama Prefecture, a young modernist, reached the local assembly in 1972 on such a campaign. Her causes of day care centers and the evils of industrial pollution suited the motto of clean elections: "*Detai hito yori dashitai hito,*" or "Let's support the person whom you want to send rather than one who wants to run herself." Said Ichikawa about Ōta, "She is a bright girl, and her supporters are all clever girls. I was impressed with them and their attitude toward the elections so I supported her by giving them campaign donations and letting them use my campaign paraphernalia."[29]

Not all who use these methods are successful. Fujita Taki, long affiliated with Tsuda College, as student, teacher, and president, shrugged her shoulders and chuckled in her special manner when discussing her unsuccessful race for a Diet seat, implying she just did not know what to do. She could not manage to spend even half the money raised by the enthusiastic Tsuda College students and alumnae who supported her. Her adherents considered that she probably carried her modest behavior too far. She did not even wear a name band across her chest when she appeared in public meetings and on television with other candidates so that voters could learn to recognize her written name (names are not written phonetically) as it would appear in the polling booth on the ballot.

Some of the big independents already in the Diet, such as Yamataka Shigeri, fell by the wayside when using this technique in the 1971 election, which wreaked such havoc nationally and locally on women independents. A year after the event she concluded that the time of the independent candidate was not yet over. But, she went on, if one wants to be a Diet member, one should be a Conservative and spend a lot of money!

In 1974 Kihira Teiko, the president of the League of Women Voters, whom Ichikawa had trained as her protégée, failed in her try as an independent for the Upper House. She struggled with the insurmountable odds of the single constituency of Tōkyō and the lack of popular recognition inevitable in the clean election process. Famed novelist Ariyoshi Sawako campaigned for her every day because she regarded Kihira as the only candidate in Tōkyō really representative of the people. It was not enough. Only in her forties, Kihira did not yet invoke the reverential homage among the women that surrounded Ichikawa like a halo. Furthermore, Kihira suffered from the unexpected reentry of

Ichikawa onto the election scene, which automatically placed her in a subordinate vote-getting position.

Ichikawa had been defeated in 1971 in a tough race fighting for the Tōkyō constituency. Her friends blamed the hazards of the race in a single constituency by comparison with the national at-large constituency. Tōkyō is a sophisticated place with many young voters who did not know her important role in the historic women's movement. Her proposals for amendment of laws on elections and political funding were not popular with the political and industrial elements. The defeat, however, gave her nationwide publicity and permitted her time to undertake extensive speaking tours to educate the public about the abuse of political funds. This cause and her increasing visibility as a charismatic figure fighting the system highlighted her 1974 campaign. Her champions were men and women students studying clean elections, consumerists, environmentalists, and those eager for improvement in the quality of life. The students, blessed with the leisure time typical of Japanese universities, organized caravans of jeeps bedecked with flags and rallied voters with the motto, "Keep on Walking, Ichikawa Fusae." Consumerists promoted her through "blue sky" market campaigning (that is, campaigning out of doors—which implies an absence of corruption). Not a single poster was put up. The mass media boosted her. The campaigners used but ¥5.3 million of the ¥12 million raised by individual donations, when ¥18 million was legally allowable. The funds remaining, as also the prize of the Magsaysay Foundation awarded in August 1974 for her service to the community, she donated to clean campaign and related research.

When the results came in, Ichikawa had garnered 1,937,448 votes, exceeded only by television personality Miyata Teru among the 112 candidates vying for 54 national seats. With this large vote came the power of its prestige. She was again a *"kyōsōsama,"* or great and honored competitor. The vote evidenced the strong public endorsement of her ideas. With her new leverage, she was better able to exert influence against big public utility corporations already under public attack for election contribution practices. In the weeks after the election the companies withdrew one by one from the Kokumin kyōkai, the fund-raising arm of the Liberal Democratic party.[30] The effect was unprecedented and propitious.

Ichikawa's uncompromising and untainted reputation in political affairs and the endorsement of the youth and reform groups had appealed to the general public. The people were disgusted with excessive campaign spending. They worried about the moral fiber of modern Japan, which had witnessed the "black mist" of corruption enveloping the parties of the right as well as the left. Ichikawa swept forward on a reaction of repugnance against the political machines.

Some asked after the 1974 election whether the Ichikawa phenomenon was merely another "personality" episode or part of a reform trend. Within three years, the Lockheed uproar and the ramifications of the "black peanuts" payoffs battered the LDP, swept away Prime Minister Tanaka, and shook the very foundations of parliamentary democracy.[31] The ensuing national attention to the reform of political practices and to the cleansing of the civic spirit, for which Ichikawa and the women's organizations had fought so long, provided a kind of unhappy vindication of their devoted efforts.

Ichikawa Fusae died in 1981, having in her last successful independent clean election campaign for a fifth term in the Upper House in 1980 become the top national at-large vote-getter, winning more than 4.5 percent of all votes cast. The story of her life is the modern history of Japanese women in their country's political life. At every stage her leadership stood for courage and undaunted pursuit of political morality. Her dedication made her in her final years the lodestar of all women— even more, an admired and trusted national figure. Masuda Reiko, editorial writer of the *Mainichi shimbun,* mourned in her eulogy:

> Never will there be another politician for whom the people will shed real tears. . . . Ms. Ichikawa Fusae was a great bright torch leading and encouraging us and providing us with hope and vitality.
>
> The loss of Ms. Ichikawa is like losing the concentration of the minds of the people who have been unceasingly seeking clean and just politics.[32]

Ichikawa Fusae's death ended an era. Her passing threw out the challenge to those who would be her worthy successors.

———————

In the court of public judgment, Japanese women routinely stand charged with the offense of indifference to politics. Statistical samplings show their interest in political affairs is actually not much lower than that of men.[33] Aroused women castigate their less responsive sisters. Said one in a speech to an assembly of foreign diplomats, "For some women to despise female students who struggle with their staves and at the same time feel easy about their own womanly indifference to politics is very strange. I think indifference is as bad as violence in politics."[34]

The complication is that these accusations take no account of the nature of the influence women do exert. Ogata Sadako has said that they limit their political role in keeping with their own particular ambitions and conscientiousness of purpose.[35] Guardianship of political

Ichikawa Fusae speaks at a street demonstration against the Lockheed scandals and for clean politics and electoral reforms, June 29, 1976. Photo courtesy Fusen kaikan.

Ichikawa Fusae addresses the plenary session of the House of Councillors in what proved to be her last interpolation, January 1979. Photo courtesy of Kyodo Photo Service.

Loyal supporters of Ichikawa Fusae (seated center) celebrate at the Fusen kaikan her victory in the House of Councillors election, June 23, 1980, with shouts of "*banzai*" and raised arms. The sign proclaims, "Victory is based on ideal elections." Photo courtesy of Kyodo Photo Service.

morality is one characteristic they cultivate. It is the public affairs alter ego of the diligent housewife: Spiritually, clean elections and honest, frugal campaign spending go hand in hand with daily sweeping of the *tatami* and careful husbanding of family finances. It is consistent with their worries about the quality of modern life and their comparisons of industrial and urban pollution with political corruption. It is rooted in the working code of women leaders as they participate in the political process.

Adherence to nonpolitical politics emerges as another bent of women's public affairs personality. This tendency in part underlies the attitudes condemned as indifference. Fearful of being duped or used by the partisan activist, they choose the safer course that refrains from public endorsement of any clear-cut political party bias.

Faithfulness in going to the polls is a third trait of women in their political lives. It is an expression of democratic participation and personal democratic fulfillment. This performance may be criticized as the mere discharging of a ritual taught in school and social education classes and absorbed as approved doctrine since the 1940s, but it is also a practice that carries power of decision in the no-nonsense count of ballots at the end of an election day. Since the last half of the 1960s, the trend in national and local elections has been consistent: The percentage of eligible women voting is greater than that of men. If the fact that the sheer number of women voters is larger than that of men is added to their other characteristics of political morality and aloofness from partisan expression, their electoral habits give women the effectiveness of the "swing vote" to wield in closely contested situations. It is the alert political party and wise politician who pays heed to the proclivities of this unencumbered majority of the voting public.

POLITICAL ACTION—
PETITIONERS AND OFFICEHOLDERS

> *Almost all members of civic action groups are housewives because action starts with problems in daily life. Housewives are the heroines of civic action. They never fail to play an important part in campaigns to protect the quality of life and the consumer and to improve educational and health problems. Many active groups have only women members. Some originated out of other women's organizations and the PTA, and some simply from the "chatter by the well" (idobata kagi).*
> *—Asahi shimbun,* May 21, 1973[36]

The women's lobby busily, ceaselessly prods the body politic into the refashioning of Japanese society. The wellspring of impulse to improve both the spiritual and physical quality of life in contemporary Japan very often arises from women, who not only "chatter by the well" but then act from such motivation and information. Issues that move them from chatter to action radiate from the assessed needs of home and family. They are inspired by a mixture of defense of the hearth, desire for self-fulfillment, and democratic awareness.

Excluded from the tight, hierarchical political mainstream, women depend primarily on reliable, traditional neighborhood ties or on their own organizations.[37] Seldom united, let alone monolithic, women ply acquired skills to exert influence. They lobby; they take up civic action; they engage in practical politics. When pressures build a sense of urgency requiring a response from reluctant seats of power, they may resort to opposition tactics.

Civic Organizations: The League of Women Voters

Before the war free-spirited, crusading women banded together in small, independent organizations, often depreciatingly labeled suffragist or emancipationist. Direct organizational descendants exist today. They still organize, educate, and fight for women's rights. They also mobilize more broadly for improvement of public and community affairs.

True to this heritage is the League of Women Voters (LWV) of Japan, one of the most important if not one of the largest of the women's civic organizations. Still active in its ranks are women identified with the early fight for feminine equality. The league founder, Ichikawa Fusae, argued in the 1970s just as vigorously as fifty years previously that ways must be found "to bring women's power into full scope." Women should "stand on their own feet in their own awareness, establishing their own subjectivity and developing their own ability." She called for "courageous women who do not yield to money, power, *giri* (obligations), and *ninjō* (sentiment)."[38]

An inheritor of this legacy is the serious, hard-working Kihira Teiko, who interweaves duties as president of the league with equivocal aspirations for a seat in the Diet. Of the same generation as Tanaka Satoko of Chifuren, for more than twenty years Kihira had faithfully served the organization and its founder-leader. Because her father had always praised Ichikawa, she went in 1949 to ask Ichikawa to find a job for her husband. Instead she found a vocation for herself.

Political Tactics. Officially nonpartisan, the league emphasizes both the deepening of women's political consciousness and civic watchdog activities. It enlightens women on political methods and issues. It rallies them to campaign to bring spartan, honest government to the people.

In anticipation of elections, members consult with candidates in ways well known to members of the U.S. league, with whom they are in touch but not formally associated. The league, often in cooperation with other like-minded organizations, invites candidates to discuss their policies and opinions through questionnaires or at candidates' open meetings. Because of Japanese election laws, such meetings must be held prior to the opening of the official campaign period—a curious regulatory logic.

At election time, the league publicizes election laws and advises voters about their rights. It is a strong advocate, as already seen, of the clean elections process. The national office distributes as many as 200,000 guidebooks of information on candidates and their positions on issues. Chapters often print local editions to highlight their own situations.

After elections, leaguers regularly discuss their concerns with the government. In Tōkyō, for instance, where the league was active in the gubernatorial election that brought Minobe Ryōkichi to office for the first time in 1967, they joined with members of other civic-minded women's groups to discuss with him issues ranging from wholesale market prices, transportation, and the nature of the Tōkyō Assembly to water supply and pollutions of all kinds. Kihira explained how they went about their consultation:

We give Minobe suggestions. At the same time we ask him questions. Sometimes he raises problems he wants the people of Tōkyō to understand. He may want us to support his plan to restrict the number of cars allowed into the city. After the last meeting on this traffic problem, for instance, we did indeed talk to the Metropolitan Police Board, which was not in favor of Minobe's plan. Sometimes cooperating with Chifuren and Shufuren in the Group for the Improvement of the Tōkyō Metropolitan Police, we sponsor a meeting and invite Minobe. At other times, only five or six organizational representatives meet with him in his offices. We may talk about his hopes to do away with public gambling. Following that meeting, our organization prepared a petition which was accepted by the chairman of the Tōkyō Metropolitan Assembly and which now obligates them to prepare appropriate legislation.

Most petitions are received by politicians and forgotten. . . . We follow up on our petitions to local governments through open letters and questionnaires to each party and in meeting with party members individually to talk with them.[39]

Although Minobe rated the capabilities of women highly and called himself "the feminist governor," Kihira lamented that he was not good at making the best use of their capabilities.[40] Nevertheless, the working relationship was close between this powerful liberal-minded executive of the biggest city in the world and his staunch female constituency.

On national issues, six nonpolitical organizations—Women's International League for Peace and Freedom, League of Women Voters, Women's Christian Temperance Union, Japan Nursing Association, Chifuren, and the Tōkyō YWCA—have cooperated since 1957 in the Diet Liaison Committee (Fujin dantai gikai katsudō renraku iinkai) to formulate joint policies. They besiege the prime minister, the Diet, the ministries, and the bureaucracy. Their well-known points of view, frequently of the hair-shirt variety, push for morality in elections, women's rights, pollution controls, and consumer problems, issues on which a skeptical, unsympathetic conservative establishment has been wont to drag its feet.

The lobbying power of women in organizations has continued to grow. At the time of the Lockheed crisis, which was moving to a climax in April 1976—a time when women were alerted to political activism as they celebrated the thirtieth anniversary of their first vote—seventeen organizations reported national lobbying. Subsequently, through enthusiasm for implementation of the National Plan of Action, forty-eight nationwide women's organizations, including labor unions, joined in the Liaison Group for the Implementation of Resolutions from the

International Women's Year Conference to present coordinated viewpoints and demand action.

Over the years prime ministers have continued to meet with the
politically conscious activists on request. Prime Minister Satō periodically
invited women leaders to his famous breakfast sessions to discuss trends
and policies. Generally, however, they were from academia and the
media, rather than the more demanding lobbyists from civic organizations, for, as one invitee noted, he recognized the hazards of an open-
door relationship with reformist women. Nonetheless, those advocating
a cause saw him and his successors when the issues warranted, and
by now such meetings are built into their routine strategy of political
lobbying.[41]

When approaching the Diet, the organized women naturally turn to
friendly sponsors to convert their petitions into legislation. Kihira indicated that it is very difficult to use the same petition methods with
the Diet as they do on the local level because, "Realistically, a petition,
if it is to have any effect at the Diet level, must be accepted by the
LDP. The fact that only one party in Japan is powerful, i.e., the LDP,
is the biggest problem we have."[42] Yet perseverance over the years has
brought successes directly attributable to their efforts, and there is
realization that these women represent both a ground swell of conscience
as well as the mood of people.

Local Chapters. As is so often noted, civic-minded women can exert
maximum influence on political affairs at the local level. The Hiroshima
league during the leadership of Bito Shizuko provides a good example.

A graceful devotee of the Noh dance and Japanese ceremonial arts,
Bito looks like a gracious housewife who would not make any waves;
her strength and determination are softened by impeccable decorum.
She came to the League of Women Voters as a PTA member interested
in supporting a woman candidate for the local Board of Education. Her
rise to leadership was possible, she explained, because she had no rank
or occupation. Her late husband helped her make the sacrifices that
are often requisite to leadership—sacrifices that stem from the suspicion
and hostility with which the league is often viewed because its work
requires critical evaluation of local politics and established political
leaders.

Reminiscences of her earlier years brought out that Bito migrated to
Korea to find a job and start a new life after the death of her first
husband. This move enabled her to break out of the restrictions of
widowhood in Japanese society and to find a second husband. As with
the five young girls sent to the United States by the Emperor Meiji,
her experiences outside the heartland of Japan helped embolden her to
undertake community responsibility after her return.

The Hiroshima league functions as much like a chapter in the United States as its Japanese cultural setting permits. Since 1960, for example, it has achieved solution of a garbage disposal issue. In a long and complicated struggle, it helped clean up malpractices of the "one-day-assemblymen," who attended only the opening day of the Assembly but collected full salary for the entire session. The league regularly sends questionnaires at election time to Assembly members, asking what they wish to do next, whether they have kept their election pledges, and if not, why not. All activities aim at fulfilling fundamental league objectives of political education of the public and safeguarding parliamentary democracy to serve people's needs. Bito's philosophy of faith bespeaks the moral strength of the league: "[I would never] compromise my principles with anyone in power when I believe I am right . . . that is the reason why the work of the league is so hard, but so important."[43]

Linking the Generations. The national leadership of the league builds its hopes for the future of the organization on this same faith. There is also recognition that the organization must keep step with the changing of generations and update its priorities to suit the mood of the times. The membership must expand—membership was about 4,000 in 1975 and some 80,000 would be needed to make it proportional in size to its U.S. counterpart—and it must increase the number of its chapters, fifty-one in 1974. Young women must be recruited to membership—a difficult task because so many now work full-time and wish to avoid domination by less educated older leaders. Kihira long ago recognized that concentration on women's welfare does not always mesh with larger national social issues and that the organization must progress from old-fashioned study techniques into a movement vibrating with the times. She has argued that

> members of LWV should organize many tiny groups here and there to cope with daily problems. . . . this will raise women's political consciousness. By solving definite problems, they learn to participate in politics. For instance, there is a group who opposed the building of a bowling alley in the middle of a residential district. . . . [knowing that] if the bowling alley goes up, they can expect more cars, snack bars and noise. . . . Not only recreational issues, but education and other matters can also give women impetus to organize groups. . . . In many cases leaders of such small groups are members of LWV. I don't think everybody should become a LWV member. Rather the important thing is for LWV members to be leaders of community movements. . . . all with similar purposes.

Kihira advocated the linking of the trained membership of her older established organization with the adherents of the newer, more spontaneous impulses of local democratic action.[44] Such a union would pass the baton of women's civic obligations from one generation to the next and simultaneously build on the strength of both experience and immediacy.

The Modern Way of the Citizen

Analyzing her own younger generation, one International Christian University modernist maintained in 1968 that "what the new woman needs to do to achieve greater equality and a sense of identity is surmount her own diffidence and find a greater dedication elsewhere, i.e., apart from her role as housewife-mother, so that she can become an important and integral part of her community."[45]

Increasingly this new woman of the last quarter of the twentieth century is finding an outlet in solving community problems, often through the modern "way of the citizen," generically termed *shimin undō.* Spending all or much of her time in the area in which her home is located, the average housewife seems a full-time citizen of the local community by comparison with her commuter husband, who comes home at night only long enough to sleep and return to his job, giving her the opportunity to become the central figure among the new "civic-type Japanese." At thirty-five this average housewife manifests the changed life-cycle of women. Her involvement is possible because of postwar democratic education, spare time, and relative affluence. Her improved ability to debate, a skill polished in PTA meetings and at her place of work, contributes to her overall competence.

Author Mishima Sumie has declared that such women are motivated to take up civic causes because they have inadequate opportunities in regular political life. Perhaps so. In contrast to long-established formal organizations like the league, *shimin undō* is an ad hoc and amorphous movement, spawned in response to short-term problems, usually local in scope. It developed as a major training ground in nonpartisan political consciousness in the late 1960s and is expected to grow in the years ahead.[46]

The dawn of each day may see as many as 2,000 to 3,000 new local civic campaigns get under way across Japan. The action invariably centers on living standards and the environment. It is generated by some negative impact on the home and kitchen by local government or political and industrial forces. It may be a fight against industrial pollution of the Tamagawa River successfully led by a thirty-three-year-old polio-paralyzed woman, or a Tōkyō suburban housewives' study-group campaign to forestall the rezoning of their semiresidential ward to permit factory expansion. It may be a class action suit against the noise of Ōsaka Airport—a legal proceeding compared in an editorial to "an army of ants attacking a huge elephant."[47]

The right to sunshine has precipitated many episodes. In Musashino, a suburb of Tōkyō, new high-rise buildings that tower over tiny family gardens set residents in motion. Typical of the complaints was the lament of a widow and mother: "I can no longer air *futon* quilts and washing won't dry outside. Maple trees in the yard started withering and the air inside the house is very humid, and it is very chilly."[48] A "right to sunshine" campaign in Chiba resulted in payment of sizable compensation. In due course a new city ordinance banned the construction of buildings of more than five stories without the consent of nearby residents. Similarly, "resident power" has won court rulings in Ōsaka, Tōkyō, and other cities. However, the very slowness of court procedures with little legal precedent has contributed to the increase in *shimin undō* activism. Large construction companies, as well as others, decry the "egoism" of these movements, which "sacrifice the welfare of all city dwellers" who need high-rise homes in crowded cities. Yet the human right to sunshine appeals to the aesthetic and to the small landowner who also demands a place in the sun—a right that could assume greater and greater importance as the nation increasingly turns to solar heating.

When violence is superimposed on the more routine techniques of civic expression, the desires of all may be frustrated. Such was the case with the Narita farmers' struggle against the new International Airport for Tōkyō in Chiba. Long protestations were of no avail, even though women wept in their appeal to the governor. Obdurate farm families dug in, siege-fashion, to resist occupation of their lands by construction machinery and to bargain for more compensation. Their cause attracted outside dissidents. Radical university students from all over the country jumped in with demonstration tactics that soon escalated to the assassination of police officers. A children's action corps was mobilized and took the field, a step that split the protagonists. Next came the massive intervention of a politically partisan national power—in this instance the Communist party supported Gensuikyō (Japan Council Against Atomic and Hydrogen Bombs), an organization that is strongly, sometimes violently, anti-establishment, regardless of the issue. The campaign illustrates the complexity of an encounter that can originate innocently in natural peasant attachment to the land and possibly exacerbated by human avarice, as solatium payments are always sizably increased by noisy protestors. However, if organized resistance becomes a tool for larger political forces, the effort can be counterproductive, with heavy losses for all.

Civic Movement: Garbage

The Suginami garbage war portrays a completely typical example of women in action on the *shimin undō* front. Historically, this issue, like prices, has brought women out from behind their *shōji* doors to confront the government. The garbage war of the late 1930s, for instance, expanded into a national project publicized by an educational play made into a movie. The stellar cast brought together Yamataka Shigeri, Kubushiro Ochimi, Akamatsu Tsuneko, Ichikawa Fusae, and others in a campaign for the "municipal cleaning" of Tōkyō. One amusing result is that for years the nickname "Garbage Grandmother" followed Yamataka, who played that role.[49] It also may well have boosted her national political career.

Forty years later the women of the Suginami ward of Tōkyō, in time-honored tradition, protested about garbage, this time relying on the modern tactics of *shimin undō*. For a long time their neighbor, Kōtō Ward, had suffered constant invasion by other wards' municipal garbage trucks carrying 70 percent of Tōkyō's waste and garbage to be dumped as landfill on Kōtō Ward's shoreline in the bay. Finally Governor Minobe in 1971 announced a "war" against the garbage problem: Each ward would share the suffering and build its own incinerator by 1975. Suginami was asked to be the first to comply. Reluctance and indecision forestalled action, and Kōtō residents built up resentment against their neighbors.

Trouble erupted in January 1973 when the Tōkyō metropolitan government suggested that a park area in Suginami be used for temporary storage of local garbage during the New Year holidays, when regular garbage trucks did not operate. Politics entered the issue. A Tōkyō assemblyman of the Liberal Democratic party, Tanaka Mitsuru, tried unsuccessfully to arouse opposition, probably to embarrass Governor Minobe, a Socialist. By March, however, Tanaka was able to warn the influential Neighborhood Association that the Tōkyō government had decided to build an incinerator plant in their park. The association distributed a handbill in opposition, but it provoked little reaction.

Meantime, some of the women became upset. There are six schools near the park, and the area had already been attacked by photochemical smog! Further, the new incinerator would require the demolition of some homes along the widened access road, and the big garbage trucks themselves would make the air pollution worse. The women forthwith organized the Society to Protect the Greenery of Wadabori Park (Wadabori no midori o mamoru kai). Said one leader, "We couldn't wait for the slowness of the Neighborhood Association and we didn't like the issue to be made use of by LDP's political tactics as before in January."

Approximately thirty members of the society, mostly housewives in their thirties and forties whose land and homes were directly threatened by the building of the incinerator plant and the access road, astutely elected as their president the vice-president of the Neighborhood Association. They elected as vice-president the man who had given them advice about making posters. For funds, the housewives turned to the two factories that would have to be evacuated when the incinerator was built. Each donated ¥45,000, or about $300. This was all the money the little society had.

During the three months from March to May 1973, when the local garbage war between the wards was at its height, the tiny group of civic activists conducted a "telephone offensive" (*denwa-kōsei*). Assigned to telephone the Socialist party ward chief, one activist, Mizutani Kakuko, fulfilled her responsibilities "precisely" at nine o'clock in the morning and was surprised that he listened quietly to her argument.

Mizutani typifies one version of a *shimin undō* woman. Of the midwar generation, with eight years of schooling, she had three children and a traditionalist husband, a blue-collar worker for Mitsubishi Heavy Industries. He did not like her to use words like "capitalist" and "citizens" (*shihonka* and *shomin*) and resisted sending their daughter to college. Although husband and wife thought differently about the role of women in community activities, in this instance her concern for her home and family prevailed.

Step by step her little group worked to rally support. Mizutani and some of her colleagues visited the ward chief in person with their petition, signed by about 2,000 residents opposed to the building of the incinerator plant in the park. The group produced fifty green sashes bearing opposition slogans to wear around their heads and three big signs on green cotton cloth to represent the green park they would lose to the incinerator. At meetings of the Tōkyō and ward government committees, they wore the green sashes on their heads. Unlike the neighboring Takaido group, the Wadabori Park Society listened quietly in silent protest, rather than shouting to disrupt the meeting. Meanwhile, Kōtō Ward's threats to blockade, by violence if necessary, Suginami trucks en route to the bay heightened the urgency of finding a solution. It was finally decided to build the incinerator at Takaido, and so the Wadabori group disbanded, not wishing to get involved permanently with political parties.

It is interesting to note that Mizutani, not unlike the younger generation, thought of excitement in life as involving times of struggle and opposition. Before the garbage war, she was aware that she had missed "the primitive time during the war and just after the war when there was little food and clothing and nothing to throw away." After the garbage war, learning through her attendance at the ward's social education classes, she turned to the consumer struggle and the "critical" commodity price problem. Said Mizutani, "We are now in the age when public opinion is quickly reflected so civic action is very important and effective. We won't sit and wait for the government's countermeasures as before. We citizens have to stand up and stop the price hike."

Mizutani's standing up is the *shimin undō* spirit that continues to have far-reaching effects for strengthening local autonomy in Japan and lessening dependence on centralized administration. In Suginami, the final agreement, reached in 1974 after eight years of dispute and negotiation about the construction of the Takaido incinerator, provided for resident representation in decision making about its design and operation. Suginami's example led populous Shinjuku Ward to erect its new incinerator in a modern, attractive high-rise building in the middle of the business district, spending extra funds to insure freedom from air pollution.[50] Fortunately, technology to do so is available at a price, and the higher price of better living is now being accepted.

More and more the voice of the organized citizen—now strongly the voice of women—demands concessions to improve or insure livable surroundings. How much the impetus of this public consciousness is greedy interest in solatium and how much is democratic concern and civic pride continues to be debated.[51] The tactics and organizational patterns deviate from the old-style dominance of single-person leadership. *Shimin undō* groups combine democratic methods with traditional anonymity and the safety of facelessness. Minobe noted that *shimin undō* cannot but result in people's "standing against the government, but such a check and balance function is a must for democratic administration." He found it very hopeful. Obviously so do about 80 percent of Japan's people, who are willing to raise up such movements to protect their interests. They insert a democratic will into modernizing the law and effecting social change.[52]

The Political Nose Count

An accepted measure of political participation is to count incumbents in elective and appointive offices, membership in recognized political parties, and numbers voting, both total and by percentage of eligibility. These figures are easily compared on the yardstick of civic duty.

For Japanese women the nose count in the Diet started at its highest with the first, history-making election in 1946, when thirty-nine out of seventy-nine women candidates made it to the House of Representatives. In 1947 eleven women were successful in the first Upper House election. Subsequently, men returned from their war duties and reestablished their previous political patterns. From 1950 on, the number of women serving in both houses remained between twenty and twenty-eight, roughly 3 percent of the seats—a level comparable to that in the United States.[53]

Below the national level, historical comparisons become difficult because of electoral changes and local administrative reorganizing, but the proportion of women to men elected is lower than at the national level. In prefectural bodies there were 23 women in 1947, 39 in 1967, and 34 in 1979. In city assemblies their numbers have more than tripled, rising from 158 in 1955 to 504 in 1979. Adding those elected in town and village assemblies brings the overall total on the local level for 1979 to 793 (see Table 5.1).

Only two women have become cabinet ministers, both appointed by Prime Minister Ikeda Hayato of the LDP. The first was Nakayama Masa, who was named minister of health and welfare in 1960. Nakayama came from an international background, having an American father and a Japanese mother. She was educated, after missionary schooling in Nagasaki, at Ohio Wesleyan University. Elected in 1947 to the House of Representatives, she won reelection six times. Wife of a lawyer, mother of four sons, she had an excellent reputation, but apparently the unrestrained energy she applied to improving welfare policies led to dismissal after only a few months. However, years later, during the ceremony for the twenty-fifth anniversary of women's suffrage she was chosen to be the representative figure on behalf of all the women pioneers receiving prizes from Prime Minister Satō.

Kondo Tsuruyo of the House of Councillors, a home economics teacher who turned politician when her brother was banned from seeking office during the Occupation, became Ikeda's second woman minister. He appointed her director of the Science and Technology Agency in 1962. Having served as parliamentary foreign vice-minister under Yoshida Shigeru, she was not without cabinet-level experience, but there was much comment about the assumed unsuitability of this post for a woman. She served for about one year.

A series of women have been appointed to vice-ministerial slots, starting with Sakakibara Chiyo, a Socialist, in the Ministry of Justice in 1948. Noda Aiko, one of the first women to become a lawyer after the war, sits on Japan's High Court, which is comparable to the U.S. Court of Appeals. Increasing numbers of women serve in appointed or commissioned local and national positions, and one of the goals of the National Plan of Action is to bring their participation up to 10 percent of the total. For many, such service is volunteer work, an extension of their activities in women's and civic organizations. Something more than 30 percent of women appointees are concentrated in the Family Courts and public and child welfare offices.[54]

Registered membership in political parties offers little evidence of the actual voting patterns of the electorate. Despite periodic recruitment campaigns, both recruiters and pollsters admit that most people are indifferent to party membership. Party regulations and the psychological burden of openly acknowledging a political preference, combined with a desire to avoid entanglement in the power struggles of the parties, keep rosters thin.

In 1971, for instance, LDP women in Shizuoka Prefecture, under the spirited leadership of Kawanobe Shizu, topped all prefectures with their membership of 11,850 out of a prefectural total of 52,784; but that year Kawanobe was elected to the Upper House by one of the largest votes in the election, some eight times the total prefectural party membership. Nationally, LDP women members numbered 144,929 out of a total of 890,584.

Other parties reported figures for 1972 as follows: Kōmeitō, 43,484 women out of a total of 93,566; Social Democrats, 2,935 out of 44,509; Socialists, 12,090 women (no report on men). The Communist party headquarters would not release any figures.

Associations related to the candidate and the many personal support organizations provide greater grassroots backing than do the parties. Katō (Ishimoto) Shidzue, as late as the early 1970s, relied on her early connections with the birth control groups and the knitting societies rather than the Socialist party mechanisms for electoral support. Even more than in the United States, membership or leadership in groups like the Rotary Club, local environmental societies, or charities provides exposure and swells voter support. In Japan, the loyalty of the ordinary member to the local leader, who in turn has a loyalty to a regional leader, is strong and persuasive.[55]

Polls about party adherence taken by the Women's Suffrage Hall, newspapers, and so on consistently show that the majority of women, even if not members, support the conservative LDP. One League of Women Voters member explained, "In the United States the Republican and Democratic parties are like the difference between Pepsi Cola and Coca Cola, and so Americans can choose. In Japan no thinking person would choose between the LDP and the Communists."[56] This has been true of national politics, but on the local level the women more often find help from leftist or progressive anti-establishment groups as they try to get answers for their problems, look for changes, and improve the quality of life—a situation little changed from the 1920s and 1930s when Japanese women struggled for rights of suffrage and liberation.

Their interest is in using the political party system primarily to get their way.

Last but not least of the nose-counting concerns is the voting turnout, where women have shown steady improvement. As noted earlier, in 1946, with 54 percent of the eligible voters, they surprised the political pundits by turning out to cast 52 percent of the votes. Over the years, with a continuing majority of eligible voters, they have improved their percentage voting rate and now lead in that aspect as well. This trend started with the ward elections in the spring of 1955, followed in 1959 with the city assembly, mayoralty, ward, and town and village elections and in 1963 with all local elections from the prefectural assemblies on down. In 1968 the women's voting rate for the eighth general election of the Upper House surpassed that of the men. Women have since then sustained their voting majority for national elections.

The independence of the women's vote, however, continues to be suspect—a journalistic harking-back to the 1940s that is long overdue for correction. Judgments formed through family experiences are condemned as sycophantic. Yet this is where women's first loyalty rests. Men are rarely criticized when their first loyalty obviously lies with their business or labor union affiliation. Polls by the Women's and Minors' Bureau and the Women's Suffrage Hall show that decision making is more often than not individual and, indeed, that most women do not know how their husbands vote—very plausible in view of other indications about lack of communication on such matters.[57]

Legislative Successes

An interview with any elected official invariably includes a question about which accomplishment has given the greatest sense of satisfaction. For Japanese women legislators, it is assumed that the answer will be some key legislation about women, as if men and women do not live in the same society. However, from their first days in the Diet, women have not agreed among themselves that their primary obligation should indeed be to women. A women's bloc has hardly existed or, at best, has been merely a conversational crossover of party lines. Even this breaking of party discipline, which is very rigid in the Japanese Diet, has not always occurred. Reality lies somewhere in the middle. Women do have certain priorities that may differ from those of men, and their evaluation of what needs reforming is made from a feminine viewpoint.

A few legislative achievements are directly attributed to women and their priorities. These usually deal with women, social welfare, and family life; but obviously final passage of any legislation means it has been supported as well by a majority of male Diet members. Over the years the women Diet members have been credited with leadership on bills on social education laws, revision of the Eugenic Protection Law (1953), national pension laws with provisions for mothers and for the aged, invalids, widows, and orphans (1959), establishment and enforcement of laws on medical facilities for alcoholics (1961), extension of welfare benefits to mothers and children (1964), and the Consumer Protection Basic Law (1968). All the women Diet members successfully promoted the 1975 legislation proposing improvement of the status of women in accordance with International Women's Year. The most frequently cited example of coordinated effort on a single issue by women in the Diet and women's pressure groups is that of antiprostitution legislation.

Licensed prostitution in prewar Japan was the major target of Christian-oriented groups, both male and female, as well as of those fighting for feminist causes and women's suffrage. The first mothers' demonstration, a march of 100 women to the Diet, was made to protest the reconstruction of the licensed prostitute quarters following the devastating fire in Yoshiwara in 1911. They lost this battle, but the incident made women humanitarians realize that they were fighting this evil "bare-handed" and that they needed the power of the vote to accomplish their aims.[58] The same sequence occurred after the 1923 earthquake, when housing for licensed prostitution was rebuilt ahead of badly needed schools, thereby rallying an even wider group. Said Yamataka Shigeri, who was at that time a newspaperwoman, "I thought it was wrong and began to pay attention to politics." She promptly organized a fight against the reconstruction and increasingly became involved in the suffrage movement.[59]

After the Pacific War and before the first landing of the U.S. military forces in 1945, the Japanese government organized a system to service the Occupation troops, systematically recruiting women—patriotically—to serve as prostitutes. From their own experience on mainland China, the authorities considered this essential for any military occupation. The women were recruited, according to Morosawa Yoko, as the "breakwater to protect Japanese women's chastity"—meaning, of course, the chastity of less needy daughters and wives.[60] General MacArthur took a stand against fraternization as well as indentured prostitution. He posited that women could not have full equal rights if they were tied by this licensed bondage, a policy that won him favor among women.

The Anti-Prostitution Law was presented to the Twenty-Second Diet by Kamichika Ichiko and eighteen others from a broad range of parties. Representatives of leading women's organizations—the YWCA, Women's Christian Temperance Union, League of Women Voters, Women's Peace Association, and Japanese Association of University Women—met the new premier in December 1955 to urge passage. The law was enacted the next year, and women's leaders hailed the event as the reward of an eighty-year fight. On the fifth anniversary of the legislation, Akamatsu Tsuneko, Ichikawa Fusae, and Oku Mumeo proposed strengthening amendments. On the tenth anniversary the women turned to a new dimension in the war against prostitution—the "Turkish bathhouse," in which masseuses routinely served as prostitutes. To assess the situation, Diet women made official inspection visits to some of the baths in Tōkyō. The publicity aroused animosity and ribald sneers, including a supposedly straight news story in the *Asahi Evening News* ridiculing them as the "Distaff Diet-women of Dullsville."[61]

In the early 1970s, when it was obvious that Okinawa would revert to Japan, women concentrated on combating prostitution, still licensed there. The Association to Help Okinawa was set up, with members of all political persuasions. They called on cabinet ministers to apply the Anti-Prostitution Law to Okinawa. They sent committees to inspect conditions and meet with the prostitutes, most of whom were in debt to the brothel managers and owners. They raised ¥5 million through a benefit performance of *kabuki* and other events for rehabilitation programs. The problem in Okinawa was not easy; local mores saw little harm in temporary service of this kind when the needed income supported the larger family and often the maintenance of the large ancestral tombs important in observance of traditional rituals.

In honor of the twentieth anniversary of the law in 1976, twenty-two organizations and Diet and prefectural representatives, cutting across all party lines, rallied to demand the end of all prostitution and to condemn Japanese tourists and businessmen who exploit women in other Asian countries. The issue remains a pivotal one for women leaders and legislators.

With ever-increasing political sophistication, women legislators have expanded their attention, effectively integrating themselves and their solutions to problems into the entire fabric of Japanese society. Diet woman Togano Satoko gave voice to this strategy in 1967: "The Diet woman shouldn't speak for women only. She should be conscious that she is representing the people. We female members can be active in what men don't notice. The most important significance of our existence is that we are not tied to any pressure groups by which men are influenced."[62]

In recent years priorities stressed by women have increasingly emerged as the domestic priorities of the population as a whole. "Chatter at the well" has turned more and more to issues of the quality of life. Sometimes the thrust is economically oriented, as seen in the consumer confrontations that forced the Consumer Protection Basic Law of 1968. Sometimes the focus is on public morality, which the phenomenon of Ichikawa so well illustrates; and sometimes, on essential community concerns. Organized, riled-up women, addressing themselves to problems affecting all aspects of the life of their country, have demonstrated that they can assemble support for their ideas.

The Local Scene

In this corrective process, a new breed of cause-oriented women leaders has arisen. Many also seek local elective office. They are not so much classic feminist reformers, elected by support of traditional women's organizations, as advocates of a representative government concerned with the better life. They are the new product of their time.

Hiyoshi Fumiko, characterized as a tiny, cheerful "kind old aunty" in her fifties, was elected to the Minamata City Assembly in western Japan as a result of her fight on behalf of the Citizens Council for Minamata Disease Counter-Operation. Formerly vice-principal of an elementary school, she became a champion of the sufferers of the "Minamata disease" when she saw the terrible ravages this industrial poisoning brought to the mother of one of her pupils. She bucked both the senior Assembly men and the powerful Chisso Company. She helped form the citizens council, the first of its kind, and ultimately carried her campaign, with left-wing support, into the political field by running for the city Assembly. In the doing, she became involved in one of the most publicized, ultimately successful civic action movements directed at the evils of industrial pollution.[63]

Ozawa Ryoko is another of the new-style advocates. She conducts much of her daily constituency affairs from a coffee shop featuring blaring electronic rock music and hanging beaded curtains, but conveniently located near the subway stop of a Tōkyō suburban line. University-educated, she learned the rudiments of political know-how observing her former father-in-law practice politics. When divorced, she gave up her child to her husband. Believing this step disqualified her as a woman and mother, she turned to politics and ran successfully for the Urawa City Assembly on an independent ticket. She espoused women's liberation and built on her membership in Beheiren (Japan Peace for Vietnam Committee), hoping to bring the antiwar movement into the community. Since assuming office, she has been proudest of her work to set up day care facilities for children of divorced parents and of parents imprisoned in antiwar demonstrations. She has also pursued her interests overseas, traveling on observation trips to the United States and Europe to talk with women leaders and give speeches about Japanese women. Concerned about anti-Japanese attitudes in

Southeast Asia, she visited Thailand to study at first hand the human basis for such antipathy.

This independent-minded, aggressive representative of the younger generation has been determined to give expression through her political career to the role of woman as something other than mother and housewife. Thereby, she has believed, she would strengthen both the women's movement and the antiwar movement, for she argued, it was the dutiful wife and mother who supported the last war by acquiescing in sending husband and sons off to battle. Although she is a controversial figure among women feminists, her dynamism and intelligence have insured that she will not be ignored.[64]

Soft-spoken Ōta Hiroko, elected to the Niiza City Assembly in Saitama Prefecture in 1972, is regarded by many as the prototype of the young, democratically educated generation beginning to make an impact on the shape of Japanese society. A graduate of Ochanomizu University, with a masters' degree in modern Chinese history from Tōritsu University, teacher of social studies, wife of an intellectual and bureaucrat, and mother of two, she has felt since her undergraduate years a "silent pressure" to engage in political action. In fact, she and her family moved to their Niiza apartment complex (*danchi*) to be free of the restrictions against political activity imposed on public servants resident in special government housing. In her new *danchi* she could follow the dictates of her heart; and shortly she was thrust forward by neighboring women into a series of battles about quality-of-life problems in this suburb of Tōkyō. First, there was the problem of bus service stopping too early. Then the newly organized women moved on to garbage disposal issues and pollution hazards arising from faulty incineration. Finally, in an attempt to meet the need for increased day care facilities, they tackled the election process.

Because a good number of the *danchi* women were also working mothers, the activist group had made a plea for additional day care facilities to the head of the local Welfare Bureau. Ōta recalls his rebuff as disdain for "noisy women." Provoked, the women, guided by a Socialist Assembly member, prepared a petition with some 4,500 signatures, requesting the Assembly to provide another day care center. They won their cause, but the incident demonstrated that they needed their own electoral representative. Realizing their inexperience in running a candidate, they sought the guidance of Ichikawa Fusae and learned about clean election tactics. In a campaign hailed as unprecedented in quality and number of supporting workers, they elected Ōta, who placed ninth among thirty candidates. Having gained wide recognition as the "housewife city councillor," Ōta wrote for a national magazine about the campaign:

Ōta Hiroko, successful candidate for the Niiza City Assembly, Saitama Prefecture, in 1972, and the day care center she and her neighbors established in their *danchi* to assist working mothers. Photos by the author.

Never before had the mothers cooperated more closely [or] . . . shown their hidden abilities to such a full extent. From that point of view, this campaign was also a comprehensive study of the mothers themselves.

Pushed forth by the hand of mothers who had regarded elections simply as the casting of a ballot, . . . I have already found a clue to the difficult problems which were never solved before. Hereafter, I'm going to fight against the city, prefecture, and national governments.[65]

The same mood of reform by April 1973 had swept progressive mayors of the Socialist-Communist alliance into all the major metropolitan cities between Tōkyō and Kōbe and even brought a reformist governor to conservative Kagawa in Shikoku, the first since 1947. This mood encouraged local Communist parties to de-emphasize ideology and adopt so-called smile tactics, concentrating on individual needs and complaints and using slogans such as "Cover Drainage Ditches," "Build More Day Nurseries," and "Ban Vehicles from Narrow Shopping Streets." In 1973, the Communists elected more than 100 women candidates to local office, and by 1979, with 330 seats, they had surpassed even those professing to be independent. With similar tactics in Diet campaigns, forty-year-old Kurita Midori succeeded in 1971 in gaining the first Communist seat in twenty-three years in normally conservative Shizuoka Prefecture. Physician Kutsunugi Takeko, after five terms in the Ōsaka City Assembly, and building on an active career devoted to improvement of women's status, education, and public welfare, shocked the LDP with her by-election victory in June 1973 for the House of Councillors. This was the first time a Communist had won an Upper House seat from an Ōsaka constituency. In the 1980 double elections for the Upper and Lower Houses, eight of the eleven women elected were Communists. Populist claims of "new morality" and "sound democratic spirit" have gained ground in the shifting political post-Lockheed era.

The emphasis of the 1970s on reform explains why so many women independent and leftist candidates come out of the activist consumer movements. Or why LDP Diet woman Santo Akiko, backed in 1974 by the electrical giant, Hitachi Corporation, recanted to endorse consumerist policies and the labor union wage offensive. The reform spirit gives strength to the clean election concept. It shows why Governor Minobe received petitions from his constituents every Thursday and launched projects like "Operation Greenery" to encourage the planting of flowers and trees to appeal to women voters of all parties.

Hata Yawara, elected in 1972 as the first progressive coalition governor of Tōkyō's neighboring Saitama Prefecture, outlined in a personal interview how he tied together elements of reform and pressures for social betterment with alert women unsatisfied with local conditions:

I recognized that women are half of the voting population, and I knew I was popular among the women. My public pledges . . . were all on subjects of interest to women. I placed priority on the people's welfare, and my five-year greenery project also won many sympathizers. My pledges were on high school problems, free medicare system for the aged and young children, welfare for mother and child families, etc. I classified women into three types: (a) women in general, (b) intellectual women, and (c) women party members. The women party members did very well for me and . . . Communist women were the most active. I walked among the people and talked to them, keeping my eyes on theirs to produce a friendly atmosphere. This proved to be very effective because no one did that before. I got a great number of votes from women. Now with more higher education, women are sloughing off feudalistic ideas, and I am expecting they will play a bigger role in politics.[66]

In his interview for *Time* magazine in May 1973, Prime Minister Tanaka admitted that problems for his party arose because of the waving of the "Green Flag" against pollution. He specifically cited the women's vote as a factor, pointing out that "women don't vote on big national issues but on things which affect their daily lives." Tanaka blamed the "frustrations of big city life" and confirmed that his party, in power so long, lagged behind in "grass roots contact with the people."[67]

Yet public opinion polls as early as 1966 had warned LDP's Prime Minister Satō of his waning popularity with women because of such domestic issues, and the LDP women in their convention in January 1972 had underscored the situation when they called for progress aiming at "a new welfare society." Finally fully alarmed, the party did begin to move. LDP's policy research institute in 1973 advocated reforms, many of which had been previously called for by the younger members of the party, and the Fukuda faction endorsed similar policies. That July the party fought a fierce and successful campaign to retain the lead in the Tōkyō Metropolitan Assembly. Candidates discussed practical urban problems and warned against strengthening progressive parties, particularly the Communists. Mobilizing too late against the tide of a disgruntled citizenry, the LDP won only a precarious seven-seat majority in the House of Councillors elections in 1974.[68]

The party crisis was a crisis of a government heeding too little the changing needs and expression of the people. It first came to a head not in the National Diet, which appears remote and inaccessible to the average citizen, but at local levels at which the voter has direct access to those in office. Only later did the urgency of reform become a lever for change on the national scene. With such recognition came realignment of LDP factions and readjustments of Socialist-Communist-Kōmeitō coalitions to attune their priorities to the reform-conscious mood of the middle and late 1970s and the concerns of the knowledgeable, active citizen. The responsiveness was clear in Prime Minister Miki's statement to the coordinators of International Women's Year: "My motto is 'simplified material life and rich spiritual life.' Seeking the understanding and cooperation of Japanese women, I should like to exert my efforts to build up a 'beautiful and peaceful Japan' in both material and spiritual terms, and thereby to contribute to world peace."[69]

The "noisy women," at first ignored in their requests for improved quality of life and morality in politics, sought redress in civic action and retribution at the polls, even moving in on a limited scale with their own candidates. In local decision making, they can no longer be shooed away to grumble harmlessly in the kitchen. Rather, they can take pride that a trend of the 1970s is expressed by the campaign slogan of a consumer-labor-cooperative coalition for its woman candidate, "From the kitchen to municipal government."[70] The well-being—and the future—of Japanese society, locally and nationally, is the healthier because of this move.

CHAPTER 6
INTERNATIONAL AWARENESS
AND COOPERATION

CONCEPTS AND ATTITUDES—
INSULARISTS AND GLOBAL SOPHISTICATES

> *Japanese women are like frogs in the well which do*
> *not know the ocean, and they are trying hard to peep*
> *out of the well at the world.*
> —Sōka gakkai housewife, Tōkyō, 1972[1]

**Self-contained in cultural security and geographic insularity, Japanese women—
and men—find rapport with the outside world difficult to achieve. To be
Japanese means to start with a uniqueness of heart and habit that is isolating.**

In the quarter century following the Occupation, the needs of Japanese
foreign policy were second in priority to policies of national reconstruction
and economic growth. The Peace Constitution and the Security Treaty
with the United States placed international responsibilities outside the
orbit of urgent national initiatives. Prime Minister Yoshida's patriarchal
leadership stressed friendship with the United States. His successors
maintained this policy, hoping for stability and a forestalling of the
tensions of distracting international encounters.

Occasionally, exceptional events alerted international sensibilities:
establishment of the Self-Defense Forces during the Korean War; renewal
of the U.S. Security Treaty in 1960; the nuclear dusting of fishermen
off Bikini Atoll; the Chinese and Soviet bomb tests of the mid-1960s
and the arrival of U.S. nuclear submarines and carriers; the Vietnam
bombings; the achievement of the second-largest GNP in the free world;
the Nixon shocks of dollar-yen revaluations, the opening of diplomatic

relations with Peking, and the brief soybean embargo; the anti-Japanese riots in Southeast Asia; and the Arab oil embargo.

Especially for women, such jolts, like alarm clocks, reawakened their dozing awareness of the strange world beyond the seas around Japan—lands and peoples remote, bewildering, and possibly unfriendly. They reacted to intrusions defensively and demonstrated a historically-based caution, preferring a low-key position. They made judgments based on the perceived ultimate effect on the human core group of children, family, and self.

There is a psychological constancy about Japanese women's attitudes on foreign policy. The extent of their education abroad and of their face-to-face contact with foreign peoples is directly proportional to their ability to relate, as individuals, to new international situations and problems.

Early Internationalists

Two Meiji policies, one purposeful and the other inadvertent, contributed to early stimulation of women's international awareness. Both involved the impact of living abroad, and, thereby, a breaking with traditional habits.

Initially, when Japan was just coming out of the Tokugawa shell, it was the Charter Oath proclaimed by the emperor that set forth the first policy design. In a burst of emancipated thinking, decision makers included women in the famous fifth precept advising the people to seek modernizing knowledge and experience throughout the world in order to strengthen Japan. Overseas, the welcome of hospitable schools and earnest friends precipitated these shy, intelligent students into mind- and personality-stretching experiences, involving not simply Western-style education but also overwhelming cultural adjustments. Independent-minded feminine leadership grew from this exposure to Judeo-Christian human ethics and from the trauma of rediscovering self and blooming in a non-Japanese society. Within Japan, repatriated women such as Tsuda Umeko and others who followed after her reinforced the work of Canadian and U.S. educational missionaries and carried on a democratizing, internationalizing process. Their decorous schoolrooms nurtured startling concepts of intercultural awareness and international cooperation. They gave spirit to a small but eventually precedent-shattering group of Japanese women who toppled the social and cultural barriers of Japanese isolation and restrictive traditions.

The second Meiji policy, which also dispatched Japanese to other lands, emerged from intensifying nationalism, a jingoism well described in the Japanese colloquialism *jingo ni ochi nai*, which urges "don't fall behind" or "be second to none." Time saw it expand from "respectable" emulation of the imperialist West during Meiji and Taishō to engulfing militarism during early Shōwa.

One unexpected by-product was the influence of overseas living, which touched and often changed the families of the men who followed in the wake of the military excursions and wars with China, Russia, and Germany to govern, engage in business, run the railroad systems, back up the occupying military, or in some way maintain the territorial occupation that spread from the Ryūkyūs to Taiwan and the Pescadores, to Korea and southern Sakalin, then to many Pacific islands, concessions in China, and South Manchuria. The recollections of the daughter of an insurance and express agent, who was born in Tientsin during World War I and grew up in the Japanese concession there, provides a bit of the flavor of this life:

> It [Tientsin] was a small city, . . . on both sides of the Pei, a yellow muddy river, where Chinese junks commuted up and down. . . . There were Japanese "Yamato" park, British "Victoria" park, and the Russian park where we used to have a picnic when I was a first year elementary school pupil. Victoria park . . . I remember in connection with an outdoor concert of the British military band given . . . on a warm summer evening. . . . Peking, about two hours' ride by train from Tientsin, had many famous spots for sightseeing. I went there on my sixth grade school excursion and visited the Grand Palace and other historical places.
>
> From what I later heard from my mother, the late Prime Minister Shigeru Yoshida was Japanese Consul General in Tientsin one time while my family lived there, and my mother sometimes met Mrs. Yoshida at a Japanese women's club when some women gathered for a Japanese music (*naga-uta*) concert. This indicates that most Japanese lived a Japanese way of life, while in contact also with a variety of nationalities. . . . The city was cosmopolitan, but each nationality had its own way of life. . . .
>
> We used to go to a sea resort in summer. The place I liked best was Peitaho. . . . Most of the summer visitors were Westerners. . . . A Russian family next door had a little girl called Clara, and we soon became friends. We talked in Chinese so there was no language problem. Clara, my sister, and I used to climb up a mulberry tree which stood just between our cottage and Clara's house and had a wonderful time eating mulberries, . . . Those were unforgettable days for me.

She returned to Tōkyō after elementary schooling and went on to graduate from Tōkyō Women's Christian College and to enjoy a career in an international setting.[2]

These overseas Japanese lived for the most part in ghettos of their own arrangement—as did the Westerners in their concessions—and were separated by custom and language as well as by policy from the indigenous population. Ogata Sadako, a child in a diplomatic family, called her early years in the late 1930s in the international settlement in China "a very isolated life" in which she knew Chinese only as servants.[3] Nevertheless, the overseas exposure led to conditioned acceptance of different ways as conceivable alternatives to ordained Japanese ways.

Some are aware of the import of their experience. Seki Fumiko, who very early supported the UN University in Japan, has enjoyed talking about her years overseas. She wrote a book about her two years in Chapel Hill, where her professor husband studied under a Rockefeller Foundation grant. She valued her early years in Peking where the "international surroundings gave me a much broader view and made me internationally minded." Her father, who worked for Japanese newspapers in China for almost twenty years, wrote in 1925 at the time of her first trip back to Japan at age seven that "Japan seems to be a wonderland" for her.[4]

Or consider Nakamaru Kaoru, a sophisticated television personality who was born in Peking in the late 1930s and graduated in international affairs from Columbia University, taking an advanced degree from its East Asia Institute. She grew up moving around in China, Japan, and Europe because her father, who was a son of the Emperor Meiji, had been asked through Prime Minister Itō Hirobumi to work with Sun Yat-sen. Her studies completed, she traveled extensively "wanting to see the world for its own sake." Her experiences led her to decide to interpret the world to Japan through television interviews with international figures; she created and produced such a program. She also decided to concentrate in one area, Yamanashi Prefecture, on an intensified adult education program on international matters. Believing, as she said, "in the oneness of the world, I wanted to popularize international affairs at the mass level"—an uncommon goal for any Japanese, man or woman.[5]

Kamiya Mieko, one of the Japanese women most admired by Tsuda College undergraduates, found her growing-up years unsettling because of the many moves her family made around Japan and then to the Palau Islands and Switzerland because of her father's career in the Ministry of Home Affairs. The shuttling between Japanese and European cultural settings and languages and the shock of alternating between strict schooling in Japan and free attitudes in the Swiss classroom caused her to speak of her "dark childhood." At a young age she came to realize "how difficult it is to introduce the culture of our own country correctly and to understand the cultures of other countries." She vividly remembered an incident during her primary schooling at the Rousseau

Seki Fumiko (right), aged seven, poses with her mother, father, and two brothers in front of their house in Peking in the spring of 1926. Photo courtesy of Seki Fumiko.

Seki Fumiko with her two daughters, Kazuko and Michiko, in 1970. Photo by the author.

Education Institute in Geneva when her teacher suggested she introduce Japan to the school by talking about how Japanese houses are made of paper and wood, and how the people take baths outside. Rejection of such cultural stereotyping led, over the years, to philosophical questioning of who she was and led her to decide that "all the people from different countries were the same human beings."

Out of such personal seeking, and through continuing studies at Tsuda, Columbia University, and Tōkyō Women's Medical College, she developed an interest in psychology. Today, she is an educator and psychiatrist and combines a loving family life with unusual, perhaps courageous, work on the frontiers of her profession, including medical work with lepers. She is a modern philosopher whose own intercultural adjustments pushed her to transcend cultural bias and conclude, "It is necessary to have warm thoughtfulness to understand human beings."[6]

Fujita Taki, who in postwar years more than any other woman has represented her country and her sex at international gatherings, tells of her childhood residences in Okinawa and Port Arthur in Manchuria. Her father, who in his position as judge was rotated around the Japanese empire, remained harshly traditional in his attitude toward her mother, but he came to believe it was essential for his daughter to receive a modern education and a very uncommon one at that, at Tsuda and at Bryn Mawr.[7]

Thus, in these outstanding personalities and others was fostered a willingness to reach out to foreign friends and institutions to build international goodwill and exchange. Reinforced with better education and obviously imbued with an adventurous inclination, their families, probably unknowingly, had nurtured in them the flexibility that welcomes new ideas.

Women in the "Shell"

Early international experiences influenced an elite group of women; it was the war pounding on those at home, followed by the Occupation, that compelled cognizance of the larger world outside Japan on the part of the mass of women. They did not go out to seek international interchange. The results of national foreign policies brought it home to them, willy-nilly.

Preponderantly it was the women, the old, and the children who suffered the immediate ravages of modern warfare in the home islands. They coped with trials of evacuation, split families, and uncertain food supplies. They endured the repeated terrors of the fire bombings of Tōkyō and other cities up and down the land, recalled by Foreign Minister Shigemitsu Mamoru as "the most frightful experience the

Japanese people have ever undergone . . . day by day Japan turned into a furnace." Death rained on them within the sanctuary of their very homes.[8]

For the women, the legacy is a deep, abiding devotion to peace—the absence of war as they experienced it. Simply, graphically, Kihira Teiko explained: "I grew up during the war and was seventeen or eighteen when it ended. So my peace is very definite. Peace for me is to change my dress into pajamas, and sleep in the same bed, in the same home and to live with my family."[9]

Then with the war's end, for the first time in their entire history, Japanese lived side by side with foreigners, who fanned out through the land in occupation. Again the women, the old, and the children at home received the initial brunt. Unlike the United States, which grew with waves of polyglot emigration, unlike Europe and much of Asia where invading, conquering hordes repeatedly overran the lands or imperialist rule and colonialism spread a veneer of alien culture, Japan had never before felt such an impact. The Occupation forced the first daily contact for the average person with the distrusted foreigner, the red-haired "barbarian" of children's rhymes of the Meiji era, the "devil" of war propaganda. Mused Kihira Teiko: "Japanese have always been in a kind of shell. The Occupation was the only time we were mixed up with foreigners. Otherwise we have not had daily opportunity for contact with foreigners. We just read and hear about them. . . . There are few Japanese who can regard foreigners as human beings."[10] Her only exceptions were those Japanese educated in Western-related schools and colleges!

The Occupation was unique in the history of such relationships. But even this single mixing provided only limited practice in intercultural give and take, for it involved primarily one nationality. It provided neither a broad international education nor a base for understanding all kinds of foreigners.[11] It was an encounter, too, that entailed at least outward deference to placate those in authority. For most Japanese, therefore, the Occupation turned only one Western type, the American man, into a living, breathing foreigner. Others tend to melt into a composite identified ubiquitously as *gaijin*, or foreign person, and they are viewed as guests, transitory and isolated by walls of courtesies from the inner interplay of ordinary Japanese life.

As late as the mid-1960s, it was possible to visit small towns in the Tōhoku, Hokuriku, and Hokkaidō and talk with Japanese who had never encountered an American woman—indeed one of any foreign nationality—in the flesh. Sparkling-eyed curiosity under such circumstances could overcome reticence. They enjoyed the opportunity to shake the American woman's hand or touch blond hair or parts of what seemed like unusual Western-style clothing, such as wools mixed with synthetics or lace-edged nylon slips. Such an afternoon's visit pried open the Japanese shell at least for a moment.

The Peace Constitution

While the human encounters of the Occupation period broadened the international outlook of insular Japanese women, another major innovation of that time gave them an excuse to turn back inward. The well-studied Constitution established a new shell for them in its peace provisions in Article IX.[12] Within its provisions they felt they could hide from the international entanglements that could lead again to the horrors of war. It offered a legal variant on their geographic and historical isolationism. Designed to forestall any tendencies toward the reoccurrence of militarism, it could equally be interpreted so as to avoid involvements in international peacekeeping. The Americans had arranged for it and, from the Japanese point of view, were forthwith responsible for making it prevail. The Japanese, in turn, were freed to reconstruct their lives and their country peaceably.

The Constitution has also provided in its emphasis on peace an important linkage of purpose between the average woman and those women leaders long active in programs of social progress and women's emancipation. In prewar society, many women and men had regarded these leaders with suspicion. Their ideas of equality seemed alien and rooted in Western ethics and foreign relationships. They were different. At times the handy, scourging labels of "socialist" and "anarchist"— foreign epithets—were indiscriminately pinned on, with the result that some did, in fact, espouse such ideologies to bolster their struggle with established society. Ultimately, as we have seen, the movement of feminist emancipation temporarily withered under repressive edicts issued by the militaristic government, a pattern of repression that bequeathed an antiwar, pacifist, anti-establishment stance to the whole Japanese feminist movement. When the victorious Americans also sponsored the "Peace" Constitution that included the rights they had been seeking, the causes of peace and women's liberation became even more closely enmeshed.

The statement delivered by Katō (Ishimoto) Shidzue on behalf of the Diet women who met with General MacArthur in June 1946 while the Constitution was under debate was prophetic. Thanking him for granting them suffrage and educating them to its use so as to establish democracy in Japan, the Diet women made clear how they and all Japanese women would use their new powers: "We Japanese women will never vote for the militarists. . . . we shall particularly emphasize the article [of our

Nakane Chie of Tōkyō University speaks about peace and international understanding at the Japanese Association of University Women–American Association of University Women Joint Seminar at Ōiso in 1970. Seated to the right is Fujita Taki; to the left is Elizabeth Wallace, leader of the AAUW delegation. Photo courtesy of Japanese Association of University Women.

new Constitution] for the permanent abolishment of war. We certainly shall stand for peace; we shall never have war again."[13]

Over the years, public support by men and women of the war-renouncing article has continued to be strong. Endorsement forms a common bond between the international elite women, with all their energies and causes, and the greater numbers still enamored of their shell.

A mid-war generation teacher of the handicapped in a prize-winning essay explained her view of Japan's role in the world. Although having renounced war in the Constitution, the nation, she maintained, "lacks confidence and forcefulness and diplomacy to press others to do the same. . . . Article IX was the best Japan could contribute to the cause of peace, and it would be unreasonable to expect more from this humble country." Not wanting Japan ever again to have a "sense of mission" to follow as it did at the time of the Pacific War, she concluded that "Japan should play the part of not doing anything, not playing any role."[14] And anthropologist Nakane Chie backstopped this approach when, in 1973, she argued against a stronger world role for Japan: "No. I think it is better not to do anything . . . for if we are set in motion toward any direction, we have just too much energy and no mechanism to check its direction."[15]

Japanese women have responded to more recent international events within this historical frame of experience. Older mainstream leaders fret, in the words of Yamataka Shigeri, that the "generation with no experience of war is troublesome."[16] Older left-inclined leaders of the Congress of Mothers note that young mothers, untouched by war, diversify and dilute their movement with pursuit of varied political and economic goals.[17] Women's organizations give organized voice to opinions on foreign policy issues, but even with the leadership, the substantive base can be rather thin. Women tend to react effectively in direct proportion to their foreign exposure.

Peace! Peace!

"Peace is a high ideal" for Japanese women, according to Ariga Michiko. "They hold it in their minds, but do not think carefully, so there is nothing practical." A well-educated war widow who struggled to professional prominence to support her growing children, she refused early on to join other scholars in an antiwar movement. She preferred to work at the causes of war where "deep in the background you see economic problems." She focused on bringing equality in economic affairs in her work at the Fair Trade Commission. "To have democracy in the economy is to maintain peace."[18]

Egami Fuji, a practical, high-powered executive, agreed with Ariga. She worried that growth of the economy meant inevitable international pressures and that the subsequent danger of economic conflict could turn into military conflict. For this reason, she opposed reinforcement of the Self-Defense Forces lest their growth diminish the chances that they will stay "only within our country." The latter point of view is widely held by women who are uneasy about any military presence, although few realize that their national budget provides proportionately less than the Swiss, whose neutral policies they admire. Egami feared that average women "just say 'Peace, Peace!' But when something happens what do they do?" She was suspicious of such advocacy, believing women react selfishly rather than from love of country. "If they don't love their own country, how can they love other countries?"[19]

More relaxed, Mishima Sumie explained that the women simply "want peace and to be friends with everyone in the world," slyly adding in a not unrelated comment, "and to have their children learn English."[20] Most Japanese hang back from international encounters on both diplomatic and personal levels because of poor language facility. Even such a personally confident, well-traveled, internationally-minded leader as Kawanobe Shizu turned away from responsibilities in foreign affairs in the Diet on the grounds "that she is not good at foreign languages."[21] Kamiya Mieko says that the communications barrier means "Japanese just look at the surface of things. They have no real contact."[22]

Such lack of contact no doubt contributes to what Kubota Kinuko has described as the "childish, dreamlike" approach to peace. She wrote a newspaper article that took her countrymen to task for their attitudes when they heaved a collective sigh of relief at the fortuitous ending of the Japan Air Lines Yōdō incident, the first of the airport hijacking and urban guerrilla warfare episodes in Japan. The five drawn-out days of the drama, watched step by step by most Japanese on television, made her realize "how ignorant we are about the severe reality of international relationships" and how readily dependent on a policy of "peace just because Japan has the Peace Constitution."[23]

The embarrassment and horror of the Japanese over the atrocities of the ultra-leftist Red Army factions in one world capital after another have been severe. Having turned from a war policy to embrace the Peace Constitution, they have agonized that these violent transgressions demonstrate a breach of faith. The shouts at Lod Airport, "The Japanese did it! Damn it, the Japanese!" seemed haunting reminders of a military past they have tried hard to overcome. They cannot understand how they can have brought forth such a travesty.

That a woman could be the guiding evil genius of these guerrillas accentuated even more strongly the aberration they represent. What made a Shigenobu Fusako, who helped mastermind the Yōdō hijacking and the Lod Airport massacre and plotted violence with the Popular Front for the Liberation of Palestine? How could a quiet, average family spawn a Nagata Hiroko, who sat as coleader in judgment on her fellow "soldiers" in the butchering torture and purge of almost half their group on a remote, freezing mountain? Even radical young women who believe in violent action, who took part in club-swinging demonstrations and lived in communes in the fortress they made of their university, cannot condone such lynchings.[24] Thoughtful mothers, aware of the frustrations of their children who would correct social injustice, condemn even as they ponder what in modern society causes such deviations.

The cause of peace is fraught with contradictions of motive and method. Its ultimate reality for most Japanese women, as for Morosawa Yoko, is simply, "peace . . . a world without wars." She has recognized, as have many other leaders, that women "would rather advocate the denial of violence than look for ways to stop war. They have not given thought to the cultural and economic facets. They are just against war because they have experienced it."²⁵ It must be emphasized that to many women international relations and international understanding are vague and unfamiliar terms. "Peace," unlike "international relations," does not seem like an abstraction. It is real. It is a policy. It is not just a goal; it is a way. It calls for neutralism in international manners of a kind that, when aggressively practiced in their own society, keeps one out of trouble.

For some women, the philosophy and advocacy of peace spring from a Christian, missionary-inspired pacifism. The YWCA has since its inception promoted this cause, often in opposition to official policies, and developed women into activists on its behalf. Mrs. Inazo Nitobe, an early twentieth-century YWCA president and educator, organized in her home the Women's International Study Club, which evolved into the Women's Peace Organization. Before the war, this organization sponsored essay contests on peace; it petitioned Premier Inukai to support the Geneva Disarmament Conference. After the war, as the Women's International League for Peace and Freedom, it took leadership in a supra-organizational demonstration to call for peace, and, in 1950, with the WCTU, YWCA, and others, petitioned John Foster Dulles for a peace treaty. Jodai Tano, who was one of those personally petitioning the U.S. secretary of state, developed a "Peace Collection" of books, which she gave to the library at the Japan Women's University, of which she became president. Her intent was to instill in the students a "real interest in international affairs" so as to "bring some earnest study of the problems that confront the world and its way to peace."²⁶

As Kawai Michi, founder of Keisen Girls School, proclaimed in giving purpose to her school in the mid-1920s, "Wars will never cease till women interest themselves in World Affairs. Then, begin with the young—with girls!"²⁷ The aim is no different for modern apartment-dwelling mothers, who believe that the most important thing they can do for international understanding is to "teach children the importance of peace," with Vietnam cited as an example of "how bad it is to have war."²⁸

For some women espousal of peace follows the lure of international Marxist ideologies, newly interpreted or long established. This path promises peace as a dream certain to come true if a socialist governmental and economic system would replace that now established. These policies find support among advocates of the "new left," some young feminists, and in varying degrees, among members of trade unions and organizations affiliated with the Socialist and Communist parties.

Women's organizations of all persuasions hail peace in their purposes and programs and crusade for it in petitions to the government or statements to the press. From Pilot International to the League of

Women Voters, the Sōhyō Labor Union Women's Association, the huge Chifuren, and the Communist-sponsored New Japan's Women's Association, the goal is everlasting peace, often to be carried out "hand in hand with all of the women of the world." Little wonder that the Liaison Group of forty-eight organizations working to implement the goals of the latter half of the UN Decade for Women found it "indispensable" to associate elimination of discrimination with the "achievement of world peace."

Peace, Ichikawa Fusae reminded representatives of the many organizations gathered to observe the twenty-fifth anniversary of women's suffrage, is an issue on which they can use their votes with effectiveness. She called it one of the three biggest problems of modern life. Kushida Fuki, director of the New Japan Women's Association, also advocated peace as one of the three pillars—the others, as with Ichikawa, were pollution and prices—integrating the emphases of the women's movement in the 1970s.[29]

Politicians well understand its vote-getting appeal. For example, the heavily solicited Nobel Peace Prize for former Prime Minister Satō Eisaku elicted the pragmatic, perhaps cynical, appraisal that it would gain the Liberal Democratic party more votes from women.[30]

Japanese women follow the ideological grail of peace much as they respond to praise of motherhood. When the two virtues are joined excitement mounts. Hiratsuka Raichō's slogan "Mothers of the World, Let's Join Hands," issued at the 1955 International Congress of Mothers, rallied sixty women's organizations to cooperate in preparing for this event. They raised money by selling 130,000 Japanese-style towels (*tenugui*) imprinted with this plea in her handwriting.[31] Unfortunately, by 1959 it had begun to be clear that the congress was entrapped in larger political and ideological struggles. Communist infiltration of the leadership was finally recognized and alienated Democratic Socialist, LDP, and hence government support. The next year, the congress passed resolutions not simply on school education and social security matters, but also on opposition to the U.S. Security Pact, restoration of diplomatic relations between mainland China and Japan, and opposition to trade liberalization.

The Women's Policy Committee of the Democratic Socialist party, well-tested in a long, precarious relationship with the Communists, commented some years later about how many women at the local level, who have "self-consciousness of less degree," were sometimes exploited by the Communists:

Their old trick is to start letting simple Japanese women speak out their difficulties and requests, then to urge them to stand up and, as they begin

to show interest in children's problems, political and economic institutions,
and the peace issue, to infuse them with the idea that only the communist
society could serve as the social structure for true emancipation of women.[32]

Ordinary women, who followed their natural enthusiasms but who went
beyond the issuance of platitudes, through lack of knowledge and
experience naively became pawns of doctrinaire political activists. Such
situations can be disheartening, building confusion about what action
to take.

However, like the incessant intoning of a single sutra by Nichiren
Buddhists to win salvation, like a humanitarian ideal brush-written
10,000 times by a pious priest and sent off from his holy mountain
temple to encourage its implementation, so the women's chanting of
"Peace, Peace!" carries the expectation that their pleas will spread this
harmonious condition over the island of Japan and throughout the
world! Their cry for peace is a pledge of faith.

The Atomic Heritage

Reactions about atomic energy parallel women's attitudes on peace.
The antinuclear position becomes subsumed within the meaning of
peace. Ask about the former, and the response is likely to dwell on
the latter.

The Hiroshima experience is one place to start arousing sentiment
for world peace, according to Shoji Masako, who escaped that bomb
because of her early-morning diligence in helping to evacuate the
university library to safer neighboring villages. Tokunaga Kikuko, who
read the warning American leaflets and escaped with her daughter from
Nagasaki to a fishing village, has urged Japanese to make use of their
unique nuclear encounter to work harder for world peace. She lamented
that too few Japanese think of Hiroshima and Nagasaki in international
terms.

Americans continue to be more self-conscious about the nuclear
bombs than the average Japanese, and the guilt appears more enshrined
in Hiroshima than in Nagasaki, for international emphasis stresses the
first use of the device rather than the repeat offense. Japanese, by
comparison, feel the guilty weight of their broader role as aggressors,
particularly on the Chinese mainland. Americans visiting Hiroshima
sometimes hear from Japanese their belief that those who died at
Hiroshima and Nagasaki served the cause of peace: Their personal
sacrifices brought the war's end. Mishima Sumie, writing in the early
1950s, expressed views often still reiterated:

But in this terrible war of Japanese spiritualism versus modern science, their long-yearned for *deus-ex-machina* finally appeared in quite an unexpected direction of heaven. He came out of the atomic bombs and spoke in a voice of the Emperor! Although I never believed in the divine protection of our island, I had yearned for intervention of some sort to bring peace. So I could not, and still cannot, help but admit that the bombs with their horrors of gigantic proportion did bring or at least speeded up, an end to our tragic war. I know some people disagree with me, and probably I am motivated by the limited experience of one who knew only the bombing of Tōkyō. But still I sincerely persist in the view. I add, however, that although the first two A-bombs of mankind intervened for peace, this will never happen again.[33]

The last sentence helps explain the permeating obsession with "peace." It shows why there is amazingly little resentment of Hiroshima-Nagasaki and why so little anti-Americanism clings to the memory. In a 1971 *Asahi* newspaper poll, for instance, 51 percent expressed "tolerance" (*Asahi*'s word) of the U.S. action. Comments typically ran, "We no longer give it a thought." "Americans had no other choice." "It was fair in war."[34]

Between the time of Mishima's statement and the poll, Japanese women showed that they would and could rise up to protest the use of nuclear bombs for purposes other than the ending of the Pacific War. The inadvertent dusting of Japanese tuna fishermen by nuclear fallout from the U.S. hydrogen-bomb tests at Bikini Atoll in March 1954 triggered the outbursts. In a classic instance of women's public affairs action, the "No More Hiroshimas" drive to collect signatures to ban the weapons and stop the testing got started in a reading-study group. This one, in Suginami Ward in Tōkyō, was headed by Tazuki Yasui. Aroused by the news, the women organized the Suginami Ban-the-Bomb-Signature Movement Association (Gensuibaku kinshi shomei undō Suginami kyōgi kai), making their leader's husband the president. In three months they had collected 200,000 signatures from 85 percent of the ward population.

After the death of one of the unfortunate crew members of the *No. 5 Fukuryū Maru*, the signature campaign assumed national proportions, spurred on by the media and organizations. In ten months 2 million signatures were gathered. One method was that of Maruki Iri and his wife Toshi, who traveled around Japan holding exhibitions, reputedly in 600 places, of pictures of the victims of the bomb. Subsequently, she set up a similar display at the International Women's Congress in Denmark and in other countries, a prelude to the first international ban-the-bomb conference in Hiroshima. The Japan Council Against Atomic and Hydrogen Bombs (Gensuikyō) came into being. The little

Japanese tourists pay their respects at the atom bomb cenotaph Hiroshima Peace Memorial in Hiroshima Peace Park. Photo courtesy of Karen Marston.

Suginami women's association had given fire to a national movement, which was then joined by Americans, British, and others to make it international.[35]

As journalist Shiraishi Tsugi and countless editorials have pointed out, the Japanese people wholeheartedly supported the initial campaign. The atomic bomb victims welcomed the meeting in Hiroshima in expectation that the emphasis would be humanitarian. Too soon such hopes died. The Communists maneuvered to seize organizational control, and Sino-Soviet rivalries dominated. The issue of approval of the Soviet Union's nuclear tests, thrust into the international conference in 1963, produced unmanageable confrontation. Dissenting Sōhyō, Socialist, and Social Democratic leaders and others left to form two other antibomb groups. Even Suginami's little Gensuibaku split. Genuine antinuclear, pacifist exponents were entrapped in the larger power vortex by Communist-Socialist forces and antigovernment pressures against LDP power and its pro-U.S. policies. Humanitarian interest in the welfare of the initial victims slipped lower and lower on the priority scale.

Rallies in ensuing years ebbed and flowed in size and sincerity of purpose. The Communist party in 1963 reportedly paid the transportation for 10,000 "activists" to attend from all over Japan.[36] Busloads of women are still brought in for the day for rallies, receiving their *obentō* lunches and some souvenir to swell the attendance. For those women, the event provides the excitement of an outing linked to an idealistic purpose. For others, politicalization of the nuclear issue has brought disappointment. One Aomori woman leader explained that skepticism about the genuineness of the peace movement caused her community group to stop sending delegates to the antibomb rallies.

Not so readily deterred was Kobayashi Hiro of Nagasaki, a long-time fighter for good causes. Although not a baptized Christian, she has spoken of the Bible as the motivation of her life and regarded Tomo no kai, the Christian friendship organization, as a lifelong influence. In 1964, disillusioned with the ideological disputes within the procommunist Gensuikyō, she, as president of the Nagasaki Chifuren, led her group out of the organization. A member of the Assembly, she acted with political courage, for whereas the bombing of Hiroshima plays a role in international politics, that of Nagasaki more strongly affects its local political scene. Kobayashi argued that for her and her membership the desire for peace led them to object to atomic bombs of all countries. She could find no rationale for regarding the bombs of socialist countries as "intended for peaceful use" by comparison with the bombs of capitalist countries, which are "for fighting." She went on record as saying of the atom bomb, "Any human being should not do such a cruelty to any human being whichever country they belong to."

Kobayashi Hiro (right) of Nagasaki talks to the First All Kyūshū-Yamaguchi Women's Conference on International Understanding in Fukuoka, May 18, 1964, about the importance of women working for the cause of peace. To her right is Sakanishi Shio. Photo courtesy of USIS/Japan.

In the 1960s–70s, in the All-Kyūshū Yamaguchi Women's Conferences on International Understanding, sponsored with the American Cultural Center, Kobayashi never let the Americans forget that they had dropped the bombs on Hiroshima and Nagasaki. She insisted that wars would cease if people were truly made aware of the horrors of war. She exhorted American women to use their influence for this cause. She has stuck by her principles and acted on them in her work with the pro–Socialist party Japan Congress Against Atomic and Hydrogen Bombs (Gensuikin) for special welfare support for the *hibakusha*, the people who experienced the bomb.[37]

Nuclear power, whether employed for peaceful or for military purposes, haunts most Japanese. Yet such power has come increasingly to be an important source of Japan's energy supplies, and village officials, alert to public fears, astutely negotiate hard for compensation before sites for nuclear power plants are agreed upon. Strong-willed fishermen in 1973 and 1974 blockaded and kept stranded at sea the Japanese-built nuclear ship *Mutsu*, forcing the promise of conversion to fossil fuels. As a kind of international *mea culpa*, the *Mutsu* was set to become, after conversion, a youth ship to carry young people on exchanges with

Southeast Asia. Arrival of U.S. nuclear submarines or the nuclear-powered aircraft carrier *Enterprise,* or the question of whether or not U.S. planes and bases in Japan or Okinawa have nuclear capabilities, is routinely viewed with alarm. As one Nagasaki woman explained at an International Women's Conference in 1968, "Nuclear subs in Nagasaki Prefecture ports remind us of the bomb. They cause consternation and threaten human rights. What is the opinion of American women?"[38]

During the 1960s, when bomb testings were much in the news and the nuclear test ban treaty was being negotiated, women's organizations singly and jointly agitated in protest. In 1961, for instance, resumption of Soviet testing in August and tests by both the Soviets and Americans in September brought reaction from organizations with wide-ranging constituencies. The pacifist Women's International League for Peace and Freedom visited both embassies and submitted letters requesting abstention from testing to President Kennedy and Premier Khrushchev. The League of Women Voters wrote the U.S. league to influence U.S. action. The conservatively inclined Chifuren and the All Japan Women's Federation sent letters of protest to both embassies. The leftist Women's Democratic Club appealed to all women to seek a halt to the testing and called for universal disarmament; in their statement, the similarly oriented Federation of Japanese Women's Organizations called for the repeal of the U.S.-Japan Security Treaty.[39]

In 1963 the League of Women Voters praised and expressed gratitude to President Kennedy, Premier Khrushchev, and British Prime Minister Macmillan for the partial nuclear test ban treaty of that August. The next year the league, as well as the Women's Democratic Club, criticized the People's Republic of China's tests, sending protest letters to Premier Zhou Enlai. France's President Charles de Gaulle, and again China, received protests in 1966. Chinese and French testing in 1973 equally did not go unheeded.

Typical of the protests, although perhaps unusually eloquent, were the arguments of the Seeds of Grass Association (Kusa no mi kai), whose members are housewives, usually progressively inclined, who contribute to family columns in newspapers. They inveighed as much against Chinese testing as against the presence of U.S. nuclear-powered submarines because as "Mothers, Pacifists . . . one cannot oppose war in general without opposing in particular the very preparations which make war possible and, indeed probable." Their appeal to President Johnson in late 1964 summarized the beliefs and fears of Japanese women, bundling together their closest concerns—military uses of nuclear energy, remembrance of the war, family, environment, especially hypothetical radioactive pollution of their staple, seafood, and the cause of peace: "As the people of the only nation who suffered from that great disaster of the atomic bombs in the past, we hate nuclear weapons [and] wish from the bottom of our heart that nuclear weapons will never bring any destruction to the world, wherever it may be."[40]

"Fires Across the River"

Secure in having renounced war "forever" by committing themselves to the Peace Constitution and a policy of antimilitarism, Japanese viewed the wars in the Middle East, Indochina, and even in Korea, one woman critic pointed out, as "fires across the river" (*taigan no kaji*). Korea, although annexed by the Japanese in 1910 and held until the end of the Pacific War, "with the sea between," was "not our country. . . . so we just watched the war there." The Japanese could continue to work, overcome their financial depression, and go on to economic growth. But, she believed, this situation helped "spoil" the Japanese, for it contributed to their unhappiness, at least "from the moral point of view."[41]

Security for Japanese, individually or as a nation, has in fact traditionally come through isolation. Tokugawa withdrawal gave strength to the shōgun and cut off threats of invasion, or at least danger of entanglement in seventeenth-century European imperialism and power struggles. Retreat into the home behind wooden shutters and barred gates bolstered hope that avenging power or seesawing conflicts of *daimyō*, samurai, or marauding *rōnin* would somehow pass by. Calling attention to oneself by propounding different viewpoints, even now in democratically educated Japan, induces some nervousness. The conventional wisdom is to mind one's own business and not reach out beyond one's established family-livelihood circle of insularity.

Obviously, fires across the river can arouse uneasiness. Converted by experience to an antiwar policy, most Japanese prefer that international fires be confined to the other side of the river so they need not assume any responsibility for extinguishing them. This preference shapes their views about "peace, peace," nuclear rejection, and overall postwar security. It influences their reaction to the U.S.–Japan Security Treaty. Along with their remembrances of the terrors of bombing, it triggered their reaction to the Vietnam conflict.

Attention to Vietnam intensified with news about U.S. bombing raids into the north—earlier reports of Viet Cong atrocities had attracted little interest. Air warfare had relevant immediacy, and the presence of U.S. air bases in Japan and larger bomber bases in Okinawa created anxieties about retaliatory attacks.[42] One Kansai woman educator, an admirer of the United States, said, "I always have an uneasy feeling toward war. When I look at the present situation in which they increase the Self-

Defense Force and the Americans use military bases here for the Vietnam war, I can't help worrying about another war. I hope the Americans will settle the war as soon as possible."[43]

In April 1965 representatives of the Liaison Council of Women's Organizations (Kokuren NGO kokunai fujin iinkai), including the Tōkyō YWCA, Japan Nursing Association, WCTU, League of Women Voters, Women's International League for Peace and Freedom, and Chifuren, met at their request with U.S. Ambassador Edwin O. Reischauer in his residence one afternoon to present a "statement of concern" for the president about the bombing of North Vietnam, to seek policy clarification, and to exchange ideas.

The next January, the Tōkyō YWCA, in one of its "Know Your World" luncheon discussions, hosted a large public meeting at which Ambassador Reischauer spoke to some 300 women representing a cross-section of organizations. Again the plea was for information to fill news gaps and counterbalance distortions in the Japanese press. The mood of the meeting, low-key and friendly, held unique poignancy because the families of both the ambassador and Mrs. Reischauer had been instrumental in the founding and development of this important Christian-based agency for women's education. Subsequently, the YWCA launched a postcard campaign pleading directly with Mrs. Lyndon Johnson and, later, with President Nixon to make efforts toward negotiation and peace.

Appeals and petitions to the prime minister, the Foreign Ministry, U.S. officials, and the U.S. Embassy to take steps to end the war continued throughout the Vietnam era. The Women's International League for Peace and Freedom, as an outgrowth of its international conference, sent an appeal in October 1965 directly to the American people—to women's organizations in the United States. The list of signers read like the roster of leaders who had fought for women's rights during earlier suffrage days. It included Fujita Taki, chairman of the Japan Committee, Pan-Pacific and Southeast Asia Women's Association; Ichikawa Fusae, president of the League of Women Voters of Japan; Kitamura Koko, president of the Japanese Association of University Women; Kubushiro Ochimi, president of the Japan Women's Christian Temperance Union; Kume Ai, president of the Japan Women's Bar Association; and Uemura Tamaki, honorary president of the Japan YWCA.

Often interpolated in the women's statements were expressions of concern about other policies. The League of Women Voters, for instance, in October 1967 urged that the United States cease bombing North Vietnam and take steps toward the reversion of Okinawa. Matsuoka Yoko, who visited North Vietnam, railed at Prime Minister Satō for involving Japan in the aggressive war in Vietnam, arguing that the policy was reviving militarism. Others, who favored closer ties with the People's Republic of China, added their voices. Hiratsuka Raichō, as president of the Federation of Japanese Women's Organizations (Nihon fujin dantai rengōkai, or Fudanren), linked the U.S. Security Treaty, the Japan–South Korea Treaty, and the Self-Defense Forces in the "vicious cycle" of aggravating tensions in Asia. She called for the abolition of the Self-Defense Forces.[44]

A few spoke to endorse the United States as a trusted friend and ally. Suzuki Sumiko, president of the independent Kōbe League of Women Voters, wrote in a letter to the author in April 1965,

> We, from our usual studies, have eyes to see what the truth is, and believe in American good faith. Thinking of today's North and South Korea and Vietnam, it was lucky that Japan was occupied only by the United States. I will be praying for those who are working hard for early realization of peace in that part of the world.

The same month Sōma Yukika supported U.S. policies, including the bombing, in an article for the most widely circulated (700,000) women's weekly in Japan, *Josei Jishin* [Women's magazine]. She continued to encourage backing of U.S. policies and visited South Vietnam to obtain first-hand information.

Throughout this period, women tended to distinguish official U.S. policy from ordinary Americans as people, particularly American women, who they felt certain would react as mothers, just as did the Japanese. The U.S. Delegation of the Women's Strike for Peace, which traveled to Indonesia in July 1965 to meet with Viet Cong and North Vietnamese representatives to consider ways of ending the strife, fulfilled this expectation and aroused considerable newspaper coverage even though the delegates stopped only briefly in Japan.

In Fukuoka in 1966, a team of women Sōhyō trade unionists reluctantly met with a visiting U.S. woman trade union representative, although the previous week their organization had helped block Ambassador Reischauer from inaugurating a new library. Arriving late, perhaps indicative of their uncertainty up to the last moment as to whether they would even come, they raised hostile questions about the U.S. role in Vietnam. Finally, the visitor exclaimed, "But you surely must know that the United States wants peace also!" When she then told them that she planned the next day to visit the Hiroshima Memorial, tears united the women in a deep emotional desire for peace.

The liking for Americans, established time after time in public opinion polls and evident in most personal encounters, provided for some women the basis for greater criticism of their friends than of the forces of North

Vietnam. In talking to Americans, Japanese women have often said, "You can be appealed to. You have a high standard of morality and democracy. The others we know won't even listen."

It was a difficult time, but the women adhered faithfully to their instincts about security, peace, and Japan's role in the world. They knew that for themselves they preferred noninvolvement, believing it would keep them safe.

The Security Treaty

The U.S.-Japan Treaty of Mutual Cooperation and Security was promulgated in 1951 and effected when the Peace Treaty was concluded in 1952. It provided protection in those uncertain days of the Korean War when Japan itself was militarily helpless. In exchange, it permitted the United States to station land, sea, and air forces within Japan's territory. For women it holds interest because it has been fundamental to their most important international concerns. It has implications for the ebb and flow of their attitudes about militarism, the Japan Self-Defense Forces, the United Nations, and the dignity of Japanese nationalism. It is pivotal in United States–Japan relations and security in Asia.

From the beginning there were questions about ambiguities among the Security Treaty, the Peace Constitution, and the Peace Treaty. These led some, such as Katō (Ishimoto) Shidzue and other right-wing Socialists, to vote in the Diet for the Peace Treaty but against the Security Treaty. Ethel B. Weed, writing Mary R. Beard about Katō and the progress of women's affairs in Japan, felt it necessary to explain this variance.[45] Such differences of opinion and interparty strife also turned the Security Treaty into a handy device for opposition parties to use to belabor the government and its pro-U.S. foreign policies.

Although in the 1950s the Security Treaty shielded the hardworking generation of Japanese who concentrated on bringing order out of the destruction of the 1940s, it continued the U.S. military presence and perpetuated the traditional Japanese dislike of the foreigner in their midst, particularly as the foreigners were now part of foreign military bases on now independent soil.

In the most inflammatory episode of the period, the 1957 "Girard Case," a forty-six-year-old—so-called elderly—woman, Saki Naka, scavenging scrap brass on a United States–leased firing range in the Mt. Fuji area at Somagahara, was accidentally killed. She was a classic "woman in the shell," who collided with the outreach of the Security Treaty into Japanese life and precipitated a much larger intergovernmental crisis.

It should be made clear that there is a historic pattern of resistance by rural people to any encroachment by the central government onto their preserve of the village and its environs. The training and practice-firing areas in the rural regions of Mt. Fuji have typically been such locales. Here women, in their role as mothers, objected before the war to the Japanese imperialist military and after the war to both U.S. and Japanese military forces.[46] The modern *shimin undō* spirit has reinforced this civic heritage.

The Shinobugusa Mothers Club in Fuji-Yoshida, Yamanashi, for example, protested in a hunger strike in the mid-1960s the Japanese government's "lack of sincerity" about the U.S. forces' drills with Little John missiles. Again, in 1973 farm wives of the area resisted use of their common-rights lands, this time against firing practices of the Japanese Ground Self-Defense Force. In a different locale, the leftist Mothers Association (Hahaoya taikai) in 1972 collected 70,000 signatures opposing U.S. use of Yokota Air Base. With the spreading out of Tōkyō's suburbs, Yokota was no longer in sparsely settled countryside. Informed by the Defense Agency that it could not act because the base existed under Security Treaty arrangements, the women turned against the source of their displeasure, the treaty. They demonstrated but ultimately gained little.[47]

Another episode in which mothers were pitted against the U.S. military in a similar suburb brought success to the women. In 1973 mothers in the Camp Zama area protested to the military authorities against the firing of salutes and early-morning bugle calls. These noises, the mothers complained, were "making the children cry and hold on for dear life."[48] The military capitulated. The issue in this instance was good neighborliness, not security!

The most serious crisis over the treaty came in 1960. Having repeatedly sought revision of the treaty, the Japanese government under Prime Minister Kishi finally achieved U.S. agreement for a new version. Among the new provisions was prior consultation in case the United States made any major changes in deployment, equipment, or use of its forces, an aspect that arose repeatedly during the period of the Vietnam war. The need for Diet approval of the treaty and the actions surrounding the vote precipitated grave political and parliamentary upheavals and the "Ampo" riots. The confrontations produced, as George Packard suggested in his study, a "kind of watershed." After this, Japanese more fully and consciously asserted sovereignty over their own future.[49]

In that tempestuous June of 1960, two women stand out: one of the young, postwar generation and one of the prewar, socially motivated emancipationists. Both were women of education, politically attuned. Each battled for her convictions, but in different ways. One was part of the crowd; the other stood apart from it. The contrast of roles illustrates a generational change in attitude, a revamped approach to democratic action.

A Tōkyō University senior and literature student, twenty-two-year-old Kamba Michiko became the martyr of the cause. Just one of the many milling about in the battling of the Zengakuren (National Federation of Students Associations) *demo*s as they stormed the gate of the Diet, she was crushed or trampled to death in the melee. She was mourned then in a "people's funeral," and the anniversary of her death still is commemorated with parades featuring her serious face in a black-draped portrait photograph. Her inadvertent "sacrifice" is used as a rallying point for demonstrations against the treaty and other current policies of the establishment.[50]

House of Councillors Diet woman Katō (Ishimoto) Shidzue, an individualist and converted socialist, rose up in her way, too, to battle for her beliefs. Two days after the Kamba incident she broke party discipline to apologize to the nation for her Socialist party, which was deeply involved in the antitreaty struggle. She publicly proclaimed her shame that Japan's new democracy faced the danger of destruction from such violence. She questioned what kind of ideology Japanese want for themselves and their children. In her letter to the press she entreated, "Let us all rise up with courage."

Many years later, Katō described the agonizing soul-searching that preceded her decision to release her letter of protest. She had just returned from a trip to Europe with the Moral Rearmament Association, on which she had studied how communist ideologues used manipulation tactics to seek their political goals. In Europe she had made speeches in which she repeatedly told what she called the story of the rabbit and the cabbage. She demonstrated her points with a big cabbage and a toy rabbit:

> There is a cabbage farm, cabbage, cabbage, cabbage . . . a lot of cabbages
> . . . and there is a rabbit getting into the cabbage farm and the rabbit
> eats the cabbage. Since the cabbages have no protection for themselves
> of any kind, they just let the cabbage be eaten. . . . The rabbit represents
> a country with ideology. The cabbage farm represents a big nation without
> any ideology . . . and it will be eaten up by the nation with ideology.
> It's a very simple story, isn't it?

Upon her return home from Europe, the press picked up this story. Within the Socialist party, she was confronted with being unfaithful to its ideology, but she continued to insist that socialism was an economic policy, "that's all!" When the antitreaty demonstrations, which she felt were communist-inspired, went on day after day, she became convinced that this was not what the new Constitution, which had ended wartime totalitarianism, meant by democracy. Recalling that time years later, she described her inner turmoil:

> This is not democracy at all. Democracy is discussion, set to take place in the building of the Constitution which is the Diet. We have to think of this Diet building as our castle or temple. Why do they have to tear down this Diet building, its gates? . . . Not only that, many encouraging messages came from China to the members of the Diet in the Socialist Party: "Go ahead, go ahead" with this demonstration. . . . We are supposed to be an independent nation. Who decided to take orders from Communist China? . . .
>
> I thought this was very serious and I had to do something. But still I had some feeling that if I stood up and said, "This is wrong," what would happen next? What would happen to my husband? I was very afraid.
>
> But everyday I was watching television, and I just couldn't wait any more. A group of MRA people also said, "If you have courage, you have to stand up now." So I wrote that statement about what I honestly believed at that time and sent it to all the newspapers. In those days the papers were rather supportive of this kind of demonstration, but the demonstrations were moving too fast and they, too, began to feel some fear.
>
> Afterwards I received thousands of letters of thanks and encouragement. . . . Only two or three said *"Bakayaro"* (crazy fool), or something like that.

The extreme wing of the Socialist party sought her expulsion from the party, but party leader Asanuma Inejiro urged that no action be taken against her.[51]

In less dramatic fashion, a few women's organizations issued public statements against the treaty: the Women's International League for Peace and Freedom because its goal is "complete disarmament"; the YWCA because the treaty seemed to assume that adjacent countries are enemies, an idea that might lead to war; the Women's League for the Protection of Human Rights because the treaty seemed incompatible with the Peace Constitution.

Yet, the angry demonstrations and a possible constitutional crisis that would damage Japan's democracy worried "the sensible Japanese people." The projected visit of President Eisenhower exacerbated fears that "rude and impolite behavior" could have fatal repercussions on Japanese-U.S. relations. The quarterly newsletter of the Women's Research Institute, speaking for the informed elite, later explained to its foreign friends:

Japanese women felt sincerely sorry for the violence committed to Mr. Hagerty by some communist members and their followers on his arrival in Japan. And though they considered it very rude of the Japanese Government to propose the postponement of the President's visit. . . . they felt relieved in the sense that the worst consequence, which might have happened, had been averted.[52]

The approach of June 1970 loomed as another potentially serious target date for violent opposition, as treaty provisions allowed either country to take action to terminate the treaty ten years after it went into effect. Whereas in 1960 constitutional aspects dominated the discussion, ten years later Vietnam, sensitivities about U.S. military bases, and awareness of Japan's position in Asia were the major influences on attitudes.

On October 14, 1969 the League of Women Voters, asserting its nonpartisan position, proffered the following statement to the government:

We cannot allow U.S. Army bases to remain in Japan, nor Japanese military power to be strengthened under the guise of self-defense, because these policies will endanger our independence [and] raise tension not only in the Far East, but throughout the whole world.

We believe that our country must strive for a peaceful world and especially try to keep Far Eastern countries secure, as stated in our Constitution. To do so, it will be necessary for us to renew diplomatic relations with the [People's] Republic of China in order to relax tensions among Far Eastern countries. We should also give energetic cooperation and assistance to southeast Asian countries in the areas of economics, technology, and culture.[53]

Interestingly, during this same period the United States League of Women Voters had recommended a softening of relations with "Red" China.

By the critical date of June 23, 1970, discussion had run its course. On the activist front, the police had learned how to contain the *demo*s so as not to repeat the hazards of 1960. They often turned out in larger numbers than the demonstrators, forming human dikes with their shields, reminiscent of *Ivanhoe*, against the flowing lines of towel-masked, helmeted demonstrators. Each side knew its accepted roles: The very ritual of the *demo* made the point and provided satisfaction. Sōhyō trade union women, for instance, staged a nighttime lantern-and-candle demonstration in November 1969. They listened to Takada Naoko, chief of the Women's Socialist party's Women's Bureau, who exhorted them to an intensified campaign against the treaty that threatened the peace and security of Japan and Asia. The nasty violence of 1960 did not need to reemerge and never did.

To give perspective about Japanese citizenry's relative inattention to foreign affairs, public opinion polls showed that sizable numbers at the height of the 1960 crisis did not seem to know about the treaty. This lack of knowledge or interest was found again ten years later, except among the younger generation.[54] Positions were taken primarily along political party lines, and women were no exception. A survey of 600 Tōkyō women carried out by the League of Women Voters after the Lower House election in 1970 showed that LDP supporters agreed with continuation; Socialist and DSP supporters agreed with their parties' position gradually to abolish the treaty; and Communist adherents wanted an immediate termination. By age, those sixty and over preferred continuation while those in their thirties, forties, and fifties preferred gradual abolition. More important was the conclusion that women's greatest concern was not security or foreign affairs, as media attention to the treaty suggested—their greatest concern was commodity prices.[55]

Increasing sophistication, greater national confidence as a result of Japan's economic leap, agreement on the return of Okinawa in 1972, and gradual relinquishment of U.S. military bases combined in the first half of the 1970s to de-emphasize the treaty as an issue. Outmoded *demos* by students were viewed as anathema and counterproductive even by the Socialist party leadership. Katō (Ishimoto) Shidzue emphasized, "We are very much annoyed with this radical mob movement. It's really destroying our intentions."[56]

The winding down of the Vietnam struggle relaxed women's fears that Japan might become involved in war. The Nixon trip to Peking, presaging a conciliatory U.S. attitude toward the People's Republic of China, undercut the progressive left. By September 1973, a public opinion survey showed that almost 67 percent of Tōkyō housewives preferred that the Security Treaty be replaced by a multilateral agreement including China and the Soviet Union as well as Japan and the United States.[57] This broadened focus has given shape to subsequent foreign affairs efforts of major women's organizations: They encouraged the peace treaty with the People's Republic of China; they continued to protest against Soviet control of the southern Kurile Islands; they took stands and rallied for disarmament and antinuclear policies; and they sought to enlarge international exchange programs.

Basically unencumbered by a sense of international tension, the women feel free—and this is their preference—to concentrate on their own status and the political health of their local and national institutions.

Japanese women's attitudes about international relations are well established, perhaps deeply entrenched. As Sōma Yukika has explained, "Japanese women think with their hearts."[58] Rational analysis is not traditional—emotion is. It is natural to cling to the ideals that sustain their basic beliefs and interests.

The historian Yamazaki Tomoko has proposed that lower-class Japanese women relate to Asia, whereas upper-class women identify with the West.[59] Ichibangase Yasuko has talked of the bipolarization by outside influences into those who are "Western-oriented" and those who are "communist-centered and have a cause"—the East-West struggle! The result, she maintained, is that only a few are independent.[60]

Despite these correlations, it is safe to say that most women are inner-centered. Only a vocal few rise to assert positions. Until schools teach more world history and international understanding to the young—Hiroshima schools, for instance, pay little or no attention to the history of the atom bomb—and until solid adult education classes enable women to catch up on international realities, traditional reactions, tempered by mass media directives, will shape the average woman's views about the world and Japan's place in it.

It is not amiss to recall the concluding lines of Yosano Akiko's "Song of Women's Suffrage" ("Fusen no uta"), written in 1930:

> Where there is woman's power,
> There will be the light of peace.[61]

INTERCULTURAL EFFORTS—
FRIENDS AND EXCHANGERS

> *In years to come the United States and Japan are going to find that the partnership that has characterized their relationship over the past three decades is going to be increasingly essential, and that one of the great challenges of the future will be that of developing a greater awareness of, and appreciation for, the variety of peoples and cultures that make up our world.*
>
> —Ogata Sadako, ambassador to the United Nations, 1979[62]

Although hesitant and shy, smiling Japanese women are successful envoys of goodwill for their nation. Despite fewer opportunities for contact with foreigners, they seem to come more readily than their men to easy, international friendships. As they step out from their glass boxes of stereotyped constraint into avenues of direct human encounter, they gain in international understanding and make friends for their country.

As Japanese women come from an intimate society in which personal loyalties bind relationships, meaningful international experiences succeed when their personal roles supersede traditional manners. Massive tourism, for instance, is merely superficially international—an outgrowth of affluence that of recent years has permitted the tightly knit group outing to spill over into more expensive outings overseas. Traveling in their jet-propelled or bus-shaped glass boxes, the tourists are still neatly separated from any real cultural interchange. They move in an animated, scenic picture-postcard world. Group tours minimize the agonies of dealing with foreigners in alien cultures.

Linguistic and cultural hurdles to international interchange are very real, as discomfitingly high for contemporary Japanese as for their forebears. They still must cope with a self-consciousness of inadequacy with respect to the mores of the West. It is one thing to study such manners in a Western etiquette class or the movies, another to essay actual practice with embarrassment close at hand in case of error. Their spoken language is often ambiguous because numerous unrelated words have the same pronunciation, creating confusion when interpreting into or from foreign languages. It is, therefore, difficult to be fully composed when making foreign friends or attending international conferences. As a Kyūshū leader explained, the old notion hovers nearby that "fear peoples the darkness with monsters."[63]

Nevertheless, varying proportions of curiosity and genuine friendliness lighten this darkness among women throughout Japan. How often do their desires come up in discussions—with farm women in a remote northern fishing village, aware of and interested in the UN Educational, Scientific and Cultural Organization (UNESCO) and its goals of mutual understanding; with young business and professional women in Takamatsu on the smallest main island groping for some way to find out how their sisters in the United States or Europe live and deal with their affairs; with university students in mid-Japan's Kinki area who ask about comparisons between their campus life and that in the United States; with the wives of the mayor and other leading officials, businessmen, and academics in a cherished garden teahouse on the edge of a sylvan pool in an old traditional city on the Japan Sea. All are eager to find out how to create world-mindedness—how often do questions of how to build understanding of others and how to make friends dominate the conversation whenever an interested, nonmonstrous foreigner appears!

The Tōkyō Summer Olympics of 1964 proved a landmark in turning international understanding from conjecture to reality; potential home-visit hostesses talked to Westerners about how best to greet and entertain foreign visitors; policemen and taxi drivers studied English; private good manners stretched to become public good manners. The 1970 Ōsaka International Exposition, with the theme "Progress and Harmony for Mankind," and the Sapporo Winter Olympics of 1972 repeated the 1964 breakthrough. To take part in person by crowding close to the reentry-blackened space capsule at the U.S. Pavilion, by applauding figure-skater Janet Lynn, or even remotely, by watching the action on television made many observers glow with a kind of international companionship.

Achievement of the second-largest GNP in the free world brought to many the realization of their country's new position of dignity in the world and some sense of the noblesse oblige that should flow from it. The GNP accomplishment prompted the perception that Japanese could no longer claim to be really "poor." For many women feeling poor, it must be explained parenthetically, is a state of mind born of a combination of deferential humility, historic sensitivity about the geographic size of the home islands, and classic concern about the family budget. At a conference held on the shores of the Japan Sea, one agricultural cooperative officer, abruptly recognizing this changed condition and its practical cross-national implications, exclaimed:"I suddenly realize that the problems our farmers are now facing do not exist in a vacuum but are closely related with the problems of other countries.

I am ashamed of myself for never before having felt that I was a member of the Asian community."[64] The shining look of discovery swept over her face as she talked. For her as for others, better understanding of the rationale for aiding the poorer peoples of Southeast Asia emerged. Unfortunately, their innate hesitancies were reinforced when the fateful Tanaka trip to Southeast Asia in 1974 excited taunting coverage in the mass media of the world about Japanese businessmen as "economic animals" and brought to the surface residual resentment about wartime brutality.

Events such as these inch open doors of awareness of the outside world and of the need to try to live with it, rather than isolated and apart. Inevitably the plea follows for "leaders" (read "teachers") to help them in their search for a new role. By themselves, as some Tōkyō suburban apartment-dwelling housewives indicated, "We have no courage."[65] However, in true Japanese fashion, once the goal is apparent, there is progress, but it is made on their own terms. Reassuringly, an Akita organization officer explained: "We are slow in accepting new things, but once given direction compatible with what we ourselves feel should be done, we bestir ourselves and plod on steadily."[66]

"Be International-Minded!"

Thinking internationally has obviously been low on the priority list of most Japanese women. It must be remembered that in 1951 it was credible for the internationally active Kubushiro Ochimi to write to friends abroad, "Internationalism is a totally new idea to the Japanese."[67] She explained the newness in terms of the history of Japan. Nakane Chie maintained that the situation stems from lack of principle. A leader from Niigata concluded that a sense of service is needed, but worried that there is no Japanese religion to provide such motivation.[68] "We have been so busy at home," explained a Mrs. Tanaka of Tōkyō, "we have had no time left over for international relations."[69]

Over the years many have tried to extend the mother-wife role to include the obligation of stretching minds and hearts across cultures—and no one more than Haru Matsukata Reischauer. Western-educated daughter of the prestigious Matsukata family, which served creatively in the Meiji era to assist Japan emerge from Tokugawa isolation, she became, during those years from 1961 to 1966 when her husband served as U.S. ambassador, a symbol of international understanding. She encouraged thinking internationally in terms that women clearly understood. Admiration of her flowed from women of all ages. Her popularity outscored that of movie stars. When she made speeches, she drew standing room only, whether the auditorium held hundreds or thousands.

Fujita Taki joins in singing with Japanese women leaders who came to see her off at the Tōkyō airport as she left to assume her duties as a member of the Japanese delegation to the United Nations, September 14, 1958. Photo courtesy of Fujita Taki.

Her ideas stirred their desires as she linked remembrance of the old Confucian three obediences with the challenge of the new:

> In this age can we not again hold up a trio of sacred ideas appropriate for this new step onto the international scene? These "three modern treasures" are first to increase study and knowledge, second to build up personal friendships with people of other cultures, and third to foster international thinking and world perspective in the home and in the community. I think in this way we help to mold the kind of society in which we would like to live.[70]

Other internationalists encourage similarly motivated study and thought. Observe the leadership of Fujita Taki who, as president of Tsuda College, finally overcame institutional traditionalism and made international studies a part of the curriculum, or that of Sōma Yukika, whose motivations derived from an international childhood and the strength of her Moral Rearmament beliefs. Follow the impact of Ogata Sadako, Akamatsu Ryoko, and the ever-growing group of women who serve on delegations to the United Nations. Watch Nuita Yoko, who follows closely the newest trends in continuing education and projects her hopes into programs geared to preparing women for a modernized, internationally oriented future. The ideas of these leaders filter into the ubiquitous study groups where ordinary women try to organize their thoughts and decide what to do.

UNESCO, since the immediate postwar years, has been one focal concept for Japanese seeking to reestablish harmonious relations among the people of the world. The preamble of its constitution lent inspiration to those eager to profess adherence to universal peace. As early as August 1948, a suprapartisan women's meeting used these ideals to plan programs to work for peace. Japan's acceptance as a UNESCO member in 1951 was viewed as a way station to full acceptance as a "peace-loving nation" via election to the United Nations itself. The specialized agency's emphasis on education provided a meritorious approach. Stimulated by the approach of the Olympic Games, prefectural education officials set up UNESCO social education classes for women in the early 1960s. Studies concentrated on mutual understanding and fundamental human rights, not hard foreign relations issues. An aura of international friendship emerged based on greater appreciation of other cultures, languages, and arts.

UNESCO activities have seemed particularly viable outside urban centers. For example, in Sendai in the Tōhoku region, the first non-governmental UNESCO Association was formed in 1947. Prefecture-wide conferences in Miyagi in the 1960s attempted to bring UNESCO into "small town, every day life." Concerned that busy housewives did not know about UNESCO—and stories of their confusing its initials with a food brand or a kind of woolen underwear had crept into discussions—organizers shifted emphasis toward encouraging education of children and youth. Or farther north, the lively combination of UNESCO social education forces and the Iwate UNESCO Association, supported strongly by the editor of the *Iwate Nippō*, a wise, grandfatherly man who had traveled overseas, made the intercultural process real. They set up a traveling seminar, busing women representatives from the U.S., British, French, Indian, and Soviet embassies across the prefecture to discuss with Iwate women, colloquium-fashion, education, work force opportunities, and family life. In turn, the foreign women gained insight into rural Japan and enjoyed special introductions to local folklore and festival dances.

This person-to-person kind of international consciousness-raising, repeated many times over and in other study sessions (not necessarily associated with UNESCO), all over the country whenever Japanese women sit down with a foreign woman guest, is the pragmatic approach they enjoy most and respond to best. Although intellectual and informed women may deplore its superficiality, they recognize that it can offer the inspiration for something more substantial. One must remember that since earliest Meiji times Japanese have been looking at others and, as a result of making comparisons—processing through what Tōkyō University's Haga Toru has called the "Japanese-filter"[71]—taking in those practices most useful to their needs.

The perceptive Sakanishi Shio, whose foreign affairs capabilities brought her appointments to the governmental commission to review the Peace Constitution and to the diplomatic problems advisory body of the Foreign Ministry, urged building intellectually on such experiences. She admonished, "Be international-minded! Don't just seek acquaintances with blue-eyes or foreigners." She encouraged "imagination." In her never-ending quest for excellence, she insisted that "Japanese women must learn to get to the bottom essence of matters."[72] Egami Fuji recommended using discussions in the spirit of UNESCO to gain understanding of themselves as Japanese. "How can we begin to have true international understanding unless we understand ourselves?"[73] Ogata Sadako wisely took the next step and raised the question of the kinds of institutional changes that are required "to internationalize Japan itself."[74]

Many of the thousands of women, from Hokkaidō to Okinawa, who took part in the regional seminars on international understanding under the joint aegis of organizations such as Chifuren, the Japan UNESCO Association, newspapers, NHK and other television companies, prefectural education bodies and the American Cultural Centers, tried over the years of the sessions from 1964 to 1971 to find human and practical responses to these challenges. The continuum of the sessions made possible the evolution of their viewpoints. In the beginning the women reacted only on a personalized, one-to-one basis. Questions such as "How do *you* deal with traffic problems?" put to U.S. and European guests dominated, for questioning is an easier technique of communication than the real interchange of discussion. Slowly the sense of community widened from neighborhood to city to prefecture and on to global perspectives. Finally, as one Western-mannered Kitakyūshū educator, who went on to sponsor international education projects herself, realized during her eighth conference, "Our community thinking should be not just as women. . . . [We must] think of the world community in global terms, too."[75]

Japanese are so used to equating "international" with the United States and Europe, that Asia, particularly Southeast Asia, came finally into the global mix almost as a surprise, perhaps because war guilt or a subliminal feeling of superiority had submerged this area below daily consciousness. "We have been too interested in the United States and Europe in the past," concluded Tokunaga Kikuko, after two days of discussion about "Progress and Stability Among the Pacific Nations." "The time has come when we should devote more attention to our neighbors in Asia." Thoughtful educator Chiba Kikuko of Odawara City reminded a similar group in the Kantō area that obviously there were war widows in the Philippines, too.[76] Talk of overseas assistance for these women began to take on some of the obligation of kinship. Some of the early reservations that surrounded the Japanese Overseas Cooperation Volunteers (JOCV) and its recruitment of young men and women gave way to awareness of its merit. The practicality of JOCV and the assistance projects of the women's organizations helped balance, as a Niigata professor phrased it, the "perhaps too beautiful" emotions of international understanding.

Japanese women tend to be doers rather than thinkers—unless immobilized by the perplexities of study. But initiative for action requires both leadership and motivation, and action is better understood and more successfully carried out when the goal is practical. Beaches at Chōshi, Japan's easternmost promontory, and beaches in California are equally threatened by Pacific oil spills. Women appreciate that cooperation to solve such international problems benefits all. However, coming to grips with centuries of prejudice about Koreans is something else. That kind of international problem requires reordering cultural attitudes and needs the leavening of long-range education—perhaps a new generation.

Soul-searching continues, epitomized by the conclusion drawn at an all-Tōhoku conference in Morioka that "international understanding is easy to say but difficult to practice." What is important is that Japanese women are taking steps to put these beliefs into practice.

Overseas Studies

The number of Tsuda Umeko's heirs—young women setting off throughout the world in the spirit of the Charter Oath—swells with the passing years. The results may be either measured in statistics or extrapolated from individual achievement. Japanese passport records indicate that steadily increasing numbers, male and female, go abroad each year to study. In 1964, 1,775 set out from Japan for academic training. In 1970, the figure was 4,659. By 1979, it had reached 13,000. Until 1972, more than one-half went to the United States; since then the proportion has been just under one-half, although the United States still draws a far larger proportion than any other country. About one in three overseas students is female.[77]

Modern women students, as before, tend to seek a liberal arts education. Interest also grows in the social sciences as offering training of more immediate vocational value. Mathematical fields and the physical sciences, especially on the graduate level, lure a few extremely bright and devoted hard workers. Most, however, pursue studies that in the long run give them competence in the English language, a route that enhances their marriageability within their own society. The English-speaking wife, more than ever before as Japan reaches out internationally through business and diplomacy, has become a public relations asset and a well-received envoy of goodwill.

At the same time, young women exposed to education that opens minds to personal and professional aspirations beyond those of the traditional housewife still find that reentry into Japanese society, as in the Meiji and Taishō eras, can be difficult and personally frustrating. The daughter of a well-educated professional couple, enjoying her college training in the United States and eager for advanced work, found her father concerned that she was getting into her marriageable mid-twenties but was not in Japan where she could become interested in a prospective Japanese husband. She returned home, was thwarted in her mass media career because her father found the unusual hours unladylike, and turned to personally less fulfilling but more decorous English teaching.

Alternatively, those who decide not to return home also create unhappiness. A Tōkyō mother, writing to the *Mainichi Daily News*, expostulated about the problem of Japanese girls' marrying Westerners when studying overseas: "Parents . . . must have sacrificed a great deal for their daughter's education . . . at first-class colleges . . . expecting the girls would be of service to the Japanese nation some day. If these young women marry Westerners one after another and do not come back, it is a big loss to this country."[78] The loss she worried about may be the ministering hand of the daughter in her older years as much as service to the nation, but it is a break in custom.

A good proportion of the women who earlier studied in the West did not get married because they could not reconcile their sense of emancipation and their career desires with a life involving traditional Japanese husbands and, perhaps even more important, traditional in-laws. Yet it is interesting to note how many who did marry and had daughters have, in turn, sent them abroad to study. There are not only the four daughters of Wellesley College–educated Uramatsu Fuki, translator into English of the *Heiki Monogatari* [Tale of the House of Taira] but also those of Katō (Ishimoto) Shidzue, Matsuoka Yoko, and, in the younger generation, Ogata Sadako. Other women, who may not themselves have studied abroad but have lived overseas, have followed suit: the daughters of Seki Fumiko and the granddaughter of Ōshima Kiyoko, for example, have studied abroad. Looking beyond the matriarchal sequence and adding the father-daughter lineage, which was initially so important in the Meiji era, one must also include international families like the Hanis and the Matsukatas.

Thus, there is a growing group of second- and third-generation families for whom overseas education of their daughters is a normal option. Each generation's experience reinforces the next. But will they be challenged to play as dynamic a role in their society as their Western-educated mothers and grandmothers? Certainly this is true of Tsurumi Kazuko, holder of a doctorate from Princeton University and professor at Sophia University, whose mother Aiko, born of the illustrious Gotō family, studied at Wellesley College.

Such women link Japan more closely to the lands beyond its shores, and there is frequently a special quality to their role. For some reason, international follow-through seems rather stronger with women who have studied or lived overseas than with men. Men's language capability is often lower—sometimes purposely lest they be depreciated by business peers as an *"eigo-zakai,"* or user of English—but this does not account for situations where all need language assistance. Girls from birth are imbued by training with more sensitivity to others; this quality, if practiced, could account for the difference in receptivity.

But even more crucial may be purpose. For men, as university (particularly graduate) students and as participants in advanced professional training programs, and certainly as entrepreneurs and business executives, the goal is precise. Accomplishment is dedicated to mounting the next rung of the upward-mobility ladder back home—knowledge gained is applied narrowly to specific objectives of personal or company advancement. Nakane Chie commented critically in 1967 when she characterized study abroad as "part of the passport to success and fame" within Japan rather than a step toward helping to bridge the "distance between the world of Japanese intellectuals and that of Western intellectuals."[79]

The activities of the International House of Japan and the various government cultural agreements and special projects, such as the U.S.-Japan cultural conferences and the more recently established Japan–United States Friendship Commission, Japan Foundation, and the Japan Council on International Education, may help ameliorate the inward orientation. Meanwhile, women students, and indeed those women of all ages who go abroad for brief educational exchanges, are likely to continue as the more amiable two-way conveyers of international friendship.

Overseas Studies: Short-termers

Miracles of twentieth-century transportation have added another dimension to the classic nineteenth-century educational interchange. Air travel requires only hours of passage from one culture to another instead of the weeks and months needed for young Umeko's ship and trains.

Young college-age women can test out in short encounters whether they wish to try the longer, full academic training abroad. For women out of school—mothers and even grandmothers—short-term overseas educational projects become quick adult education courses in comparative socio-politico-economic practices and cultures. Sometimes these are linked with participation in international seminars and gatherings. Internationally implanted ideas, received first hand, are more usefully transplanted into Japanese society.

After the war ended, it will be recalled, Uemura Tamaki, a Christian minister and president of the national YWCA, was the first Japanese selected to go to the United States on a short-term leaders' program. Some 1,100 followed during the Occupation era, mostly men. The 1950s imitated the trend of the late 1940s, with most interchange visitors going to the United States under U.S. auspices. Australia, the United Kingdom, the USSR, the People's Republic of China, and others began inviting women leaders. Sponsorships grew as private and government interests opened more and more opportunities.

In the 1960s the Ministry of Education started its overseas observation trips to Europe and the United States and, subsequently, to South and Southeast Asia, sending some ten to twenty women each year. The ministry concentrated on organization leaders and gradually, year by year, included representatives from all over the country. Alumnae of these trips, by 1977 numbering about 300, finally organized their own International Women's Education Association (Kokusai fujin kyōiku shinkōkai). This organization, rather than the ministry, now plans the annual tours. The ministry continues some subsidy, but the program has graduated in initiative from the public to the private sector.

The marriage of Crown Prince Akihito and Princess Michiko in 1959 inspired the prime minister's office to establish the Japanese Youth Goodwill Mission Program to broaden views and foster cooperation. With this program the government's attention to people-to-people diplomacy grew, and it enlarged international cultural exchanges of all kinds, with emphasis on student and youth programs. The centennial anniversary of the Meiji restoration prompted inauguration of Youth Ship sailings, initially to South and Southeast Asia, for these "floating universities" had caught the popular imagination. Ironically, the Youth Bureau of the prime minister's office at first excluded girls, giving reasons reminiscent of the Meiji-era doctrine that girls and boys over seven years of age should not go to school together. Irate youth organizations soon corrected that! By 1976 some 30 percent were young women.

Tours with a study overtone for young and old are now the vogue. Events such as the United Nations International Women's Year conferences in Mexico City and Copenhagen offer a raison d'être for trips with an educational function. In the same vein, a number of women's organizations, trying to establish friendship and exchanges with mainland Chinese women, sent off a group in December 1976 under their project "Fujin no tsubasa," or Winged Women. Almost routinely the concentrated eye-opening, exhilarating experiences of valid educational trips, whatever the locale, produce the excitement of learning that bubbles out on return home to be shared widely. Reports, articles, books, speeches, and television appearances abound in the months that follow. Practical programs for their own women's organizations or community institutions result, as illustrated by some who have gone to the United States. Toda Satsuki, then director of the Ōsaka Women's Education Center, returned with revised concepts of adult and community education that helped lay the groundwork for study programs on countries participating in Expo 70 and for hospitality-friendship projects during the event itself. Morioka Fumi of the *Kōbe shimbun* stimulated more systematic volunteer services with cancer patients and in hospitals. The list is as long as the roster of those combining study with travel.

Better understanding of what makes Americans and other foreigners tick makes these women more incisive, modern members of their own democratic society. One LDP official concluded that she "went to the States to see Japan. . . . I feel as if I came back with homework to do—to improve the Japanese situation." Sōhyō trade union women reported unexpected awareness of why different historical backgrounds made Americans and Japanese think differently about policy decisions. They now better understand the problems of the capitalist economy as it exists in both Japan and the United States.

The ratio of women to men who go on in-depth educational tours is not high, as the latter receive the bulk of both Japanese and foreign government grants and also benefit from corporate and business training-observation programs. For example, from 1953 to 1982 in the United States Leaders Program, the oldest postwar program and thus a classic, only 116 women participated compared with 1,268 men. The U.S.-Japan Labor Exchange fared even worse. In its first twenty years, up to 1982, the program involved 734 people; only five Japanese women's teams, totaling 20 women, were sent, and the number of U.S. trade union women sent to Japan was even smaller. Both U.S. and Japanese unions consistently discriminate.

On special foreign governmental short-term tours for leaders, some women are cautiously hostile, skeptical of how they will be treated or of what they can learn. DSP's Taguchi Sachiko, for example, did not really wish to attend the Harvard International Seminar, even though asked by her party to apply. Her application papers in 1969 purposely criticized the United States and its policies, but to her surprise she was

Japanese women trade unionists visit the United States under a labor leaders' exchange program and attend the national conference of the AFL-CIO. Photo courtesy of USIS/Japan.

accepted. The viewpoints gained by her summer in Massachusetts contributed, she acknowledged later, to her continued international seasoning.[80]

For most who cross the Pacific to the United States, there is a desire to compare standards and observe activities of American women, particularly in fields of current interest: family relationships, modernized home living, youth programs, volunteerism, political participation, civic-mindedness, consumerism, continuing education, care of the aged, and the like. Almost inevitably, whatever the period and focus of the tour, the ending of the observation trip is, in the words of a Ministry of Education group, the "true time of beginning."[81]

Internationalism at Work

International pioneering for Japanese women has now started a reverse-flow stage. The mission inspired by the fifth principle of the Charter Oath, starting in Meiji times, emphasized the receiving aspects of the "inter" part of international. The mutuality aspect of "inter," the giving out of self and resources, is what is new. Those who put this kind of internationalism to work are no less modern pioneers of Japan than were the early Meiji travelers.

For a people that is often characterized by foreigners in phrases like "Oh, you never *really* get to know them," or "Oh, you never get invited into their homes," the move away from self-preoccupation becomes a drastic and occasionally traumatic reversal of role. Their venturing forth becomes a heartwarming extension of the human spirit that underlies friendship and understanding between people no matter what their land, no matter what their culture. It occurs on many levels.

Sometimes it is an individual who finds a cause of service and gives herself to it. To exemplify: When Hashimoto Sachiko, a Meiji woman born in Shanghai, discovered Red Cross ideas and ideals in 1948, she felt that "suddenly everything fell into place. The light within me shined and shined. I had found my life's work." With this light, she devoted herself to the Junior Red Cross and youth work. Her creative leadership finally received the recognition of the International Red Cross when in 1972 it awarded her the Henry Dunant Medal, its highest honor. She was the first Asian and one of only two women to be so honored up to that time. The award cited her most significantly for organizing "Konnichiwa '70," a technical seminar for youth in the Pacific area to consider their responsibilities to country and world community.

It is possible that some of the young people she nurtured grew up to find personal reward in the JOCV, the small but growing technical guidance program started in 1965. One twenty-two-year-old volunteer, preparing to teach the Japanese language in India, explained that in the JOCV she would not be restrained by old-style customs and would have a chance to do what she wanted. In her two-year tour in India she knew, "I will be lonely, but it is not such a long time if we accomplish some purpose."[82]

Or sometimes it is a Japanese family that slides open the doors of its home to welcome foreign friends into its intimate circle: A young family in Wakayama receives its overseas guests for an unforgettable evening of conversation, home-cooked food, and the goodwill of song when the father and young son get out their guitars to encourage fellowship, climaxing their musical duo with a moving offering of "We Shall Overcome." Rotary Club exchange students in Sendai or Niigata, summer exchanges of many programs in Kyōto or Takamatsu, and others throughout the country find knowledge and love as families receive foreign foster sons and daughters into their lives. In the early 1960s, home hospitality was a rare phenomenon, but every year the number of international hostesses has grown.

One of the earliest groups to experiment with home hospitality was the Tōkyō YWCA. Its project, "Mothers to Southeast Asian Students in Japan," got started in 1961. Learning that the students from these countries who had won Japanese government scholarships to study in Japan were unhappy and not satisfied with their living conditions, Ōtsuki Yuka and the YWCA's International Relations Committee launched a "foster adoption" program in which volunteer foster mothers adopted one student each. The concept proved successful, and the YWCA expanded the undertaking. It offered personalized help, professional counseling, outings, and always the warmth of a home to go to. In the first twelve years the program involved more than 200 Japanese families and some 500 students from twenty-four Southeast Asian countries. It was part of the mood beginning in the early 1960s, when, as a YWCA leader explained, the association "turned its eyes toward the world."[83]

There are more and more examples of women's associations launching projects of outgoing goodwill. The Tōkyō Pilot Club supports a U.S. pilot exchangee on an educational trip to Japan. Chifuren, sensitive to health conditions in South and Southeast Asia, raises funds for vitamins for children in Bangladesh. Or the National Women's Association of Agricultural Cooperatives appeals to its 2.8 million members for donations to provide "Clean Water for Children in Cooperatives Around the World."

When the Japanese Association of University Women (JAUW) in 1974 sponsored the large XVIII Triennial International Conference of the International Federation of University Women, the members rallied all their pioneering spirit and courage to organize and manage this major intercultural event, held in Asia for the first time. With so many of the members themselves products of the Tsuda heritage, the group is signally aware of international relationships. By 1965, under the leadership of Ogawa Yoshiko, diplomat's wife and intellectual, the association had started intensive, carefully devised study programs on Southeast Asia, also supporting a few women graduate students from that area. The JAUW's sponsorship of the conference symbolized the contemporary advancement of Japanese women into the international community of women.

In the summer of 1970, encouraged by the experienced Fujita Taki, the association organized a joint international seminar with the American Association of University Women. One hundred thirty-one Japanese from twenty prefectures and thirty-one Americans gathered together at an academic hostel overlooking the Pacific. Their agenda set deliberations on (1) how to promote international understanding, especially between the United States and Japan; (2) education and student movements; and (3) urbanization and public hazards. Because of this experience,

Japanese women realized that they could successfully plan and execute an international venture of considerable size. It emboldened them to take on the greater responsibilities of the world conference in 1974, with 1,000 university women coming from thirty-nine countries. Led by their president, the conscientious and caring Ōshima Kiyoko, a strong Meiji woman, they raised financial support from government and private sources, provided travel scholarships for many from less developed countries, opened up home hospitality, and involved the officials and political power structures of Tōkyō and Kyōto. They were gracious hostesses to their peers from around the world. The election at the conference of Takano Fumi, professor at Tsuda College, as a vice-president of the International Federation acknowledged their capacities for international involvement, and subsequently her election as president reaffirmed Japanese powers of international leadership.

Princess Michiko's hope for the future, expressed at the gala inaugural meeting of the International Federation of University Women in a beautiful, fan-ornamented Tōkyō ballroom, set the tone of the conference. She herself projected the potential of the newly outreaching spirit of Japanese women and called for the realization of a new world: "With the deep sense of identity throughout our past and the present we are now all together in our realization that we stand at the threshold of what might be called a 'global age' on a united front in search of right direction for future progress of mankind."[84]

In the in-depth interviews of the hundred or more Japanese whose ideas and experiences have gone into personalizing this study of Japanese women, the final question asked was always, "What would you like to say about Japanese women to the rest of the world?"

Preponderantly the response was a plea for understanding—understanding of them, their history, and their heritage. The desire was for foreign women to get to know the real Japanese woman better. Ichibangase Yasuko, lamenting that the foreign image of Japan has been only of "geisha, Fuji-san, and the life of top ladies," called for appreciation of the *danchi* people, those working in factories, and farm women. Kamiya Mieko hoped for the realization that would change other people's image of the Japanese women away from that of the "humble and self-effacing woman who has no real will of her own to that of individuals thinking and facing all kinds of problems with their own minds." Thus will come the knowledge that there is a great diversity of women in Japan, and not just one image. Kobayashi Hiro hoped that many people would come to Japan to gain such understanding.[85]

Princess Michiko, escorted by Ōshima Kiyoko, president of the Japanese Association of University Women, enters the opening plenary of the XVIII Triennial International Conference of the International Federation of University Women in Tōkyō, August 13, 1974. Seen walking directly in back are Dr. Bina Roy of India, president of the IFUW, and Takano Fumi, who became president in 1981. Photo courtesy of Ōshima Kiyoko.

If these hopes are to be realized, the burden of effort must fall more and more on the Japanese themselves. Since the early 1970s Japan has firmly entered a new era of international exchange. International conventions of Lions, patent attorneys, scientists, environmentalists, physicians, university women, and so on fill the hotels and spread their delegates and families up and down the islands. The Japanese government, awakened to its Pacific international obligations, brings Asian Women's Bureau representatives, for example, to a fully paid International Labour Organisation regional workshop to exchange ideas on women workers. The United Nations University pulls intellectuals. The fascination of the world with the miracle of Japan's progress lures many observers to her shores. There is, as Ichibangase realized, a desire to see the natural beauty of Japan, its gardens, Mt. Fuji. There is also an interest to meet and get to know the Japanese, women as well as men, and not simply the geisha.

Many of the best, the brightest, the most interested and sympathetic are coming to Japan all the time. Without further hesitancy all Japanese can, if they wish, lower those barriers hitherto created by their isolating sense of uniqueness. While retaining cultural traditions and distinction, they can now accept true friendship, understanding, and fellowship as equal and participating citizens of the world.

PART 3
DESIGNS FOR THE FUTURE

IWY's Mexico City Conference left us two things: one is the World Plan of Action. This action plan is a "treasure mountain" for women, as a Japanese woman reporter called it, and we have to keep excavating for this treasure all during the next ten years. . . . At the Mexico Conference, I quoted Hiratsuka Raichō's, "In the beginning, woman was the sun. She has now lost her light, and she has become the moon that shines only when it reflects the other light. We now have to restore the true sun, no longer to be the pale moon." I think this, then, is the very time, come again, for us to restore the true sun.

—Fujita Taki, "Towards Tomorrow," November 22, 1975[1]

For Japanese women, International Women's Year (IWY) coincided with the thirtieth anniversary of their enfranchisement. It made 1975 a particularly appropriate benchmark for assessing how far they had come with their emancipated role and for setting goals for the forthcoming decade of action. It linked in propitious Japanese combination hopes for the future with the underlay of the past.

In Mexico City, at the formal meetings of the United Nations International Women's Year Conference and at the often passionate events of its satellite, the Tribune, Japanese women could be observed performing very much in the character and spirit of the many contemporary variations they represent.

Internationally experienced and revered *sensei* (teacher) Fujita Taki headed the official delegation. Moriyama Mayumi, forceful, energetic director of the Women's and Minors' Bureau, and the women section chiefs of the Ministries of Education, Agriculture, and Social Welfare, who funnel ideas and projects to women and their organizations throughout Japan, served, giving practical support. Ten women Diet members, representing all political points of view, participated as observers. Their presence underscored their contribution in cosponsoring the resolution, unanimously passed by both houses of the Diet, that

---

Photo opposite: Although this pensive high school girl from Sapporo evokes the heritage of the women authors of Heian times and poets and social critics of subsequent centuries, equally she is heiress to the riches of the "treasure mountain" of the U.N. Decade of Women to which Fujita Taki alludes in her November 22, 1975, assessment of the future of Japanese women (quoted above). Photo courtesy of Karen Marston.

dealt with the "Enhancement of the Social Status of Women in International Women's Year."

Across Mexico City at the Tribune, organization members, clustered in groups, briefly attended the big Tribune plenaries, looked around and followed their tour guide across the broad plaza to hurry on to sightseeing spots. Feminist Tanaka Mitsu in "mod" dress and a few like-minded cohorts scheduled one of the individually organized meetings at the Tribune to publicize their point of view. Seemingly unaware that Fujita Taki, who was with difficulty climbing the stairs on her crutches to their upper-story meeting, had arrived to endorse them, they cut their session short because of insurmountable language barriers, their ideas largely uncommunicated to feminists of other nationalities. In the Tribune's intense politicizing, which generated heated discussions edging close to physical encounter, Matsui Yayori, world-traveled newswoman, joined the multinational leadership that overcame argumentative splintering to prepare the demands for action finally presented to Helvi Sipila, UN secretary general for IWY. Matsui's activism helped consolidate the Tribune's efforts; in the future, with conviction and intelligence, her progressive voice may similarly crystallize her sisters' needs within Japan.

At home, starting in 1974, the women's organizations and the government planned and organized action on what the National Committee for United Nations Non-governmental Organizations of Women aptly labeled "Women's Questions in the Contemporary Age." Celebrations of the thirtieth anniversary on April 10, 1976 of women's first vote further stimulated women to focus on society's issues as they rallied in cooperative mass meetings in recognition that "a woman's vote changes politics!"

The Prime Minister's Advisory Council on Women, in its major report of November 1976, called for full awareness of how "economic development, scientific improvement and technological innovation have greatly changed the social environment." It placed on women obligations to "choose for themselves a life which is substantial" and to be responsible both as independent individuals and as members of society. The report urged women to overcome their own latent idea of sex discrimination, think about the whole of society, and foster the spirit to contribute to it. But it also recognized that these goals required (1) improvement in the legal status of women; (2) increased participation of women on equal footing with men in all political, economic, social, and cultural activities; (3) respect for maternity and protection of the health of women; (4) insuring of economic stability of the aged; and (5) promotion of international cooperation. To realize these policies, the council proposed research, legislation, education, training, and full, progressively oriented action by government at all levels, organizations, mass media, trade unions, and individuals themselves. It asked for the "cooperation of men and women to bring about happiness not only of women themselves but of the whole society."[2]

Forward-looking public and private advisory groups have followed through to promote IWY-era philosophy about the status of Japanese women. They have outlined practical proposals to correct discrimination and speed fulfillment of the IWY slogan "Remove sex-discrimination and strengthen women's power."

This mobilization to improve the status of women, by comparison with that of the Occupation thirty years ago, is intrinsically Japanese. There has been no duress imposed from the outside. Further, the Japanese government has endorsed this advocacy and is committed to providing organizational and financial support. Thus, policies and activist measures are interwoven as naturally as possible into the Japanese design of society in the last quarter of the twentieth century.

For Japanese women, who respond with greater ease to an extended time frame, setting these goals within the IWY framework of a decade's span also establishes a schedule for accomplishment that is innately comfortable and hence more viable. Their plea for time to think about and make adjustments, so often reiterated since the upheaval of the war and the Occupation, can find realization in a tempo of their own as they mold what they believe their IWY-era life-style and role should be.

There is little reason, if analyses of past development are projected forward, to anticipate many surprises. The initial five years of IWY have shown that the trends are firmly established—as are the inherent complexities of getting the sun of Japanese women to shine forth. Sometimes it seems that the first requirement is simply to get the Japanese to open their eyes to see the rays of sun—the abilities, or "genius," of Japanese women, as Hiratsuka phrased it. Then it would be easier to observe how they are already lighting and cultivating with their renewed capacities many aspects of Japanese society.

Japanese women possess a uniformity in their self-understanding and the direction they wish to move that may be unique in the developed world. Universal literacy and widespread elementary and secondary schooling have established one important base of this uniformity. But also, because individualism is frowned upon, each step of advancement is taken most satisfactorily by the group as a whole. Given this proclivity, their cultural homogeneity, and their educational strength, Japanese women digest change and develop more or less in unison. This may in part explain why so often they are viewed in stereotype. This process does not produce many fireworks or encourage flashy, spectacular leaders who, in other cultural settings, may actually represent themselves rather than women of their countries. It does insure that the progress the Japanese women make has depth and strength—and a kind of universality of accomplishment.

The preceding pages tell of the interplay between the general female population and their leaders, including the difficulties of natural cooperation among the leaders and their groups—a problem that hampers women's cause. What of future leadership? Given the three age blocs of women—Meiji matriarchs, midway generation, and young modernists—the tradition-breaking trailblazing of the individualistic leadership of Hiratsuka, Ichikawa, Oku, Katō, Fujita, and Sakanishi is coming to an end. The young modernists, whatever their exceptional promise, are still unproven by Japanese standards. They must wait for some tempering of time before there can be broad acceptance of the guidance they undoubtedly can and will give. For the next period leadership seems likely, therefore, to be pluralistic. Such women as the well-trained Ichibangase Yasuko, Kihira Teiko, Moriyama Mayumi, Nuita Yoko, Ogata Sadako, Tanaka Satoko, and Takahashi Nobuko will use the system. They are orderly builders and strengtheners rather than disruptive innovators. Their leadership insures sustained progress, effectively attuned to the slowly but surely evolving general population of women. They represent a generation of women achieving success within rather than apart from the system.

This may not be the style of action to shake Japanese men into real perception of their women and the directive force they give in Japanese life. Most men struggle with a kind of tunnel-vision, focusing mind and energy on their careers. Yet male awakening is essential to a breakthrough to partnership. Much more than public relations gestures is called for. There is need to go beyond platitudinous acknowledgment of constitutional status to learn how very able and contributive the women can be—and indeed are—in the work place, in government, and in the community. In times of crisis and adversity, like the earthquake of 1923 or the war, society has unquestioningly accepted women's performance of duty. But women cannot accuse the men of ignoring their talents if they do not themselves insist on breaking the communication barriers by building bridges across the bipolarized life-styles of men and women. Without many such bridges, the "balanced status" of "women as partner of the male," which Taguchi Sachiko held up as the Japanese ideal—by comparison with the Western "equal status"— is not really possible.

Meantime, and importantly, although it may not be obvious to their men—or even to foreign observers of this vital nation—the women are the prognosticators of change in Japan. Equally, in most periods, they regulate the tempo of change. Closer to the daily life of family and community, they are the bellwethers of practical problems that emerge to require national remedy. At the local level they have pioneered procedures for coalition politics, which may become important nationally. The concerns of their little study groups, of their neighborhood *shimin undō*, of their organizations, which are their mechanisms of power, of their petitions to local and national authorities—these are frequently the tiny black clouds on the horizon warning of encroaching storms. Note their early worries about environmental pollution of various kinds; about the quality-of-life balance between concentration on escalating GNP and welfare needs; about consumerism, not only on price issues but on urgent matters of safety and health; about corruption in government and the need for clean political life and elections. At heart they are conservative. They are sensitive to dangers that threaten the security of the family and its setting in society. As guardians of their country's domestic well-being, they become as well the architects of social change. This role flows from the creativity of citizenship, which the women themselves do not fully realize—nor does the leadership of Japan even begin to understand it. Too often officials regard women's intrusion into policy formulation as a nuisance when they should study women's ideas as guidelines for legislative and administrative action. It is precisely because women are not a special-interest group and because their concerns are not politically motivated that their priorities are all the more important. Herein lies the true value of women's fulfillment of democratic responsibility and their gift to postwar Japan. Their sensitivity may, in the future, help guide Japan in the family of nations.

Japanese women now more than ever can choose their own way, individually or in organized lobbies for their causes. Like women in most nations, they are a majority "minority." They have the basic constitutional and legal rights to make of themselves what they will. Their own consciousness-raising, particularly since the early 1970s, is broadening the scope of this awareness. Moreover, this enlarging consciousness is paralleled at an accelerating rate by adjustments in institutional processes. Court judgments on rights in the work force and on the economic value-equivalent of the housewife's work, as well as legislation on Civil Code revision, health and welfare of mothers, and employment insurance, illustrate expanding societal recognition of their rights. International Women's Year brought confirmation of such change: No less a leader than Ichikawa Fusae optimistically described the progress as "beyond expectation."

The momentum of the 1970s, building on the many transitions of attitude, life-style, economic affluence, and community experience of

These smiling high school girls from Urawa embody the outward-look-ing, outward-reaching approach to life that is typical of increasing num-bers of modernized Japanese women in the closing decades of the twen-tieth century. Photo by the author.

the 1960s, has moved women into a brighter era in the 1980s. Opportunity opens to the penetrating light of their intelligence and activism. As Fujita Taki exhorted, "This, then is the very time, come again," when Japanese women can expect to step forth, resplendent, into their society— no longer the hidden sun.

APPENDIXES

APPENDIX A
CHRONOLOGY OF EVENTS
CONCERNING JAPANESE WOMEN

Date	Events Concerning Women	General Events
	LEGENDARY ERA (traditional dates)	
B.C. 660		Emperor Jimmu ascends the imperial throne
A.D. 200	Empress Jingō invades Korea	
	HISTORICAL ERA	
Kantō Era		
A.D. 188	Himiko becomes queen	
538		Introduction of Buddhism
592	Suiko empress (592-628)	
593		Regency of Prince Shōtoku
604		17-Article Constitution
642	Kōgyoku empress (642-645)	
645		Taika Reforms
655	Saimei empress (655-661)	
687	Jitō empress (687-697)	
701		Taihō Legal Code (Taihō Ritsuryō)
707	Gemmyō empress (707-715)	
Nara Era		
710		Capital moved to Nara
712		Kojiki
715	Genshō empress (715-724)	

311

Date	Events Concerning Women	General Events
720		Nihon-shoki
729	Kōmyō becomes empress of Emperor Shōmu	
749	Kōken empress (749-758)	
759		Manyōshū concluded
764	Shōtoku empress (764-770)	

Heian Era

794		Capital moved to Kyōto
858		Regency of Fujiwara Yoshifusa
ca. 1000	Sei Shōnagon's Pillow Book	
ca. 1004	Lady Izumi's diary	
1010	Lady Murasaki's diary	
ca. 1011	Lady Murasaki's The Tale of Genji	
1016		Regency of Fujiwara Michinaga
1060	Sarashina Diary	
1185		Defeat of Heike at Dan-no-ura

Kamakura Era

1192		Minamoto Yoritomo founds shogunate
1219	Hōjō Masako's era as "nun-shōgun"	
1232		Jōei Code
1244		Tales of Heike
1277	Abutsuni's travel diary	
1333		End of Kamakura shogunate

Ashikaga Era

1338		Ashikaga Takauji's shogunate
1467		Ōnin Wars
1543		Arrival of Portuguese and introduction of guns
1549		Francis Xavier introduces Christianity
1568		Oda Nobunaga controls Kyōto
1573		End of Ashikaga shogunate
1585		Toyotomi Hideyoshi becomes ruling ministe

Date	Events Concerning Women	General Events
1587	Hosokawa Gracia Tamako christened	Toyotomi Hideyoshi bans Christian missionaries

Edo Era

Date	Events Concerning Women	General Events
1600		Battle of Sekigahara
1603	Izumono Okuni plays kabuki	Tokugawa Ieyasu becomes shōgun
1639		Policy of isolation imposed
1672	Kaibara Ekken's Higher Learning for Women	
1853		Commodore Matthew C. Perry arrives
1858		U.S. Consul Townsend Harris negotiates Commercial Treaty
1868		Meiji Restoration

Meiji Era

Date	Events Concerning Women	General Events
1868		Charter Oath
1870	Ferris School established	
1871	First five girls sent to United States to study	Ministry of Education established
1872		Tomioka Spinning Factory founded Fukuzawa Yukichi's Encouragement of Learning
1874	Tōkyō Women's Normal School established	
1877		Tōkyō University established
1880		Japanese translation of New Testament
1881	Kishida Toshiko makes political speeches	
1884	Ogino Ginko, first woman medical doctor	Rokumeikan flourishes
1885	Fukuzawa Yukichi's Concepts on Japanese Women Fukuda (Kageyama) Hideko arrested Peeress School established	
1886	Hiratsuka Raichō born Tōkyō Women's Christian Temperance Union established	
1887		Peace Preservation Law (Hoan jorei)

Date	Events Concerning Women	General Events
1889		Imperial constitution
1890		First imperial Diet Imperial Rescript on education
1892	Katō (Ishimoto) Shidzue born	
1893	Ichikawa Fusae born	
1894	Higuchi Ichiyō's Comparing Heights	Sino-Japanese War
1895	Oku Mumeo born	
1899	Fukuzawa Yukichi's Shin onna daigaku [New Women's Higher Learning]	
1900	Tsuda Umeko founds Girls' English School (Tsuda College) Yoshioka Yayoi founds Tōkyō Women's Medical School	Peace Preservation Police Law (Chian keisatsu hō)
1901	Japan Women's University established Patriotic Women's Association Yosano Akiko's Tangled Hair	
1902		Civil Code Anglo-Japanese Alliance
1904		Russo-Japanese War
1905	Japan YWCA established	
1907	Fukuda (Kageyama) Hideko's Sekai fujin magazine	
1908	Hani Motoko's Fujin no tomo magazine	
1910		Annexation of Korea
1911	Hiratsuka Raichō publishes Seitō [Bluestocking magazine] and establishes Seitō sha (Bluestocking Society)	

Taishō Era

1913	Tōhoku University admits women students	Yūai kai established
1914		Japan enters World War I
1915	Miura Tamaki sings Madam Butterfly in London	
1916	Fujin kōrōn magazine	

Date	Events Concerning Women	General Events
1916	Yūai kai Women's Section established	
1917	Shufu no tomo magazine	
1918	Tōkyō Women's Christian College established	Toyama rice riots
1920	New Women's Association established	Japan joins League of Nations Japanese celebrate first May Day
1921	Hani Motoko's Freedom School established Yamakawa Kikue establishes Red Wave Society	
1922	Peace Preservation Law Article 5 revised Visit of Margaret Sanger	
1923	Federation of Women's Association of Tōkyō established	Kantō earthquake
1924	Women's Suffrage League established	
1925	A Sad History of Women Workers published	Peace Preservation Law (Chian ijihō) Universal Manhood Suffrage Law passed

Shōwa Era

Date	Events Concerning Women	General Events
1926	Women textile workers' strikes	
1928	Pan Pacific Women's Conference, Honolulu	
1931		Manchurian Incident
1932	Women's National Defense Association established	
1933		Japan leaves League of Nations
1936		February Rebellion
1937	Japanese Association of University Women established	China Incident
1938	Protection of Mother-and-Child Law	
1941		Pearl Harbor
1942	Great Japan Women's Organization established	
1945	League of Women of New Japan established	Atom-bombing of Hiroshima Potsdam Declaration Pacific War ends

Date	Events Concerning Women	General Events
1946	Women's suffrage achieved	New Shōwa Constitution
	Women's Democratic Club established	Yoshida Shigeru elected prime minister
	Women students admitted to national universities	
	Abolition of licensed prostitution	
1947	First International Women's Day	Labor Standards Law
		New civil code
	Women's and Minors' Bureau established	Katayama Tetsu elected prime minister
1948	Housewives Association established	Yoshida Shigeru elected prime minister
	Eugenic Protection Law	
1949	First Women's Week	
	Family Courts established	
1950	League of Women Voters (former League of Women of New Japan) established	Korean War
1951		U.S.-Japan Peace Treaty
		U.S.-Japan Security Treaty
1952	National Federation of Regional Women's Organizations established	End of Occupation
		Margaret Sanger visits Japan
1953	Revision of Eugenic Protection Law	
1954	Ōmi Kenshi women silk workers strike	U.S. Bikini Atoll hydrogen bomb tests dust Japanese fishermen
	Suginami Ban-the-Bomb-Signature Movement Association established	
1955	First Mothers' Congress	
1956	First National Conference of Trade Union Women	Japan joins United Nations
	Anti-Prostitution Law passed	
1957		Kishi Nobusuke elected prime minister
		Girard Case
1959	Crown Prince marries Shōda Michiko	

Date	Events Concerning Women	General Events
1960	Nakayama Masa appointed minister of health and welfare Radical woman student Kamba Michiko killed	U.S.-Japan Security Treaty riots Ikeda Hayato elected prime minister Ideal Election Campaign Association founded
1962	Women's Suffrage Hall built	
1963	First Consumer Conference	
1964	Mother and Child Welfare Law	Satō Eisaku elected prime minister Olympic Games in Tōkyō
1966	Suzuki v. Sumitomo Cement Company: first court decision against forced early retirement for marriage Mother and Child Health Law	"Ideal Image of a Japanese" report of Central Council for Education
1967	ILO Convention #100 on equal pay adopted	Minobe Ryōkichi elected governor of Tōkyō
1968	Percentage of women voting exceeds that of men for the first time	University student riots Consumer Protection Basic Law
1969	Women exceed 50 percent of elementary school teachers	Achieved world's third-ranking GNP
1970	Women consumers boycott color television "Women's lib" movement initiated Government of Japan hosts Seminar on Women's Problems for Asian Women Public Administration Officials Industrial Home Work Law	Ōsaka International "Expo"
1971	Housewives Association and National Federation of Regional Women's Organizations boycott of Shiseido cosmetics	Nixon "shocks"
1972	Survey Commission on the Status of Women established Working Women's Welfare Law	Tanaka Kakuei elected prime minister Winter Olympics in Sapporo

Date	Events Concerning Women	General Events
1972		Return of Okinawa to Japan
1973	Women consumer groups force abandonment of synthetic protein projects	World energy crisis
1974	Chūpiren established Japan's Women's Hall completed	Miki Takeo elected prime minister
1975	International Women's Year Child-Care Leave Law Japanese women Alpinists scale Mt. Everest	
1976	Appointment of Ogata Sadako as first woman minister in Diplomatic Corps	Lockheed scandals Fukuda Takeo elected prime minister
1977	National Plan of Action of the International Decade of Women announced National Women's Education Center opened	
1978		Ōhira Masayoshi elected prime minister
1980	Japan signs UN Convention on the Elimination of all Forms of Discrimination against Women Takano Fumi elected president, International Federation of University Women Takahashi Nobuko appointed first woman ambassador	Suzuki Zenko elected prime minister Civil Code amended to enhance wives' legal inheritance status
1981	Revised Civil Code and Domestic Proceedings Law become effective	
1982		Nakasone Yasuhiro elected prime minister

APPENDIX B

NUMBER OF WOMEN ELECTED TO HOUSE OF REPRESENTATIVES AND HOUSE OF COUNCILLORS AND VOTING RATES BY SEX, 1946–1980 (ELECTION YEARS ONLY)

Year	House of Representatives[a]			House of Councillors[b]				Total Number of Women in Diet
	Number of Women Elected	Voting Rate, % (female)	Voting Rate, % (male)	Number of Women Elected	Number of Women in House of Councillors	Voting Rate, % (female)	Voting Rate, % (male)	
1946	39	67.0	78.5					39
1947	15	61.6	74.9	11	11	54.0	68.4	26
1949	12	67.9	80.7					23
1950				5	12	66.7	78.2	24
1952	12	72.8	80.5					24
1953	9	70.4	78.4	10	19	58.9	67.8	28
1955	8	72.1	78.0					27
1956				5	15	57.7	66.9	23
1958	11	74.4	79.8					26
1959				8	13	55.2	62.6	24
1960	7	71.2	76.0					20
1962				9	17	66.5	70.1	24
1963	7	70.0	72.4					24
1965				9	17	66.1	68.0	24
1967	7	73.3	74.8					24
1968				5	13	69.0	68.9	20
1969	8	69.1	67.9					21
1971				8	13	59.3	59.1	21
1972	7	72.5	71.0					20
1974				8	18	73.6	72.7	25
1976	7	74.1	72.8					25
1977				8	16	69.3	67.7	23
1979	11	68.6	67.4		15			26
1980	9	75.4	73.7	9	17	75.4	73.7	26

[a] The term of office in the House of Representatives is for a maximum of four years. The entire house, however, may be dissolved by the passage of a nonconfidence resolution. A general election must be held within forty days of dissolution.

[b] The term of office in the House of Councillors is six years, with one-half the members standing for election every three years.

APPENDIX C

PARTY AFFILIATION OF WOMEN DIET MEMBERS, 1946–1980 (ELECTION YEARS ONLY)

House of Representatives

Party	1946	1947	1949	1952	1953	1955	1958	1960	1963	1967	1969	1972	1976	1979	1980
Liberal	5	3	{2	2	1	1	{3	{2	{2	{3	{3	{2	{1	{1	
Democratic		3													
Socialist	8	9	5	6	7	6	8	4	4	3	2	2	3	2	2
Democratic Socialist								1	1	1					
Communist	1		3								1	2	2	8	7
Progressive	6														
Kōmeitō											2				
Minor parties	10		2	1	1	1									
Independent	9											1	1		

House of Councillors

Party	1947	1950	1953	1956	1959	1962	1965	1968	1971	1974	1977	1980
Liberal	4	4	1	{3	{5	{8	{7	{3	{4	{3	{6	{6
Democratic	3	5	2									
Socialist	3	5	4	4	5	4	4	4	5	3	2	2
Democratic Socialist							1	2	2			
Communist							1	1	1		5	5
Kōmeitō								1	1		2	2
Ryōkufu-kai	3	1	1									
Minor parties	2	2	2	4							1	1
Independent	1	1	4	1	2	4	4	2		1	1	1

APPENDIX D
OBJECTIVES OF ANNUAL WOMEN'S WEEK

The Women's and Minors' Bureau sponsors an annual national meeting in Tōkyō to commemorate the election day on April 10, 1946, when Japanese women first exercised their franchise. One or more preselected objectives or themes are the subject of study and discussions at hundreds of preparatory meetings throughout the country. Local groups send one or more delegates to discuss, debate, and try to reach consensus at the national forum. The official topics illustrate the evolution and growing maturity of women's concerns, starting with introspection about self, home, and community, moving on to awareness-building about society and national problems, and finally to equal political responsibility with men for national and international affairs.

Year of Meeting	Themes
1949	To understand the laws pertaining to the emancipation of women
	To clarify the factors which hinder improvement in the status of women
	To disseminate information about facilities which are useful to bring about improvement in the status of women
1950	To abolish feudalistic practices in the home and in places of work
	Let's learn about our rights and duties
1951	To raise women's civic consciousness
	To promote civic activities among women
1952	To renew awareness of the status of women and to encourage such awareness
1953	To establish independent-minded activity among women
1954	To cultivate women's ability
1955	To cultivate women's ability as members of society--in personal relations, the

Year of Meeting	Themes
	community and working places--and as molders of public opinion
1956	To use the power of women especially to build a happy home
1957	To use the power of women especially to establish modern human relationships
1958	To use the power of women through activities carried out in a cooperative way
1959	To establish among women a sense of independence and independent activities, especially in group relationships
1960	To organize an independently planned daily schedule
1961	To contribute to the growth and development of the next generation, especially to mold good character as members of the society
1962	To reexamine our lives in this rapidly changing society and to endeavor to nurture a new life order
1963	To have women foster social conscience in order to build a happy society
1964	To understand the role of the home and family in modern society: the problem of industrialization and the home
1965	To have women examine the present condition of our culture and contribute toward its betterment in the future
1966	To look at the role of women today in a changing society
1967	To make full use of women's talents
1968	To make full use of women's talents as good members of society
1969	To make use of women's talents to plan a full and independent life
1970	To use women's talents through participation in society and fulfillment of responsibility in the home
1971	Rights and duties of women today on the twenty-fifth anniversary of women's suffrage
1972	Status of women--its present situation and problems
1973	Thinking about Japan--the role of women and the future of society
1974	Consider Japan: Future of its society and the role of women
1975	Promoting equality of the sexes and the social participation of women with responsibility for their contribution to the economic, social, and cultural aspects of society and the peace of the world

Year of Meeting	Themes
1976	A ballot cast by a woman can change politics
1977	Promoting equality of the sexes with emphasis on reviewing social customs
1978	Promoting equality of the sexes with emphasis on social conventions and developing new life attitudes
1979	Promoting equality of the sexes emphasizing the widening of women's activities in all fields
1980	Equality for men and women and promotion of women's participation in society
1981	Co-participation of male and female in every dimension of life: home, workplace, community
1982	Co-participation of male and female in every dimension of life: the responsibility to build a future society

APPENDIX E
MAJOR WOMEN'S ORGANIZATIONS IN JAPAN

	Date Founded	Number of Branches (1975)	Member- ship (1975)
Japan Women's Christian Temperance Union (Nihon kirisutokyō fujin kyōfūkai)	1886	123	4,443
Young Women's Christian Association of Japan (Nihon kirisutokyō joshi seinenkai)	1905	55	17,000
Japan Section of Women's International League for Peace and Freedom (Fujin kokusai heiwa jiyū renmei Nihonshibu)	1921	11	700
Association of Subscribers to the Fujin-no-Tomo (Zenkoku tomo no kai)	1930	159	25,000
Women's Social Education Association of Japan (Nihon joshi shakai kyōikukai)	1937	5	--
League of Women Voters of Japan (Nihon fujin yūkensha dōmei)	1945	51	4,000
Japanese Women's Democratic Club (Fujin minshū kurabu)	1946	95	5,600
Japan Nursing Association (Shadan hōjin Nihon kango kyōkai)	1946	120	100,000
Housewives Association of Japan (Shufu rengōkai [Shufuren])	1948	460	--
Japanese Association of University Women (Daigaku fujin kyōkai)	1948	28	3,000

	Date Founded	Number of Branches (1975)	Member-ship (1975)
National Widows' Association of Japan (Zenkoku mibojin dantai kyōgikai)	1950	47	840,000
Japan Women's Bar Association (Nihon fujin hōritsuka kyōkai)	1950	--	220
National Council of Women's Organizations of Agricultural Cooperatives (Zenkoku nōkyō fujin dantai kyōgikai)	1952	5,000	2,800,000
National Council of Federation of Regional Women's Clubs (Zenkoku chiiki fujin dantai renraku kyōgikai [Chifuren]	1952	25,000	6,400,000
Pan-Pacific and Southeast Asia Women's Association, Japan Committee (Han taiheiyo tōnan Asia fujin kyōkai Nihon iinkai)	1952	--	100
National Association for Improvement of Life (Kurashi no kai zenkoku rengōkai)	1953	35	4,800
All Japan Buddhist Women's Association (Shadan hōjin zen Nippon bukkyō fujin renmei)	1954	75	13,000
Japan Liaison Council for the National Congress of Mothers (Nihon hahaoya taikai renrakukai)	1955	47	--
National Committee for United Nations Non-Governmental Organizations of Women (Kokuren NGO fujin iinkai)	1957	10	--
Japan Women's Union (Nihon josei dōmei)	1959	--	--
National Federation of Business and Professional Women's Clubs of Japan (Nihon yushokufujin kurabu rengōkai)	1959	18	800

	Date Founded	Number of Branches (1975)	Member-ship (1975)
National Council of Women's Department of Fishery Cooperatives (Zenkoku gyōgyō kyōdō kumiai fujin-bu renraku kvōaikai)	1959	1,269	40,000
All Japan Women's Federation (Zen Nihon fujin renmei)	1960	35	62,000
Japan Democratic Women's Association (Nihon minshū fujin no kai)	1961	35	5,000
Japan Women's Conference (Nihon fujin kaigi)	1962	245	50,000
New Japan Women's Association (Shin Nihon fujin no kai)	1962	1,700	135,000
Association for Consumer Sciences (Shōhikagaku rengōkai)	1964	34	11,000
Lib Shinjuku Center (Lib Shinjuku senta)	ca.1973	--	--
International Women's Education Association of Japan (Kokusai fujinkyōiku shinkōkai)	ca.1975	5	300

Notes

Preface

1. Lafcadio Hearn, *Japan: An Attempt at Interpretation* (Tōkyō: Charles E. Tuttle Co., 1955), p. 361.

2. Kuwahara Takeo, "Studies of Japan by Foreign Youths," *Mainichi Daily News* (Tōkyō), 9 July 1972, p. 3.

3. The Japanese Women's Commission for the World's Columbian Exposition, *Japanese Women* (Chicago: A. C. McClurg and Co., 1893), p. 3.

4. Editorial, *Japan Through Women*, 7, no. 33 (January–April 1954):1.

5. Alice Mabel Bacon, *Japanese Girls and Women* (Boston and New York: Houghton Mifflin, 1902), Preface.

6. Mary R. Beard, *The Force of Women in Japanese History* (Washington, D.C.: Public Affairs Press, 1953), Preface.

PART 1. BACKGROUND: THE LOOM OF HISTORY

Chapter 1. The Way of Tradition

1. *The Manyōshū* (New York: Columbia University Press, 1965), pp. 67–68.

2. Harada Tomohiko, *Nihon josei shi* [History of Japanese women] (Tōkyō: Kawade, 1965). Harada makes the historical judgment; the women themselves build on the legends.

3. Tsunoda Ryusaku, Wm. Theodore de Bary, and Donald Keene, comps., *Sources of Japanese Tradition* (New York: Columbia University Press, 1958), pp. 5–9.

4. "A History of Japanese Women," *Japanese Women* (bimonthly publication of the Woman's Suffrage League of Japan, Tōkyō) 3, no. 4 (July 1940):2. A member of the Asiatic Society of Japan in 1873 deprecated the *Kojiki* as "the work of a female peasant." See Basil Hall Chamberlain, trans., *Kojiki: Records of Ancient Matters* (Tōkyō: Asiatic Society of Japan, 1973), Foreword (hereafter cited as *Kojiki*).

5. Tsunoda et al., *Sources of Japanese Tradition*, p. 14.

6. "A History of Japanese Women," *Japanese Women* 3, no. 3 (May 1940):2.

7. Charles S. Terry, "Legend and Political Intrigue in Ancient Japan: Shōtoku Taishu," in *Great Historical Figures of Japan*, Murakami Hyōe and Thomas J. Harper, eds. (Tōkyō: Japan Culture Institute, 1978), pp. 1–15.

8. *The Manyōshū*, pp. 17–18.

9. Edward Seidensticker, trans., *The Gossamer Years: A Diary of a Noblewoman of Heian Japan* (Tōkyō and Rutland, Vt.: Charles E. Tuttle Co., 1964), p. 33. (hereafter cited as *The Gossamer Years*).

10. Ibid., p. 61.

11. See Ivan Morris, *The World of the Shining Prince: Court Life in Ancient Japan* (New York: Alfred A. Knopf, 1972) for a perceptive study of Heian society.

12. *The Gossamer Years*, pp. 60, 121.

13. Ibid., p. 38.

14. Annie Shepley Omori and Doi Kochi, trans., *Diaries of Court Ladies of Old Japan* (Tōkyō: Kenkyusha Co., 1935), p. 123 (hereafter cited as *Diaries of Court Ladies of Old Japan*).

15. Sei Shōnagon, *The Pillow-Book of Sei Shōnagon*, trans. Arthur Waley (London: George Allen & Unwin, 1928), p. 147.

16. Ibid., p. 118.

17. *Diaries of Court Ladies of Old Japan*, p. 49.

18. Ibid., p. 52.

19. Ibid., p. 158.

20. For Murasaki Shikibu's diary, see Ibid., pp. 71–150.

21. Murasaki Shikibu, *The Tale of Genji*, trans. Edward C. Seidensticker (New York: Alfred A. Knopf, 1981), p. 41 (hereafter cited as Seidensticker, *Genji*).

22. Lady Murasaki, *The Tale of Genji*, trans. Arthur Waley (London: George Allen & Unwin, 1935), pp. 21–37.

23. Seidensticker, *Genji*, p. 26. The Seidensticker and Waley translations of Lady Murasaki's classic provide rather different interpretations of her work. That of Seidensticker is less romantic, and in its completeness it reveals greater complexities in the lives of women in the Heian era. For an excellent review of the Seidensticker translation, see Helen C. McCullough, *Monumenta Nipponica* (Sophia University, Tōkyō), 32, no. 1 (1977):93–110.

24. The *Sanjū*, or "three obediences," originally came from the writings of the Chinese philosopher Lieh Tzu. It appears in Japanese literature in the *Gempeiseisuiki* [Record of the rise and fall of the Minamoto and Taira]. See Joyce Ackroyd, "Women in Feudal Japan," *Transactions of the Asiatic Society of Japan* (Tōkyō), 7, no. 3 (1959).

25. See Nitobe Inazo, *Bushidō: The Soul of Japan: An Exposition of Japanese Thought* (Rutland, Vt., and Tōkyō: Charles E. Tuttle Co., 1969) for an interpretation of the traditional samurai spirit. Chapter 14 considers "The Training and Position of Woman."

26. Wakamori Taro and Yamamoto Fujie, *Nippon no joseishi* [A history of Japanese women], 4 vols. (Tōkyō: Shuei-sha, 1965), 2:55–56.

27. Ibid., 2:67–177. For Hōjō Masako's claim as founder of the *bakufu* government, see Kenneth D. Butler, "Woman of Power Behind the Kamakura

Bakufu: Hōjō Masako," in *Great Historical Figures of Japan,* pp. 91–101.

28. Wakamori, *Nippon no joseishi,* 2:235–304.

29. Ackroyd, "Women in Feudal Japan," p. 50.

30. Quoted in Fujikawa Asako, *Daughter of Shinran* (Tōkyō: Hokuseido Press, 1964), pp. 18–19.

31. Quoted in Ishimoto Shidzue, *Facing Two Ways: The Story of My Life* (New York: Farrar & Rinehart, 1935), p. 342.

32. Quoted in the Japanese Women's Commission for the World's Columbian Exposition, *Japanese Women* (Chicago: A. C. McClurg and Co., 1893), p. 6.

33. Ackroyd, "Women in Feudal Japan," pp. 54–55. Statement is attributed to the Regent Nochi No Jō.

34. Ibid., p. 55. Taken from *Nihon kyōiku bunko (Jokun hen)* [Japanese Education Series (Precepts for Women)], pp. 62–63.

35. Ishimoto, *Facing Two Ways,* p. 325.

36. Sōma Yukika cited this in her speech on the history of Japanese women delivered at the College Women's Association Seminar in Tōkyō, 1971.

37. Ishimoto, *Facing Two Ways,* p. 38.

38. Quotations from the *Onna daigaku,* in *Women and Wisdom of Japan* (London: John Murray, 1914). The quotation in the above paragraph is the opening of the *Onna daigaku* as translated by Basil Hall Chamberlain (p. 33).

39. Quoted in Karasawa Tomitaro, *Kyōshi no rekishi* [History of teachers] (Tōkyō: Sōbun-sha, 1958), p. 105.

40. Shiga Tadashi, "Historical View of the Education of Women Before the Time of Meiji," *Education in Japan: Journal for Overseas* (International Educational Research Institute, Hiroshima University) 6(1971):13–14.

41. Okada Rokuo, *Japanese Proverbs* (Tōkyō: Japan Travel Bureau, 1955), p. 77.

42. See Charles J. Dunn, *Everyday Life in Traditional Japan* (Tōkyō: Charles E. Tuttle Co., 1972), for a colorful portrait of the era.

43. George B. Sansom, *Japan: A Short Cultural History* (New York: Appleton-Century Company, 1931), p. 471.

44. See J. E. De Becker, *The Nightless City or the History of the Yoshiwara Yūkwaku* (Rutland, Vt., and Tōkyō: Charles E. Tuttle Co., 1971), for a turn-of-the-century history and sociological study of Yoshiwara.

45. The playwright is Fukuchi Genichiro, known under the nom de plume of Ochi Koji. Ibid., pp. 19–20.

46. Scholars continue to debate the extent of "modernizing" influences developed during the period of Japanese feudalism. For countervailing views over the years, see the works of William Elliot Griffis, John Whitney Hall, and John W. Dower.

Chapter 2. The Way of Modernization

1. Yoshikawa Toshikazu, *Tsuda Umeko den* [Biography of Tsuda Umeko] (Tōkyō: Tsuda dōsōkai, 1956), p. 201.

2. The slogan signified the change from the restrictions of Tokugawa feudalism. See Joseph M. Kitagawa, "Religions and Cultural Ethos of Modern

Japan," in *Selected Readings in Modern Japanese Society*, George K. Yamamoto and Ishida Tsuyoshi, eds. (Berkeley: McCutchan Publishing Corp., 1971), pp. 188–189.

3. Pat Barr, *The Deer Cry Pavilion: A Story of Westerners in Japan 1868–1905* (London: Macmillan, 1968), pp. 12–13. Quotation translated by Arthur Waley.

4. Alice Mabel Bacon, *Japanese Girls and Women* (Boston and New York: Houghton Mifflin, 1902), p. 186.

5. Mary R. Beard, *The Force of Women in Japanese History* (Washington, D.C.: Public Affairs Press, 1953), pp. 157–160. See also *Michi o kiri hiraita josei-ten* [Women pioneers since the beginning of the Meiji era] (Tōkyō: Nippon keizai shimbun-sha, 1968), n.p.

6. "Black Butterfly" comes from Sanford Goldstein and Shinoda Seishi, trans., *Tangled Hair* (Lafayette, Ind.: Purdue University Studies, 1971), p. 114. The poem for her brother is a translation from Tohya Yumiko, "Women of Japan," *Mainichi Daily News* (Tōkyō), 11 July 1969. Asked which Japanese woman she most admired, Yamakawa Kikue named first the novelist Higuchi Ichiyō because of her sympathetic understanding of the poor. Second, Yamakawa chose Yosano. Interview with Yamakawa Kikue, 19 January 1973. The students are from Tsuda College and Kyūshū University. Writing on nationalism in Japan in *Chūō Kōron* in 1951, Maruyama Masao maintained that Yosano's poem for her brother was not an indictment against war but an expression of family-clan loyalty in the face of a military conscription policy that exempted the eldest son in deference to the family system. Ivan Morris, ed., *Thought and Behavior in Modern Japanese Politics* (New York: Oxford University Press, 1963), pp. 147, 154–156.

7. Valid statistics are difficult to find. The *Japan Statistical Yearbook* does not give total figures for the early period. The end-of-century figure comes from John K. Fairbank, Edwin O. Reischauer, and Albert M. Craig, *East Asia: The Modern Transformation* (Boston: Houghton Mifflin, 1965), p. 260. Later statistics are from Ishimoto Shidzue, *Facing Two Ways: The Story of My Life* (New York: Farrar & Rinehart, 1935), pp. 269–270.

8. "Kakochō ni miru kōjo tachi" [The spinning girls in the obituary], *Asahi shimbun* (Tōkyō), 7 November 1972, p. 15. At the one-hundredth anniversary of the founding, a memorial service was held for the sixty-five girls who died in the Tomioka Spinning Factory. Tohya Yumiko, "Women of Japan: Meiji Era (2)," *Mainichi Daily News* (Tōkyō), 26 July 1969. See Sidney L. Gulick, *Working Women of Japan* (New York: Missionary Education Movement of the United States and Canada, 1915), pp. 61–86, for a contemporary account of the factory girls' lives.

9. In 1970–1971, I visited Toyama a number of times to help plan one of the women's conferences on international understanding that dealt with pollution problems and international responsibilities. Toyama women delighted in retelling this early example of their action to correct public problems.

10. Herbert Passin, *Society and Education in Japan* (New York: Bureau of Publications, Teachers College, and East Asian Institute, Columbia University, 1965), p. 13. This is a useful overview of education from late Tokugawa, including

pertinent statistics. See also Hiratsuka Masunori, *Joshi kyōiku shi* [History of education for girls] (Tōkyō: Teikoku chihō gyōsei gakukai, 1965).

11. "Waseda Welcomes Women students," *Japan Advertiser* (Tōkyō) 23 December 1938, p. 4. For practical data on Japan's educational system, see Japan, Ministry of Education, Science and Culture, Research and Statistics Division, Minister's Secretariat, *Japan's Modern Educational System: A History of the First Hundred Years* (Tōkyō, 1980).

12. Samuel M. Hilburn, *Gaines Sensei: Missionary to Hiroshima* (Kōbe: The Friend-sha, 1936), p. 46. Nannie B. Gaines founded Hiroshima College for Girls.

13. For the complete "Preamble to the Fundamental Code of Education" of 1872, see Passin, *Society and Education in Japan,* pp. 209–211.

14. Fukuzawa Yukichi, *An Encouragement of Learning,* trans. David A. Dilworth and Hirano Umeyo (Tōkyō: Sophia University, 1969), p. ix.

15. Ibid., p. 4.

16. Inoue Hisao, "A Historical Sketch of the Development of the Modern Educational System for Women in Japan," *Education in Japan* 6(1971):15–16.

17. Hiratsuka, *Joshi kyōiku shi,* pp. 276–279. See Fukuzawa Yukichi, *The Autobiography of Fukuzawa Yukichi,* trans. Kiyooka Eiichi (Tōkyō: Hokuseido Press, 1960) for a delightful, often amusing account of his reactions to changing events. Despite Fukuzawa's espousal of women's rights, he maintained a conservative home and educated his own daughters in the traditional way. As he grew older, he moved generally toward a more conservative viewpoint.

18. Bacon, *Japanese Girls and Women,* p. 309.

19. Hiratsuka Masunori is the educational historian referred to.

20. Shibukawa Hisako, "An Education for Making Good Wives and Wise Mothers," *Education in Japan* 6(1971):50–53.

21. Ibid., p. 54–55. The 1939 Imperial Rescript to Young People and the Ministry of Education Order of 1943 exhorted such goals; textbooks of moral education, such as the cited material for seventh-grade girls, provided for special responsibilities for girls. See Passin, *Society and Education in Japan,* pp. 259–269, for extracts from the morals textbooks.

22. Kawahara Shizuko, "Awakening of the Meiji Woman," *Asia Scene,* January 1962, p. 45.

23. Ishimoto, *Facing Two Ways,* p. 362. Tsuda Umeko later wrote of her awe at the visit.

24. Tsuda was inspired to make her decision as a result of helping Alice Mabel Bacon write her book on Japanese women. Yamazaki Takako, "Tsuda Umeko," in *Nihonjin no hyakunen* [One hundred years of the Japanese] (Tōkyō: Sekai bunka-sha, 1971), 3:90.

25. Mishima Sumie, *My Narrow Isle: The Story of a Modern Woman in Japan* (New York: John Day Company, 1941), p. 65.

26. Ibid., p. 140.

27. Interviews with Tsuda College graduate students, 25 February 1972.

28. Interview with Shiraishi Tsugi, 18 August 1972.

29. Mishima, *My Narrow Isle,* pp. 107–108.

30. Interview with Nishida Koto, 25 July 1972.

31. Interview with Mishima Sumie, 15 February 1972.

32. See *Pioneer Women Educators of Japan: 24 Leaders of the Century* (Tōkyō: Japanese Association of University Women, 1970). See also *Michio kiri*. My own interviewing showed the same phenomenon, in which Christian heritage or early overseas experience or both became factors in motivating leadership.

33. Hoshina Ai, formerly president of Tsuda College.

34. Charles W. Iglehart, *A Century of Protestant Christianity in Japan* (Rutland, Vt., and Tōkyō: Charles E. Tuttle Co., 1959), pp. 126–127.

35. Popular comment often recounted. See Bacon, *Japanese Girls and Women*, and Hiratsuka Masunori, *Joshi kyoiku shi*.

36. There is good historical material on the WCTU. See the Sophia Smith Collection on the WCTU, including a 1923 article on Yajima Kaji by Mrs. Henry Topping of Yokohama; *Pioneer Women Educators*, pp. 61–64; and Iglehart, *Protestant Christianity in Japan*, passim.

37. Shiraishi Tsugi and Watanabe Matsuko provided information and insight into its historical role. For the commenting foreigner, see Emma Sarepta Yule, "Japan's New Woman," *Scribners*, 1921, p. 358 (Sophia Smith Collection).

38. Ishimoto, *Facing Two Ways*, pp. 272–273.

39. Yanagida Kunio, *Japanese Manners and Customs in the Meiji Era*, trans. Charles S. Terry (Tōkyō: Ōbun-sha, 1957), p. 250.

40. Kaneda Kazue, "Concepts of Women in the Taishō Era as Seen in the *Yomiuri shimbun*," research paper (Ochanomizu University, n.d.). Quotations are from Nishida Keishi, director of Tōkyō Jogaku-kan, and Tanahashi Ayako, president of the Higher Girls' School.

41. *Japan Year Book* (1926), p. 239, as quoted in Iwasaki Yasu, "Why The Divorce Rate Has Declined in Japan," *American Journal of Sociology*, January 1931, p. 577; and Ishihara Kiyoko, "A Glimpse of the Working Population of Women," *Japanese Women* 2, no. 2 (March 1938):2. *Japanese Women* is a bimonthly publication of the Women's Suffrage League of Japan, Tōkyō.

42. Cited in Iwasaki, "Divorce Rate," pp. 572–573.

43. Miyake Yasuko's article in *Trans-Pacific*, 24 July 1926, p. 8, as quoted in Ibid., p. 580.

44. Interview with Shiraishi Tsugi, 18 August 1972.

45. "Divorces Were High in Meiji Era," *Japan Times* (Tōkyō), 28 October 1971.

46. Ito D., wife of a coal millionaire of Kyūshū, was White Lotus. Her poem is included in the collection entitled *Fumiye*, the term given to a form of persecution of suspected Christians. Ozaki Yukio, "Some Contemporary Japanese Poets" (n.p., December 1920), p. 1077, Sophia Smith Collection.

47. Hiratsuka Raichō wrote that *Seitō* members came to be called "new women" by mistake. The press thought because they discussed the "new women" of the theater they admired them, which Hiratsuka said was false. Hiratsuka Raichō, *Genshi josei wa taiyō de atta* [In the beginning a woman was the sun] (Tōkyō:Ōtsuki shoten, 1971), pp. 369–370. Ichikawa Fusae indicated that by 1920 Hiratsuka favored the "new women" name because it had become a useful label. Interview with Ichikawa Fusae, 13 April 1973. During the *Seitō*

period, Japanese used the phrase *"atarashii onna,"* which is the Japanese reading of the written *kanji.* The later organization used the Chinese reading of *"shin fujin."*

48. Yosano Akiko's poem "Wondering Thoughts" in the first issue of *Seitō* characterized the changing women in these now famous terms: "The mountain--moving day is coming. . . . All sleeping women now are awake and moving." *Seitō* 1 (September 1911):1–2.

49. Yoshikawa, *Tsuda Umeko-den,* p. 294. Tsuda discussed the Bluestocking women in her lecture "Women's Movement in Japan" at the YWCA Summer School, 1915.

50. The appeal against Satan is a popular quote. Yamakawa Kikue cited Kawai Michi's use of it in her autobiography. Yamakawa Kikue, *Onna nidai no ki* [Chronicle of two women] (Tōkyō: Heibon-sha, 1972), p. 155. The counter-campaign was named the Truly New Women's Organization (Shin shin fujin kai). It caused hardly a ripple.

51. Hiratsuka Raichō, "New Woman," *Chūō Kōron,* January 1913, trans. Yamamoto Kazuko, in Wakamori Taro, *Nihon no josei shi* [History of Japanese women] (Tōkyō: Shuei-sha, 1966), 4:426–428.

52. "Death of a Suffragette," editorial, *Mainichi Daily News* (Tōkyō), 28 May 1971.

53. Interview with Yamakawa Kikue, 19 January 1973.

54. For more information on Itō Noe, see Miyamoto Ken, "Itō Noe and the Bluestockings," *Japan Interpreter* 10, no. 2 (Autumn 1975):190–204. The article contains a useful bibliography.

55. Yamakawa Kikue, "The Woman's Movement," *Shakai shugi kenkyū,* September 1922. She and her husband published this monthly study bulletin. Her unease about Hiratsuka's concept is discussed in an interview with Takenishi Hiroko, *Hito to kiseki* [Man and his life] (Tōkyō: Chūō kōron-sha, 1970), p. 196.

56. Kobayashi Tomie, "Raichō sensei to watakushi" [Raichō and I], in Hiratsuka, *Genshi josei wa taiyō de atta,* p. 625.

57. Kanamori Toshie, "Nihon no jinmyaku: fujin undō" [Personalities of Japan: Women's movement], *Yomiuri shimbun* (Tōkyō), no. 24 (series ran from 2 April 1971 to 20 June 1971). For a feminist view of Kishida, see Sharon L. Sievers, "Feminist Criticism in Japanese Politics in the 1880's: The Experience of Kishida Toshiko," *Signs: Journal of Women in Culture and Society* 6, no. 4 (Summer 1981):602–616.

58. Interviews with radical women students of Kyūshū University, 29 March 1972, and with Tanaka Mitsu, 30 May 1972. See also Tanaka's autobiography, *Inochi no onna tachi e* [To my spiritual sisters] (Tōkyō: Tabata shoten, 1972).

59. Fukuda is undoubtedly best remembered for this statement. Katayama Tetsu, "An Outline of Women's Movement," *Japanese Women* 2, no. 5 (September 1939):2. For the emotion of the woman see her autobiographical writings. Fukuda Hideko, *Warawa no han seigai* [Half of my life], White Series 61 (Tōkyō: Iwanami bunko, Iwanami shoten, 1958); also *Warawa no omoide* [My memories].

60. The Japanese Women's Commission for the World's Columbian Exposition, *Japanese Women* (Chicago: A. C. McClurg and Co., 1893), pp. 150–151.

61. The Girls High School Act of 1899 provided for one hour per week of civics out of a curriculum of twenty-nine hours of classes in the third and fourth years of high school. A 1921 debate in the House of Peers revealed continuing governmental reluctance to foster political education in secondary education generally. See Robert A. Scalapino, *Democracy and the Party Movement in Prewar Japan: The Failure of the First Attempt* (Berkeley and Los Angeles: University of California Press, 1962), pp. 295–305, for the 1921 debate and a discussion of education and the Peace Preservation Laws.

62. Bacon, *Japanese Girls and Women*, pp. 296–330.

63. Katō (Ishimoto) Shidzue organized the Reijitsu kai (Bright Sunshine Society) in the mid-1920s to raise funds for the activist suffragists and formed Raisho kai (Coming Light Society) to study "contemporary thought and problems," i.e., birth control. Ishimoto, *Facing Two Ways*, pp. 231–233, 355–357. Yamawaki Fusako, educator and wife of a House of Peers member, organized the Fujin dōshi kai (Women's Comrade Association) to promote suffrage. Beard, *Women in Japanese History*, p. 163.

64. Matsuoka Hideo, "1922 Women's Movement: Demand by 'New Women' for Equal Rights," *Mainichi Daily News* (Tōkyō), 15 September 1968. The quotation is from Hiratsuka.

65. Interview with Nakamura Kii, Oku Mumeo's daughter, 21 March 1972.

66. Kamichika Ichiko, *Josei shisōshi* [History of feminine thought] (Tōkyō: Sangen-sha, 1949), pp. 198–199. The translation is from Lavonne Mehrenberg, "The New Women: A Study of the *'Seitō'* and the *Shin Fujin Kyōkai* and the Women Who Pioneered These Japanese Women's Movements," Master's thesis, University of Michigan, 1971, pp. 91–92.

67. Ichikawa Fusae, "Woman Suffrage Movement in Japan," *Women of the Pacific, Being a Record of the Proceedings of the First Pan-Pacific Women's Conference Which Was Held in Honolulu from the 9th to the 19th of August 1928, Under the Auspices of the Pan-Pacific Union* (Honolulu: Pan-Pacific Union, 1928), pp. 201–204 (Sophia Smith Collection).

68. Adachi Kinnosuke, "The New Women of Nippon," *Woman Citizen*, November 1926, p. 15.

69. Kanamori, "Nihon no jinmyaku," no. 29, 8 May 1971.

70. Oku Mumeo, *Akekure* [Day and night] (Tōkyō: David-sha, 1957), essay no. 3, part 2.

71. Interview with Fujita Taki, 12 April 1973.

72. This is a recurring theme with many of the women I talked with during my years in Japan, including those interviewed for this book, such as Fujita Taki (Tōkyō), Gotō Masa (Hokkaidō), and Bito Shizuko (Hiroshima).

73. Interview with Nakamuri Kii, 21 March 1972. Also see Matsuoka, "1922 Women's Movement."

74. Ichikawa, "Woman Suffrage Movement in Japan," p. 201.

75. Matsuoka, "1922 Women's Movement."

76. Shiraishi Tsugi, "Women in the Upper House," *Japan Times* (Tōkyō), 28 March 1964; Ishimoto, *Facing Two Ways*, pp. 237–243.

77. Adachi, "New Women of Nippon," pp. 16, 41.

78. Yamakawa, "Woman's Movement," pp. 3–4. She clarified her position in an interview (19 January 1973). She feared conservative elements would take advantage of universal, including female, suffrage to accomplish their own purposes.

79. Kanamori, "Nihon no jinmyaku," no. 30, 9 May 1971. Fujita Taki told me about Magara's "borrowed baby."

80. Women leaders of the time of the earthquake all have special stories to tell. See, for instance, Kawai Michi, *My Lantern* (Tōkyō: private printing, 1939), pp. 154–167; Ishimoto, *Facing Two Ways,* pp. 244–254; and Mary R. Beard, "The New Japanese Women," *Woman Citizen,* 1924. Beard continued close contact with Japanese women leaders. At Katō's urging, she later turned materials originally collected for the history of Japanese women for an encyclopedia of women into her book *The Force of Women in Japanese History.*

81. Yoshikawa, *Tsuda Umeko-den,* p. 297. Both Yamakawa (19 January 1973) and Katō (8 September 1972) described this Russian relief program in personal interviews with me. The former analyzed the famine as a socialist, emphasizing that even in a natural disaster the common people suffer. She felt the appeal for donations would bring greater understanding of the Russian Revolution. Katō viewed the campaign in a humanitarian framework and welcomed its success as a demonstration of what Japanese women could do if they put their energies to a good purpose.

82. Katō has spoken and written extensively about her birth control beliefs and personal philosophy. See, for example, her autobiography, *Facing Two Ways,* pp. 350–351, and her speech at the conference of the Western Pacific Region of the International Planned Parenthood Federation, Tōkyō, 13 October 1970.

83. Vital statistics are from the Ministry of Health and Welfare. For the relationship between the statistics and birth control issues, see *Japan's Experience in Family Planning—Past and Present* (Tōkyō: Family Planning Federation of Japan, Inc., March 1967); and *Family Planning in Japan: Twenty Years of Public Opinion Survey on Family Planning* (Tōkyō: Japanese Organization for International Cooperation in Family Planning, 1970).

84. Ishimoto, *Facing Two Ways,* pp. 230–231. There are discrepancies in dates and personnel between her autobiographical recollections and the historical files she organized at the offices of the Planned Parenthood Association of Japan.

85. Beard, *Women in Japanese History,* pp. 167–173.

86. Matsuoka Yoko, *Daughter of the Pacific* (New York: Harper and Brothers, 1952), pp. 119–133. Her trip to Manchuria provides one reaction to this issue.

87. Interview with Katō (Ishimoto) Shidzue, 8 September 1972.

88. Yule, "Japan's New Woman," p. 349; Barbara Bliss, "The Chrysanthemum Cauldron: Women and Children in Japan," *Liberal Woman's News,* January 1927, p. 169; Ishimoto, *Facing Two Ways,* p. 370.

89. Gauntlett C. Tsune, "Fodder for Thought," *Japanese Women* 3, no. 4 (July 1940):1.

90. *Pioneer Women Educators,* pp. 22–24; quotations from Shiraishi, "Women in the Upper House."

91. Katayama Tetsu, "The Political Position of Women," *Japanese Women* 2, no. 6 (November 1939):2.

92. Adachi, "New Women of Nippon," p. 42.

93. Ide Kikue, "Legal and Political Relationships of Women of Japan Today—An Interpretation," in *Women of the Pacific, Being a Record of the Proceedings of the First Pan-Pacific Women's Conference Which Was Held in Honolulu from the 9th to the 19th of August 1928, Under the Auspices of the Pan-Pacific Union* (Honolulu: Pan-Pacific Union, 1928), pp. 194–197 (Sophia Smith Collection).

94. Ibid., p. 200.

95. Ichikawa, "Woman Suffrage Movement in Japan," p. 204. The resolution had been passed earlier at the fifth national conference of the Woman's Suffrage League, April 1927.

96. Interview with Katō (Ishimoto) Shidzue, 8 Sept. 1972. Mary T. Shapiro, "Japanese Women Are Waging an Earnest Fight for Equal Suffrage," *New York Times*, 13 March 1930. Story datelined 1 March 1930, Tōkyō. The Sophia Smith Collection has extensive, if uneven, material on the Japanese suffrage movement, especially as seen through the eyes of visiting Americans.

97. Hugh Keenleyside and A. F. Thomas, *History of Japanese Education and Present Educational System* (Tōkyō: Hokuseido Press, 1937), p. 237.

98. "The Sino-Japanese Incident and the Activities of Japanese Women," *Japanese Women* 1, no. 1 (January 1938):3.

99. "13 Items for Home Practice," *Japanese Women* 1, no. 2 (March 1938):4.

100. Intense rivalry developed between the Patriotic Women's Society and the more egalitarian Women's National Defense Association. See Richard J. Smethurst, "The Army, Youth, and Women," in *Learning to Be Japanese*, Edward R. Beauchamp, ed. (Hamden, Conn.: Linnet Books, 1978), pp. 157–162.

101. "Foreign Correspondence," *Japanese Women* 3, no. 3 (May 1940):3–4.

102. "Asahi-shō no hitobito #4" [Recipients of the Asahi Prize, No. 4], *Asahi shimbun* (Tōkyō), 8 January 1973.

103. See Hatano Isoko and Hatano Ichirō, *Mother and Son: A Japanese Correspondence* (London: Chatto & Windus, 1962), as an illustration of the spirit and courage of one woman and her child during the war years of hardship.

104. For an assessment depicting the underutilization of women workers during the war, see Thomas R. H. Havens, "Women and War in Japan, 1937–45," *American Historical Review* 80, no. 4 (October 1975):913–934.

105. Kawai Michi, *Sliding Doors* (Tōkyō: Keisen jogaku-en, 1950), pp. 50–51.

106. Ōtsuki Masao, "Japanese Womanhood," *Nippon Times* (Tōkyō), 9 February 1945, p. 4.

107. See Gwen Terasaki, *Bridge to the Sun* (Harmondsworth, Middlesex: Penguin Books, 1962) for a humanized, autobiographical account by an American married to a Japanese diplomat of the multitude of living adjustments during the war and the Occupation.

108. Mishima Sumie, *The Broader Way: A Woman's Life in the New Japan* (New York: John Day Co., 1953), p. 239.

109. Faith in the role Japanese women could play in their society was, according to all of his intimate colleagues, a personal belief of General MacArthur's

and not just an official policy. See Russell Brines, *MacArthur's Japan* (Philadelphia and New York: J. B. Lippincott, 1948), pp. 47–50; Courtney Whitney, *MacArthur: His Rendezvous with History* (New York: Alfred A. Knopf, 1956), pp. 213, 290–292; and Kawai, *Sliding Doors*, pp. 84–87, who reported General Bonner Fellers on this subject.

110. Whitney, *MacArthur*, p. 243.

111. "Statement to the Japanese Government Concerning Required Reforms," 11 October 1945, in Supreme Commander for the Allied Powers, General Headquarters, Report of Government Section, *Political Reorientation of Japan, September 1945 to September 1948* (Washington, D.C.: Superintendent of Documents, Government Printing Office, 1949), 2:741 (hereafter cited as *Political Reorientation*).

112. Douglas A. MacArthur, *Reminiscences* (New York: McGraw-Hill Book Co.), pp. 305–306. Beard quotation from Mary R. Beard to Ethel B. Weed, 10 July 1946, Sophia Smith Collection.

113. *Political Reorientation*, 1:186.

114. Sakanishi Shio, "Women's Position and the Family System," *Annals of the American Academy of Political and Social Science*, November 1956, p. 131. Shimomura Juichi, president of Peeress School, Shibata Minoru of Kyōto Imperial University, Tanigawa Tetsuzo of Hosei University, and Ishikawa Ken of the School for Women Teachers held back. *Fujin gaho*, a women's magazine, found political party leadership restrained about women's taking part in general political affairs. SCAP, Publications Analysis, no. 8 (2 February 1946), pp. 1–3.

115. Ichikawa Fusae wrote a series of articles entitled "Status of Women: Japan and the USA" for *Asahi shimbun* after visiting the United States in 1970. They reflect this pride of long and faithful struggle for suffrage and, not unnaturally, also some resentment that suffrage finally came during a foreign occupation. She said that Prime Minister Shidehara responded, in answer to MacArthur's instructions about enfranchising women when the two men met the day after his first cabinet meeting on 9 October 1945, that the cabinet had decided on that step the previous day.

116. *Asahi shimbun*, 25 September 1945; Fujioka Wake A., trans., "Women's Movements in Postwar Japan" (selected articles from *Shiryō: Sengo nijū-nen shi* [Source book on twenty postwar years in Japan], Tsuji Seimei, ed. [Tokyo: Nippon hyōron-sha, 1966], pp. 602–615), mimeographed, Research Publications and Translations, Institute of Advanced Projects, East-West Center, 1968, pp. 1–4.

117. Ichikawa's views appeared in *Fujin kurabu* in SCAP, CIE, Publications Analysis, no. 8 (2 February 1946), p. 2.

118. Ichikawa's radio broadcast to the United States, 26 April 1940, after her return from China expressed regret at previous neglect of getting to know women elsewhere in Asia while concentrating on "absorbing Occidental civilization." She called her visit to China "the first tangible step of Japanese women's active support of the Konoye Declaration." Text is printed as "On My Return from China," *Japanese Women* 3, no. 3 (May 1940):1. The quotation (and other material) is from an interview, 13 April 1973.

119. "Election Digest," *Mainichi Press* (Ōsaka), 18 April 1947.

120. Matsuda Kaiko, *Fujin asahi,* in SCAP, CIE, Publications Analysis, no. 27 (8 April 1946), p. 2.

121. Interview with Egami Fuji, 29 May 1972.

122. Interview with Frances Baker Blakemore, former CIE Exhibits Branch chief officer, 18 July 1972.

123. Nishiyama Shiro, in *Shinsei Nippon,* in SCAP, CIE, Publications Analysis, no. 27 (8 April 1946).

124. Interview with Ethel B. Weed, 19 April 1972.

125. Frank Kelley and Cornelius Ryan, *Star-Spangled Mikado* (New York: Robert M. McBride & Company, 1947), p. 164.

126. Interview with Murashima Kiyo, 4 April 1971.

127. Interview with Katō (Ishimoto) Shidzue, 8 September 1972.

128. SCAP, CIE, Publications Analysis, no. 8 (2 February 1946), pp. 1–2.

129. Katō Etsuo's cartoon in *Fujin gaho,* in ibid., no. 77 (3 October 1946), p. 4.

130. Ethel B. Weed, "Japanese Women," mimeographed, personal files, n.d., pp. 4–5.

131. *Political Reorientation,* 2:321.

132. MacArthur, *Reminiscences,* p. 305. His remembrance of the number of votes this woman received is obviously incorrect: No one received that many. This error doesn't spoil the tale, however.

133. See Appendix D for the list of objectives of the Annual Women's Week.

134. Oku wrote her autobiography in a twenty-article series for the newspaper column, "Watakushi no rirekisho" [My history], *Nihon keizai shimbun* (Tōkyō), 24 January 1958–16 February 1958. "Family Election Campaign" was article thirteen. The articles subsequently appeared in book form: *Watakushi no rirekisho* [My personal history], vol. 6 (Tōkyō: Nihon keizai shimbun-sha, 1958).

135. SCAP, CIE, Publications Analysis, no. 151 (8 March 1948), p. 6.

136. Interview with Katō (Ishimoto) Shidzue, 8 September 1972. Ichikawa Fusae said the club, which lasted only six months, was her idea, but that the Socialists soon left it because of party policy. Interview with Ichikawa Fusae, 13 April 1973.

137. Ethel B. Weed to Mrs. Dick, 25 June 1946, in Ethel B. Weed file, Sophia Smith Collection.

138. *Political Reorientation,* 2:752.

139. *Tōkai shimbun,* 9 May 1947, in SCAP, CIE, Analysis and Research Division, "Prefectural Press Analysis," no. 140 (23 May 1947), p. 4.

140. Hirose Kanihei's cartoon in *Manga,* in SCAP, CIE, Publications Analysis, no. 77 (3 October 1946), p. 4.

141. Sakanishi, "Women's Position and the Family System," pp. 132–133.

142. Further breakdown revealed that more females approved (60 percent) than did males (56 percent). High approval came also from the unmarried, both male and female, and from the urban sections. *Political Reorientation,* 1:216–217.

143. Agatsuma Sakaye, "The Emancipation of Women in Civil Law," *Sekai shuhō,* in SCAP, CIE, Publication Analysis, no. 38 (9 May 1946), p. 3.

144. See comments of Hata Ikuhiko on the influence of so-called Midwestern democracy, derived from Thomas Jefferson, Andrew Jackson, and William Jennings Bryan, in the SCAP bureaucracy, which influenced Japanese thinking during the Occupation, in *The Occupation of Japan: Economic Policy and Reform,* Proceedings of a Symposium Sponsored by the MacArthur Memorial, April 13–15, 1978, Lawrence H. Redford, ed. (Norfolk, Va.: The MacArthur Memorial, 1980), pp. 25–27.

145. *Demokurashii* is felt to be somewhat "sophisticated" in mood and carries the sense of equality of personal relations and a balancing of obligations. There is just a trace of embarrassment in its use, an inheritance from the Occupation. *Minshūshugi* is used especially in discussions of politics and government in the schoolroom. This word came into the Japanese language early in the century when such concepts were first being discussed by intellectuals, and it was best avoided during the rise of the militarists in fear of reprisal because it had gained a negative connotation. The adjectival form—*minshūteki,* "democratic"—has now been incorporated into socialistic and communistic jargon with the result that it has a "leftist feeling." For "community," if *shakai* is used, the translation becomes "society." "Region" and "nation" call for elaboration of *shakai.* The author is not a Japanese-language specialist, but these findings represent the result of many hours of discussion with experts and ordinary, interested Japanese trying to discover how to explain democratic living. Nishiyama Sen, a well-known interpreter, and Gotō Yumi, who is interested in "citizenship" issues, both formerly with U.S. Information Service, Tōkyō, and Dr. Kubota Kinuko, a political scientist, provided much assistance about interpretive translations.

146. Interview with Kubota Kinuko, 14 July 1972.

147. There is much literature on the Communists in the Occupation. See Robert A. Scalapino, *The Japanese Communist Movement, 1920–1966* (Berkeley and Los Angeles: University of California Press, 1967), Chapter 2; Evelyn S. Colbert, *The Left Wing in Japanese Politics* (New York: Institute of Pacific Relations, 1952). Hashiguchi Toshiko spoke of "a tiny group" in an interview, 25 May 1972, based on her Occupation-era experiences in the Japan Federation of Press Workers' Unions.

148. A 1953 study of mixed-blood babies by the Ministry of Welfare showed the problem to be smaller than popular discussion suggested. The February 1953 survey showed 3,289 babies abandoned by their fathers but mostly living with their mothers or other relations; 200-plus in homes run by missionaries; and 482 in Japanese child welfare institutions. Lloyd B. Graham, "Those GI's in Japan," *Christian Century,* 17 March 1954, p. 330.

149. Relations between Japanese women and American GIs prompted much comment in the press and by other observers. See, for instance, Mishima, *The Broader Way,* pp. 165–175; Brines, *MacArthur's Japan,* p. 298; and Kawai, *Sliding Doors,* pp. 86–89.

150. Ihara Usaburo in *Shufu no tomo,* in SCAP, CIE, Publications Analysis, no. 38 (9 May 1946), p. 6.

151. *Jiji Press* conducts monthly public opinion polls in which the Japanese rank in order the foreign countries they like and dislike. Until 1965 the United States consistently ranked as most liked. That year Switzerland became first.

Between 1965 and 1977 the position of the United States fluctuated primarily between second and third position, along with France and Britain. Since 1977 the United States and Switzerland have run neck and neck for most-liked honors. A 1982 Japanese government public opinion poll about popular perception of Japan's Asian neighbors showed mention of affinity for China (73 percent), followed by South Korea (40 percent) and the USSR (8 percent). The United States was also included and the "friendly count" was 71 percent. From the *Japan Times* (Tōkyō), in "What Others Say: Japan's Asian Tilt," *Christian Science Monitor,* 19 November 1982.

152. This section on CIE's women's affairs programs reflects many conversations over the years and many interviews with women active at that time, including Ethel B. Weed, Martha Tway Mills, and Frances Baker Blakemore of CIE and Egami Fuji, Katō (Ishimoto) Shidzue, Shiraishi Tsugi, and Tokunaga Kikuko.

153. Interview with Katō Taka, 24 March 1971.

154. Personal files of Martha Tway Mills.

155. For this and the preceding paragraph, see "Women's Movements in Postwar Japan," pp. 19–23; Kanamori, "Nihon no jinmyaku," nos. 39 (21 May 1971), 42 (26 May 1971), and 43 (27 May 1971). Conversations with Katō (Ishimoto) Shidzue and Matsuoka Yoko offered points of view at variance with each other about the break-up of the original leadership. After Matsuoka resigned to go to the United States in 1949, Kushida Fuji of the Communist party became president.

156. Ethel B. Weed to Mary R. Beard, 15 October 1946, Sophia Smith Collection, discusses the establishment of the Women's Bureau.

157. Interview with Yamakawa Kikue, 19 January 1973. During the 1930s, when her socialist husband had been under police surveillance and imprisoned, Yamakawa had withdrawn from activism and retired to the country to farm and produce quail to sell eggs. Labor specialist Tanino Setsu became head of the Women in Industry Section and [Niijima Ito, head of the General Women's Section] under Yamakawa.

158. Koyama Takashi, *The Changing Social Position of Women in Japan* (Paris: UNESCO, 1961), p. 110.

159. For an analysis by a member of the Labor Division of SCAP, see Theodore Cohen, "Labor Democratization in Japan: The First Years," in Redford, *Occupation of Japan.*

160. Koyama, *Changing Social Position of Women,* pp. 98–133. Official work force statistics resume as of 1947 after the interruption during the closing war years.

161. Interviews with Ariga Michiko, 17 July 1972; Nakagome Fumi, 30 June 1972; Shoji Masako, 4 April 1972; and Saisho Yuriko, 20 June 1972. See the latter's autobiography, *Career Woman—My Way* (Tōkyō: Simul Press, 1979).

162. MacArthur, *Reminiscences,* p. 283.

163. Iglehart, *Protestant Christianity in Japan,* pp. 303–304; Mainichi Daily News (Tōkyō), 15 April 1947.

164. Interview with Shoji Masako, 4 April 1972.

165. Interview with Ethel B. Weed, 19 April 1972.

166. Whitney, *MacArthur*, pp. 291–292.

PART 2. FABRIC OF CONTEMPORARY TIMES

Chapter 3. Social Patterns

1. Tohya Yumiko, "Women of Japan: Modern Age," *Mainichi Daily News* (Tōkyō), 2 September 1969.

2. Sakanishi Shio, "Barbour Scholar," *Our Michigan* (Ann Arbor: University of Michigan Sesquicentennial, 1966), p. 6.

3. Muramatsu Toshio, "Her Poems Reflect Pathos of Person Who Has Lived Vicissitudinous Life," *Yomiuri* (Tōkyō), 19 January 1971. The woman is Fukuda Kazue.

4. Alice Mabel Bacon, *Japanese Girls and Women* (Boston and New York: Houghton Mifflin, 1902), p. 102.

5. At the end of the 1970s some 70 percent of households were nuclear. The Ministry of Health and Welfare reported that a 1978 survey showed that 73.4 percent of those 65 years of age and over live with their children. See regular reports by the Ministry of Health and Welfare for assessment of trends.

6. About 12 percent of the aged runaways committed suicide. Causes given were illness, 26.3 percent; family incompatibility, 21.9 percent; and vocational or business reasons, 4.4 percent. "12% of Aged Runaways End in Suicide, Police Report," *Yomiuri* (Tōkyō), 15 April 1973. The suicide rate for women over 65 years of age in 1975 was 52 per 100,000; for those over 75 it was higher, 73.7 per 100,000. See also Sister Rose Marie Cecchini, "Women and Suicide," in *Women in Changing Japan*, Joyce Lebra, Joy Paulson, and Elizabeth Powers, eds., (Boulder, Colo.: Westview Press, 1976), pp. 263–296.

7. Murakami Hyōe, *Chūō Kōron*, December 1965, as reported by Amano Yosei, "From the Magazines: Japan's 'Lost' Generation," *Mainichi Daily News* (Tōkyō), 26 November 1965.

8. Ichibangase Yasuko, "Mondai teiki sono shiten" [Presentation of problems-viewpoints], in *Sengo fujin mondai shi* [Postwar history of women's problems], Ichibangase Yasuko, ed. (Tōkyō: Domesu shuppan, 1971), p. 21.

9. Sumiya Etsuji, president of Dōshisha University, "Women's Role in the Modern Age," lecture given at the Chifuren National Conference, Kyōto, 1972. Sumiya analyzed women's progress using the 1949 Women's and Minors' Bureau survey on the status of women (hereafter cited as *1949 Survey*). See also Koyama Takashi, *The Changing Social Position of Women in Japan* (Paris: UNESCO, 1961), pp. 145–152.

10. Statistics Section, Ministry of Welfare, *Statistical Yearbook*, provides figures on divorce since 1900. The divorce rate, which rose after World War II, declined from 1950 to 1965, then increased, albeit slightly, to a record high in 1980. The rate is still lower than those in other industrial countries, hovering around 1 percent. For causes of divorce see Ministry of Labor, Women's and Minors' Bureau, ed., *Me de miru fujin no ayumi* [Pictorial history of women] (Tōkyō: Domesu shuppan, 1971), pp. 44–45 (hereafter cited as *Pictorial History*). The

three principal causes for divorce given by women in 1968 were infidelity, violence, and personal incompatibility. By the time of a 1979 survey, the reason most often given by women was economic problems.

11. Prime Minister's Office, Information Section, *Fujin ni kansuru ishiki chōsa* [Opinion survey on women: A report of survey made in October 1972] (Tōkyō: Prime Minister's Office, Information Section, 1973), 1:52–55 (hereafter cited as *Prime Minister's Report*).

12. "Life Is Hard for Middle-Age Unmarried Women in Tōkyō," *Japan Times* (Tōkyō), 11 May 1973. The Tōkyō survey of 1973 reported that 46 percent of women without spouses felt this way. A 1975 report showed a continuing trend. See "The Women of Japan—Past and Present," *About Japan*, Series 5 (Japan: Foreign Press Center, July 1977), pp. 19–20.

13. *Family Planning in Japan: Opinion Survey by the Mainichi Newspapers* (Tōkyō: Population Problems Research Council, Mainichi Newspapers, 1970). The 1975 survey covers opinion for 1950 to 1975, with analysis of results, and has useful demographic charts.

14. See Katō (Ishimoto) Shidzue and Mary R. Beard files, Sophia Smith Collection, including MacArthur to Halliom Bosworth of New York, 6 April 1950, which explains his point of view.

15. Katō Shidzue, "Birth Control Movement," mimeographed, 1947, Katō (Ishimoto) Shidzue files, Sophia Smith Collection.

16. Haruhara Matsuko appealed on behalf of fifteen unmarried young men, aged twenty to thirty. "What the Japanese Are Saying," *Yomiuri* (Tōkyō), 28 March 1973.

17. Shiraishi Tsugi, "A Woman's Viewpoint," *Japan Times*, 8 July 1967.

18. Douglas Overton talked about Florence Powdermaker and her recommendations in an interview, July 1972. *1949 Survey*, cited in Sumiya, "Women's Role," showed that 30 percent of women considered "irrational" housekeeping as a hindrance to their progress.

19. *Prime Minister's Report*, 1:122–123. The projection for the 1980s was made in early 1980 by the *Nihon keizai shimbun*.

20. Interview with Kaneko Atsuo, 30 March 1972.

21. One may ask whether the "education mama" syndrome has not been a major motivation in raising the national mean IQ score of Japanese youth, who now have a better than ten-point lead over U.S. and European children, bringing some 10 percent of Japan's population to the IQ level found among successful professionals. Philip J. Hilts, "Young IQs in Japan Rising Smartly," *Washington Post*, 13 June 1982.

22. Attitudes of "young modernists" given here reflect many sources: personal interviews, commentary of trained observers, and books and articles written by those in this age group. Note especially the regular series of public opinion surveys and white papers released by the Prime Minister's Office on women and on youth. For one analysis of this age group, see Susan J. Pharr, "The Japanese Woman: Evolving Views of Life and Role," in Lewis Austin, ed., *Japan: The Paradox of Progress* (New Haven, Conn., and London: Yale University Press, 1976), pp. 301–327.

23. Takano Etsuko, *Hatachi no genten* [Viewpoint of a twenty-year-old] (Tōkyō: Shincho-sha, 1971), p. 8.

24. This is a strongly prevailing attitude, expressed, for example, in an interview with Kamiya Mieko, psychiatrist and educator, 28 September 1972, and ten years later by Higuchi Keiko in her "Bringing up Girls: Start Aiming at Love and Independence—(Status of Women in Japan)," manuscript, ca. 1981.

25. Takano, *Hatachi no genten*, passim.

26. Interview with Kyūshū University graduate and radical activist, 29 March 1972.

27. Interviews with Fukuoka's Iwataya Department personnel director and staff, 30 March 1972. Interviews with Shiraishi Tsugi (18 August 1972) and Mishima Sumie (15 February 1972) showed similar points of view.

28. Isobe Machiko, "The Changing Role of Women," 23rd Annual National Intercollegiate English Oratorical Contest, June 1969.

29. For attitudes of college-educated women see Yamamoto Kazuyo, "Kōtō kyōiku o uketa fujin no genjō" [Present situation of women with higher education], *Ningen kenkyū*, no. 6 (Tōkyō: Educational Society of Nihon joshi daigaku, n.d.), passim.

30. Tanaka Mitsu, *Inochi no onna tachi e* [To my spiritual sisters] (Tōkyō: Tabata shoten, 1972), p. 144.

31. "Female Dominance" (Josei jōi), *Neo Lib*, 15 April 1973, p. 3.

32. Murata Kiyoaki, "Liberate Whom? Women's Lib Movement Unlikely to Take Roots in Japan," *Japan Times*, 5 February 1971. Personal conversations, like articles, continue to reveal media and male resistance. See Takie Sugiyama Lebra, "Sex Equality for Japanese Women," *Japan Interpreter* 10, no. 2 (Autumn 1975):284–295; "Meet the Japanese: The Japanese Women's Movement: The Long Road to Equality," *Focus Japan*, February 1979.

33. Women in Arita, 17 November 1970, objected to an NHK television documentary on the feminist movement. In Arita, ceramics capital of Japan, women work throughout the ceramic industry, which is organized so that they can work part-time and can, therefore, readily combine chores in the home with labor responsibilities. It makes a difference.

34. Tanaka Mitsu, "Inochi no tsuyosa ga hoshii" [I want a stronger spirit], *Fujin Kōrōn*, June 1973, pp. 159–160.

35. Sakanishi Shio recognized the problem early and counseled young women to study some specific profession, such as pharmacy, to secure a better chance of breaking through the special job hurdles facing college-educated women.

36. Statistics on women's education are available from the Ministry of Education; Women's and Minors' Bureau, Ministry of Labor; and the Office for Women's Affairs in the Secretariat of the Prime Minister's Office.

37. *1949 Survey*, cited in Sumiya, "Women's Role."

38. Tanino Setsu, "The Status of Japanese Women in the World," *Kokusai bunka*, December 1964, p. 2.

39. The steel worker is Kaneko Katsuo, as quoted by Keyes Beech, "Hard Work Earns Japan Leisure and New Woes," *Yomiuri*, 1 January 1973. By 1980, 38 percent of wage earners were on a five-day week, an increase of 30 percent

since 1975. "Housewives Spending Less Time on Household Chores," *Information Bulletin* (Japan, Ministry of Foreign Affairs, Public Information and Cultural Affairs Bureau), 15 May 1981, pp. 14–15 (hereafter cited as "Housewives").

40. Two out of three salaried workers' wives felt this way, according to a Fuji Bank survey, 1972. Since then, the number of those engaging in leisure activities, especially women, has continued to increase. See 1980 Survey, NHK Public Opinion Research Institute in Tōkyō, in "Housewives."

41. Ibid.

42. *Prime Minister's Report*, 1:56. Forty percent of women and 47 percent of men answered "*mā mā*," that is, "uncertain." Women above sixty years of age and under twenty-four had the highest percentage of free time.

43. Tsujimoto Yae, president of Chifuren, Ōsaka, in 1964, discussed her members' approach this way. She considered this progress over the past. See *Opinion Poll on Women* (Japan: Foreign Press Center, February 1977), pp. 16–19.

44. Fifth Kyūshū-Yamaguchi International Women's Conference, sponsored by the Nagasaki Prefectural Liaison Council of Women's Associations and the Fukuoka American Cultural Center, 23–24 May 1968.

45. "Philosophy of Leisure," editorial, *Asahi Evening News* (Tōkyō), 30 April 1971.

46. Shogunate Government Bulletin for farmers, 1659, cited by Saito Shintaro, "Spare Time on Increase for Japanese Housewives," *Mainichi Daily News*, (Tōkyō) 30 October 1970.

47. Ueda Kanji, *Volunteer tsukuri* [Volunteer recruitment] (Ōsaka: Volunteer kyōkai, May 1967), pp. 1–3. These ideas were not original with him, having been frequently expressed by old-timers in women's affairs like Katō (Ishimoto) Shidzue or educators like Ichibangase Yasuko and Kamiya Mieko.

48. Ogawa Keizo of Fukuoka to the author, May 1966. Her volunteering concentrated on affairs of the government corporation apartment in which she lived.

49. *A Report on the How-Do-People-Spend-Their-Time Survey* (Tōkyō: NHK Radio and TV Culture Research Institute, 1963), passim; *Prime Minister's Report*, 2:18–19, 22–23; and *Opinion Poll on Women*, pp. 9–12.

50. Makino Fusako, *Byōin volunteer katsudo no jissai* [Present situation of volunteer activity at the hospitals] (Ōsaka: Ōsaka Volunteer Association, 1970), passim; and Makino Fusako, ed., *Volunteer no ayumi* [What the volunteers did] (Ōsaka: Byōin volunteer renrakukai, 1973), passim. See also Makino Fusako, "Byōin hōshi volunteer katsudo no tsuite" [On hospital volunteer activity], *Nihon joi kaishi* [Japanese Women Doctors Association organ], 15 June 1969, p. 7; "Aru nakama #36, shufu no byōin hōshi group" [Housewives volunteer hospital group], *Mainichi shimbun* (Tōkyō), 12 September 1966; and "Through a Looking Glass: Women Volunteers," *Mainichi Daily News* (Tōkyō), 21 January 1973.

51. Yoshikawa Toshikazu, *Tsuda Umeko den* [Biography of Tsuda Umeko] (Tōkyō: Tsuda dōsōkai, 1956), p. 297.

52. For a listing of principal women's organizations, see Appendix E. USIS/Japan compiled in 1966 a catalog of national organizations to which women belong, now available in Japan File, Sophia Smith Collection. For background,

see Kanamori Toshie, "Nihon no jinmyaku: fujin undō" [Personalities of Japan: Women's movement], *Yomiuri shimbun* (Tōkyō), 2 April 1971–20 June 1971; Morosawa Yoko, *Onna no sengo shi* [Postwar history of women] (Tōkyō: Mirai-sha, 1971), passim; and *Pictorial History*, p. 42.

53. The PTA is an illuminating institution through which to study neighborhood and family life in Japan. For the PTA's place in adult education see Komada Kinichi, "The Organization of Social Education (Including P.T.A.)," *Education in Japan* (International Educational Research Institute, Hiroshima University) 5(1971):83–95; for its role in the community see Ezra F. Vogel, *Japan's New Middle Class: The Salary Man and His Family in a Tokyo Suburb* (Berkeley: University of California Press, 1971), pp. 109–113; and for its training of women see Higuchi Keiko, "The PTA—A Channel for Political Activism," *Japan Interpreter* 10, no. 2 (Autumn 1975):133–140.

54. Sakanishi Shio thus encouraged the women leaders at the International Women's Conference on Community Affairs, Fukuoka, 18 May 1964.

55. National Committee, YWCA, "Present Status and Main Problems of Japanese Women," *Japanese Women* 1, no. 6 (November 1938):3.

56. Japan File, Sophia Smith Collection. The observer was Mrs. William Barclay Parsons of the International Council of Women; the Japanese was Tsujimoto Yae.

57. Japanese Association of University Women, Pan-Pacific and Southeast Asia Women's Association, Japan Women's Bar Association, Japan Section of the Women's International League for Peace and Freedom, League of Women Voters of Japan, Japan Women's Christian Temperance Union, Japan YWCA, Japan Nursing Association.

58. Interview with Kamiya Mieko, 28 September 1972.

59. Interviews with Kawanobe Shizu, 26 September 1972, and Uchino Umeko, 30 March 1972, provided the leadership quotations. Conversations with Toda Satsuki, former director of Ōsaka City Women's Hall, and with the director, Sakamoto Muneko, 1 June 1972, were useful for administrative viewpoints. Personal observation and experience with women leaders at many levels provided basic perspective.

60. Interview with Yamataka Shigeri, 6 April 1972.

61. The Congress of Mothers (Hahaoya taikai) draws large numbers of "mothers" to its annual convention, some 12,000 in Sendai in 1972. It is "ideological," as the Japanese say, with political overtones suggesting communist influences. See Kanemori, "Nihon no jinmyaku," nos. 35–43, 15–27 May 1971.

62. Interview with Egami Fuji, 29 May 1972. Kawai Michi, *Sliding Doors* (Tōkyō: Keisen jogaku-en, 1950), p. 18, described wartime Japan as a "nation blind-folded."

63. Interview with Mishima Sumie, 15 February 1972.

64. Interview with Tokunaga Kikuko, 30 March 1972.

Chapter 4. Economic Enterprise

1. Letter to Fujita Suzue, in "Here in Japan: Women's Horizons Are Widening," *Mainichi Daily News* (Tōkyō), (no month or day) 1965.

2. A Labor Ministry survey, released in June 1972, showed that a majority of men and women wage earners placed priority on work above home life and leisure, although this was less true of workers under age nineteen. The *1975 White Paper on Youth* reports youth's attitude as "I'll be able to make a living whatever I do." *JIWMP News: Current Information on Women and Minor Workers in Japan* (Tōkyō: Japan Institute of Women's and Minors' Problems), March 1976, pp. 9–14 (hereafter cited as *JIWMP News*).

3. See, typically, "High-School Coeds Being Wooed for Jobs by Banks," *Asahi Evening News* (Tōkyō), 11 July 1973; Tazawa Hideko, employed by Tōkyō Tanker Company to work on the world's largest tanker, *Nisseki Maru*, in "Names in the News: Happy About Going to Sea," *Asahi Evening News* (Tōkyō), 30 December 1970.

4. The Prime Minister's Office and the Women's and Minors' Bureau of the Ministry of Labor regularly provide statistical data. See also "Japanese Industrial Relations Series: Problems of Working Women" (Tōkyō: Japan Institute of Labour, 1981). Regarding upward mobility in management, see the Prime Minister's Office, *Outline of Results Concerning Women's Participation in Decision-Making Process*, S-79-13 (Japan: Foreign Press Center, June 1979).

5. "Japanese Women: To What Extent Have They Invaded Men's Realms?" *Sunday Mainichi Magazine*, 9 April 1972, pp. 36–40. Translation is from U.S. Embassy, Tōkyō. "Women's Status," editorial, *Daily Yomiuri* (Tōkyō), 3 February 1978.

6. Watanabe Kei, *Onna hitori no ikikata* [How a woman lives alone] (Tōkyō: Shufu to seikatsu-sha, 1973), p. 3.

7. "Woman Announcer Fights Discrimination," *Japan Times* (Tōkyō), 5 September 1976.

8. Higuchi Keiko, in an interview, 8 March 1972, discussed this phenomenon. The Yokohama strike, 19 January 1972, involved 500 women, representing about 3,500 prefectural clerks. The 1975 Tōkyō protest was reported in "Tea, Sympathy Still Expected of Fem Workers," *Mainichi Daily News* (Tōkyō), 12 October 1976.

9. Interview with Kageyama Hiroko, 11 July 1973. For an early, well-publicized episode on attitudes toward clerical inefficiency that brought public reaction, see "Nara Women Workers, Unite! Gov. Says You're Inefficient," *Asahi Evening News* (Tōkyō), 21 March 1966. Consideration of women as "supplementary" is the terminology of the 1980s. Ministry of Labor, *Employment of Female Workers in Enterprises*, S-81-15 (Japan: Foreign Press Center, December 1981), pp. 11–14.

10. Takahara Sumiko, "Shimedasareta joshidaigaku sotsugyasei" [Why female college graduates are unwelcome], *Fujin Kōrōn*, September 1964, pp. 66–69. Nagoya Kazuhike, "Japanese Magazine Highlights: Unwanted: Girls with College Education," *Mainichi Daily News* (Tōkyō), 25 August 1964. During International Women's Year Diet members Ichikawa Fusae and Tanaka Sumiko presented proposals to NHK and the private radio-television companies asking for improvement in status. It is a continuing problem, but the situation has been improving. See Ministry of Labor, *Employment of Female Workers in Enterprises*, pp. 3–5.

11. "Manpower Policy and Education in Japan (II)," *Japan Labor Bulletin* 9, no. 8 (August 1970):5–8.

12. "Japanese Women."

13. Kageyama Hiroko, speaking at the "Womanpower *Taikai*" Conference, 4–5 November 1970. The other 30 percent, she said, depends on "women's consciousness."

14. Conversation after conversation supports this theme. See "Japanese Women" and Nan Robertson, "The Life of a Japanese Journalist in New York," *New York Times*, 20 February 1981.

15. Interview with Saisho Yuriko, 20 June 1972. See her autobiography, *Women Executives in Japan: How I Succeeded in Business in a Male-Dominated Society* (Tōkyō: YURI International Inc., 1981).

16. The issue of women teachers is readily discussed. Interview with Shoji Masako, 4 April 1972. See also "Women Teachers," editorial, *Mainichi Daily News* (Tōkyō), 26 June 1973. On the Nikkyōsō struggle for equal pay, see Kanamori Toshie, "Nihon no jinmyaku: fujin undō" [Personalities of Japan: Women's movement], *Yomiuri shimbun* (Tōkyō), no. 52, June 1971.

17. Conversation with Sakanishi Shio, 12 July 1973.

18. Interview with Maeda Sumiko, 26 July 1972.

19. "Opinion Poll on Women" (Japan: Foreign Press Center, February 1977), pp. 6–8. Interview with Nakagome Fumi, 30 June 1972. "Female Labor in Japan, Its Present and Future," *Mitsui Bank Monthly Review* 17, no. 12 (December 1972):9. For husbands' complaints, see Prime Minister's Office, Information Section, *Fujin ni kansuru ishiki chōsa* [Opinion survey on women: A report of survey made in October 1972] (Tōkyō: Prime Minister's Office, Information Section, 1972), 1:182–185.

20. Ibid. *Fujin ni kansuru,* 1:148–149. See also "Survey on the Real Situation of Female Workers" of the Conference of Labor Unions for the Promotion of Policy, released 6 February 1982, as reported in "Persistent Feelings of Sexual Discrimination," *Asahi shimbun* (Tōkyō), 7 February 1982 (translation by U.S. Embassy, Tōkyō) (hereafter cited as "Survey on the Real Situation").

21. The Ministry of Labor poll of 1973 showed that nearly 90 percent favored such leave for working women and helped the successful legislative fight in April 1976.

22. Kobayashi Shigeru, *Motivational Management: Its Exploration in Sony* (Tōkyō: Japan Management Center, 1969); "Yōji-kyōiku no jissen hōtoku" [Report: Experiment in education for young children], *Kenkyū kiyo*, no. 5, July 1972; and "Yōji ni okeru Mugakunen-sei no kokoromi" [An experiment in a nursery school nongrade system], *Kenkyū kiyo*, no. 6, July 1973. Conversations with Kobayashi, Uchida-*sensei*, and officials of Sony and a visit to the Atsugi Plant provided first-hand information.

23. Dōmei women's conference (Zenkoku fujin no tsudoi) first met in 1960. Sōhyō's conference (Hataraku fujin no chūō shukai) goes back to 1955. Their purposes are similar, but each follows policies and political action in keeping with its sponsor. Dōmei has links with the Social Democratic party, Sōhyō with the Socialist party.

24. Interview with Maeda Sumiko, 26 July 1972.

25. Arousing "consciousness" of working women perennially comes up in talks about their status in the work force, whether with women workers, section chiefs, personnel officials, or social critics. Ariga Michiko kept returning to the need for *"ikigai"* in an interview, 17 July 1972. See also interview with Kyūshū Matsushita Electrical Union Members, 29 March 1972.

26. Comment made to visiting U.S. trade unionists, 18 May 1965.

27. Interviews in 1972 with Kyūshū Matsushita Electrical Labor Union members revealed that 23 percent of women thought menstruation leave necessary and 50 percent used it. Both men and women union members understood that the issue provided leverage for obtaining other benefits. "Survey on the Real Situation" found that only 30 percent of women workers used menstruation leave. See also Alice H. Cook and Hayashi Hiroko, *Working Women in Japan: Discrimination, Resistance, and Reform,* Cornell International Industrial and Labor Relations Report No. 10 (Ithaca: New York State School of Industrial and Labor Relations, 1980), pp. 18–21, 67–75.

28. Ministry of Labor, Women's and Minors' Bureau, *Hanrei ni miru fujin no nōryōku-hyoka to rōdōken* [Evaluation of women's ability and rights of labor in court decisions] (Tōkyō: Rōdōhōrei kyōkai, 1970), Chart 15, p. 98.

29. Even within the judicial system there were problems. In 1970 women trainees at the Supreme Court's Judicial Officer Training Institute protested discrimination in making them judges. The Supreme Court's Personnel Bureau in July 1970 said, "Women, physically-handicapped persons and those over thirty-five years old are not welcomed as judges." The grouping is similar to the prewar legal classification of women with the physically handicapped and mentally retarded.

30. Kaji Chizuko, "Teinensei-hanketsu ni miru danjo-sabetsu" [Sex discrimination seen in retirement trial], *Fujin tembō,* April 1973, p. 1.

31. A survey by the Ministry of Labor in 1980 of 7,000 companies with thirty or more employees provided the one-out-of-five figure. *Japanese Women* (Tōkyō: Fusen kaikan), no. 46 (1 September 1981), pp. 2–3.

32. Interview with Takahashi Nobuko, 8 November 1973; and "Madame Ambassador," *Japan Pictorial* 3, no. 3 (1980):32–35. The U.S.-Japan Joint Study grew out of a visit of U.S. Labor Department officials with their counterparts in Japan, September 1973. On the IWY see *Fujin mondai kikaku shishin kaigi iken* [Opinion of the Advisory Council on Women's Affairs] (Tōkyō: Prime Minster's Secretariat, 6 November 1976); *JIWMP News,* May 1976, pp. 1–8.

33. Shiraishi Tsugi, "A Women's Viewpoint," *Japan Times,* 13 February 1971.

34. For comparisons of trends, see International Labour Organisation and United Nations reports, and specialized geographic studies, such as those by the Council for Cultural Cooperation, Council of Europe; and the Commission of the European Communities.

35. Oku Mumeo, *Watakushi no rirekisho* [My personal history], vol. 6 (Tōkyō: Nihon keizai shimbun-sha, 1958), article 20 (hereafter cited as *My History*).

36. Ibid., Vol. 6, articles 14, 15. Interviews with Nakamura Kii, daughter of Oku Mumeo, 21 March 1972, and Nomura Katsuko, 2 March 1972.

37. The Dai-Ichi Kangyō Bank in 1972 measured conditions in Japan against those in the United States, Britain, West Germany, and France, covering forty-one indicators grouped by eleven categories, with U.S. figures as the basic index of 100. Results placed Japan at the bottom in waterworks, sewage systems, public park space, air pollution, traffic congestion, congested subways, diet, and housing. Japan's best marks came in clothing consumption, health, and safety—although not in traffic fatalities.

38. "Why Land Prices in Japan Are High," editorial, *Japan Stock Journal* 17, no. 840 (2 July 1973):12. The National Land Agency posts land prices annually. It administers the National Land Law, which provides regulations for overall utilization of land and land transactions.

39. For a succinct wrap-up, see Japan, Ministry of Foreign Affairs, Public Information and Cultural Affairs Bureau, *Facts about Japan*, "Social Security," Code no. 05401, March 1981.

40. Morosawa Yoko, *Onna no sengo shi* [Postwar history of women] (Tōkyō: Mirai-sha, 1971), article 9.

41. In 1972 one in three Japanese families had telephones, totaling more than 20 million, to match Europe in distribution. Demand caused long delays—up to one year or more—in new installation.

42. Mishima Sumie, *My Narrow Isle: The Story of a Modern Woman in Japan* (New York: John Day Co., 1941), p. 234.

43. Interview with Morosawa Yoko, 25 May 1972.

44. Interview with housewives of Minami-Urawa *danchi*, 17 May 1972. Studies of cost-of-living inflationary patterns are widely available, but they often show discrepancies. For instance, in April 1973, MITI produced one showing that Tōkyō ranked twenty-first among thirty-four major cities in cost of living. *Asahi shimbun*, assisted by Sumitomo Bank and Kansai University, released one in July 1973 placing Tōkyō highest, with Ōsaka comparable to New York in third place. OECD assessed Japan's price-increase rate for the year ending April 1973 at 9.7 percent, followed by Britain (9.2 percent), France (6.8 percent), and the United States (5.1 percent). By the end of the 1970s Tōkyō still led in cost of living. See regular reports of the Economic Planning Agency on consumer trends and the *Japan Labor Bulletin*.

45. "Satō Quizzed by Housewives," *Japan Times*, 20 November 1964.

46. Interview with Egami Fuji, 29 May 1972.

47. "Hada samui yen taikoku" [Our opinion: The chilly big country of the yen], *Shufuren tayori*, no. 265 (15 September 1971).

48. Conversation with Tanaka Satoko after the meeting with the Economic Planning Agency director-general in April 1973. The event was widely covered in all the major newspapers.

49. The Ministry of Labor's annual White Paper on Labor, July 1973, focused on the peril of inflation for the worker's standard of living. A survey by the National Livelihood Center in September 1973 showed that 90 percent of the Japanese believed they belonged to the "middle class" by virtue of their income, vocations, and education rather than family background. In 1962 the figure was about 65 percent.

50. Oku Mumeo, *Akekure* [Day and Night] (Tōkyō: David-sha, 1957), essay no. 1.

51. The 1973 Construction White Paper called for such new guidelines.

52. "Woman Appeals to Emperor," *Japan Times*, 1 November 1973.

53. Conversations with Takada Yuri, 18 July 1973, and Nakamura Kii, 21 March 1972. For Takada's role in the consumer movement, see *My History*, articles 17, 18, and 20; Kanamori, "Nihon no jinmyaku," Nos. 7 (8 April 1971), 8 (9 April 1971), and 9 (10 April 1971). Takada was featured by *Mainichi Daily News* in a special supplement, "Dawning of the Era of International Consumerism," 12 December 1970.

54. Interview with Uchino Umeko, 30 March 1972.

55. Interview with Hosokawa Kou, 17 October 1972.

56. Tazaki Toshiko, in "Tanaka Satoko," *Sankei shimbun* (Tōkyō), 11 March 1969. My own conversations with innumerable Chifuren leaders, and with Tanaka herself, substantiate this point of view.

57. Interviews with Tanaka Satoko, 21 March 1972 and 22 November 1976; "Consumers Seize Economic Initiative," Supplement, *Mainichi Daily News* (Tōkyō), 12 December 1970.

58. Conversation with Tanaka Satoko, 25 July 1973. Her meeting with the executives was covered in *Asahi shimbun*, 13 July 1973, and "Consumer Power," editorial, *Mainichi Daily News*, 18 July 1973. *Japan Economic Journal* (11, nos. 534 and 535 [20 and 27 March 1973]) carried a two-part series, "Consumerism Takes on Big Business."

59. By comparison, women trade unionists in the Kyūshū Matsushita Electric plant said they knew little about the double pricing problem. They were "proud" of their company. The male chief of the union explained that a special distribution system was necessary if Matsushita was to compete with the supermarkets. Interview with members of Kyūshū Matsushita Electrical Labor Union, 30 March 1972.

60. Interviews with Ariga Michiko, 17 July 1972; Tanaka Satoko, 21 March 1972; Yamataka Shigeri, 6 April 1972. Almost every interview that touched on consumer action included comment on the television issue.

61. "Battle Is Planned to Win Hearts of Japanese Women," *Asahi Evening News* (Tōkyō), 3 May 1971. Shiseido's financial statement of 1972 showed a profit of Y11.4 billion, more than 1,400 times greater than that of Chifuren. For industry-wide figures in the 1980s, see "The Competitive World of Cosmetics Marketing," *Focus Japan* (Tōkyō: JETRO), December 1981, pp. 1–2.

62. Interview with Nakagome Fumi, 30 June 1972.

63. *Encyclopaedia Britannica* faced a very difficult time over its aggressive sales techniques in door-to-door merchandising. Curtailment of the cosmetic industries is probably an offshoot of the *Britannica* fracas.

64. Valuable for this section on the cosmetics resale campaign were the interviews with Tanaka Satoko (21 March 1972), Yamataka Shigeri (6 April 1972), and Nakamuri Kii (21 March 1972), for explanations of the consumers' aims; and with Miya Yooichi, director of Shiseido, and Kouga Fujiko, who was in charge of training and field tests, on 7 June 1972 for information about

Shiseido. Kouga Fujiko is a young woman who has moved successfully into management.

65. Interview with Egami Fuji, 29 May 1972.

66. Interview with Ariga Michiko, 17 July 1972.

67. Interview with Higa Masako, 31 May 1972. The author spent an afternoon with her and visited her Shufuren kaikan and the related nursery and child-care center in Ōsaka. See her autobiography, *Onna no tatakai* [A woman's battle] (Tōkyō: Nihon jitsugyō shuppan-sha, 1971), on her early life.

68. Interview with Higa Masako, 31 May 1972.

69. Interview with Nakauchi Isao, 16 June 1972. His book, *Waga yasui uri no tetsugaku* [*My philosophy of selling cheaply*] (Tōkyō: Nihon keizai shimbun-sha, 1972), pp. 160–164, carries details on his ideas about beef production.

70. Both Higa Masako and Ariga Michiko indicated that Japanese women do not learn enough about international economics and its effect on them. Perhaps because Higa was born in Okinawa, her awareness of life beyond Japan proper was strong.

71. "Japan Consumer Move Growing in Popularity," *Japan Times*, 28 September 1972.

72. "Nipponese Naderism Fascinates the West," *Asahi Evening News* (Tōkyō), 24 April 1971.

73. The Economic Planning Agency's survey of consumer organizations, October 1972, showed that 75 percent conducted education programs, 50 percent did surveys, 38 percent carried out testing, 33 percent acted as grievance committees, and 37 percent engaged in lobbying.

74. Interview with Yamamoto Matsuyo, 21 February 1971.

75. Interview with Nomura Katsuko, 2 March 1972. "Nomura Katsuko," *Hataraku hito* [Working person], 18 June 1969.

76. "Consumerism Takes on Big Business," *Japan Economic Journal*, 20 March 1973.

77. "Japanese Enterprises Being Awakened to Social Roles," *Mainichi Daily News* (Tōkyō) 16 June 1976; and Koji Kondo, "The Trend of the Consumer's Movement and Women's Role," *Keizai* (Tōkyō: Shin-Nihon shuppan-sha), no. 96, April 1972.

Chapter 5. Political Process

1. Interview with Ichikawa Fusae, 13 April 1973.

2. The conference was the Fifth Consultation on the Contemporary Woman, Ōsaka, 2 November 1964. Haru Reischauer, wife of the U.S. ambassador, was the keynote speaker.

3. The quotations in this section come from direct personal interviews, 1971–1973, with the persons cited. Each concept expressed, however, is representative of ideas heard repeatedly by the author from Japanese women in many conversations, discussions, and conferences from 1963 to the late 1970s.

4. For the development of the thinking of Matsuoka Yoko, see her autobiography, *Daughter of the Pacific* (New York: Harper & Brothers, 1952).

5. Katō (Ishimoto) Shidzue in her autobiography told of her personal struggle to find a rewarding philosophy of life and break with form for form's sake. Ishimoto Shidzue, *Facing Two Ways: The Story of My Life* (New York: Farrar & Rinehart, 1935), p. 315 and passim. Modern youth do also. For a recent comment, see Susan Chira, "Against the Japanese Grain," *New York Times Magazine*, 20 May 1982, pp. 28–46.

6. Prime Minister Yoshida was concerned that postwar teachers were without "any guiding spirit" and so trying to teach democratic education "without much confidence." Yoshida Shigeru, *The Yoshida Memoirs: The Story of Japan in Crisis*, trans. Yoshida Kenichi (London: William Heinemann, 1961), pp. 170–171. For the pre–Pacific War policy of education for political indoctrination, see Herbert Passin, *Society and Education in Japan* (New York: Bureau of Publications, Teachers College, and East Asian Institute, Columbia University, 1965), pp. 149–160. For discussion of the modern implications of the issue the following were helpful: interviews with Izumoi Chizuko, 21 July 1972; Ōta Hiroko, 22 June 1972; and with some bright, conservatively oriented students of Urawa Girls' High School, 17 May 1972.

7. *Niigata nippō* [Niigata City], 25 June 1967. The author observed and tried to find some satisfactory answers in this remarkable discussion.

8. "Sugoi shufu benkyō netsu" [Remarkable housewives study at fever pitch], *Asahi shimbun* (Tōkyō), May 1972. The age breakdown was forties, 54 percent; thirties, 26 percent; fifties, 14 percent; twenties, 3 percent. See also Ichikawa Fusae, ed., *Sengo fujinkai no dōkō* [Trends of women's circles in the postwar period] (Tōkyō: Fusen kaikan, 1969).

9. *Iwate nippō* (Morioka), 7 March 1967. The statement, heard by the author, illustrated a moment of civic revelation not just of the farm woman speaker but of the group. From this conference flowed a series of excellent adult education initiatives.

10. Ichibangase Yasuko emphasized this link between social education and electoral practices.

11. A text compiled by the Ministry of Foreign Affairs states: "The law emphasizes the importance of political knowledge and of religious tolerance in the development of sound citizens, but it specifically prohibits any link between political parties or religions and education." Ministry of Foreign Affairs, comp., *Japan of Today* (Tōkyō: International Society for Education Information, 1970), p. 93. Interviews with Toda Satsuki and Sakamoto Muneko, 1 June 1972, provided details of program development procedure and the social education philosophies. My own observations over the course of a decade or more in prefectures all over Japan confirm the delicacy involved in combining political studies and social education programs.

12. The author attended the Social Education Conference, Takamatsu, 14 March 1966, at which this Tadotsu City program was detailed, receiving great commendation for its fresh approach. The mayor announced that in the next year the women's programs would expand into consideration of economic and world problems.

13. Kawakami Sueko, "Achievements and Tasks," *Bulletin of the International Council of Social Democratic Women* (London) 3, nos. 1-2 (January-February 1975):4 (Sophia Smith Collection).

14. "New Japan Women's Organization," *Asahi Evening News* (Tōkyō), 4 May 1973.

15. *Shokuba ni okeru nikkyō no fujin kakutoku senjutsu* [The Communist party's strategy for recruiting women at working places], *Nihon seiji keizai kenkyūyo* (Tōkyō: Japan Institute of Economic and Political Affairs), 10 April 1972.

16. Interview with Katō (Ishimoto) Shidzue, 2 September 1972; "Grass Roots Activities of Political Parties, *Mainichi Daily News* (Tōkyō), 21 June 1971.

17. Interviews with Hashiguchi Toshiko, 25 May 1972, and Soma Yukika, 20 January 1972. The author had many conversations with Soma about women in politics and how they fared in the different parties.

18. Interview with Matsuoka Yoko, 9 April 1973. Her philosophy is given in Matsuoka Yoko, *Shinryaku-sabetsu to tatakau Ajia fujin kaigi* [Asian Women's Conference to Fight Against Aggression and Discrimination], report of the conference held 22–23 August 1970, Tōkyō (Shinryaku-sabetsu to tatakau Ajia fujin kaigi, 25 October 1970).

19. Kobayashi spoke of "long and short noodles" at the First Kyūshū-Yamaguchi International Women's Conference on Community Affairs, Fukuoka, 28 May 1963. She described her rationale and personal history in an interview in Nagasaki, 28 March 1972.

20. Interview with Hachiya Yumiko of the Women's Section of Sōka gakkai, 30 November 1972.

21. For instance, see "Japan Women Think Politics Is Man's Job, Poll Discloses," *Japan Times* (Tōkyō), 11 February 1967. In 1976, 37 percent of women polled thought more women should run for office at all levels. *Opinion Poll on Women* (Japan: Foreign Press Center, February 1977), pp. 21–22.

22. Interview with Ogata Sadako, 19 June 1972.

23. Interview with Kawanobe Shizu, 26 September 1972. The author visited Shizuoka repeatedly in the late 1960s and early 1970s and observed Kawanobe in action, talking with many of her adherents.

24. The Green Wind Society slowly lost its considerable power and membership and to all intents and purposes ended in 1965. Many, such as Oku, joined because they believed that Upper House members should belong to no political party.

25. Interviews with four women in the Diet, *Tōkyō shimbun*, 18 December 1963.

26. Kihira Teiko elucidated the rules of clean elections in a discussion-interview, 21 July 1972. Women who had taken part "as a voter-supporter" talked about their own experiences. See also "Ichikawa suisenkai" [Association to endorse Miss Ichikawa], *Asahi shimbun* (Tōkyō), 7 July 1965, and Ichikawa Fusae's "Editorial," *Fujin tembō* [Women's outlook], May 1974, p. 14, about the campaign to send Kihira Teiko to the House of Councillors.

27. Fujioka Wake A., trans., "Women's Movements in Postwar Japan" (Selected articles from *Shiryō: sengo nijū-nen shi* [Source book on twenty postwar

years in Japan], Tsuji Seimei, ed. [Tōkyō: Nippon hyōron-sha, 1966], pp. 602–615), mimeographed, East-West Center, 1968, pp. 33, 35.

28. "The Victory of Clean Election," *Japan Through Women* (Tōkyō) 6, no. 30 (April-May 1953).

29. Interview with Ichikawa Fusae, 13 April 1973.

30. The Tōkyō Electric Power Co., which had donated ¥30 to ¥40 million a year to LDP, and the Hokuriku Electric Power Co. led the way. Reasons given for the changed policy were the public nature of the power company, business and management difficulties, and consumer-shareholder pressures. After reform of the Kōkumin kyōkai, March 1975, donations resumed.

31. "Black peanuts" was a phrase used in the media to refer to the illegal donations in the Lockheed case, "black" signifying corruption, "peanuts," units of money. For a useful discussion of the LDP in the 1970s, see Taketsugu Tsurutani, "The LDP in Transition? Mass Membership Participation in Party Leadership Selection," *Asian Survey* (Berkeley: University of California Press) 20, no. 8 (August 1980):844–859.

32. Masuda Reiko, editorial, *Mainichi shimbun* (Tōkyō), 12 February 1980.

33. A survey by the Prime Minister's Office in 1973 asking people how much they were interested in political affairs showed the following: Of a total of 16,645 women, 3 percent responded that they were deeply interested; 13 percent fairly interested; 54 percent, somewhat interested; 28 percent, hardly interested; and 2 percent, unknown. Parallel questioning of 2,413 men gave the following corresponding figures: 11 percent; 32 percent; 44 percent; 12 percent; and 1 percent. *JIWMP News: Current Information on Women and Minor Workers in Japan* (Tōkyō: Japan Institute of Women's and Minors' Problems) 1, no. 1 (August 1974):4 (hereafter cited as *JIWMP News*). By 1976, 18 percent of women thought they took sufficient interest in politics; 67 percent thought they did not. *Opinion Poll on Women*, p. 20.

34. Tohya Yumiko, "Japanese Women in Politics—Past and Present," speech to American Friends Service Committee's diplomats luncheon, Tōkyō, 16 September 1969.

35. Interview with Ogata Sadako, 19 June 1972. Also conversations in August 1974.

36. "Mezameru Shomin" [Awakened citizens], *Asahi shimbun* (Tōkyō), 21 May 1973.

37. Barbara Ward, ed., *Women in the New Asia* (Amsterdam: UNESCO, 1963), p. 73. In her introduction to this UNESCO study on women in Southeast Asia, Ward maintained that political power in those societies is mainly a "male prerogative." The study did not include Japan.

38. Interview with Ichikawa Fusae, 22 March 1972.

39. Interview with Kihira Teiko, 21 July 1972.

40. The March 1973 *Fujin tembō* [Women's outlook] p. 15, listed 88 women appointees to the Metropolitan Government Councils out of a possible 681. They were top-flight women, many representing key women's organizations.

41. Interview with Kihira Teiko, 21 July 1972.

42. In July 1972, for example, the LWV, with a cross-section of women's organizations, petitioned Prime Minister Tanaka on (1) the landing of U.S. B-52 airplanes on Okinawa after action in Vietnam; (2) price problems in light of his scheme for the "remodeling" of Japan; and (3) the need for LDP use of political funds. In November 1981 the Liaison Group for IWY lobbied Prime Minster Suzuki on women's appointments and administrative and fiscal reforms. *Japanese Women,* the newsletter of the Women's Suffrage Hall, Tōkyō, routinely carries stories on policy statements presented to prime ministers.

43. Interview with Bito Shizuko, 3 April 1972. The author worked with the Hiroshima league and observed its membership in operation over a period of years in the late 1960s and early 1970s.

44. Interview with Kihira Teiko, 21 July 1972. She believed so much in *shimin undō;* she said she would rather work for that cause than run for political office. For a study of young women, see Susan J. Pharr, *Political Women in Japan: The Search for a Place in Political Life* (Berkeley, Los Angeles, and London: University of California Press, 1981).

45. Mary Muro, "Towards The New Japanese Woman," paper prepared for Japanese History II, International Christian University, 2 December 1968.

46. The prime minister's survey of women in 1973 revealed that 40 percent were willing to take part in "neighborhood and civic movements." *JIWMP News* 1, no. 1 (August 1974):3. Political scientist Matsushita Keiichi, a leading writer on *shimin undō* and a founder in March 1971 of the intellectual journal Shimin, highlighted the role of women in the movement. See also Shinohara Hajime, "Josei no jitsuryoku towa nani ka" [What is women's ability], *Mainichi shimbun* (Tōkyō), 6 October 1967. "The Japanese Today:(37) Civic Campaigns are Frequent in Japan Nowadays," *Asahi Evening News* (Tōkyō), 29 March 1972. By comparison, Kageyama Hiroko dismissed the feminine *shimin undō* role with "behind every woman there is a man." Conversation on 11 July 1973. As so often happens in Japanese, the use of *"shimin"* by comparison with other possible words for "people" carries nuance: *Asahi* pointed out that the LDP talks to *kōkumin,* the Socialists and DSP to *shimin,* Kōmeitō to *shomin,* and Kyosanto-Communist party to *jinmin.* Reputedly, *kōkumin* carries an "old-fashioned" feeling; *shimin* a sophisticated feeling; *shomin* feels like the man-in-the-street; and *jinmin* has an aggressive feeling. *"Sōryushi"* [They say that], *Asahi shimbun* (Tōkyō), 13 July 1973, evening edition.

47. "Trends Toward Mass Suits," *Mainichi Daily News* (Tōkyō) 5 March 1974.

48. This was one of hundreds of complaints publicized in the mass media. "Many Involved in Disputes," *Japan Times,* 11 April 1972.

49. Interview with Yamataka Shigeri, author of the play, 6 April 1972. She delighted in her nickname. Kanamori Toshie, "Nihon no jinmyaku: fujin undō" [Personalities of Japan: Women's Movement], *Yomiuri shimbun* (Tōkyō), nos. 3 (4 April 1971), 4 (5 April 1971), and 5 (6 April 1971).

50. Conversations with Mizutani Kakuko, spring 1973. Newspapers were filled with the Suginami events. In May 1973 *Asahi shimbun* (Tōkyō) ran the series "Jūmin undō" [Civic action], which grew out of a questionnaire submitted

to civic action groups. Of 627 who responded, 38 groups were composed solely of women; 40 percent stressed women's leadership. Katsudo Terado was quoted in the 21 May 1973 article.

51. Older analysts tended to be more negative about the spirit of *shimin undō*, emphasizing its selfish aims; younger ones viewed it as a strengthened democratic process resulting from the "gift of the Occupation," as Kubota and others have called the new talent of personal expression and speaking out.

52. Minobe so spoke at the Tōkyō gubernatorial candidates meeting, 13 March 1971, sponsored by the Diet Liaison Committee of Women's Organizations. The Economic Planning Agency's White Paper on Japanese Home Life, released in 1971, reported the 80 percent and associated it with postwar democratic reforms and high economic growth. The Social Affairs Research Institute public opinion survey in May 1973 on "autonomy consciousness" of Tōkyō citizens found that the general reaction was, "Tōkyō is not a comfortable place in which to live." See *Asahi Evening News*, (Tōkyō), 12 July 1973. Matsushita Keiichi believed civic action would change the traditional quality of Japanese politics, calling it *shimin kakumei*, or "civic revolution." "Shimin sanka to hōgakuteki shikō" [Citizen's participation and its juridical thought], *Sekai* (June 1973), in Kono Kenji, "Rondan jihyō" [Editorial platform], *Asahi shimbun* (Tōkyō), 28 June 1973.

53. See Appendix C for numbers of women elected to the Diet and their party affiliations.

54. For a breakdown of men and women in official posts, 1950–1969, see Ichibangase Yasuko, ed., *Sengo fujin mondaishi* [Postwar history of women's problems] (Tōkyō: Ōtsuki shoten, 1971), p. 304. "The Second Report on the National Plan of Action," issued in June 1980 by the Prime Minister's Office, revealed that the number of women in government councils had increased from 2.4 percent in 1975 to 4 percent in 1979.

55. For a classic study of the development of group allegiance, with the Beppu Chifuren as a case study, see Gerald L. Curtis, *Election Campaigning Japanese Style* (New York and London: Columbia University Press, 1971), pp. 158–177.

56. Conference for Women on International Understanding on "The Role of Women in Good Government," Hiroshima, 21 May 1968.

57. The Women's and Minors' Bureau poll in 1955 showed that 75 percent of women voted according to their own dictates. The Research Institute of Women's Problems of the Women's Suffrage Hall in 1960 indicated that 49.5 percent did not know how their husbands voted; of the remainder, 17.5 percent voted differently from their husbands, showing that 67 percent were completely independent. A Clean Election Federation survey in 1969 indicated that 15.9 percent consulted with their family. The Fusen kaikan report in 1975 simply commented that women's independent judgment about voting prevails.

58. "How Christian Women Worked for Suffrage in Japan," *Japan Through Women*, 1947.

59. Interview with Yamataka Shigeri, 6 April 1972.

60. Morosawa Yoko, *Onna no sengo shi* [Postwar history of women] (Tōkyō: Mirai-sha, 1971), sections 2, 13.

61. Japan's Dowager Dietwomen Declare Righteous War on Turkish Baths," *Asahi Evening News* (Tōkyō), 18 June 1966.

62. "The Number of Dietwomen Doesn't Increase," *Mainichi shimbun* (Tōkyō) 9 February 1967.

63. Nakamura Kyoichi, "Pollution in Japan, i.e., Minamata, Fighting Assembly Woman," *Mainichi Daily News* (Tōkyō), 27 April 1972.

. 64. Interview with Ozawa Ryoko, 17 May 1972. During the 1970s both the Japanese and U.S. press carried stories on her activities.

65. Ōta Hiroko, "Hoiku mondai de shigi ni tosen shita watakushi" [I was elected to the City Assembly on the day nursery issue], *Fujin kōrōn*, May 1972, p. 133. Interview with Ōta Hiroko (22 June 1972) and subsequent conversations.

66. Interview with Hata Yawara, 19 September 1972.

67. "Kakuei Tanaka: 'The U.S. Comes First,' " *Time*, 7 May 1973, p. 71. The mid-1966 *Mainichi* poll showed that only 28.8 percent of the people polled supported the Satō cabinet; the figure included a drop of 6.7 percent among women. Those between twenty and forty were particularly unhappy. By September 1973 Tanaka's popularity had fallen to 26 percent from his 1972 high of 53 percent, with 22 percent of women supporting him compared with 31 percent of men. Editorial, *Mainichi Daily News* (Tōkyō), 14 June 1966; "*Mainichi* Public Opinion Survey: Price Issue Causes Fall of Tanaka Cabinet Popularity" and "Tanaka's Popularity Drops: *Mainichi* Poll," *Mainichi Daily News* (Tōkyō), 30 September 1973.

68. For analysis of the 1974 elections, see Michael K. Blaker, ed., *Japan at the Polls: The House of Councillors Election of 1974* (Washington, D.C.: American Enterprise Institute for Public Policy Research, 1976). By 1979 women's organizations and the Citizens' Groups for Promotion of Ideal Elections had mobilized to pinpoint for defeat specific LDP candidates suspected of corruption. *Japanese Women*, no. 43 (1 March 1980), p. 2.

69. Statement of 19 February 1975, *JIWMP News* (March 1975), pp. 4–5. LDP promises were still being made by Prime Minister Ohira, who said in June 1980 that restoration of political morality would be his principal campaign slogan.

70. Interview with Mizuno Sumiko, 17 October 1972.

Chapter 6. International Awareness and Cooperation

1. Interview with group of housewives, active members of *Sōka gakkai*, 30 November 1972. The comment plays on an old Japanese proverb, "I no naka no kawazu taikai o shirazu" (the frog in the well knows no ocean).

2. Uchitori Kikuyo, a colleague at the U.S. Embassy in Tōkyō, at my request wrote some of her childhood recollections, August 1974.

3. Interview with Ogata Sadako, 19 June 1972.

4. Interview with Seki Fumiko, 8 February 1972. The quotation comes from articles written by Fujiwara Kamae, her father, for *Shin Shina* and *Peking nijū-nen* [Twenty years in Peking] (Tōkyō: Heibon-sha, 1959).

5. Conversation with Nakamaru Kaoru, 6 September 1974, in Washington, D.C. Direct quotation is from Vivienne Kenrick, "Personality Profile," *Japan Times* (Tōkyō), 18 September 1972.

6. Interview with Kamiya Mieko, 28 September 1972. She wrote about her childhood and professional motivation in "My Thought and My Climate," *Asahi shimbun* (Tōkyō), 13–17 December 1971.

7. Interview with Fujita Taki, 12 April 1973.

8. Devastation in Tōkyō from firebombings was worse than the 1923 earthquake. The Shigemitsu quote is from Don Oberdorfer, "Tokyo Recalls 1945 'Rain of Fire' With Sadness, Little Anger," *Washington Post*, 10 March 1975. Most memoirs of individuals who stayed in Tōkyō and other firebombed cities strike similar reactions—horror, numbness, and practically no anti-American reaction.

9. Interview with Kihira Teiko, 21 July 1972.

10. Ibid.

11. Interview with Ethel B. Weed, 19 April 1972. Martha Tway Mills, a CIE education officer in the Kansai, concurred. Once she raised international understanding with a school group and the discussion warranted press coverage. *Mainichi Daily News* (Ōsaka), 19 September 1946.

12. Article IX of the Constitution reads:

Aspiring sincerely to an international peace based on justice and order, the Japanese people forever renounce war as a sovereign right of the nation and the threat or use of force as means of settling international disputes.

In order to accomplish the aim of the preceding paragraph, land, sea and air forces, as well as other war potential, will never be maintained. The right of belligerency of the state will not be recognized.

13. Mary R. Beard, *The Force of Women in Japanese History* (Washington, D.C.: Public Affairs Press, 1953), p. 176.

14. Endo Hiroko's essay, "Japan's Role in the World," sponsored by the magazine *Nippon*, was reviewed in Amano Yosei, "From the Magazines: Japan's Role in the World," *Mainichi Daily News* (Tōkyō), 2 February 1966.

15. Nakane Chie interview in *Newsweek*'s international edition, 7 October 1973. "Japan Warned of International Role," *Mainichi Daily News* (Tōkyō), 9 October 1973.

16. Interview with Yamataka Shigeri, 6 April 1972.

17. Kanamori Toshie, "Nihon no jinmyaku: fujin undō" [Personalities of Japan: Women's Movement], *Yomiuri shimbun* (Tōkyō), no. 42, 26 May 1971.

18. Interview with Ariga Michiko, 17 July 1972.

19. Interview with Egami Fuji, 29 May 1972.

20. Interview with Mishima Sumie, 15 February 1972.

21. Interview with Kawanobe Shizu, 26 September 1972.

22. Interview with Kamiya Mieko, 28 September 1972.

23. Kubota Kinuko, "Heiwa e no michi" [Road to peace], *Tōkyō shimbun*, 8 April 1970.

24. Interview with Kyūshū University women graduates, 29 March 1972.

25. Interview with Morosawa Yoko, 25 May 1972.

26. Jodai Tano's March 1971 thank-you letter, sent to those who remembered her at Christmas.

27. Kawai Michi, *My Lantern* (Japan: Private printing, 1939), p. 169.

28. Interview with high-school-educated housewives of Minami-Urawa *danchi*, Saitama, 17 May 1972.

29. *Japanese Women* (Tōkyō: Women's Suffrage Hall), no. 29 (January 1971), pp. 1–2, reported on Ichikawa; Kanamori, "Nihon no jinmyaku," no. 43, 27 May 1971, discussed Kushida.

30. Attributed to retired LDP Diet member Kajima Morinosuke of Kajima Corporation. Don Oberdorfer, "High-Level Campaign Led to Satō's Nobel," *Washington Post*, 12 October 1974.

31. Kanamori, "Nihon no jinmyaku," no. 38, 20 May 1971.

32. "Actual Situations of the Activities of Women's Organizations in Japan Particularly on Communist Activities," mimeographed, Women's Policy Committee of Democratic party statement issued about 1963.

33. Mishima Sumie, *The Broader Way: A Woman's Life in the New Japan* (New York: John Day Co., 1953), pp. 58–59.

34. Ten to 20 percent of the Hiroshima and Nagasaki junior high school students did not know who dropped the bombs. "Nuclear Allergy Unrelated to Feeling Toward the U.S.," Japan and America series, no. 119, *Asahi Evening News* (Tōkyō), 2 March 1972.

35. Kanamori, "Nihon no jinmyaku," no. 37, 18 May 1971.

36. Murata Kiyoaki, "The State of the JCSP," *Japan Times*, 9 January 1964.

37. Interview with Kobayashi Hiro, 28 March 1972. I talked with her many times after 1964 about the atom-bomb issue. For the story of the Nagasaki Chifuren withdrawal from Gensuikyō see *Nagasaki-shi fujinkai tayori* [Newsletter of the Women's Association of Nagasaki], 15 March 1964.

38. Fifth All Kyūshū-Yamaguchi Women's Conference on International Understanding, Unzen, 27 May 1968. Ambassador Edwin O. Reischauer's disclosure in spring 1981 that U.S. naval vessels with nuclear arms had indeed visited Japanese ports precipitated heated public and parliamentary reaction, but also some very healthy debate of the nuclear issue. See Komori Yoshihisa, "Japan and A-Weapons," *New York Times*, 5 November 1981.

39. "Japanese Women's Organizations Are Against Nuclear Tests," *Japanese Women*, no. 14 (March 1962):2.

40. Typically, five members of the organization met with U.S. Embassy officers in Tōkyō to discuss their letter. Correspondence between the women and the author about peaceful uses of nuclear power continued after the meeting.

41. Interview with Egami Fuji, 29 May 1972.

42. Opinion polls regularly measure Japanese attitudes toward security, the U.S.-Japan Security Treaty and so on. See, for example, studies of Douglas H. Mendel, Jr., such as "Japanese Defense in the 1970s: The Public View," *Asian Survey* 10, no. 12 (December 1970):1046–1055.

43. Interview with Sakamoto Muneko, 1 June 1972.

44. "Japanese Women Intellectuals Condemn Policy of Reviving Militarism," Tōkyō dateline press release, 15 December 1965, of the Peking New China

News Agency International Service in English, carried the comments of Matsuoka, Hiratsuka, et al. from the magazine *Japan*.

45. Ethel B. Weed to Mary R. Beard, 3 December 1951, Sophia Smith Collection.

46. Carter Aiko, *On Being a Woman in Japan* (Tōkyō: Femintern Press, January 1975), pp. 4–5. Japanese media periodically have carried stories of the protests of Mt. Fuji–area women.

47. Report given at the Tōkyō hahaoya taikai conference, 24 July 1972.

48. Official complaint to Headquarters, United States Army, Japan (USARJ), *Pacific Stars and Stripes* (Tōkyō), 12 July 1973.

49. George R. Packard III, *Protest in Tokyo: The Security Treaty Crisis of 1960* (Princeton, N.J.: Princeton University Press, 1966), pp. 303–351.

50. For a vivid portrayal of a young college woman and her involvement in university activism, see the novel by Albery Nobuko, *Balloon Top: A Novel of Growing Up in Japan* (New York: Pantheon Books, 1978).

51. Interview with Katō (Ishimoto) Shidzue, 8 September 1972. For her letter, see *Asahi shimbun* (Tōkyō), 17 June 1960.

52. *Japanese Women*, no. 10 (Summer 1960), p. 2.

53. Ibid., no. 28 (February 1970), p. 1.

54. Douglas H. Mendel, Jr., "Japan Reviews Her American Alliance," *Public Opinion Quarterly* 30, no. 1 (Spring 1966):4–9. In 1960 only one in three knew the facts about the treaty. The Kyōdō Survey, January 1969, showed 49.3 percent of those polled ignorant or indifferent to the treaty and only 40.7 percent, mostly young people, aware that the pact could be acted upon in 1970. See "Most People Not Apprehensive About War, Poll Shows," *Japan Times*, 9 January 1969; also monthly *Jiji* press opinion polls.

55. "Bukka ga kanshin no moto" [Prices of commodities are target of interest], *Tōkyō shimbun*, 4 March 1970.

56. Interview with Katō (Ishimoto) Shidzue, 8 September 1972.

57. Survey, "Japan-U.S. Relations in the Age of Multi-Powers," conducted by *Sankei shimbun* (Tōkyō), reported in *Business Japan*, September 1973. An editorial in *Asahi shimbun*, 28 December 1975, commented on the "tidal change" within the DSP, Kōmeitō, and JSP, causing them to rely on the Security Treaty to provide a stabilized status quo.

58. Sōma Yukika, speech to the Fifth All Kyūshū-Yamaguchi Women's Conference on International Understanding, Unzen, 27 May 1968. She urged action based on "concrete reality."

59. Yamazaki Tomoko, *Chi to senketsu ajai josei koryūshi* [Love and blood— the history of female exchange in Asia] (Tōkyō: Sansei-do), which is frequently cited by feminists, e.g., interview with Morosawa Yoko, 25 May 1972.

60. Interview with Ichibangase Yasuko, 23 May 1972.

61. Written for the First All-Japan Conference on Women's Suffrage, 27 April 1930. Yosano Akiko created the words and Yamada Kosaku, the music. See Ichikawa Fusae, *Watakushi no fujin undō* [My women's movement] (Tōkyō: Akimoto shobō, 1972), pp. 130–131.

62. Ogata Sadako, "Challenge to Partnership: Japan and the United States in the Twenty-first Century," opening address, Japan Today Symposium, Wash-

ington, D.C., 1979, *International Exchange News* (Meridian House International) 23, no. 3 (Spring 1979):11.

63. Interview with Uchino Umeko, 30 March 1972.

64. Satō Ko, vice-chairman, Women's Section of the Akita Prefectural Agricultural Cooperative, Niigata-Toyama-Nagano Tri-Prefectural International Women's Seminar, Niigata, 9–10 July 1970.

65. Interview with high-school-educated housewives of Minami-Urawa *danchi*, 17 May 1972.

66. Nikaido Kiyo, vice-chairman, Akita Prefectural Liaison Council of Organizations, Sixth Tohoku Regional Seminar for Women on International Understanding, Akita, 6–7 July 1970.

67. Editorial, *Japan Through Women* 4, no. 23 (September-October 1951):3.

68. Niigata-Tōyama-Nagano Tri-Prefectural International Women's Seminar, Niigata, 9–10 July 1970.

69. Tōkyō representative, Kantō Area Women's Conference on International Understanding, Yokohama, 25–26 June 1970.

70. Haru Reischauer, "Japanese Women in World Perspective," mimeographed, First Tōhoku Regional Conference for Women on International Understanding, Sendai, 7 December 1965.

71. Haga Toru, quoted in "The Blossoming of Education for Women," Japan and America series, *Asahi shimbun* (Tōkyō), 27 January 1971.

72. Sakanishi Shio, "Practical Ways in Developing International Understanding," First Tri-Prefecture Women's Conference on International Understanding, Shizuoka, 15 May 1967.

73. Egami Fuji, Third Tōhoku Regional Seminar for Women on International Understanding, Aomori, 14 September 1967.

74. Ogata, "Challenge to Partnership," p. 11.

75. Yamaguchi Nobuko, Eighth Kyūshū-Yamaguchi International Women's Conference, Kirishima National Park, Miyasaki, 10–11 June 1971.

76. Tokunaga Kikuko, president of Fukuoka Prefectural Mothers Liaison Council, Seventh Kyūshū-Yamaguchi International Women's Conference, Fukuoka, 29–30 June 1970; and Chiba Kikuko, Kantō Women's Conference on International Understanding, Yokohama, 25–26 June 1970.

77. Japan, Foreign Minister's Office, Migration Bureau, Passport Section publishes material on those receiving passports. See also Japan, Ministry of Justice, *Annual Statistical Yearbook for Immigration and Emigration Control.*

78. "Japanese Girls Studying Overseas," *Mainichi Daily News* (Tōkyō), 9 May 1966. See Takao Tokuoka, "Japanese Still Sensitive to Int'l Marriages," ibid., 5 February 1978, for a review of polls and sociological studies in 1967 and 1974 on this issue. *Kokusai kekkon*, or interracial marriage, is not popular.

79. Nakane Chie in *Chūō Kōron*, May 1967, as discussed by Tsunezo Sasai in "From the Magazines: Weak Spots of Intellectuals," *Mainichi Daily News* (Tōkyō), 19 April 1967. For Japanese adjustment internationally, see also Nakane Chie, *Tekiō no jōken: Nihonteki renzoku no shikō* [Criteria for adjustment: The Japanese continuum mentality] (Tōkyō: Kōdan-sha, 1972).

80. Interview with Taguchi Sachiko, 20 October 1972.

81. Japan, Ministry of Education, Social Education Bureau, *Report on Women's Overseas Education Observation Tour* (Tōkyō, 1965).

82. "Japan Overseas Volunteers Working Throughout World," *Yomiuri* (Tōkyō), 24 September 1972. Conversations with these volunteers revealed they had remarkable determination to make their own lives. By joining the JOCV, most knew they had started a career outside the mainstream, making acceptance and reentry into Japanese society very difficult.

83. Shiraishi Tsugi, "60th Anniversary Celebrations Begin Sunday: YWCA, Pioneer in Training Leaders, Looks to New Nat'l, Int'l Challenges," *Japan Times,* 16 October 1965. In 1972 the Education Ministry adopted the "foster parent" system for foreign students to help them "adjust themselves to their surroundings and to understand Japan and the Japanese well."

84. Congratulatory Address, opening ceremonies, 13 August 1974, in *International Federation of University Women, XVIII Triennial Conference,* report of the conference held in Tokyo and Kyōto, 13–19 August 1974 (Tōkyō: Japanese Association of University Women, n.d.), pp. 10–11.

85. Interviews with Ichibangase Yasuko (23 May 1972), Kamiya Mieko (28 September 1972), and Kobayashi Hiro (28 March 1972).

PART 3. DESIGNS FOR THE FUTURE

1. *Kiroku kokusai fujin-nen Nihon taikai* [Report: International Women's Year Japan Mass Meeting) (Tōkyō: Kokusai fujin-nen Nihon taikai zam-mu seiri iin-kai, 1976], pp. 13–14.

2. Japan, Prime Minister's Office, *Fujin mondai kikaku suishin kaigi iken* [Opinion of the Advisory Council on Women's Affairs] (Tōkyō, 1976). See also Japan, Headquarters for the Planning and Promoting of Policies Relating to Women, *National Plan of Action* (Tōkyō, January 1977).

Bibliography

The literature about or by Japanese women is more extensive than might be expected. Much of it is informal and in Japanese. It consists heavily of memoirs and articles in publications of women's organizations, often unprofessionally annotated and scattered; some is reproduced in mimeographed or simply processed, limited editions. The most sizable primary resource collection, including photographs, is at the Fusen kaikan (Women's Suffrage Hall) in Shinjuku in Tōkyō, but these files are still inadequately catalogued. Much historical material was destroyed during World War II. As a result, some of the earlier material, such as that in the Sophia Smith Collection (Women's History Archive, Smith College, Northampton, Mass.), is not available in Japan. This collection also offers unique research opportunities in its files of personal papers of women associated with Japan. I found the Japanese collections at the University of Michigan and the Library of Congress greatly helpful. However, some of the most important and interesting materials are still coming from the hands of individuals and organizations—primary sources certainly in the lore of women.

The Japanese government is a rich source of statistical data and public opinion survey reports on modern Japanese women, their lives, and their point of view, particularly on their own status. Broad-gauged materials are available from the Office for Women's Affairs of the Prime Minister's Office and the Women's and Minors' Bureau of the Japanese Ministry of Labor. The Women's Education Section, Social Education Bureau of the Ministry of Education, and the Home Living Improvement or women's section of the extension services of the Ministry of Forestry and Agriculture offer excellent information in their specialized areas. The Headquarters for the Planning and Promoting of Policies Relating to Women is responsible for efforts being made under the National Plan of Action and for publications pertaining to the United Nations Decade for Women.

Listed below are readings that elaborate subjects discussed in this book; the footnotes contain additional items, including newspaper references. The national and regional Japanese press often provides helpful clues about developments not systematically discoverable through library or other research channels. Obviously the listing is incomplete, but many listings will lead to other sources.

GOVERNMENT PUBLICATIONS

English

Japan, Foreign Office, Division of Special Records. *Documents Concerning the Allied Occupation and Control of Japan.* Vol. 2, *Political, Military and Cultural.* Tōkyō, March 1949.

Japan, Ministry of Education. *Japan's Growth and Education: Educational Development in Relation to Socio-Economic Growth.* Tōkyō, July 1963.

Japan, Ministry of Education, Japanese National Commission for UNESCO, ed. *The Role of Education in the Social and Economic Development of Japan.* Tōkyō, 1966.

Japan, Ministry of Education, Science and Culture, Research and Statistics Division, Minister's Secretariat. *Japan's Modern Educational System: A History of the First Hundred Years.* Tōkyō, 1980.

Japan, Ministry of Foreign Affairs. *Status of Women in Modern Japan: Report on Nationwide Survey.* Tōkyō, 1975.

Japan, Ministry of Home Affairs. *Election System in Japan.* Tōkyō, 1970.

Supreme Commander for the Allied Powers (SCAP), General Headquarters, Civil Information and Education Section (CIE), Media Analysis Division. *Publication Analysis* Series.

Supreme Commander for the Allied Powers, General Headquarters, Civil Information and Education Section, Public Opinion and Sociological Research Division. *Current Japanese Public Opinion Surveys.*

Supreme Commander for the Allied Powers, General Headquarters, Report of Government Section, *Political Reorientation of Japan, September 1945 to September 1948.* 2 vols. Washington, D.C.: Superintendent of Documents, Government Printing Office, 1949.

United States, Department of Labor, Employment Standards Administration and Women's Bureau. *The Role and Status of Women Workers in the United States and Japan: A Joint United States–Japan Study.* Washington, D.C.: Government Printing Office, 1976.

United States, Department of State. *Occupation of Japan: Policy and Progress.* Pub. 2671, Far Eastern Series 17. Washington, D.C.: Superintendent of Documents, Government Printing Office, n.d.

Japanese

Japan, Ministry of Labor. Women's and Minors' Bureau. *Fujin kankei nenpyō 1868–1968* [A chronological table concerning women]. Tōkyō, 1968.

———. *Fujin rōdō no jitsujo* [The situation of women workers]. Annual publication, series beginning 1952. English version published under title *Women Workers in Japan.*

———. *Me de miru fujin no ayumi* [Pictorial history of women]. Tōkyō: Domesu shuppan, 1971.

Japan, Prime Minister's Office. *Fujin mondai kikaku suishin kaigi iken* [Opinion of the Advisory Council on Women's Affairs]. Tōkyō, 1976.

Japan, Prime Minister's Office, Council for Women's Problems. *Fujin taisaku kankei keihi shiryō* [Government expenditures for women's projects]. Tōkyō, March 1972.

Japan, Prime Minister's Office, Information Section. *Fujin ni kansuru ishiki chōsa: seron-chōsa hōkoku-sho* [Opinion survey on women: A report of survey made October 1972]. 4 vols. Tōkyō, March 1973.

Nagoya, Nagoya City Board of Education. *Nagoya-shi ni okeru fujin hōshi katsudo sokushin hōsaku no matome* [Report on methods to improve women's volunteer activities in Nagoya]. 1972.

BOOKS AND PAMPHLETS

English

Albery, Nobuko. *Balloon Top: A Novel of Growing up in Japan.* New York: Pantheon Books, 1978.

Aston, W. G., trans. *Nihongi: Chronicles of Japan from the Earliest Times to A.D. 697.* Rutland, Vt., and Tōkyō: Charles E. Tuttle Co., 1972.

Austin, Lewis, ed. *Japan: The Paradox of Progress.* New Haven, Conn., and London: Yale University Press, 1976.

Bacon, Alice Mabel. *Japanese Girls and Women.* Boston and New York: Houghton Mifflin, 1902.

————. *A Japanese Interior.* Boston and New York: Houghton Mifflin, 1894.

Baike, Wren, ed. *Young Japan Views Uncle Sam: A Collection of Opinions on America.* Rutland, Vt., and Tōkyō: Charles E. Tuttle Co., 1965.

Barr, Pat. *The Deer Cry Pavilion: A Story of Westerners in Japan 1868–1905.* London: Macmillan, 1968.

Battistini, Lawrence H. *Postwar Student Struggle in Japan.* Tōkyō: Charles E. Tuttle Co., 1956.

Bazel, Karen, trans. *Confessions of Lady Nijo.* Garden City, N.Y.: Anchor Press, 1973.

Beard, Mary R. *The Force of Women in Japanese History.* Washington, D.C.: Public Affairs Press, 1953.

Beauchamp, Edward R., ed. *Learning to Be Japanese.* Hamden, Conn.: Linnet Books, 1978.

Benedict, Ruth. *The Chrysanthemum and the Sword: Patterns of Japanese Culture.* Tōkyō: Charles E. Tuttle Co., 1954.

Boserup, Ester. *Women's Role in Economic Development.* London: George Allen & Unwin, 1970.

Brines, Russell. *MacArthur's Japan.* Philadelphia and New York: J. B. Lippincott, 1948.

Buck, Pearl S. *The People of Japan.* New York: Simon and Schuster, 1966.

Burks, Ardath W. *The Government of Japan.* New York: Crowell, 1972.

_____ . *Japan: Profile of a Postindustrial Power.* Boulder, Colo.: Westview Press, 1981.

Chamberlain, Basil Hall, trans. *Kojiki: Records of Ancient Matters.* Tōkyō: Asiatic Society of Japan, 1973.

Cohen, Jerome B. *Japan's Economy in War and Reconstruction.* Westport, Conn.: Greenwood Press, 1973.

Cook, Alice, H., and Hayashi Hiroko. *Working Women in Japan: Discrimination, Resistance, and Reform.* Cornell International Industrial and Labor Relations Report No. 10. Ithaca: New York State School of Industrial and Labor Relations, 1980.

Cressy, Earl Herbert. *Daughters of Changing Japan.* New York: Farrar, Straus & Co., 1955.

Cummings, William K. *Education and Equality in Japan.* Princeton, N.J.: Princeton University Press, 1980.

Curtis, Gerald L. *Election Campaigning Japanese Style.* New York and London: Columbia University Press, 1971.

Danly, Robert L. *In the Shade of Spring Leaves: The Life and Writings of Higuchi Ichiyo, a Woman of Letters in Meiji Japan.* New Haven, Conn.: Yale University Press, 1981.

De Becker, J. E. *The Nightless City or the History of the Yoshiwara Yūkwaku.* Rutland Vt., and Tōkyō: Charles E. Tuttle Co., 1971.

De Forest, Charlotte B. *The History of Kōbe College.* Nishinomiya: Kōbe College, n.d.

Doi Takeo. *The Anatomy of Dependence.* Tōkyō: Kodan-sha, 1971.

Dore, Ronald. P., ed. *Aspects of Social Change in Modern Japan.* Princeton, N.J.: Princeton University Press, 1967.

_____ . *City Life in Japan.* London: Routledge and Kegan Paul, 1958.

_____ . *Education in Tokugawa Japan.* Berkeley and Los Angeles: University of California Press, 1965.

Dufourcq, Elizabeth B. *Les femmes japonnaises.* Paris: Denoel Gonthier, 1969.

Dunn, Charles J. *Everyday Life in Traditional Japan.* Tōkyō: Charles E. Tuttle Co., 1972.

Duverger, Maurice. *The Political Role of Women.* Paris: UNESCO, 1955.

Enchi Fumiko. *The Waiting Years.* Translated by John Bestor. Tōkyō and Palo Alto, Calif.: Kodan-sha International, 1971.

Fairbank, John K., Reischauer, Edwin O., and Craig, Albert M. *East Asia: The Modern Transformation.* Boston: Houghton Mifflin; Tōkyō: Charles E. Tuttle Co., 1965.

Family Planning in Japan: Twenty Years of Public Opinion Survey on Family Planning. Tōkyō: Japanese Organization for International Cooperation in Family Planning, 1970.

Fujikawa Asako. *Daughter of Shinran.* Tōkyō: Hokuseido Press, 1964.

Fukuzawa Yukichi. *The Autobiography of Fukuzawa Yukichi.* Translated by Kiyooka Eiichi. Tōkyō: Hokuseido Press, 1960.

_____ . *An Encouragement of Learning.* Translated by David A. Dilworth and Hirano Umeyo. Tōkyō: Sophia University, 1969.

Griffis, William Elliot. *The Mikado's Empire*. New York: Harper and Brothers, 1887.

Gulick, Sidney Lewis. *Working Women of Japan*. New York: Missionary Education Movement of the United States and Canada, 1915.

Hall, John W. *Japan from Prehistory to Modern Times*. New York: Delacorte Press, 1971.

Hall, John W., and Beardsley, Richard K. *Twelve Doors to Japan*. New York: McGraw-Hill Book Company, 1965.

Hane, Mikiso. *Peasants, Rebels, and Outcasts: The Underside of Modern Japan*. New York: Pantheon Books, 1982.

Hani Setsuko. *The Japanese Family System: As Seen from the Standpoint of Japanese Women*. Tōkyō: Nihon taiheiyō mondai chōsakai, 1948.

Hatano Isoko and Hatano Ichirō. *Mother and Son: A Japanese Correspondence*. London: Chatto & Windus, 1962.

Hearn, Lafcadio. *Japan: An Attempt at Interpretation*. Tōkyō: Charles E. Tuttle Co., 1955.

Higuchi Chiyoko. *Her Place in the Sun: Women Who Shaped Japan*. English version by Sharon Rhodes. Tōkyō: The East Publications, 1973.

Hilburn, Samuel M. *Gaines Sensei: Missionary to Hiroshima*. Kōbe: The Friend-sha, 1936.

Iddittie, Junesay. *When Two Cultures Meet: Sketches of Postwar Japan 1945–1955*. Tōkyō: Kenkyū-sha, 1955.

Iglehart, Charles W. *A Century of Protestant Christianity in Japan*. Rutland, Vt., and Tōkyō: Charles E. Tuttle Co., 1959.

Ishimoto Shidzue. *East Way, West Way: A Modern Japanese Girlhood*. New York: Farrar & Rinehart, 1936.

————. *Facing Two Ways: The Story of My Life*. New York: Farrar & Rinehart, 1935.

Jansen, Marius, ed. *Changing Japanese Attitudes Towards Modernization*. Princeton, N.J.: Princeton University Press, 1965.

Japanese Women's Commission for the World's Columbian Exposition. *Japanese Women*. Chicago: A. C. McClurg & Co., 1893.

Japanese University Women: Issues and Views. Vols. 1 and 2. Tōkyō: Daigaku fujin kyokai (Japanese Association of University Women), 1974.

Japan's Experience in Family Planning—Past and Present. Tōkyō: Family Planning Federation of Japan, Inc., March 1967.

Kaibara Ekken. *Women and Wisdom of Japan*. Introduction by Takaishi Shingoro. London: J. Murray, 1914.

Kajima Ume. *Michi Haruka: Milestones on My Pathway*. Tōkyō: Kajima Institute Publishing Company, 1963.

Kawai Kazuo. *Japan's American Interlude*. Chicago: University of Chicago Press, 1960.

Kawai Michi. *My Lantern*. Tōkyō: Private printing, 1939.

————. *Sliding Doors*. Tōkyō: Keisen jogaku-en, 1950.

Kawai Michi and Ochimi Kubushiro. *Japanese Women Speak: A Message from the Christian Women of Japan to the Christian Women of America*. Boston: Central Committee on the United Study of Foreign Missions, 1934.

Kerkup, James. *Japan Behind the Fan*. London: J. M. Dent & Sons, 1970.

Kidder, J. Edward. *Japan: Before Buddhism*. New York: F. A. Praeger, 1966.

Koyama Takashi. *The Changing Social Position of Women in Japan*. Paris: UNESCO, 1961.

Lebra, Joyce, Paulson, Joy, and Powers, Elizabeth, eds. *Women in Changing Japan*. Boulder, Colo.: Westview Press, 1976.

Little, Frances. *The Lady of the Decoration*. New York: Century Co., 1906.

MacArthur, Douglas. *Reminiscences*. New York: McGraw-Hill Book Co., 1964.

Madden, Maude Whitmore. *Women of the Meiji Era*. New York: Fleming H. Revell, 1919.

The Manyōshū. New York: Columbia University Press, 1965.

Maruyama Masao. *Thought and Behavior in Modern Japanese Politics*. Expanded edition, edited by Ivan Morris. London, Oxford, and New York: Oxford University Press, 1963.

Matsuoka Yoko. *Daughter of the Pacific*. New York: Harper & Brothers, 1952.

Mishima Sumie. *The Broader Way: A Woman's Life in the New Japan*. New York: John Day Co., 1953.

————. *My Narrow Isle: The Story of a Modern Woman in Japan*. New York: John Day Co., 1941.

Morley, James William, ed. *Dilemmas of Growth in Prewar Japan*. Princeton, N.J.: Princeton University Press, 1971.

Morris, Ivan. *The World of the Shining Prince: Court Life in Ancient Japan*. New York: Alfred A. Knopf, 1972.

Morris, Ivan, trans. *As I Crossed a Bridge of Dreams. Recollections of a Woman in Eleventh Century Japan*. New York: Dial Press, 1971.

Murakami Hyōe and Harper, Thomas J., eds. *Great Historical Figures of Japan*. Tōkyō: Japan Cultural Institute, 1978.

Lady Murasaki. *The Tale of Genji*. Translated by Arthur Waley. London: George Allen & Unwin, 1935.

Murasaki Shikibu. *The Tale of Genji*. Translated by Edward C. Seidensticker. New York: Alfred A. Knopf, 1981.

Nakane Chie. *Japanese Society*. Berkeley and Los Angeles: University of California Press, 1970.

Nitobe Inazo. *Bushidō: The Soul of Japan: An Exposition of Japanese Thought*. Rutland, Vt., and Tōkyō: Charles E. Tuttle Co., 1969.

Norman, Henry. *The Real Japan: Studies of Contemporary Japanese Manners, Morals, Administrations and Politics*. London: T. Fisher Union, 1892.

Okada Rokuo. *Japanese Proverbs*. Tōkyō: Japan Travel Bureau, 1955.

Okakura Kazuzo. *The Book of Tea*. Rutland, Vt., and Tōkyō: Charles E. Tuttle Co., 1965.

Omori, Annie Shepley, and Doi Kōchi. *Diaries of Court Ladies of Old Japan*. Tōkyō: Kenkyū-sha Co., 1935.

Packard, George R. III. *Protest in Tokyo: The Security Treaty Crisis of 1960*. Princeton, N.J.: Princeton University Press, 1966.

Passin, Herbert. *Society and Education in Japan*. New York: Bureau of Publications, Teachers College, and East Asian Institute, Columbia University, 1965.

Patrick, Hugh, and Rosovsky, Henry, eds. *Asia's New Giant: How the Japanese Economy Works*. Washington, D.C.: Brookings Institution, 1976.

Pharr, Susan J. *Political Women in Japan: The Search for a Place in Political Life*. Berkeley, Los Angeles, and London: University of California Press, 1981.

Pioneer Women Educators of Japan: 24 Leaders of the Century. Tōkyō: Japanese Association of University Women, 1970.

Plath, David W. *Long Engagements: Maturity in Modern Japan*. Stanford, Calif.: Stanford University Press, 1980.

Redford, Lawrence H., ed. *The Occupation of Japan: Economic Policy and Reform*. Proceedings of a Symposium Sponsored by the MacArthur Memorial, 13–15 April 1978. Norfolk, Va.: The MacArthur Memorial, 1980.

————. *The Occupation of Japan: Impact of Legal Reform*. Proceedings of a Symposium Sponsored by the MacArthur Memorial, 14–15 April 1977. Norfolk, Virginia: The MacArthur Memorial, 1978.

Reischauer, Edwin O. *Japan Past and Present*. Tōkyō: Charles E. Tuttle Co., 1964.

————. *The Japanese*. Cambridge, Mass., and London: Belknap Press of Harvard University Press, 1977.

Reischauer, Edwin O., and Fairbank, John K. *East Asia: The Great Tradition*. Boston: Houghton Mifflin: Tōkyō: Charles E. Tuttle Co., 1966.

Saisho Yuriko. *Career Woman—My Way*. Tōkyō: Simul Press, 1979.

————. *Women Executives in Japan: How I Succeeded in Business in a Male-Dominated Society*. Tōkyō: YURI International, Inc., 1981.

Sano Chiyo. *Changing Values of the Japanese Family*. Catholic University, Anthropological Series no. 18. Westport, Conn.: Greenwood Press, 1958.

Sansom, George B. *Japan: A Short Cultural History*. New York: Appleton-Century Company, 1931.

Scalapino, Robert A. *Democracy and the Party Movement in Prewar Japan: The Failure of the First Attempt*. Berkeley and Los Angeles: University of California Press, 1962.

————. *The Japanese Communist Movement, 1920–1966*. Berkeley and Los Angeles: University of California Press, 1967.

Scalapino, Robert A., ed. *The Foreign Policy of Modern Japan*. Berkeley and Los Angeles: University of California Press, 1977.

Schwantes, Robert S. *Japanese and Americans: A Century of Cultural Relations*. New York: Harper & Brothers, 1955.

Sebald, William J., and Brines, Russell. *With MacArthur in Japan: A Personal History of the Occupation*. New York: W. W. Norton, 1965.

Seidensticker, Edward, trans. *The Gossamer Years: A Diary of a Noblewoman of Heian Japan*. Tōkyō and Rutland, Vt.: Charles E. Tuttle Co., 1964.

Sei Shōnagon. *The Pillow-Book of Sei Shōnagon*. Translated by Arthur Waley. London: George Allen & Unwin, 1928.

Silberman, Bernard S., ed. *Japanese Character and Culture: Selected Readings*. Tucson: University of Arizona Press, 1962.

Straellen, H. V. *The Japanese Woman Looking Forward*. Tōkyō: Kyō Bun Kwan, 1940.

Sugimoto Inagaki Etsu. *A Daughter of the Samurai*. Rutland, Vt. and Tōkyō: Charles E. Tuttle Co., 1966.

Summary of Thirteenth National Survey of Family Planning. Series no. 25. Tōkyō: Population Problems Research Council, Mainichi, 1975.

Tanaka Kazuko. *A Short History of the Women's Movement in Modern Japan*. Tōkyō: Femintern Press, 1974.

Tanizaki Junichiro. *The Makioka Sisters*. New York: Universal Library, 1966.

Terasaki, Gwen. *Bridge to the Sun*. Harmondsworth, Middlesex: Penguin Books, 1962.

Thayer, Nathaniel B. *How the Conservatives Rule Japan*. Princeton, N.J.: Princeton University Press, 1969.

Tsunoda Ryusaku, de Bary, W. Theodore, and Keene, Donald, comps. *Sources of Japanese Tradition*. New York: Columbia University Press, 1958.

Tsurumi Kazuko. *Social Change and the Individual: Japan Before and After Defeat in World War II*. Princeton, N.J.: Princeton University Press, 1970.

Varley, H. Paul. *Imperial Restoration in Medieval Japan*. New York: Columbia University Press, 1971.

Vogel, Ezra F. *Japan's New Middle Class: The Salary Man and His Family in a Tokyo Suburb*. Berkeley: University of California Press, 1971.

Ward, Barbara E., ed. *Women in the New Asia*. Amsterdam: UNESCO, 1963.

Ward, Robert E. *Political Development in Modern Japan*. Princeton, N.J.: Princeton University Press, 1968.

Whan, Vorin E., Jr., ed. *A Soldier Speaks: Public Papers and Speeches of General of the Army Douglas MacArthur*. New York: Frederick A. Praeger, 1945.

Whitney, Courtney. *MacArthur: His Rendezvous with History*. New York: Alfred A. Knopf, 1956.

Yamada Waka. *The Social Status of Japanese Women*. Tōkyō: Kokusai bunka shinkokai, 1935.

Yamamoto, George K., and Ishida Tsuyoshi, eds. *Selected Readings in Modern Japanese Society*. Berkeley: McCutchan Publishing Corp., 1971.

Yanagida Kunio. *Japanese Manners and Customs in the Meiji Era*. Translated by Charles S. Terry. Tōkyō: Ōbun-sha, 1957.

Yazaki Takeo. *Social Change and the City in Japan: From Earliest Times Through the Industrial Revolution*. San Francisco: Japan Publications, 1968.

Yosano Akiko. *Tangled Hair*. Translated by Shinoda Seishi. Lafayette, Ind.: Purdue University Studies, 1971.

Yoshida Shigeru. *The Yoshida Memoirs: The Story of Japan in Crisis*. Translated by Yoshida Kenichi. London: William Heinemann, 1961.

Yoshikawa Eiji. *The Heiki Story*. Translated by Uramatsu Wooyenaka Fuki. Rutland, Vt., and Tōkyō: Charles E. Tuttle Co., 1956.

Japanese

Akamatsu Ryōko, ed. *Joshi rōdō hanrei* [Decisions on women workers]. Tōkyō: Gakuyōshobō, 1976.

Fujin sansei kankei shiryōshu [Data on female suffrage]. Tōkyō: Fusen kaikan, 1965 and 1975.

Fukuda Hideko. *Warawa no han seigai* [Half of my life]. White Series 61. Tōkyō: Iwanami bunko, Iwanami shoten, 1958.

Gauntlett Tsune. *Shichijū-shichinen no omoide* [Memories of seventy-seven years]. Tōkyō: Uemura-shoten, 1949.

Harada Tomohiko. *Nihon josei shi* [History of Japanese women]. Tōkyō: Kawade, 1965.

Higa Masako. *Okusama butai funsen-ki: Shōhisha undō 20 nen* [A record of war of housewives legion: Twenty years of consumers' activism]. Ōsaka: Kansai shufu rengōkai, 1967.

————. *Onna no tatakai* [A woman's battle]. Tōkyō: Nihon jitsugyō shuppansha, 1971.

Hiratsuka Masunori. *Joshi kyōiku shi* [History of education for girls]. Tōkyō: Teikoku chihō gyōsei gakukai, 1965.

Hiratsuka Raichō. *Genshi josei wa taiyō de atta* [In the beginning a woman was the sun]. Tōkyō: Ōtsuki shoten, 1971.

————. *Watakushi no aruita michi* [The road I walked]. Tōkyō: Shin hyōron-sha, 1955.

Ichibangase Yasuko, ed. *Sengo fujin mondai shi* [Postwar history of women's problems]. Tōkyō: Domesu shuppan, 1971.

Ichikawa Fusae. *Ichikawa Fusae no jiden—senzen hen* [The autobiography of Ichikawa Fusae—The prewar period]. Tōkyō: Shinjuku shobō, 1974.

————. *Watakushi no fujin undō* [My women's movement]. Tōkyō: Akimoto shobō, 1972.

————. *Watakushi no seiji shōron* [My views of politics]. Tōkyō: Akimoto shobō, 1972.

Ichikawa Fusae, ed. *Sengo fujinkai no dōkō* [Trends of women's circles in the postwar period]. Tōkyō: Fusen kaikan, 1969.

Ikeda Daisaku. *Josei shō* [On women]. Tōkyō: Daisan bunmei-sha, 1971.

Kageyama Hiroko. *Josei no nōryoku kaihatsu* [The development of women's ability]. Tōkyō: Nihon keiei shuppankai, 1968.

————. *Okusama no arubaito* [Women's "arbeit"]. Tōkyō: Kobun-sha, 1964.

Kamichika Ichiko. *Josei shisōshi* [History of feminine thought]. Tōkyō: Sangen-sha, 1949.

Karasawa Tomitaro. *Kyōshi no rekishi* [History of teachers]. Tōkyō: Sōbun-sha, 1956.

Katō Tomiko. *Joshi kōmuinzo no tenkan: shokuba no hana kara jitsuryokusha e* [Image-change of women civil servants]. Tōkyō: Gakuyo shobō, 1971.

Kawanobe Shizu. *Watakushi no mita Amerika no kurashi* [American living as I saw it]. Shizuoka: Fujin seikatsu bunka kenkyūsho, 1964.

Kiroku: kokusai fujin-nen Nihon taikai [Report: International Women's Year Japan mass meeting]. Tōkyō: Morishita, 1976.

Komyuniti 3: Chiiki shakai to fujin [The community 3: Community and women]. Tōkyō: Chiiki shakai kenkyūsho, 1964.

Kuroyanagi Tetsuko. *Madogiwa no totto-chan* [The little girl who looked out of the window]. Tōkyō: Kōdansha, 1981.

Makino Fusako. *Byōin Volunteer katsudō no jissai* [Present situation of volunteer activity at the hospitals]. Ōsaka: Ōsaka volunteer kyōkai, byōin volunteer hoshikai, 1970.

Makino Fusako, ed. *Volunteer no ayumi* [What the volunteers did]. Ōsaka: Byōin volunteer renrakukai, 1973.

Matsuoka Yoko. *Shinryaku-sabetsu to tatakau Ajia fujin kaigi* [Asian Women's Conference to Fight Against Aggression and Discrimination]. Report of the conference held 22–23 August 1970, Tōkyō. 2 vols. Shinryaku-sabetsu to tatakau Ajia fujin kaigi, 25 October 1970.

Michi o kiri hiraita josei ten [Women pioneers since the beginning of the Meiji era]. Tōkyō: Nippon keizai shimbun-sha, 1968.

Miyagi Eisho. *Nihon josei shi* [History of Japanese women]. Tōkyō: Yoshikawa kobun-sha, 1962.

Morosawa Yoko. *Onna no sengo shi* [Postwar history of women]. Tōkyō: Mirai-sha, 1971.

Murakami Nobuhiko. *Meiji josei shi* [The history of Meiji women]. 3 vols. Tōkyō: Riron-sha, 1970–1972.

Nakane Chie. *Tekiō no jōken: Nihonteki renzoku no shikō* [Criteria for adjustment: The Japanese continuum mentality]. Tōkyō: Kōdan-sha, 1972.

Nakauchi Isao. *Waga yasui uri no tetsugaku* [My philosophy of selling cheap]. Tōkyō: Nihon keizai shimbun-sha, 1972.

Nihon shufu yūkensha dōmei: 30 nenkan no nenpyō [Japan's League of Women Voters: A 30-year chronology]. Tōkyō: Nihon fuji yūkensha dōmei: sōritsu 30-shūren kinen gyōji: tokubetsu iinkai, 1975.

Okasan no hyaku-nen shi [One-hundred-year history of mothers]. Tōkyō: Yomiuri shimbun-sha, 1968.

Oku Mumeo. *Akekure* [Day and night]. Tōkyō: David-sha, 1957.

———. *Watakushi no rirekisho* [My personal history]. Vol. 6. Tōkyō: Nihon keizai shimbun-sha, 1958.

Sakanishi Shio. *Ikite manabu* [Live and learn]. Tōkyō: Raichō-sha, 1967.

———. *Minshū shakai no okeru shimin* [Citizens in a democratic society]. Tōkyō: Minshū kyōiku kyōkai, 1965.

———. *Minshū shugi ni tsuite* [On democracy]. Tōkyō: Shakai kyōiku kyōkai, 1964.

Seki Fumiko. *Chapperu hiru monogatari* [Story of chapel hill]. Tōkyō: Seishin shobō, 1966.

Shufu no okori: o kokkai e! [Send women's anger to the Diet]. Tōkyō: Kihira Teiko suisenkai, 1974.

Shukan Shincho. *MacArthur no Nihon* [MacArthur's Japan]. Tōkyō: Shincho-sha, 1970.

Takano Etsuko. *Hatachi no genten* [Viewpoint of a twenty-year-old]. Tōkyō: Shincho-sha, 1971.

Takeda Kiyoko, ed. *Gonin no sensei tachi* [Five teachers]. Tōkyō: Nihon kiri-sutokyōdan shuppanbu, 1960.

Takenishi Hiroko. *Hito to kiseki* [Man and his life]. Tōkyō: Chūō kōron-sha, 1970.

Tanaka Mitsu. *Inochi no onna tachi e* [To my spiritual sisters]. Tōkyō: Tabata shoten, 1972.

Teruoka Yasutaka and Tawara Moeko. *Josei to shokugyō* [Women and jobs]. Tōkyō: Yukei-sha, 1969.

Ueda Kanji. *Volunteer tsukuri* [Recruitment of volunteers]. Ōsaka: Volunteer kyōkai Ōsaka bureau, 1967.

Wakamori Taro and Yamamoto Fujie. *Nihon no josei shi* [A history of Japanese women]. 4 vols. Tōkyō: Shuei-sha, 1965.

Watanabe Kei. *Onna hitori no ikikata* [How a woman lives alone]. Tōkyō: Shufu to seikatsu-sha, 1973.

Yamakawa Kikue. *Onna nidai no ki* [Chronicle of two women]. Tōkyō: Heibon-sha, 1972.

Yamamoto Kazuyo. *Kōtōkyōiku o uketa fujin no genjō* [Present situation of women with higher education]. Ningen kenkyū no. 6. Tōkyō: Education Society of Japan Women's University, n.d.

Yoshikawa Toshikazu. *Tsuda Umeko den* [Biography of Tsuda Umeko]. Tōkyō: Tsuda dōsōkai, 1956.

ARTICLES AND PERIODICALS

English

Ackroyd, Joyce. "Women in Feudal Japan," *Transactions of the Asiatic Society of Japan* (Tōkyō: Asiatic Society of Japan) 7, no. 3 (November 1959).

Adachi Kinnosuke. "The New Women of Nippon," *Woman Citizen*, November 1926.

Beard, Mary. "The New Japanese Women," *Woman Citizen*, January 1924.

Bliss, Barbara, "The Chrysanthemum Cauldron: Women and Children in Japan," *Liberal Woman's News*, January 1927.

Fujii Harue. "Education for Women: The Personal and Social Damage of Anachronistic Policy," *Japan Quarterly*, 29, no. 3 (July-September 1982).

Gauntlett, C. Tsune. "Fodder for Thought," *Japanese Women*, July 1940.

Havens, Thomas R. H. "Women and War in Japan, 1937–45," *American Historical Review* 80, no. 4 (October 1975).

Higuchi Keiko. "Japanese Women in Transition," *Japan Quarterly* 29, no. 3 (July-September 1982).

"A History of Japanese Women," *Japanese Women*, July 1940.

Ichikawa Fusae. "On My Return from China," *Japanese Women* 3, no. 3 (May 1940).

————. "Woman Suffrage Movement in Japan." In *Women of the Pacific, Being a Record of the Proceedings of the First Pan-Pacific Women's Conference Which Was Held in Honolulu from the 9th to the 19th of August 1928, Under the Auspices of the Pan-Pacific Union*. Honolulu: Pan-Pacific Union, 1928 (Sophia Smith Collection).

Ide Kikue. "Legal and Political Relationships of Women of Japan Today—An Interpretation." In *Women of the Pacific, Being a Record of the Proceedings of* the First Pan-Pacific Women's Conference Which Was Held in Honolulu from the 9th to the 19th of August, 1928, Under the Auspices of the Pan-Pacific Union. Honolulu: Pan-Pacific Union, 1928 (Sophia Smith Collection).

Inoue Hisao. "A Historical Sketch of the Development of the Modern Educational System for Women in Japan," Education in Japan (Hiroshima: International Educational Research Institute, Hiroshima University) 6 (1971).

Jones, H. J. "Japanese Women and the Dual-Track Employment System," Pacific Affairs 49, no. 4 (Winter 1976-1977).

Katayama Tetsu. "An Outline of Women's Movement," Japanese Women 2, no. 5 (September 1939).

Kawahara Shizuko. "Awakening of the Meiji Women," Asia Scene, January 1962.

Komada Kinichi. "The Organizations of Social Education (Including P.T.A.)," Education in Japan 5 (1971).

Lifton, Robert Jay. "Individual Patterns in Historical Change: Imagery of Japanese Youth," Journal of Social Issues 20, no. 4, (October 1964).

Miyamoto Ken. "Itō Noe and the Bluestockings," Japan Interpreter 10, no. 2 (Autumn 1975).

Murray, Patricia. "Ichikawa Fusae and the Lonely Red Carpet," Japan Interpreter 10, no. 2 (Autumn 1975).

Sakanishi Shio. "Japan Since Recovery of Independence," The Annals of the American Academy of Political and Social Science, November 1956.

Shibukawa Hisako. "An Education for Making Good Wives and Wise Mothers," Education in Japan 6 (1971).

Shiga Tadashi. "Historical View of the Education of Women Before the Time of Meiji," Education in Japan 6 (1971).

Shimbori Michiya. "Comparison between Pre- and Post-War Student Movements in Japan," Sociology of Education, Fall 1963.

Sievers, Sharon L. "Feminist Criticism in Japanese Politics in the 1880's: The Experience of Kishida Toshiko," Signs: Journal of Women in Culture and Society 6, no. 4 (Summer 1981).

"The Sino-Japanese Incident and the Activities of Japanese Women," Japanese Women, January 1938.

Takeuchi Hiroshi. "Working Women in Business Corporations—The Management Viewpoint," Japan Quarterly, 29, no. 3 (July-September 1982).

Tanino Setsu. "The Status of Japanese Women in the World," Kokusai bunka, December 1964.

Yamakawa Kikue. "The Women's Movement," Shakai shugi kenkyū, September 1922.

Young Women's Christian Association, National Committee. "Present Status and Main Problems of Japanese Women," Japanese Women, November 1938.

Japanese

"Fujin no tekishoku ni tsuite" [On occupations suitable to women], Fujin mondai konwakai kaihō, no. 6, 1967.

Fujin tembō [Women's outlook], A monthly organ of Women's Suffrage Hall, beginning in 1954 (Tōkyō: Fusen kaikan).

"Josei Joi" [Female dominance], *Neo Lib* (Tōkyō: Chūpiren), 15 April 1973.

Morosawa Yoko. "Sabetsu no itami kara" [Out of the pain of discrimination], in *Chosha ni kiku: Jinbun kagaku e no michi* [Authors talk: A way to cultural sciences] (Tōkyō: Mirai-sha, 1972).

Ōta Hiroko. "Hoiku mondai de shigi ni tosen shita watakushi" [I was elected to the city Assembly on the day nursery issue], *Fujin kōrōn*, May 1972.

Tanaka Mitsu. "Inochi no tsuyosa ga hoshii" [I want a stronger spirit], *Fujin kōrōn*, June 1973.

Yamazaki Takako. "Tsuda Umeko," in *Nihonjin no hyakunen* [One hundred years of the Japanese] (Tōkyō: Sekai bunka-sha, 1971).

UNPUBLISHED MATERIAL

English

Fujika Wake A., trans. "Women's Movements in Postwar Japan." Selected articles from *Shiryō: sengo nijū-nen shi* [Source book on twenty postwar years in Japan], Tsuji Seimei, ed. (Tōkyō: Nippon hyōron-sha, 1966), pp. 602–615. Mimeographed. Research Publications and Translations, Institute of Advanced Projects, East-West Center, 1968.

Gaddis, John Wilson. *Public Information in Japan Under American Occupation: A Study of Democratization Efforts Through Agencies of Public Expression* (These presentée à l'université de Genève pour obtenir le grade de docteur ès sciences politiques, Université de Genève, 1950).

Higuchi Keiko. "Bringing Up Girls—Start Aiming at Love and Independence— (Status of Women in Japan)." Translated by Tomii Akiko. Manuscript, ca. 1981.

Mehrenburg, Lavonne. "The New Women: A Study of the 'Seito' and The Shin fujin kyōkai and the Women Who Pioneered These Japanese Women's Movements." Master's thesis, University of Michigan, 1971.

Reischauer, Haru. "East and West Do Meet." Speech to the Massachusetts Division of the American Association of University Women, Boston, 6 May 1967.

Tanaka Sumiko. *For Women's Hour NHK, 5 September 1951*. Mimeographed speech. Washington, D.C.: U.S. Department of Labor, 1951.

Weed, Ethel B. "Japanese Women." Mimeographed. Personal files.

Japanese

Kaneda Kazue. "Concepts of Women in the Taishō Era as Seen in the *Yomiuri shimbun*." Research paper, Ochanomizu University, n.d.

Sumiya Etsuji. "Women's Role in the Modern Age." Speech to the Chifuren National Conference, Kyōto, 1972.

PERSONAL INTERVIEWS

From 1963 to 1973, while I served in the U.S. Foreign Service in Japan, I had conversations with hundreds and met with, in conferences and discussion groups, many thousands of Japanese women to consider the problems and issues discussed in this book. A personal journal, notes, and tapes taken during such meetings constitute a record of these encounters. The names of people who should be listed as sources would take far too many pages. The following individuals kindly met with me in lengthy interviews specifically about the book in the period 1971–1973. Since then I have talked and corresponded with many of these as friends, in the United States, at international conferences, and in Japan. With a few obvious exceptions, the identification given these interviewees is that of their position in the first half of the 1970s at the time and place of formal interview.

Individual Interviews

Name	*Position*	*Location*
Akamatsu Ryoko	Chief, Women Workers' Section, Women's and Minors' Bureau, Ministry of Labor	Tōkyō
Ariga Michiko	Commissioner, Fair Trade Commission	Tōkyō
Bito Shizuko	President, Hiroshima League of Women Voters	Hiroshima
Blakemore, Frances	Exhibits Officer, CIE, Occupation period	Tōkyō
Brown, Don	CIE Officer, Occupation period	Tōkyō
Egami Fuji	Director, Tōgō Women's Student Center; former director, Program Inspection Board, Japan Broadcasting Corporation (*NHK*)	Tōkyō
Fujita Taki	President, Tsuda College	Tōkyō
Fujitani Atsuko	Chief, Kyō-no-onna daigaku (Today's Women's University); social critic	Kyōto
Gotō Masa	President, Hokkaidō Consumers Union	Sapporo
Hata Yawara	Governor, Saitama Prefecture, Socialist party	Saitama
Hashiguchi Toshiko	Assistant to political commentator Mitarai Tatsuo; editor-publisher of *Fujin Seminar*	Tōkyō
Higa Masako	President, Kansai Shufuren	Ōsaka
Higuchi Keiko	Social critic; specialist in feminist issues	Tōkyō

Hirose Hamako	President, Hiroshima Jogakuin College	Hiroshima
Hosaka Fumiko	Niiza City assembly woman, Communist party	Saitama
Hosokawa Kou	Urawa City assembly woman, independent; President of Urawa Shufukai (Housewives Association)	Saitama
Ichibangase Yasuko	Assistant professor, Japan Women's University and principal of attached senior high school	Tōkyō
Ichikawa Fusae	Pioneer suffragist; member, House of Councillors, independent	Tōkyō
Ishii Kikusaburo	Director, Shitennoji Gakuin College	Ōsaka
Kageyama Hiroko	Director, Koenji Division, Telephone and Telegram Corporation; founder, Womanpower Taikai	Tōkyō
Kamei Hikaru	Governor, Fukuoka Prefecture, Liberal Democratic party	Fukuoka
Kamiya Mieko	Professor, Tsuda College; psychiatrist	Ashiya and Tōkyō
Kaneko Atsuo	Bureau Chief of Culture, *Nishi-Nihon shimbun*	Fukuoka
Katō Shidzue (formerly Baroness Ishimoto)	Member, House of Councillors, Socialist party	Tōkyō
Katō Taka	Former Tōkyō YWCA secretary	Hayama
Kawanobe Shizu	Member, House of Councillors, Liberal Democratic party	Shizuoka
Kawashima Chikara	Professor of English, Niigata Junior College for Women	Niigata
Kazuo Iwama	Deputy president, Sony Corporation	Atsugi
Kihira Teiko	President, League of Women Voters of Japan	Tōkyō
Kobayashi Hiro	Nagasaki Prefectural assembly woman, Socialist party; president, Nagasaki Gensuikin	Nagasaki
Kubota Kinuko	Professor of Political Science, Seikei University	Tōkyō
Maeda Sumiko	Director of Women's Section, Zen-nittsu labor union	Tōkyō
Matsuoka Yoko	Social critic	Tōkyō
Mills, Martha Tway	CIE Education Officer, Occupation period, Ōsaka	Washington, D.C.
Mishima Sumie	Author; teacher, Tsuda College	Tōkyō
Mizuno Sumiko	Urawa City assembly woman, independent	Urawa
Morioka Fumi	Editorial staff, *Kōbe shimbun*	Kōbe

Morioka Toshi	Newspaperman, *Kōbe shimbun*	Kōbe
Morosawa Yoko	Social critic; writer on women's affairs	Tōkyō
Murai Takako	Professor, Tsuda College	Tōkyō
Murashima Kiyo	Member, House of Councillors (1st Diet), independent	Niigata
Nakagome Fumi	President, International Inspection Co.	Tōkyō
Nakamura Kii	Daughter and secretary of Oku Mumeo; vice-president, Shufuren	Tōkyō
Nakauchi Isao	President, Dai'ei, Inc.	Tōkyō
Nichols, Walter	Former cultural attaché, U.S. Embassy	Tōkyō
Nishida Koto	Former professor, Tsuda College	Kamakura
Nomura Katsuko	Executive Committee member, Tōkyō Metropolitan Consumers Center	Tōkyō
Nuita Yoko	Director, Bureau of Social Welfare, Tōkyō Metropolitan Government	Tōkyō
Ogata Sadako	Professor of international relations, International Christian University; delegate to United Nations	Tōkyō
Ogawa Yoshiko	Member, Japan Association of University Women; researcher	Tōkyō
Ōta Hiroko	Niiza City assembly woman, independent	Saitama
Oshima Kiyoko	President, Japan Association of University Women	Tōkyō
Overton, Douglas W.	Special adviser to the president, Institute for International Studies and Training	Shizuoka
Ozawa Ryoko	Urawa City assembly woman, independent	Saitama
Saisho Yuriko	Chair of Board, Nippo Marketing & Advertising Co.	Tōkyō
Sakamoto Muneko	President, Ōsaka Women's Hall	Ōsaka
Sakanishi Shio	Social critic; member, National Security Council	Oiso
Seki Fumiko	Director, JAUW Sapporo Branch; member, Board of Education	Sapporo
Seki Michiko	University student; daughter of Seki Fumiko	Sapporo
Seki Kazuko	University student; daughter of Seki Fumiko	Sapporo
Shiraishi Tsugi	Reporter, *Japan Times*; specialist in women's activities	Saitama
Shoji Masako	Professor of education, Hiroshima University	Hiroshima

Sōma Yukika	Social critic	Tōkyō
Taguchi Sachiko	Research associate, International Department, Japan Democratic Socialist party	Tōkyō
Takahashi Nobuko	Director, Women's and Minors' Bureau, Ministry of Labor	Tōkyō
Takano Fumi	Professor of English, Tsuda College; vice-president, International Federation of University Women	Tōkyō
Takasugi Tazuko	President, Hokkaidō Federation of Women's Organizations	Sapporo
Tanabe Sachiko	Bureau chief of education, RKB Mainichi Broadcasting Co.	Fukuoka
Tanaka Mitsu	Leader of "Women's Lib," author and social critic	Tōkyō
Tanaka Satoko	Secretary-general, Chifuren	Tōkyō
Toda Satsuki	Former president, Ōsaka Women's Hall	Ōsaka
Tokunaga Kikuko	Member, Board of Education, Fukuoka	Fukuoka
Uchino Umeko	Vice-president, Chifuren (All-Japan); president, Fukuoka Federation of Women's Organizations	Fukuoka
Ushijima Kunie	President, Saga Chifuren; Saga Prefectural assembly woman, independent	Saga
Weed, Ethel B.	Women's officer, CIE, Occupation period	Connecticut
Yamakawa Kikue	Director, Women's and Minors' Bureau, Ministry of Labor (1947–1951); founder Sekirankai; Socialist	Fujisawa
Yamamoto Matsuyo	President, Home-Family-Community-Life Research Institute	Tōkyō
Yamataka Shigeri	President, Chifuren; former member, House of Councillors, independent	Tōkyō

Group Interviews

Name	*Description*	*Location*
Iwataya Department Store	Personnel officials	Fukuoka
Kōmeitō	Nakajima Nobue, candidate, 1969 House of Councillors election, and other Kōmeitō secretariat officials	Tōkyō

Kyūshū University students	Radical student leaders	Fukuoka
Kyūshū Matsushita Electric Co.	Union-member women workers and union officials	Fukuoka
Ministry of Education	Izumoi Chizuko, specialist, and Shikuma Atsuko, section chief, Women's Education Section, Social Education Bureau	Tōkyō
Shiseido	Miya Yooichi, director, Technical Division, and Kouga Fumiko Fumiko, general manager, Beauty Research and Salon Operations Division	Tōkyō
Sōka gakkai	Women members: three housewives and four working women	Tōkyō
Sony Corporation	Uchida-*sensei*, head of the nursery school, and working mothers	Atsugi
Tsuda College Students	Graduate and undergraduate students	Tōkyō
Urawa High School	Five students	Saitama
Urawa housewives	Five housewives with high-school-level education and five housewives with college-level education	Saitama

Index